Advances
in **COMPUTERS**
VOLUME 8

Contributors to This Volume

Lionello A. Lombardi
R. Narasimhan
Thomas N. Pyke, Jr.
Naomi Sager
Jean E. Sammet
T. B. Steel, Jr.

Advances in
COMPUTERS

EDITED BY
FRANZ L. ALT
National Bureau of Standards
Washington, D.C.

AND

MORRIS RUBINOFF
University of Pennsylvania
and
Pennsylvania Research Associates
Philadelphia, Pennsylvania

VOLUME 8

ACADEMIC PRESS · New York · London – 1967

Copyright © 1967, by Academic Press Inc.
ALL RIGHTS RESERVED.
NO PART OF THIS BOOK MAY BE REPRODUCED IN ANY FORM,
BY PHOTOSTAT, MICROFILM, OR ANY OTHER MEANS, WITHOUT
WRITTEN PERMISSION FROM THE PUBLISHERS.

ACADEMIC PRESS INC.
111 Fifth Avenue, New York, New York 10003

United Kingdom Edition published by
ACADEMIC PRESS INC. (LONDON) LTD.
Berkeley Square House, London W.1

Library of Congress Catalog Card Number: 59-15761

Second Printing, 1968

PRINTED IN THE UNITED STATES OF AMERICA

Contributors to Volume 8

Numbers in parentheses indicate the pages on which the authors' contributions begin.

LIONELLO A. LOMBARDI, *University of Rome, Rome, Italy (247)*

R. NARASIMHAN, *Computer Group, Tata Institute of Fundamental Research, Bombay, India (189)*

THOMAS N. PYKE, JR., *Center for Computer Sciences and Technology, National Bureau of Standards, Washington, D.C. (1)*

NAOMI SAGER, *Institute for Computer Research in the Humanities, New York University, New York (153)*

JEAN E. SAMMET, *IBM Corporation, Cambridge, Massachusetts (47)*

T. B. STEEL, JR., *System Development Corporation, Santa Monica, California (103)*

Preface

In this volume, as in its predecessors, the editors' selection of topics has been guided by two principles: to present a mixed fare as an antidote to the virus of overspecialization in the computer field, and at the same time to give primary emphasis to areas of outstanding active development. The "keynote" of the present volume is programming languages, the subject which is more and more clearly recognized as the "key" to the use of computers.

Earlier volumes of Advances in Computers have brought surveys of programming languages for business and data processing applications, of procedure-oriented programming as used mainly for scientific problems, and of languages for handling (natural) languages. Also there has been a comprehensive review of developments in Eastern Europe, and a critique of processors for programming languages. This array of articles is continued in the present volume with a description of languages for dealing with mathematical formulas, a unified theoretical treatment of programming languages from an advanced viewpoint, an exposition of one elaborate system for mixed symbolic and numerical computation, and a discussion of standards for computers in general and their languages in particular.

The papers by Narasimhan and Lombardi belong to the small minority of articles in Advances in Computers which are not expository surveys. Narasimhan presents a "metatheory," i.e., a theory of the ways in which programming languages may be described; and this turns out to be the same as the ways in which the computers themselves can be described. It gives us the tools for examining what can or cannot be expressed in a given language, and for exhibiting relations between natural (human) and formal (computer) languages, and between language design and systems design. Lombardi outlines a language—or, if we prefer to call it that, a computer—which accepts problems whose formulation is still incomplete and is supplied in instalments ("increments"), and which at each stage goes as far toward solution of the problem as is possible with the information available to it at the time. A somewhat restricted version of Lombardi's proposals has been implemented (interpretively, of course).

The paper by Jean Sammet surveys, compares, and evaluates the existing programming systems for algebraic operations on formulas, a field in which she has pioneered. A status report on the efforts to establish standards for computers, peripheral devices, codes and—above all

—programming languages, is given by T. B. Steel, the chairman of one of the principal groups concerned with this problem.

To offset in part this emphasis on prgramming languages, we have included two papers on other subjects of high current interest. The treatment of human languages on computers, especially for automatic translation and for communicating with computers in English, has already been surveyed in Volume 1 of this serial publication, and one aspect of it was discussed in Volume 7. This time, Naomi Sager gives a comparison of different methods for grammatical analysis of sentences with emphasis on her own successful approach to the problem. Again, the subject of multiple computing has been discussed repeatedly in past volumes of Advances in Computers, under the names of multiprogramming, multiple or highly parallel systems. These are all different modes of batch processing. By contrast, in the present volume T. N. Pyke writes about on-line time sharing, which, usually in connection with remote access and man-machine interaction, seems to be on the verge of revolutionizing the computer field.

FRANZ L. ALT
MORRIS RUBINOFF

April, 1967

Contents

CONTRIBUTORS v
PREFACE vii
CONTENTS OF PREVIOUS VOLUMES xi

Time-Shared Computer Systems
Thomas N. Pyke, Jr.

1. The Time-Sharing Concept 1
2. Design of the Time-Shared Computer System . . . 14
3. Over-all Systems Considerations 31
4. The Use of Time-Shared Systems 36
5. The Future of Time Sharing 39
   References 42

Formula Manipulation by Computer
Jean E. Sammet

1. Introduction 47
2. Technical Issues in Formula Manipulation . . . 51
3. Technical Issues as Applied to FORMAC 78
4. Applications 95
   References 99

Standards for Computers and Information Processing
T. B. Steel, Jr.

1. Introductory Comments 103
2. The History of Standardization 104
3. Modern Industrial Standardization 109
4. Summary 151
   References 151

Syntactic Analysis of Natural Language
Naomi Sager

1. Linguistic Basis for Computations	153
2. A Procedure for Left-to-Right String Decomposition of Sentences	157
3. The String Program	163
References	186

Programming Languages and Computers: A Unified Metatheory
R. Narasimhan

1. Introduction	189
2. Simple Computation Processes	196
3. Hierarchical Computation Processes	217
4. Relevance of the Approach to the Design of Computing Systems	225
5. Concluding Remarks	240
References	244

Incremental Computation
Lionello A. Lombardi

Introduction	248
1. General Concepts	250
2. Syntax	270
3. Memory Organization	276
4. Operation of the Incremental Computer	290
Appendix: Properties of Forms	327
References	332
AUTHOR INDEX	335
SUBJECT INDEX	339

Contents of Previous Volumes

Volume 1

General-Purpose Programming for Business Applications
    CALVIN C. GOTLIEB
Numerical Weather Prediction
    NORMAN A. PHILLIPS
The Present Status of Automatic Translation of Languages
    YEHOSHUA BAR-HILLEL
Programming Computers to Play Games
    ARTHUR L. SAMUEL
Machine Recognition of Spoken Words
    RICHARD FATEHCHAND
Binary Arithmetic
    GEORGE W. REITWIESNER

Volume 2

A Survey of Numerical Methods for Parabolic Differential Equations
    JIM DOUGLAS, JR.
Advances in Orthonormalizing Computation
    PHILIP J. DAVIS AND PHILIP RABINOWITZ
Microelectronics Using Electron-Beam-Activated Machining Techniques
    KENNETH R. SHOULDERS
Recent Developments in Linear Programming
    SAUL I. GASS
The Theory of Automata, a Survey
    ROBERT MCNAUGHTON

Volume 3

The Computation of Satellite Orbit Trajectories
    SAMUEL D. CONTE
Multiprogramming
    E. F. CODD
Recent Developments in Nonlinear Programming
    PHILIP WOLFE
Alternating Direction Implicit Methods
    GARRETT BIRKHOFF, RICHARD S. VARGA, AND DAVID YOUNG
Combined Analog-Digital Techniques in Simulation
    HAROLD K. SKRAMSTAD
Information Technology and the Law
    REED C. LAWLOR

Volume 4

The Formulation of Data Processing Problems for Computers
    WILLIAM C. MCGEE
All-Magnetic Circuit Techniques
    DAVID R. BENNION AND HEWITT D. CRANE
Computer Education
    HOWARD E. TOMPKINS
Digital Fluid Logic Elements
    H. H. GLAETTLI
MULTIPLE COMPUTER SYSTEMS
    WILLIAM A. CURTIN

Volume 5

The Role of Computers in Election Night Broadcasting
   JACK MOSHMAN
Some Results of Research on Automatic Programming in Eastern Europe
   WLADYSLAW TURSKI
A Discussion of Artificial Intelligence and Self-Organization
   GORDON PASK
Automatic Optical Design
   ORESTES N. STAVROUDIS
Computing Problems and Methods in X-Ray Crystallography
   CHARLES L. COULTER
Digital Computers in Nuclear Reactor Design
   ELIZABETH CUTHILL
An Introduction to Procedure-Oriented Languages
   HARRY D. HUSKEY

Volume 6

Information Retrieval
   CLAUDE E. WALSTON
Speculations Concerning the First Ultraintelligent Machine
   IRVING JOHN GOOD
Digital Training Devices
   CHARLES R. WICKMAN
Number Systems and Arithmetic
   HARVEY L. GARNER
Considerations on Man versus Machine for Space Probing
   P. L. BARGELLINI
Data Collection and Reduction for Nuclear Particle Trace Detectors
   HERBERT GELERNTER

Volume 7

Highly Parallel Information Processing Systems
   JOHN C. MURTHA
Programming Language Processors
   RUTH M. DAVIS
The Man-Machine Combination for Computer-Assisted Copy Editing
   WAYNE A. DANIELSON
Computer-Aided Typesetting
   WILLIAM R. BOZMAN
Programming Languages for Computational Linguistics
   ARNOLD C. SATTERTHWAIT
Computer Driven Displays and Their Use in Man/Machine Interaction
   ANDRIES VAN DAM

Time-Shared Computer Systems

THOMAS N. PYKE, Jr.*

Center for Computer Sciences and Technology
National Bureau of Standards
Washington, D.C.

1. The Time-Sharing Concept	1
1.1 Introduction	1
1.2 Definitions	2
1.3 Types of Time-Sharing Systems	5
1.4 Evolution of Time Sharing	6
2. Design of the Time-Shared Computer System	14
2.1 Central Processor	14
2.2 Memory	16
2.3 Remote Terminals	22
2.4 Communications	24
2.5 Interfacing of Remote Terminals	26
2.6 Scheduling	27
2.7 Accounting	31
3. Over-all Systems Considerations	31
3.1 Hardware Systems Configurations	31
3.2 Software Executives	33
3.3 System Reliability	34
4. The Use of Time-Shared Systems	36
4.1 Appropriateness of Applications	36
4.2 Typical Applications	37
4.3 Man-Machine Interaction	38
5. The Future of Time Sharing	39
5.1 The Acceptance of Time Sharing	39
5.2 The Time-Sharing Utility	40
5.3 Man-Computer Symbiosis	41
Bibliography	42

1. The Time-Sharing Concept

1.1 Introduction

Interest in the design and use of time-shared computer systems has become widespread during the last several years. A number of experimental systems have attracted considerable attention, while several

---

*All statements herein are made on the personal responsibility of the author in his capacity as a private individual.

special-purpose systems have been serving operational needs in a variety of areas. This interest has prompted many computer manufacturers, universities, and government agencies to envision a new generation of computers capable of time-shared operation.

Close study of the time-sharing systems that are in operation and of the designs for systems now being implemented reveals the apparent trends in the time-sharing field. What characteristics do these systems have in common? What are the strengths and weaknesses of current systems and how might they be improved? For what applications are these systems best suited? By a thorough examination of the techniques involved in the design of time-sharing systems and the problems met when using them, these questions may be answered.

1.2 Definitions

Before delving into the details of time-sharing systems, several terms shall be defined. This will help the reader to be aware of the way in which the author uses these terms, since they have been used in many different ways as the field has developed. It is hoped that the definitions given here satisfy each term's usage in the mainstream of current time-sharing technology.

It is first necessary to identify the salient properties of a time-sharing system.

> Time-sharing is the simultaneous access to a computer system by a number of independent users.

A computer system may include one or more central processing units (CPU's), a primary memory, one or more mass memories, and input-output (IO) equipment of several types. The CPU and many IO controllers, channels, or similar devices are each capable of executing instructions serially from a single instruction stream, usually transmitted to the unit from the primary memory. Any device having this capability is a *processor*, and time-sharing systems usually have two or more such processors capable of concurrent operation. It is important to note the difference between this general notion of processor and that of a CPU, which can execute a wide range of instructions, including arithmetic and logic operations. Other processors in a system may have limited arithmetic capabilities, but their principal function is peripheral service to the CPU. A collection of processors and memories together with data transfer mechanisms is a computer system. Each part of the system is known as a resource of the system. The term *computer* is usually applied to a system having a CPU, a primary memory, and some IO capability.

So far as users of a time-sharing system are concerned, they each appear to be the sole user of the system. This apparently simultaneous access is an illusion resulting from the speed mismatch between the relatively show human user and the fast computer. A reaction time on the order of one-tenth of a second for each user would give the system sufficient time to service each user for a period of several milliseconds without any user noticing a delay, even if all requests are made simultaneously. This phenomenon requires, of course, that the number of users be appropriately limited. The system is being time-multiplexed with respect to the users.

The reference to independent users in the definition of time-sharing implies that users be capable of working on independent problems if they so desire. Some special-purpose systems may not satisfy this requirement. For some applications of general-purpose systems there may be a need to interconnect two or more users for multiconsole operation, thus surrendering console independence for the duration of such operation.

The term *user*, as it has been applied so far, is a human being having access to the system through a man-machine interface. This interface may be called a console or a terminal, and it may be located physically near or very distant from the computer system. In either case, to interact with a computer system at rates satisfying his response characteristics, the user must be on-line with the computer.

> An on-line user is one directly connected to the computer system.

The direct connection may be any communication link having negligible delay relative to the interaction rate.

A time-sharing system with on-line users, operating so that all users' response requirements are met, is said to be operating in real-time.

> Real-time system operation is that in which a particular response time requirement is met by the system.

This general definition is satisfied by the rather nebulously defined response requirement of a human being, which may vary from a few tenths of a second to several seconds or more, depending on his use of the system.

A system in which a human user is on-line and which operates in real-time with respect to the user can interact in a conversational manner with the human. This is an important characteristic of time-shared systems.

For systems satisfying more rigid response requirements, such as process control systems, the term *real-time* has had a more strictly defined meaning. Rosenberg [60] has used the term *critical real-time* to distinguish this sense.

> Critical real-time system operation is that in which a strict time dependency requirement is met by the system.

A critical real-time system responds to its users, or its environment, quickly enough so that it may actually influence or control its environment.

Besides allowing on-line, real-time operation, a time-sharing system can serve all users better by making full use of all system resources. The varying loads of individual users upon the system resources can be balanced so that all resources are used most of the time. As previously defined, these resources include processors capable of parallel operation. In such a system an individual program could attempt to keep all processors busy or this function could be relegated to a supervisory program. In a time-sharing system, as in a multiprogrammed batch processing system, the supervisory program is given this function. Since it is not usual for any one program to require all of the system resources at a given time, it is the job of the supervisory program to interlace operation of two or more programs in the system at the same time.

> Multiprogramming is the simultaneous execution of two or more programs in one computer system.

A characteristic of this type of operation is that any program need not be completed before another is begun. In a time-sharing system, a program may be a user's program, a segment of a user's program, or a system program. In general, a program is an instruction stream which is executed serially by a processor in a computer system.

Processors and memories have been defined as separate entities within a computer system. There is not necessarily a direct connection between any processor and any particular memory. Two terms are used to describe operation of a system with more than one processor.

> A multiprocessor system is a computer system having more than one central processing unit.

> Multiprocessing is the operation of a multiprocessor system.

In current usage, a multiprocessor system usually has a number of banks of primary memory, each capable of direct connection with each CPU. This is the system configuration employed by several time-sharing systems now being implemented.

1.3 Types of Time-Sharing Systems

Time-sharing systems span a spectrum from very specialized to completely general. They may be placed into two classes: dedicated and general purpose.

The class of dedicated systems can be further divided into two categories.

The first kind of dedicated system is that restricted to the solution of a single problem or set of problems. Users may request execution of a routine from a library within the system. This request may be in the form of a call for a function, such as a reservation request in an airlines reservation system. Specially designed terminals are sometimes employed, so that specific functions can be requested by users not familiar with the system. The users may or may not be independent of each other, and they can execute the same functions and have access to a common data base. Each user may be aware of other users either implicitly, recognizing that there is some other external source of data or control in the system, or explicitly, if the user is able to communicate with specific terminals other than his own through the system.

Examples of dedicated systems of this kind are centralized department store systems, with terminals for sales personnel to record transactions, and banking systems, in which tellers may directly query the system for the status of accounts and credit or debit them. Specialized on-line inventory control systems and some restricted information retrieval systems fall into this category.

A second kind of dedicated system gives the users the capability of submitting programs for execution, but these programs can be written in only one language. The system is dedicated to efficient execution of programs in this language. A program, consisting of a sequence of statements in the programming language, may be entered, edited, and either executed or stored for later execution. In some systems programs are translated into machine language before execution; in others execution is interpretive. This kind of system gives the user more freedom than the first kind, since he can specify sequences of available system functions through statements in the programming language.

Examples of one-language systems are JOSS [69], BASIC [16], and QUICKTRAN [36]. Each of these provides convenient scientific computing service for engineers and scientists.

The general-purpose time-sharing system can execute programs submitted in any of several languages. Through at least one of these languages, an assembly or machine language, there must be access to system resources at a very detailed level. By writing an appropriate program at this level, any user can generate a subsystem, perhaps a compiler or assembler, that may be stored for access by other users. Included in the resources that may be tapped by the low level program must be a call for supervisor routines that control io at remote terminals and provide other systems services. Thus, each subsystem can cause a user terminal to take on a new appearance. A general-purpose system can have an indefinitely large number of different appearances because of this subsystem generation capability.

General-purpose systems usually have a large mass memory in which programs and data may be stored by users for later access by themselves or other users. A basic library of service routines, including editing and debugging aids, is stored in this memory. Since all users have access to the mass memory, the system promotes communication among users. As the system is used, it grows by the contributions of its users.

Examples of general-purpose systems are CTSS at MIT [*10*], the ARPA-SDC system [*66*], and systems at Carnegie Institute of Technology [*8*], the University of California at Berkeley [*42*], the University of Pennsylvania [*57*], and the National Bureau of Standards [*58*].

1.4 Evolution of Time Sharing

The earliest reference the author has been able to find to a system having characteristics resembling the modern time-shared computer is the Bell Telephone Complex Computer [*3*]. Placed in operation in New York in 1940, the computer had three operator consoles, each capable of independent use of the machine. A relay computer, it was designed to help in the solution of filter network problems. Using this system, G. R. Stibitz and Samuel B. Williams succeeded in demonstrating the feasibility of operating a computer remotely over a teletypewriter circuit at a meeting of the American Mathematical Society in Hanover, New Hampshire in 1941.

The first reference to the time-sharing concept as it is known today was by Strachey in a 1959 paper [*73*], in which he proposed that the central processor and one or more io devices function simultaneously by time-multiplexing the memory. Further, he suggested an engineer's console, at which maintenance and routine engineering services are provided at the same time as normal user service. Strachey recognized several problems that arise in such a system, including the need for separation of control functions available to the system supervisor from those available to users. He proposed that the executive or supervisor be located in a microprogrammed read-only memory, so that privileged instructions are accessible only to the supervisor.

At about the same time that Strachey delivered his paper, a group at Massachusetts Institute of Technology had become interested in the time-sharing concept. Among these people was McCarthy, who talked of the potential use of such a system as a community utility [*47*]. McCarthy, Corbato, and others generated plans to develop a large-scale experimental facility on the IBM 7090 then at MIT [*10, 12, 26*].

Before describing these first efforts, two groups that each developed smaller systems during this period should be mentioned. J. Dennis and associates at MIT and a group at Bolt, Beranek, and Newman [*5*] both felt that the DEC PDP-1 computer was very well suited to be the CPU of a time-sharing system. The two groups proceeded to design and implement similar systems. Operation at Bolt, Beranek, and Newman began slightly before MIT, and both were actually running before the larger MIT system was on the air.

Since the MIT large-scale effort has been the backbone of the spread of the time-sharing concept, a brief description of its development is included here. A desire to be able to use the existing utility routines, including compilers and assemblers, within the framework of the new time-sharing system led to the addition of a second 32,000-word core bank to the IBM 7090. This was required since many of the existing routines used most of the original memory and memory demands would probably increase in the future. Thus, the system is called the Compatible Time-Sharing System (CTSS).

Besides this major change, a memory relocation register was added, so that programs can be written as if they are to be executed in base address zero. The supervisor loads the relocation register, so that correct reference is made to the actual memory locations during user program execution by hardware addition of the contents of this register to each memory address before access to memory. The supervisor is free to move programs in memory without the user's knowledge because of this feature. An interrupt clock was added, so that control is returned to the supervisor after a user has an adequate share of processor time. Completing the internal modifications, a protected mode of operation was installed; while the processor runs in this mode, direct execution of IO or other privileged instructions results in a trap to the supervisor. Any reference outside the user's designated area of memory causes a similar trap. This latter protection was implemented by the addition of upper and lower bounds registers, loaded by the supervisor, that are compared to all memory references while a user program is running.

The IBM 7090 was updated to an IBM 7094 and the system configuration was expanded to include disk files, drums, and an IO system that can connect to a large number of remote terminals, including some terminals requiring more extensive service than simple typewriter-like devices. Figure 1 shows a recent CTSS equipment configuration.

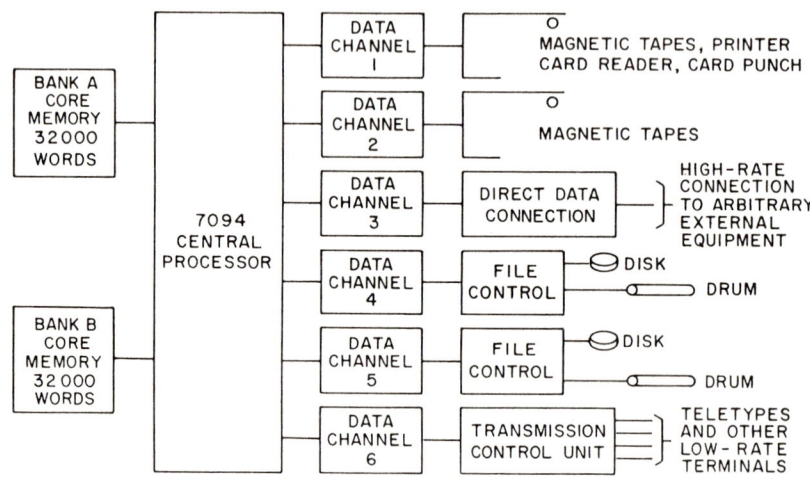

Fig. 1. A recent CTSS equipment configuration.

There are six data channels, each of which can operate concurrently with the CPU. Two of these connect to the usual magnetic tape units and other peripheral devices. A third provides a direct data connection for remote terminals requiring a very high data rate. Two channels are used for access to drum and disk files. Drum storage is used for swapping the active programs in and out of the B core, while the disk file is used as the system mass memory. Before the addition of the drum the transfer time of 32,000 words from core to disk was about 2 sec. Use of the drum decreases this time by an order of magnitude.

The sixth channel connects to an IBM 7750 transmission control unit, which is itself an independent computer consisting of a processor and an internal core memory. This control unit connects to the MIT private branch exchange which connects through telephone lines to users throughout the campus and at remote locations. Users of TWX and Western Union services may also dial into the system.

Besides assisting the IBM 7094 with format control and other bookkeeping for the remote terminals, the memory in the IBM 7750 has been used as an overflow from the A core supervisor. It has been necessary to store output to the terminals in this memory while awaiting transmission to the terminals. This is not so desirable as inclusion of the buffer in the 7094 memory, but the size of the supervisor grew beyond original expectations and space in the A core became limited.

Another use of the 7750 is to establish connection of higher speed terminals to the system in the place of several lower speed devices. A PDP-1 computer with attached display has been used in this capacity, linked by means of a 1200-bits/sec Dataphone connection.

The terminals at MIT include more than 50 Model 35 Teletypes and more than 50 IBM 1050 terminals, variations of the IBM Selectric typewriter. At any one time, the system can handle 24 or more of these terminals. The large number of terminals available in excess of 24 provides convenience of access to the system from locations remote from the MIT Computation Center.

The heart of the Compatible Time-Sharing System is the supervisory program. It handles all communication throughout the system, scheduling of time-sharing activity, movement of data and programs to and from the B core, bookkeeping for user files, and system accounting. Service by the supervisor is requested by a user at a console or from his program by the execution of system commands. Execution of a command causes a copy of the appropriate system routine to be copied from mass memory into the user's core image, and during his share of CPU time the routine is executed.

The system contains in excess of 500,000 lines of code, of which 50,000 have been written specifically for the system. It has been a massive effort, and has benefited from the dynamic growth by user contributions to the system, of which a general-purpose system is capable.

The CTSS has been in operation since November 1963, on a 24 hour a day basis. Many enthusiastic users, most of them on the MIT campus, have used the system for numerous applications. Many of the applications mentioned in Section 4.2 have been programmed in some form on the system. The CTSS's nature is experimental; it has functioned as a research tool; and it has been of prime interest to all who view the potential of more advanced time-sharing systems.

The development of CTSS was accompanied by the genesis of Project MAC (for Machine Aided Cognition or Multiple Access Computer) at MIT. Under the direction of R. M. Fano, the project is dedicated to the exploration of the intimate collaboration between human users and a computer in the solution of problems, in which the two parties contribute their best capabilities [26]. As a first step in this exploration, a copy of the original CTSS was made and has been operational for the last few years along with the original CTSS at the MIT Computation Center. The MULTICS system, which will be described later, is the outcome of the first phase of the project. It is a system designed from the ground up for time-sharing.

Another large-scale general-purpose time-sharing system is the ARPA-SDC Time-Sharing System (TSS), which has been operational at the System Development Corporation since June 1963 [65, 66]. Its design was based partially on ideas developed at MIT and at Bolt, Beranek, and Newman. The principal computer used by TSS is the AN/FSQ-32, a large-scale machine with primary memory divided into banks. Because of this memory configuration, a fast IO capability, a powerful instruction repertoire, and an extensive interrupt system, this computer was a very likely candidate for a time-sharing system.

Figure 2 shows the configuration of the ARPA-SDC system. The

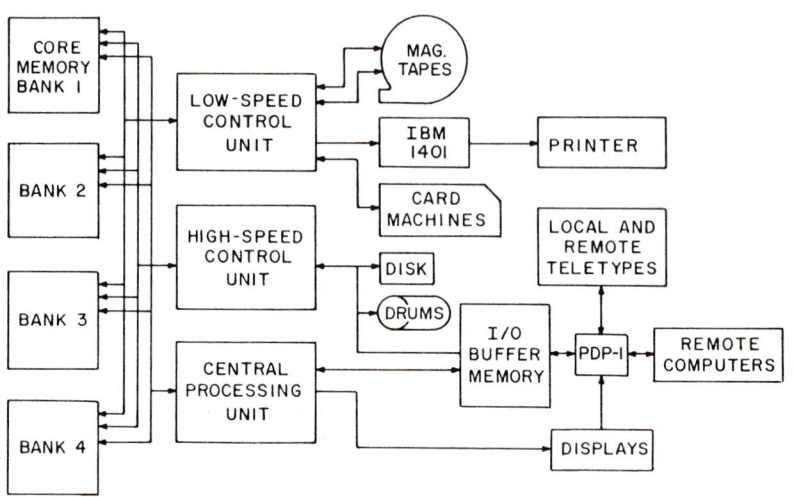

FIG. 2. The ARPA–SDC system.

processor-memory relationship is very similar to that designed into second generation time-sharing systems. Most important is the possible independent access to each memory bank by each of the processors. Each bank of memory contains 16,000 words (48 bits each) and there is a separate bank for interfacing to the PDP-1. The low-speed control unit can handle operation of several IO devices at once, in multiplexed fashion. The high-speed unit services only one device at a time because the individual bandwidth requirement of these devices approaches that of primary memory. The PDP-1 services the remote terminals, including Teletypes and displays, as well as other remote computers.

Other features not shown in the diagram are a memory protection mechanism on a bank at a time basis and an interval clock that can be controlled by the supervisory program.

A time-sharing executive similar to the supervisor in the CTSS is used to control system operation. There is a set of basic commands with which the user requests service. He may enter and call for the execution of programs in a number of languages. The executive controls allocation of memory space, use of the CPU, and the swapping of programs to and from a drum memory. Call of commands in TSS generates a request to the supervisor, resident in one of the core banks. The command programs residing there are called by all users, so there need not be separate copies made for each execution. Subsystems, including translators and interpreters for several programming languages, are called as service routines in TSS. These routines are copied for each user and run as his active program.

Considerable experience has been obtained with the system and new languages have been added; means for debugging and running programs interactively have been emphasized. Also of importance is the *link* capability, which allows intercommunication among users and the simultaneous access by more than one user to a single program.

Still another general-purpose system, at the Carnegie Institute of Technology, has been operational for some time [8]. Although not a time-sharing system by strict application of the definition, a number of on-line users can simultaneously input and edit programs in any of several languages and then request program execution. The system then queues these programs for execution in a serial manner, so that delays of from a few minutes to an hour or more may be experienced before the completion of any program, even one requiring minimal computation. Users return to the on-line consoles at a later time to obtain the output from their programs.

The Carnegie Institute of Technology system allows on-line input of programs for fast batch processing. The difference between this system and the two systems previously described is that an individual program is allowed to run to completion, while in the others every program is sliced so that each program runs for a short period during a system cycle. To provide fast program completion for short programs, yet allow execution of larger, more time-consuming ones, it is necessary to operate the CPU in a time-sliced manner.

At least three one-language dedicated time-sharing systems have been placed in operation, each serving scientific-type users. The Johnniac Open-Shop System (JOSS) at the Rand Corporation provides access in such a language at any of several specially designed consoles, each consisting of a typewriter and a set of control switches [68]. Its design features ease of use and has thus attracted a large number of users. An early version of JOSS ran on the JOHNNIAC computer, a small machine with a 4096-word core and a relatively slow drum. This version, operational since May 1963, suffered from implementation on an aging vacuum tube machine, but demonstrated the feasibility of the operation of such a system on an appropriately modified small computer. A later version of JOSS runs on a DEC PDP-6 system.

The Dartmouth Time-Sharing System has been used by a large group of undergraduates, faculty, and remote users for a variety of applications [*16*]. Its language, BASIC (Beginners' All-purpose Symbolic Instruction Code), is easy to use and allows a FORTRAN-like program to be entered and stored or executed.

The Dartmouth system consists of a GE-235 CPU and a Datanet 30 communications controller which communicate with each other primarily through a mutually accessible disk file. The Datanet 30 is attached to the remote consoles, Model 35 Teletypes, and acts also as the master executive for the system, while the GE-235 performs all translations and program executions. Operational since 1964, the system has been effective for processing small jobs. The simplicity of the BASIC language has been a valuable asset.

The first commercial entrance into time-sharing was the IBM QUICKTRAN service. Another one-language system, a FORTRAN-like language usable from remote IBM 1050 stations, allows the generation, storage, and execution of programs. The system runs on an IBM 7044 [*36*].

Two other systems, both allowing general-purpose operation within the framework of a research facility, are the CORD system at the National Bureau of Standards and the Berkeley Time-Sharing System at the University of California [*42, 58*].

The CORD (Computer with On-line Remote Devices) system runs on a modified MOBIDIC B computer system, consisting of two CPU's, a disk file, and two IO channels. The system is designed to handle a half dozen terminals ranging from typewriters to remote display systems. A file system is readily accessed by a generalized set of system commands. The executive resides in one processor and controls IO for remote terminals and the execution of system commands. The other processor executes user programs in a time-sliced fashion.

The Berkeley Time-Sharing System runs on an SDS-930, renamed the SDS-940 when modified so that memory can be paged and appropriate protection mechanisms included. The system can serve up to 32 users at a variety of terminals and emphasizes on-line program debugging techniques.

During the development and operation of these systems the design principles for efficient time-sharing systems have become clearer, and a new generation of systems, in which the components are expressly designed for time-sharing, has begun to emerge. Several manufacturers have announced such computers. Some propose radical changes, while others incorporate many of the features available on the earlier time-sharing systems.

An important example of these new systems is MULTICS (Multiplexed Information and Computing Service), a general-purpose system being developed by Project MAC at MIT [*11, 33, 77*]. The initial system is being implemented on the GE-645 computer system, a GE-635 extensively redesigned to meet MULTIC's requirements.

Figure 3 shows an example of a MULTICS system configuration. A

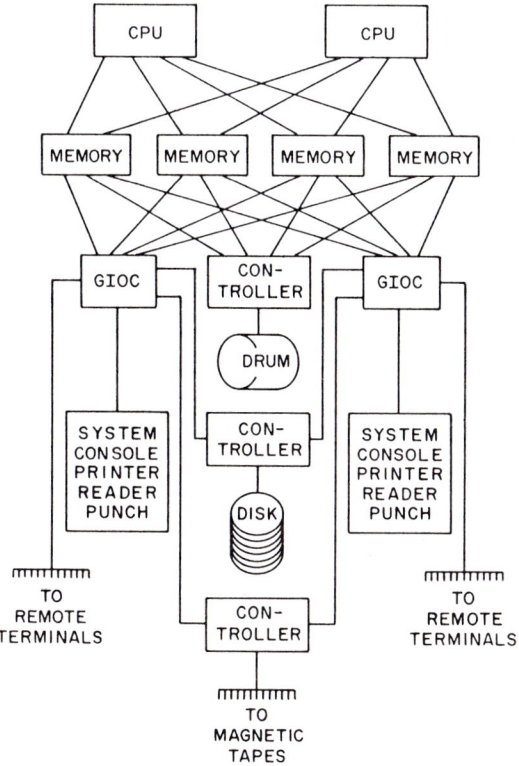

FIG. 3. A typical MULTICS configuration.

maximum of eight CPU's can each connect to any of the memory modules. Two Generalized Input-Output Controllers (GIOC's) also can connect to any memory module. The GIOC's interface with disk and tape controllers, other system peripheral equipment, and the remote terminals. A drum memory connects through a special controller directly to any memory module to provide immediate backup for the core memory. All intrasystem communication is done by means of *mailboxes* in the memory modules together with CPU interrupts.

A novel feature of the GE-645 is the addressing mechanism. All programs in the system are organized as sets of program segments, each of variable length. The segments, in turn, are broken into pages of either of two sizes. A user is aware of the segmentation, but the paging is done by the system without his knowledge in such a manner that swapping of programs and data in and out of primary memory is minimized. A mapping from the logical address given by a program to a corresponding physical address, described in Section 2.2, is done by system hardware and software.

There is a capability for dynamic linking of segments at run time, so that the burden on the programmer is minimized and maximum flexibility is maintained. Another feature is that the entire system is being written in the PL/1 language, and once the system is operational there will be little difference in appearance between systems programs and a user's PL/1 programs.

The design features of this system, which will be discussed in more detail in later sections, have been strongly influenced by the CTSS. The new MULTICS system is still intended to be a research tool, but it is designed to provide useful service to a large number of users while operating in this capacity.

Time-sharing systems other than those mentioned in this section have been developed. Representative samples of those in operation and those being implemented have been described, and others will be referenced in later sections when examining specific contributions to the development of time-sharing technology.

2. Design of the Time-Shared Computer System

2.1 Central Processor

One of the reasons that the time-sharing concept gained popularity when it did was that advancing technology reached the threshold necessary to seriously consider building a workable time-sharing system. Reliable computer operation at high speeds, accompanied by advances in machine organization, has been a major factor in reaching this threshold. There are several requirements that the CPU of a time-sharing system must meet, and most of these depend on recent technological advances.

Since a number of users must be served simultaneously in a time-sharing system, a fast CPU is required to provide satisfactory service on a centralized basis. The speed of a CPU in executing a particular program is a function of the instruction repertoire, the memory cycle time, and the CPU organization. Most of the advances in central processor technology have had a direct bearing on time-sharing. More powerful instructions, more parallel operation in arithmetic units, more index registers, and more ingenious capabilities for inter-register operations are all significant.

Along with the necessary threshold of central processor technology, certain additions must be made to a CPU to adapt it for use in a time-sharing system. It shall suffice here just to mention memory protection and memory relocation, since they will be covered in more detail in the next section. Some of the schemes for memory relocation, such as paging and segmentation, involve considerable modification of the processor addressing mechanism.

Other CPU additions include a more powerful interrupt mechanism. The processor interrupt mechanism, coupled with specially designed interfaces for remote terminals and for other peripheral equipment, must provide intimate connection on a real-time basis with these external devices. An important interrupt is the clock. Two types of clocks are used, an interval timer and a time-of-day clock. A programmable interval timer is desirable, although a fixed interval is sufficient, provided it is very short, on the order of 20 msec. This timer is used by the scheduler to control resource allocation. The time-of-day clock should be capable of interrogation by the system at any time, both for the system's and any user's needs.

Since a single CPU can execute either a supervisory program or a user program, there must be some provision for preventing the user from harming the supervisor or causing other forms of system failure. The usual way of doing this is to have the processor operate in a slave mode when a user program is running and to return it to a master mode when running the supervisor. In the slave mode certain instructions are illegal, such as all IO and halt operations. Input-output is done by subroutine call to the supervisor, so that no one user program can tie up any IO device, preventing its use by others. No program should be allowed to physically halt the processor, since a processor halt would halt all user programs as well as the supervisor. A halt operation in a user program should cause the supervisor to change the status of the program with respect to the scheduling routines.

Such a protected mode of operation introduces a means of checking for illegal operations or illegal memory accesses by a user. These illegal requests may be intentional or they may be unintentional, as can happen during program debugging. Furthermore, there must be some protection from system error, both hardware and software. Hardware errors, such as parity violation, can be detected and should cause an interrupt or trap to the supervisor so that appropriate action can be taken.

System software errors are much more difficult to detect. It has become evident the last several years that large systems are almost never fault-free. In a time-sharing system the software executive is very complex. When debugging such a system it is often impossible to re-create a system error, so it can take considerable effort to isolate errors.

It is now realized that the overall hardware-software system will never be completely debugged. Terms such as *mean time between failure* and *mean time between discontinuity* have been used to measure the reliability of systems. If it is acknowledged that all contingencies may never be accounted for, then the design of the CPU, as well as other parts of the system, must consider the minimization of loss when a failure occurs. This is a *failsoft* capability rather than *failsafe*. The component causing a failure is isolated and any part of the system executive that appears to be damaged is reloaded. Damage to active programs in the system must be minimized in this process.

To anticipate such problems, elaborate schemes have been devised to continually store in mass memory the programs and data that have been entered into the system. The design of the processor must enable such schemes to be implemented conveniently. The processor must detect faults of various kinds and be capable of taking any necessary action.

In still another aspect of processor design, a means must be provided for switching from program to program easily. The status of the CPU for a given program must be stored and another loaded. This includes swapping the program counter and all other operating registers. Various methods have evolved for accomplishing this, including the use of a program status word to indicate all of the CPU conditions that might be needed by a user program.

When switching programs, there is also the problem of interrupting a program without disturbing the execution of any instruction. This can be done by interrupting after the completion of the instruction being executed when the interrupt signal occurs. There is a problem, however, if the processor is executing an *execute* instruction, which may chain several levels deep. It is necessary to interrupt the CPU somewhere in this chaining process. Because a program error may result in an indefinitely continuing cycle in this chaining process, there must be a way of interrupting before instruction completion if the supervisor is to maintain control of the CPU. A similar problem is encountered if multilevel indirect addressing is allowed. The processor must be capable of interruption in the middle of instruction execution, and, upon return to a program, either continuing from this point or from the beginning of the instruction execution chain.

2.2 Memory

Memory in a time-sharing system can be described as a hierarchy of storage devices, from the fastest and smallest to the slowest and largest. Primary memory, at the top of this hierarchy, is usually core storage.

Magnetic drum has a sufficiently high data transfer rate and storage capacity to be used as an immediate backup for the primary memory. Bulk core, usually slower than primary memory, disk files, magnetic tapes, and other mass memory devices complete the hierarchy.

There are other types of memory in the system that are not included in this hierarchy. These are storage devices in the CPU and other processors, including registers, scratch-pad memories, and read-only memories for microprogrammed operation. All of these types of memory usually have cycle times faster than storage external to the processors. The speeds of these devices and the processor organization of which they are an integral part directly affect the operation of the time-sharing system.

The primary memory of the time-sharing system, that which the CPU's are capable of directly addressing, is usually a set of random-access core banks. In some small systems there may be only one bank, while in large systems the number of banks may be so large that complex addressing mechanisms are required in the CPU's to access them.

Multiple banks of core memory for computer systems have been developed both as a technical expedient and as an organizational necessity for high-speed operation. There are technical limitations on the size of a core bank if it is to operate with a cycle time on the order of 1 or 2 μsec. These limitations usually allow a maximum bank size of 4096 words and sometimes it is desirable to use even smaller banks.

When using a primary memory with multiple core banks, a complete addressing mechanism and data input-output channel can be set up for each bank; then, all banks can operate simultaneously. Core banks operating in this manner can be overlapped or interleaved to reduce the effective cycle of time of the entire memory. This necessitates the assignment of successive memory addresses to different core banks, so that a CPU requesting two or more words from contiguous addresses can obtain them simultaneously from different banks. This technique may halve or even further decrease the effective memory cycle time.

The effect of overlapping not only allows a single CPU to have simultaneous access to two or more banks, but also, in a time-sharing system where there are two or more processors operating in parallel, several processors may access different primary memory banks at the same time. This allows the parallel execution of a program from one bank while swapping another bank with backup memory, helping to minimize system overhead due to swapping.

Another reason for the division of memory into banks in a time-sharing system is the gain in reliability. Since each bank is independent, if one bank fails only a portion of memory is lost. Interconnections between processors and primary memory must be arranged so that a faulty core bank causes a minimum of interference with system operation.

It is desirable to have a very large primary memory in a time-sharing system, so that several programs and part of the supervisor may reside there at the same time. This minimizes swapping of programs between primary and backup memories. The designers of the first systems recognized this objective, but were forced to fit the concept to existing machines. Swapping of programs in the CTSS is an expedient employed primarily because sufficient primary memory is not available. At SDC, where the system has several memory banks (see Fig. 2), there is sufficient room in primary memory for the supervisor and some programs, but it is still necessary to swap programs when available memory is full.

The designers of systems currently being implemented, such as MULTICS [77], still foresee a need for some swapping. This swapping takes place within the over-all notion of the trickling of inactive programs down the hierarchy of memories and the percolating of more active programs up the hierarchy. In such a system, it is essential that reference to programs and data be made by some name or designation other than physical address, and that the supervisor be given control of the movement of information up and down in the memory hierarchy.

A problem that arises when swapping programs to and from primary memory is that the movement of one program from primary to backup memory leaves a hole in the primary memory that may not be large enough for a program to be moved to the primary from the backup memory. The supervisor must allocate primary memory so that holes are filled in an optimum way. It is generally inefficient to execute core-to-core transfers of programs to close or enlarge holes in primary memory. Other means for memory management centered around the paging of primary memory are more desirable.

Associated with the memory management problem is the effect on programs of being loaded into different memory locations after each swap with backup storage. Some type of memory address relocation must be employed. A simple solution to this problem is the relocation register, loaded by the supervisor, as used in the CTSS. All programs are written as if they are to be loaded into memory address zero. At run time the contents of the relocation register is added to each address used by the program before memory reference is made.

A means for handling the relocation task and the memory management problem at the same time is the use of a paged memory. The concept of paging was first used on the ATLAS computer for the simulation of a large core memory by a small core and drum [38]. It was used for the same purpose in the ACCESS computer, developed at the National

Bureau of Standards. Paging involves the fragmentation of the user's image of primary memory into a number of blocks or pages. When space is needed in primary memory, only the number of pages needed are placed in the backup storage. These stored pages may be returned as required to any available page of primary memory. Furthermore, if a bit is associated with each page of primary memory to indicate whether the user has written in that page since the last time it was copied from backup storage, only those pages that have been modified since their last memory swap need to be stored again.

To remove the burden from the user of addressing pages of memory every memory address in a user's program is translated by the system into its actual physical address. This translation might be entirely hardware or it may require assistance from the supervisor. The memory the user thinks he is using is a virtual memory, and he is unaware that it may be scattered about in the physical memory. Several methods have been developed to accomplish this mapping from virtual to physical memory.

A very simple method is employed by the Berkeley Time-Sharing System and is included in the SDS-940 computer [42]. The high order 3 bits of the 14-bit virtual address are used to select one of eight registers. These registers, previously filled by the supervisor, each contain the high order 5 bits of a physical address. These 5 bits, attached to the 11 low order bits of the virtual address, those bits not used to select a register, form a 16-bit physical memory address. Any one user has access to 8 pages of the entire 32-page memory. Since each page is 2048 words in size, the user has access to 16,384 words of the 65,536-word memory. The translating or mapping proceeds without delaying the access to memory, and the register loading by the supervisor is done quickly with four instructions.

A more elegant mapping process is used in the GE-645 computer for MULTICS [33]. A similar method is employed by the IBM System/360 Model 67 [7]. In both systems an additional level of addressing sophistication is introduced. Every program is broken into segments, each of which consists of pages. The division into pages is not seen by the user, but he must decide which parts of his program and data are to be individual segments. During program execution he may refer by name to segments other than the one being used, so that dynamic linking of segments is possible. By the user's segmentation of each program, the amount of primary memory and other high level storage required at any time is minimized. An important consequence of the ability to segment programs is the increased efficiency with which a programmer can handle small parts of a large problem rather than tackling the entire problem at once. This capability is similar to the ability to compile parts of a large program separately and then to be able to run them as one large program with assistance from the system to link the parts together.

In the MULTICS system, each user has a descriptor segment, which is used to reference all of his other segments. The descriptor segment itself may be paged by the system. A segment can be specified by a number indicating a relative position in the descriptor segment. This position contains the segment descriptor corresponding to the given number.

The segment descriptor contains the physical address of the segment or, if the segment is paged, the location of the table in which its pages are defined. In addition, the segment descriptor contains such control information as the accession limitations of the segment.

A logical or virtual memory address, as specified in a user's program, has two parts. The low order part becomes the low order part of the physical address, as in the Berkeley system. The high order part specifies the name of the segment and the logical page address. The name of the segment is the segment's relative position in the user's descriptor segment, and the logical page address is the relative position in the page table in which is found the high order bits of the physical address. The base address of the page table is found in the segment table which is referenced through the descriptor segment. The programmer need only be concerned with the segment name and can use the remainder of the address as if the segment is a contiguous section of memory, since paging is done automatically.

If this complex mapping procedure were to be executed for each memory reference, each such reference would require one memory cycle for access to the segment table and another for the page table, in addition to the final access to the memory word desired. To alleviate this problem there are eight associative registers attached to the high order part of the register containing the logical address. When a memory reference is made, the high order bits of the logical address as well as those of the physical address determined by the mapping procedure are stored in one of these eight registers. Then, if another reference is made to the same segment and page after the first reference, the associative lookup determines this immediately by comparison of the logical address register to the associative registers and transfers the physical address from the appropriate register into the memory address register. Up to eight pages can be actively referenced in this manner without the time-consuming mapping process.

Operation of this segmentation and paging mechanism is expected to add a small percentage to the program execution time. There is also a loss of memory space, since the segment and page tables for each user program must be stored. While a program is running, parts of these tables must occupy primary memory. The gain in flexibility and general system operation has been judged sufficient to merit this loss in CPU speed and memory capacity.

Some of the thought that has led to the swapping of programs on a page-by-page basis between primary and backup memories may be revised if bulk core is used instead of drum or disk. Wilkes has proposed a method for swapping one word at a time, so that unnecessary transfers between two random-access devices are minimized [*80*]. Other methods for mapping virtual to physical memory will undoubtedly be developed as larger and more sophisticated memory systems are required. Advocates of simplicity and speed will compete with those designing complex addressing mechanisms. Both will be attempting to minimize the interfacing problems between primary and backup memories, attempting to integrate them in an efficiently operating system.

So far in this section, backup or secondary memory has been used as an extension of primary memory in such a way that programs or pages of programs are swapped between the memories during time-shared CPU operation. When used in this manner, there is usually an image of each user's active program in the backup memory, and appropriate parts of this image are copied into primary memory before program execution. Both drum and disk memories have been used as immediate backup storage; however, the data transfer rate to and from a drum is usually faster than that of a disk file. Access time to a specified word for drum memory is shorter than for most disk files, since each track or channel has its own head. Most disk files have one head per disk, so that a positioning time for the head to reach the specified track must be added to the rotation time required for the particular word to appear under the head. The effect of this rotation time can be minimized by hardware and software techniques which consider the position of the head relative to the drum or disk. Using a disk file, the transfer of 32,000 words to or from memory, assuming optimum programming to minimize latency delay, may require two or three seconds. This time can be reduced by an order of magnitude with a drum.

Another important use of secondary memory is for long-term program and data storage. It may also be used for storing parts of the supervisor until they are needed, thus minimizing the supervisor's primary memory requirement.

All of the secondary memory devices discussed so far are connected on-line to the system, so that the delay in accessing any program or data is determined by supervisor scheduling as well as electronic and physical delays in the storage devices. If magnetic tape is used at the low end of the heirarchy, it has a different characteristic. A human system operator must be given a message to load a particular tape on a specified tape unit. The access time for tape data may include the delay while such a message is typed out, the time required to find the tape, transporting it to the tape unit, and loading it.

2.3 Remote Terminals

Access to a time-shared system is by means of a remote terminal or console connected on-line to the system. Typical consoles have been designed around electric typewriters, alphanumeric displays, and graphical displays. Considerations in the design and selection of remote terminals include:

(1) *Convenience to the user*. The man-machine interface must conform to man's needs for the particular use he desires to make of the system. It must minimize the effort required to enter programs and data into the system and display computer output clearly and effectively. The user should be able to type or otherwise input to the system at his own speed and the system output must be at a rate commensurate with the user's assimilation of the data.

(2) *Minimization of terminal cost*. The meaning of this consideration must be determined for each application and for each system. In general, while the system itself is shared by all users, there must be one terminal for each user, so the cost of a terminal must be multiplied by the number of users and added to the cost of the rest of the system before considering the economics of time-sharing. Because cost is of prime importance in the design of any system, and since terminal cost is multiplied in this manner, it is desirable to provide the cheapest terminal that satisfies the other considerations.

(3) *Minimization of burden on system*. Although a principal justification for time-sharing is the sharing of a central computer system, the burden placed on the system by each terminal should be minimized so that a maximum number of users can be served simultaneously and better service given to those being served. This goal may be in direct conflict with the goal of minimizing terminal cost, but it is an essential consideration. It becomes particularly important when using display-type terminals, in which the potential load on the system is much greater than for typewriter-like terminals. With such display devices, the inclusion of a buffer and local logic may minimize the total system cost and increase its operating efficiency.

(4) *Minimization of communication costs*. The cost of the communication line between the terminal and the computer system can be significant, especially if the terminal is located miles or even thousands of miles from the computer. The design of the terminal, the interface of

the line to the terminal, and the interface of the line to the computer system all determine the communication line requirements. Additional hardware at the terminal can minimize the load on the line as well as on the computer system. The greater the length of the line between the terminal and the system, the higher the cost, and the greater the justification for increasing terminal cost to help reduce the load on the communication line.

Typewriter-like devices are the most widely used terminals in current time-sharing systems. These may be electric typewriters with a few added control functions or a conventional teletypewriter. A typewriter terminal provides input by a keyboard containing numerals, the alphabet, and numerous special characters which are used in various ways in existing time-sharing systems. Although occasional special characters have similar meaning in two or more systems, there has been little attempt to standardize their usage. For a person who has access to several systems it is a challenge to remember the conventions of each. Teletypewriter output is hard copy and is produced one character at a time, as in normal typewriter operation. The maximum character rate for such terminals is 10 to 15 characters/sec. This is quite ample for manual typing, but slow for punched tape input and for large amounts of output.

Typical problems that arise when using typewriter terminals on a time-sharing system include the design of the conversation between man and machine so that a minimum of typing is required and so that the output is limited. Fast typists can usually establish a rapport with the system that lets them converse freely. Hunt and peck typists often experience difficulty maintaining a satisfactory interaction rate. For this reason, after a user is familiar with a system it is usually possible for him to abbreviate many typed statements. At the same time, an experienced user is satisfied with abbreviated output messages. However, he must learn to make optimum use of the limited output. Obtaining an assembly listing of a fairly large program, for instance, might take ten or more minutes. As a substitute, the user could either print out only part of such a listing or have the entire listing printed on a system line printer for later reference.

Since the characters of a typical typewriter can be uniquely represented by 6 to 8 bits per character, at a maximum rate of 15 characters/sec, the transmission requirement is about 90 to 120 bits/sec. A standard telephone line, having a potential capacity of more than 2000 bits/sec, is more than sufficient to tie such a terminal to the system. A TWX or TELEX link is often cheaper, since the line capacity is just sufficient for Teletype transmission. Teletype terminals can connect directly to TWX or TELEX networks with interfaces provided by Bell Telephone or Western Union. Teletypes and other typewriter terminals can be interfaced with conventional telephone lines using Bell Telephone Dataphones. A Dataphone at the computer provides an interface between the telephone line and the system.

Teletypes available for time-sharing systems include Models 33 and 35. Model 33 is intended for limited duty application, while Model 35 is qualified for substantial usage. A Model 37 Teletype, extending the capability of Model 35 to include upper and lower case letters as well as other added functions, will soon be available. All of these terminals use standard ASCII code. Other available terminals include the IBM 1050, which is designed around an IBM Selectric typewriter. This unit contains a number of control buttons and indicators and usually requires a Dataphone connection to the computer system.

Remote terminals having additional capability are available, usually costing more than a basic typewriter console. A cathode ray tube display can output a page of text in a few seconds, can include editing functions for modifying the displayed text, and can operate with a telephone line connection to the system. Additional cost is encountered, however, if hard copy is desired. Such an alphanumeric display generally requires a control unit and a remote buffer memory. With substantial buffer memory and appropriate local logic, such a terminal can allow limited input, output, and editing to be done locally, without burdening the communication line or the computer system.

A cathode ray tube terminal capable of graphical display provides two-dimensional output to the user. Using light pens and other marker devices, graphical input can also be provided. With such a device, including some local logic, a substantial amount of off-line work can be done, and the time-sharing system is used only for extensive computation and for storage and retrieval of data and programs. Devices such as MAGIC (Machine for Automatic Graphics Interface to a Computer) provide the services of a small computer as a part of the terminal [59]. Since a graphical display can be a severe load on the system without such capability at the remote terminal, interest is growing rapidly in the use of small processors at the terminals.

2.4 Communications

Steps that may be taken to reduce communication line costs by proper remote terminal design were discussed in the last section. These costs can usually be reduced by placing the remote terminals closer to the time-shared system. When considering the types and costs of communication links, the subject of reliability, including error detection and correction, is important.

An advantage of using the telephone or other existing network for connecting to a time-sharing system is the resulting wide accessability to the system. However, the farther a remote terminal is located from the system, the higher the toll expense. In much of the interaction between a typical typewriter terminal user and the system the line remains idle, while the user ponders his next move or the system delays before responding to the user. During these periods it is common to leave the full capacity line connected between the terminal and the system. For a user to temporarily disconnect, he must go through a complicated calling procedure to again gain system access. If the system does not automatically maintain an available interface, the user may find himself locked out of the system by other users who may occupy the limited number of system interfaces during his period of disconnection.

Although the terminal and system interface are wasted during such idle periods, if the user is relatively close to the system the additional communication cost is minimal. A desire to service a large number of users over a wide geographic area leads to consideration of a set of time-sharing systems distributed over the area, so that a user need not communicate over very long distances. Since access may be desired to files in a distant system, wide-band communication links among such systems could allow users to share the costs of common communication capabilities, thus minimizing the cost per user. Networks of computer systems organized in this manner are discussed in Section 5.2.

Typical communication lines used by remote terminals for access to time-sharing systems suffer from noise problems. Bursts of noise, transients on the line, are common. To minimize the effect of such noise, various error-detecting and error-correcting schemes may be employed. Some of these employ hardware at the system and as part of the terminals. Others depend on the software and on sufficient communication between users and the system for assurance that messages are received correctly.

A simple hardware parity check at both ends of the communication line can indicate when characters are garbled during transmission. Teletypewriters can be equipped with parity generation and detection mechanisms. There is, however, no standard established for such devices, and some systems use odd parity and others even, while still others leave the parity bit on or off continually. A time-sharing system can be designed to serve users having a variety of these types of remote terminals. The system can neglect the parity bit altogether. It can require those terminals having common characteristics to connect to particular system interfaces. Or it can allow all terminals to connect to any interface, and then sense the parity coming from the terminal and modify its operation with respect to the currently connected terminal accordingly.

Another means for assuring error-free operation is a full duplex link between the terminal and the system. When a user depresses a key at his typewriter terminal an appropriate code is transmitted to the system. Either hardware or a combination of hardware and software at the system responds by echoing back the character so that it is printed at the terminal. The user observes that what is being printed is what he has typed and is assured that the communication link is operating properly, since the probability that an incorrect transmission to the system was canceled by an incorrect transmission back to the terminal is very small. In full duplex operation the user must be cognizant of the individual characters being printed, and, since this requires concentration, it is possible for occasional single character errors to escape his detection. Furthermore, there is usually no check made on characters being transmitted from the system to the user. Substantial extra hardware may be required at the line-system interface for full duplex operation. This is so when the system allows two separate paths from the terminal all the way into the system, with feedback completed by software means. If the echoing loop is completed in hardware near the point where the communication line meets the system, this additional hardware can be negligible; however, this configuration checks only the line, while the other checks the operation of the entire interface.

Finally, an effective method for assuring error-free operation uses the man-computer conversational capability. As the system receives a command or other message from the terminal, it replies with a confirming message. This procedure can correct mistakes in understanding on the part of the user or the system, as well as trivial communication line errors. If the system fails to understand a command that it has received, it may either ask that it be repeated or attempt to guess its most probable interpretation and then ask the user to verify its assumption.

2.5 Interfacing of Remote Terminals

Having already discussed the terminals and the communication lines between them and the system, this section discusses the design of the interface between the communication lines and the time-sharing system. The interface design depends on the type of remote terminal, the type of communication line, the part of the system to which it is to be connected, and the amount of internal buffering and logic that is desired.

For servicing typewriter terminals, the interface must be capable of receiving 10 to 15 characters/sec and either storing them in an internal memory or relaying them to a system memory. In a sense, the interface is a processor; it functions in parallel with the CPU's and other processors in the system. Special controllers, such as the IBM 7750 and the GE Datanet 20, are actually internally programmed processors which interface directly to the communication lines.

The interface may have register storage for one character per terminal, in which case it must continually dump characters into primary memory or interrupt a CPU to perform this function. However, the interface may have delay line, core, or other internal storage capable of storing an entire string of characters before interrupting a CPU. In this case, the interface must either compare all characters to some break character, a carriage return, for instance, or it must count characters so that its memory does not become overfilled. A character-by-character input gives the system more flexibility, since the supervisor software can allow exchanges requiring only single characters.

The input task of the interface is either to respond to characters immediately as they are received from the terminal or to scan or poll all lines so that every line is scanned at least once every 100 msec. This suffices to receive characters at the fastest rate a teletypewriter terminal is capable of generating.

The output task is either to interrupt a CPU at intervals during transmission to obtain the next character to be sent to a terminal or to store an entire message and to transmit it sequentially to the terminal.

An interface for a terminal having a faster data rate may require larger buffers, more frequent interrupts, and faster circuitry. Its organization can be similar to that of a typewriter terminal interface. As mentioned in Section 1.4, controllers such as the IBM 7750 can service one higher rate device in place of several slower ones with a minimum of modification.

All interfaces must be designed to meet worst-case conditions. In the worst case a delay in transmission to a device may be allowed, but the data must not be lost. Likewise, either the interface must be able to accept long strings of characters at the maximum terminal generation rate or it must have the capability of turning the remote terminal's transmission controller on and off as the system digests the input at its own rate. This latter approach has been chosen in some systems for punched-paper tape input at a remote terminal; the system turns the terminal tape reader on and off as necessary.

2.6 Scheduling

Allocation of CPU time is done by the system scheduler. Some schedulers employ an algorithm that is designed to maximize system operating efficiency, reducing overhead caused by swapping and other supervisor functions. Others emphasize service to the users at the expense of system efficiency. Most schedulers recognize both of these goals and attempt to provide satisfactory user service while maintaining efficient operation.

The scheduler cycles among all active user programs in some manner, giving each a slice of CPU time at appropriate intervals. A program is active if its execution has been initiated and it is not yet completed. While a program is active it may require several slices of CPU time before its completion. Besides the scheduler restriction on the CPU time allotted to a program, the program itself may be temporarily halted or blocked before the end of its time slice. This blocking may be initiated by a system command call by the user program, requiring the suspension of the program until the completion of specified supervisor routines. In some systems, such a call does not necessarily cause the program to be blocked. In the NBS CORD system, for instance [58], the user program has the option of continuing operation in parallel with system command execution or waiting for the supervisor to complete the command. If such flexibility is allowed, either a separate CPU must be provided for the execution of system commands or such supervisor programs must be executed in a time-shared manner as if they are scheduled as additional user programs. This type of system command call is very similar to the generation of a task which can be run in parallel with a user's main program. With such a capability, any user might have a number of programs in operation simultaneously.

A simple means for scheduling in a time-sharing system is the round robin. Every active program is given a slice of processor time in turn as the system cycles among them. The slice of time is called a quantum, and the parameters for a round robin scheduling algorithm are the quantum time and the cycle time. For a given quantum time, the number of users determines the minimum cycle time. If program swapping is required in a system, the shorter the quantum, the more often swapping is necessary, and the higher the system overhead. However, since lengthening the quantum to minimize this overhead increases the cycle time, for a given number of active users, the quantum time cannot be chosen arbitrarily large for more efficient operation. A rule often applied is that the cycle time should be no longer than one human reaction time, which is about one-tenth of a second. For a request demanding a minimum of processor time, less than one quantum, this guarantees a response to the user within his reaction time. For a request demanding more CPU time, several cycles may be required, several program swaps may be involved, and a delay will probably be noticed by the user.

To compensate for the loss in efficiency experienced when longer programs require a number of swaps before their completion, a combination of round robin and priority scheduling can be used. The CTSS scheduler operates in this manner [10]. When a user request for service occurs the system estimates the program running time, considering the physical size of the program in its prediction. On the basis of this estimate each program is placed in a priority level, longer programs in lower levels. Programs in the higher priority levels are given short time quanta at frequent intervals, while those in lower levels are run less often for a longer period. If a program is not completed at the end of its allotted quantum, it is placed in the next lower priority level. This dynamic priority level assignment takes advantage of the information gained by the system during program execution to refine the estimate of program running time. The priority within each level may be determined by the order in which the program arrives at the level or by the order of arrival of the initial request for service [54]. This scheduling algorithm attempts to maximize system efficiency, yet give highly interactive programs the necessary shorter cycle time.

In both the simple round robin and in the multilevel priority scheduler consideration is given to the number of user programs active at a given time. The quantum may be adjusted as the system runs so that efficiency is optimized while meeting some minimum interaction requirements. As the number of active programs grows the quantum may be decreased. In systems where a programmable interval timer is not available, such modifications of effective quantum may be effected by allotting programs some multiple of the basic clock interval. Thus, a program may be allowed to continue after being interrupted by the clock if the scheduler assigns it a multiple interval quantum. In this type of system it is desirable to have a very short clock interval.

Scheduling algorithms for time-sharing systems are similar in concept to monitor operation in a batch processing installation. In the simplest installation, programs are run sequentially without regard to their size or projected run time. In others, express service is given for programs having a short maximum run time, so that the turnaround time for such programs is minimized. As in a time-sharing system, the more interactive users, those demanding less service per job, are given priority over other users. These installations usually allow the programmer to specify the predicted run time, so indicating his priority. It may be desirable to give the user similar control of his priority in a time-shared system. This has been proposed for the MULTICS system [31], where, in addition to the user's assignment of priority based on expected run time per interaction, he may judge his program's importance relative to others being run in the system. Priority assignment in this manner may prove useful, especially if a firm guideline is given for user assignment of priorities and some type of enforcement procedure is employed. In batch processing installations the normal enforcement procedure is to shove programs off the system when they exceed the time limit. The problem is more complex in a time-shared system, and there is some doubt that a user would assign himself a lower priority for the sake of system efficiency, especially if he notices a degradation in service; there will have to be some means of prodding him to assist the system.

The scheduling discussed so far applies primarily to the sharing of a CPU by a number of user programs. The system resources include other processors and devices that must also be shared in some optimum manner. One way of approaching total system scheduling is to make the most efficient use of the most expensive resources when there is a choice to be made by the system supervisor. This approach must be tempered by considering the effects of user interaction requirements on the allocation of all system resources.

Analyses have been made of schedulers in operation and those that have been proposed. Estimates of queuing problems or waiting lines in various parts of the system have been made by the observation of activity in operating systems and the extrapolation to larger systems using the data obtained, and by the simulation of systems assuming reasonable probability distributions of loads on the system. Such analyses are quite important, since the capacity of a system is determined by the operation of the scheduler under various operating conditions.

In the selection of a scheduling algorithm and of the parameters for its operation a worst-case approach could be used. The system could be designed to give some optimum level of service to a designated maximum number of users. If this is done, however, the system would be inefficiently used during periods when the load is not at a peak. This wasted capacity may be minimized by designing for some average load and providing slightly degraded service during peak load periods. The design may still specify maximum load conditions corresponding to the most degraded service that the system should provide.

A network of time-shared computer systems, as described in Section 5.2, can allow systems to share computing capacity. When one system experiences a peak load condition it can borrow spare capacity from other systems through the communication network linking all systems, so that each system scheduler need not be so concerned with the peak load consideration. Such a network may have a peak load condition for the entire set of systems, however, and may suffer degradation at various points in the network when this condition occurs.

2.7 Accounting

In most time-sharing systems the cost of operation must be distributed among the users. The system supervisor is in a position to determine the relative amount of use of each system resource by each user and to compute charges accordingly. An accounting or charging algorithm may be very simple, simply estimating charges, or it may be very elaborate, considering detailed system operation.

A first approximation to the actual distribution of system usage can be attempted by measuring the amount of CPU time accrued by each user, similar to charging techniques for batch processing systems. Since programs make varying demands on other parts of the system, this may not be the fairest way of dividing the expenses. The amount of IO processor usage, the amount of primary and backup storage used, the amount of system overhead required because of special requirements of a user, as well as the CPU time, should all be considered.

Since accounting routines which consider all these criteria may grow to the point where they become a substantial part of system overhead, some compromise must be made between sophistication and first approximation. Some overhead of this type is essential in most time-sharing systems. Little work has been reported in this area, but it is foreseen that the newer systems will incorporate accounting routines of all types. This will be especially important for the systems which will operate in a nonexperimental environment, in which satisfactory distribution of cost is essential.

3. Over-all Systems Considerations

3.1 Hardware Systems Configurations

A motivation for time-sharing is the economic gain through centralization. A large, fast computer can serve a number of users, each of whom could not keep such a machine busy. This motivation is the same as that which has caused batch processing installations to obtain the largest computer commensurate with their needs rather than several smaller computers. The disadvantages of centralization include the dependence upon a single source of computation capability and a potential loss in privacy because of the shared use of facilities. The design of most time-sharing systems attempts to minimize the effects of these inherent liabilities of centralized operation.

Decisions in the system design concerning the number of processors, the function of each processor, and the physical relation of processors to each other directly influence the performance of the system. The simplest system has one CPU which performs all supervisory and user program execution in addition to directly controlling IO for backup memory and remote terminals. An additional processor for IO can remove considerable burden from the CPU, increasing the total system capability. The IBM 7750 used in CTSS is an example of this type of configuration [26]. This system has, in addition, processors (data channels) for access to backup memory and other peripheral devices in parallel with CPU operation. If further capability is given to the communication or remote terminal IO controller, still more burden can be removed from the CPU. In the Dartmouth Time-Sharing System and in the NBS CORD system the communications controller functions as the system executive [16, 58]. Control of the CPU and even the execution of system commands is done in the executive processor. It is not usually necessary to include floating point and other extended CPU operations in such an executive and communications processor.

If the additional processor or processors contain internal memory and introduce considerable extra cost their use may not be justified in terms of increased system capability. However, if the additional processor uses the same primary memory that the CPU or CPU's require, and if the total system gain is substantial, their introduction may be justified. Present technology dictates that processor cost is small compared to memory and peripheral equipment. With the advent of integrated circuits and other cost-reducing techniques this trend should become even more apparent, so that the addition of a properly designed processor to a system may be an even better means for increasing system capability with little added cost.

Multiple CPU's have been included in the design of some time-sharing systems currently being implemented [7, 11]. In these systems, a large primary memory is multiplexed by the multiple processors. One reason for the use of multiple CPU's is that technology is reaching a standstill in the development of faster, more powerful, single CPU's. Multiple CPU's within a system, provided they are used efficiently, can substitute for such powerful processors. As CPU organizational and other technological advances gradually increase the single processor capability, a multiprocessor environment can still multiply the total computing power in a given system.

In a multiprocessor system, the number of processors and the amount of primary and backup memory must be chosen so that the entire system is balanced. As a system grows, all parts of it must grow together. With such a configuration the factors determining maximum size are of interest. The larger the system, the more the centralization of computing power accentuates the risks associated with common facilities.

However, the larger the system, the greater the justification for complex reliability and security measures that can improve system operation. The larger the number of processors and memory banks, the larger the number of interconnections, and the more complex the conflict resolving circuitry. Interlocking problems associated with the multiplexing of memory banks may introduce delays as additional levels of logic are required.

The very existence of multiple processors in a system is a type of reliability through redundancy. This added reliability can be realized only by appropriate hardware interconnections so that the failure of a processor does not incapacitate other parts of the system. If the software supervisor is capable of floating from one CPU to another, system degradation can be accomplished gracefully when any processor fails.

3.2 Software Executives

The executive or supervisor in any time-sharing system has several functions. All supervisor and user programs must be scheduled so that system resources are employed efficiently. Control of remote terminal communication and accounting procedures for each user are supervisor functions. Maintenance of the files in the mass memories and references to these files may require a large subsystem for file control. Management of space in the primary memory, including decisions for program swapping, is the supervisor's responsibility.

In a system such as CTSS the executive and one or more user programs reside in some portion of primary memory at the same time. Any user may make requests for service from the executive by a call for a system command. The executive language is composed of the set of system commands available on a particular system. These commands and the resulting messages or data returned to the user constitute the communication between the user and the executive.

Commands usually consist of a command identifier and a set of parameters. A command can be generated by a user at a remote terminal, or a user program can call a command to initiate terminal IO or other supervisor-controlled functions by setting up a parameter vector and executing a call to the system. This capability is required to prevent user programs from directly tying up system resources for long periods of time.

The system command call may be executed in any of several ways. A subroutine call, employing a TSX or similar instruction, as in CTSS, can cause a trap to the executive. The execution of one of a special set of instructions may cause such a trap to a location in the supervisor appropriate for the particular service desired. If there is a supervisor program for a particular command resident in the primary memory, the supervisor transfers control to that program. If, as usually occurs in CTSS, there is no such resident program, the command program can be loaded into the primary memory as the user's program, while his main program is stored temporarily. A copy of the appropriate system command program must be made for each execution. Command execution in this manner eliminates the possibility of the continuation of the user program concurrently with the running of the command routine. In other systems, such as the ARPA-SDC system, the continued presence of reentrantly coded system command routines in primary memory allows several users to use the same copy of the command program, conserving system memory space and saving copying and transfer time for command routines.

Because user programs can call system commands, a given user program may be a sequence of such calls. This is treated as a special case in some systems, in which sequences of commands can be given names and called in a manner similar to that used to call the basic commands. In ODIN these sequences are called clichés [27]; in CTSS the process is called the chaining of commands; and in others, the generation and use of macrocommands.

An important executive function is control of mass memory files. Information storage and retrieval in the backup memories is handled with varying sophistication. Some systems have elaborate control of file name directories for individual users and allow users to link to each other's files [15]. Others emphasize requests of the file system on the basis of logical combinations of descriptors to obtain stored programs and data [57]. All systems attempt in some way to optimize the use of space in the available backup memories, distributing it among all system users.

3.3 System Reliability

An operational time-sharing system must experience continuity of operation over long time periods. Both system hardware and software must be capable of reliable service to users upon demand. There is a greater dependence on reliability in time-shared operation than there is with batch processing. In a conventional installation, a system failure may cause the turnaround time to rise from a few hours to several hours. The programmer has sufficient time to leisurely modify his plans with such a slowly reacting system. When conversing interactively with a system which suddenly experiences a failure, the user is immediately at a loss. If such failure occurs frequently, operation can be frustrating. Since a large number of users may be on-line, all of their time will be wasted when the system goes down.

There are several potential sources of failure in a time-sharing system. They include hardware, system software, and user program failure. Protection must be provided for the system against faulty user program operation. The user must be protected against failure of his own program, which he might not recognize, and against failure of another user's program which may run astray. Since a common use of time-sharing systems is for the on-line debugging of unproved programs, this protection is an absolute necessity.

Section 2.1 referred to the increased reliability of processors and other system components currently available. The use of such components is essential for the successful operation of any system operating in a real-time environment. Since, for most components, there is an estimated probability of failure which is larger than that desired for the total system, operation of all parts of the system cannot be made entirely failsafe. The availability of multiple CPU's, multiple memory banks, and even multiple paths connecting remote terminals to the system can assist in maintaining continuity of operation. With sufficient redundancy and with appropriate means for disconnecting faulty components from the remainder of the system a failsoft capability can be maintained. That is, in the event of failure of a limited number of system components, graceful degradation of system performance can be obtained without disruption of the entire system's operation.

The system software necessary to perform such a degradation automatically would be very complex, taking into account all of the possible contingencies. Some of the dedicated time-sharing systems, such as the airline reservation systems, have a backup capability which approaches an automatic failsoft mechanism. However, in most such systems and in all of the operational and proposed general-purpose time-sharing systems the failsoft capability depends on the action of a human operator to assist in determining the failure and the recovery procedure. Work will continue the next several years to develop means for systems to detect failures, compensate for them, and indicate a plan for repairing the faulty component.

The reliability of system software is a very special problem, for a time-sharing executive is one of the most complex programs that can be written for a computer. A system is usually constructed in a modular fashion, so that various parts of the executive can be developed simultaneously by several programmers. The modules are tested separately and then linked together into the operating system. Because requests for service originate from parts of the system at unpredictable intervals, it is difficult to test all of the possible sequences of activity within the executive system. When an error is noted during debugging of an executive it is usually difficult to recreate the state of the system when the error occurred. Debugging the system is many times a problem in piecing together the evidence of several errors in an attempt to develop a pattern.

These complications in the design and testing of the executive have led to a concession by systems designers that such systems will never be completely debugged, especially those operating in an experimental environment, where changes in the system occur frequently. It is necessary to protect the system against executive failure by providing means to detect a failure, to reload damaged parts of the executive program, and to restart the system. All of this must be done while minimizing the loss to users of the system.

Protection of the system from user program error is quite simple compared to these system problems. Methods have been devised for preventing damage caused by faulty programs. These means for protection from program error have been discussed in other sections. They include protection from illegal memory access, from the execution of illegal instructions, and from usurping large amounts of CPU time.

4. The Use of Time-Shared Systems

4.1 Appropriateness of Applications

A time-shared computer system is best suited for handling applications involving continued interaction between man and computer. Computer applications may be placed in a spectrum based on interaction requirements. On one end are those needing no interaction during problem solution and for which long turnaround time poses no great restriction. These might be production runs to be executed at infrequent intervals or large programs which require considerable processor time and for which a user would not wait for a solution, even if he had the system all to himself. At the other end of the spectrum is the problem which depends on the computer to service some process in a critical real-time relationship. Between these extremes lie all of the problems that can be solved on a computer system.

Because long, noninteractive programs introduce excessive system overhead, as discussed in Section 2.6, running them in a time-shared mode is not usually efficient. For many shorter programs the time-shared mode of operation is relatively efficient, provides easy access to the system, reduces turnaround time, and allows conversational operation. For a large class of problems solution is not even possible without being on-line to a time-sharing system.

4.2 Typical Applications

Many applications for time-shared computer systems are in the general category of program testing. A principal use anticipated by early system designers has been the entering and debugging of programs. Programs are entered in any language appropriate for use from a remote console and, during the program input, as well as during the debugging period, editing functions for inserting, deleting, or modifying lines of the program can be used. Once the program is debugged, it can be stored for later execution or it can be run immediately.

On-line program debugging has been done for some time with small computers. Techniques are well known for inserting breakpoints so that program performance can be monitored and for obtaining temporary dumps of a few words of memory during program debugging runs. Symbolic debugging aids that allow reference to a program in the source language have been developed. In some systems, modifications in source language can be compiled or assembled, and inserted into the proper position in the original program without the necessity of recompiling or reassembling the entire program [*25, 40*].

Experiments in on-line information storage and retrieval have been conducted on time-sharing systems. Work has been done to integrate a storage and retrieval capability into the system itself, so that its file system can operate in a very general manner [*57*]. In other experiments, substantial subsystems have been devised to demonstrate the benefits of interaction between man and machine in both the storage and retrieval processes [*51*]. In more advanced systems, such as those anticipated in Section 5.3, the information retrieval capability is very important within the time-sharing system, since the system becomes a sophisticated message store and forward center, in which the messages may contain information of all types.

The development of teaching machine subsystems within the framework of time-sharing systems provides experimental results that contribute to this important field. Teaching machines can be both developed and used as part of a general-purpose time-sharing system. The programs can be changed easily and the results monitored by the system, so that feedback from student to teacher is enhanced. Programs for testing are also being developed in a manner similar to those for teaching machines.

The preparation of text for program input or for publication can be done easily at an on-line console. Text editing and automatic line justification can be readily programmed, and the prepared text can be delivered at the remote terminal or sent to peripheral line printers.

Another use of general or partially dedicated time-sharing systems is in a management information system for any organization. Corporations, universities, and government agencies require information transfer among elements of the organization. Inputs to a management system might be both external to the organization and feedback from parts of the organization after analysis of the external input. Executives would have instant access to records and to a computation facility for assistance in analyzing the records. Through the system the executives could indicate their decisions to others in the organization, so that the system functions not only as a data gathering mechanism but as a command and control center.

4.3 Man-Machine Interaction

Conversational interaction can be realized between man and machine in a time-sharing environment. In this conversation the interaction can be maintained at a rate best suited to the man's needs for a particular application. For the solution of some problems, the man may want to guide the machine, to monitor its progress as closely as possible. At other times, he may desire to let the machine lead the conversation. Considerable research is being done to analyze the factors involved in the man-machine communication process.

Examples of the problems which arise are found in the typical use of a time-sharing system. Suppose that a new user assumes a position at a remote console. The system can be designed to teach him all he needs to know to solve his problem. As the conversation begins, the computer will have to lead the man and to be quite detailed in its explanation of how to use the system. As the man becomes more experienced, the system's part of the conversation can become less verbose, eliminating the boring and sometimes frustrating wait while the computer outputs something the user already knows. By this adaptation to a user's needs the interaction can proceed at a faster rate.

Since the system is potentially much faster than the man, it may be necessary to restrain it from pushing the user too fast. Consider the person using a system to help gather information for a decision that he must make. The system may be able to gather and display the information at speeds which are orders of magnitude faster than the man could have done by talking with people and studying reports. The man may have all of the information necessary to make a decision in five minutes instead of two days; he may be forced to make each decision in a shorter period of time. With such assistance, more decisions can be made by the same man during each day's work. But what is the effect on the poor man who must assimilate the information and make decisions much faster than before? Will the man be subject to so much pressure that he cannot make good decisions? Will the type of man in decision-making positions change to conform to the needs of such a system? These questions will be answered as on-line systems become more widely used in management environments.

Several languages have been developed which are intended especially for use with an on-line system. One such language, Weizenbaum's ELIZA [78], can function as a psychotherapist, and may be an indication of future subsystems that soothe frayed nerves and help a user unwind after an intense session with the computer.

5. The Future of Time Sharing

5.1 The Acceptance of Time Sharing

The time-sharing concept developed primarily in the academic community. It has been heavily supported by government research funds in an attempt to plant the seed for later, commercially feasible systems. As such, the first generation systems have been implemented on available equipment which was poorly designed for efficient time sharing. Measures of overhead and other indicators of efficiency have been unfavorable in some of these systems. The extensive use of the experimental time-sharing systems has shown, however, numerous benefits that can be derived from on-line operation. The introduction of a new generation of computer systems designed for efficient time sharing has been part of an exponentially intensifying fervor in the computer field. A mere mention of a new computer brings the question "Can it be time-shared?"

It is now evident that a large number of time-sharing systems will be placed into operation in a variety of settings. At many of these installations the new mode of operation will be accepted enthusiastically. At others, where the computing load is not appropriate, there may be a quick return to batch processing.

It is also evident that many of the inefficiencies of the early systems will be reduced considerably in the newer systems. The extent of the increased efficiency, and the benefits of the techniques discussed in Section 2 that are being incorporated in the new systems, remains to be determined.

The experimental systems, from which the field began, will continue at the forefront of an advancing technology, while operational systems will remain soundly in the background, watching the experiments, noting their mistakes, and capitalizing on their accomplishments. Applications of the systems will increase many times their present number as the use of time-sharing becomes widespread, and the network of computers and the very close relationship between man and machine described in the next two sections may very well be realized.

5.2 The Time-Sharing Utility

A large general-purpose time-sharing system with many remote terminals presents, as resources available to users, not only the collection of processors and memories, but also the contents of its memories. The system provides storage for problems and data as well as a source of computing power.

This combination of resources can be tapped by anyone having access to the system through a remote terminal, so that computer power is distributed in a manner similar to the distribution of power from an electrical generating station to the individual subscribers. Early generating stations were crude and had few customers. Time-shared systems are at this stage today, but they have a much greater potential than the simple electrical utility. Not only can computer power be tapped, but, since the connection is two-way, there can be feedback to the system, input to its memories, so that the effective power of the system increases with time. Depending on the number and kinds of users, the size and organization of the long-term storage, and the selectivity in accepting new information, as well as interconnections with other similar utilities, a system can grow into a very powerful utility.

In Section 3.1 limitations have been mentioned on the size of single time-sharing systems. These and other limitations may prevent a computer utility from growing to a size at which full advantage may be taken of the accumulation of information within the system. Even if technological limitations are eliminated, there may be restrictions based on the political implications of such a large system.

An alternative to the accumulation of information in a single system, the size of which is limited, is the interconnection of a number of systems into a network. With wide-band communication links among the systems, any system could query another, so that the total amount of information in the *super-system* is available to each user. There need be duplication of information only when delays might be experienced in obtaining frequently used data or when political or security reasons require the operation of a single system if the network becomes inoperative.

Such a network of computer systems can share computing power and temporary memory space. Each system can be designed to meet its average local requirements, and loads can be averaged among systems in the network which do not experience peak loads at the same time. Capacity can be borrowed similar to the way electrical power is transferred from city to city today.

Provided the network is designed properly, operation of the vast super-system on a decentralized basis would give it a high reliability, since the failure of a single system need not affect others in the network. The interconnections must be designed carefully to prevent a catastrophic failure of the super-system. The 1965 northeastern United States power blackout is an example of what might happen if sufficient precautions were not taken.

The creation of a super-system of time-shared computers could, if properly designed and used, link together enormous amounts of knowledge, the work of many thousands of people in many fields. If the system could be made to assist in the organization of knowledge so that it is easily accessed, it could be the communication link necessary to keep up with the technological world which is enveloping man. It could save untold amounts of duplicated effort and bring together disciplines that may otherwise never have found common ground.

5.3 Man-Computer Symbiosis

The effective use of any time-sharing system requires successful interaction between man and the system. Licklider, in March 1960, introduced the term *man-computer symbiosis* as the working together of man and computer, each doing what it can do better, so that the resulting partnership "will think as no human brain ever thought and process data in a way not approached by the information-handling machine we know today" [43]. Since this was written, man has taken a step toward this partnership. It may seem to be a very small step compared with the vivid projection made by Licklider, but, through the use of time-shared systems, man and machine are now beginning to interact in a more flexible and comfortable manner than they ever have before.

There has been considerable speculation concerning the role that man will play in advanced man-machine systems. This discussion of time-sharing ends with a few thoughts about this important question. In the world today, dominated by governments, corporations, and other large impersonal organizations, individual men are beginning to feel more and more insignificant. If the successful interaction of man and machine furthers the relegation of man to an insignificant position, it must be regarded with extreme caution. If, however, this symbiosis can be made to assist man to fulfill his greatest potential, then it must be vigorously pursued.

Acknowledgments

The author wishes to express his appreciation to those individuals who have encouraged and assisted him in the investigation of time-sharing systems. Particular thanks are due Messrs. J. A. Cunningham, P. Meissner, J. H. Wegstein, and the entire staff of the NBS Computer Technology Section, which has developed the NBS CORD time-sharing system.

Bibliography

1. Adams, C. W., Responsive time-shared computing in business—its significance and implications. *AFIPS Conf. Proc.* **27**, 483–488 (1965).
2. Allen, T. R., and Foote, J. E., Input output software capability for a man-machine communication and image processing system. *AFIPS Conf. Proc.* **26**, 387–396 (1964).
3. Andrews, E. G., Telephone switching and the early Bell Laboratories computers. *Bell System Tech. J.* **42**, 341–353 (1963).
4. Arden, B. W., Galler, B. A., O'Brien, T. C., and Westervelt, F. H., Program and addressing structure in a time-sharing environment. *J. Assoc. Computing Machinery* **13**, 1–16 (1966).
5. Boilen, S., Fredkin, E., Licklider, J. C. R., and McCarthy, J., A time-sharing debugging system for a small computer. *AFIPS Conf. Proc.* **23**, 51–57 (1963).
6. Codd, E. F., Multiprogramming. *Advan. Computers* **3**, 78–155 (1962).
7. Comfort, W. T., A computing system design for user service. *AFIPS Conf. Proc.* **27**, 619–626 (1965).
8. *Computation Center User's Manual.* Carnegie Inst. of Technol., Pittsburgh, Pennsylvania.
9. Corbato, F. J., System requirements for multiple access, time-shared computers, TR-MAC-TR-3, M.I.T., Cambridge, Massachusetts, 1964.
10. Corbato, F. J., Daggett, M. M., and Daley, R. C., An experimental time-sharing system. *AFIPS Conf. Proc.* **21**, 335–344 (1962).
11. Corbato, F. J., and Vyssotsky, V. A., Introduction and overview of the MULTICS system. *AFIPS Conf. Proc.* **27**, 185–196 (1965).
12. Crisman, P. A. (ed.), *The Compatible Time-Sharing System: A Programmer's Guide*, 2nd ed. M.I.T. Press, Cambridge, Massachusetts, 1965.
13. Critchlow, A. J., Generalized multiprocessing and multiprogramming systems—status report. *AFIPS Conf. Proc.* **24**, 107–126 (1963).
14. Culler, G. J. and Fried, B. D., The TRW two-station, on-line scientific computer: general description, in *Computer Augmentation of Human Reasoning*, (M. Sass, ed.), pp. 65–87. Spartan, Baltimore, Maryland, 1965.
15. Daley, R. C., and Neumann, P. G., A general-purpose file system for secondary storage. *AFIPS Conf. Proc.* **27**, 213–229 (1965).
16. Dartmouth time-sharing system, Dartmouth College Computation Center, Hanover, New Hampshire, October, 1964.
17. David, E. E., Jr., and Fano, R. M., Some thoughs about the social implications of accessible computing. *AFIPS Conf. Proc.* **27**, 243–247 (1965).
18. Davis, M. R., and Ellis, T. O., The RAND tablet: a man-machine graphical communication device. *AFIPS Conf. Proc.* **26**, 325–331 (1964).
19. Dennis, J. B., A multiuser computation facility for education and research. *Commun. Assoc. Computing Machinery* **7**, 521–529 (1964).

20. Dennis, J. B., Segmentation and the design of multiprogrammed computer systems. *IEEE Intern. Conv. Record.*, **13**, Pt. 3, 214–225 (1965).
21. Dennis, J. B., and Glaser, E. L., The structure of an on-line information processing system. *Proc. 2nd Conf. Inform. System Sci.*, *1965*, pp. 1–10. Spartan, Baltimore, Maryland, 1965.
22. Dennis, J. B., and VanHorn, E. C., Programming semantics for multiprogrammed computation. *Commun. Assoc. Computing Machinery* **9**, 143–155 (1966).
23. Dunn, T. M., and Morrissey, J. H., Remote computing—an experimental system, part I: external specifications. *AFIPS Conf. Proc.* **25**, 413–423 (1964)
24. Engelman, C., MATHLAB: a program for on-line machine assistance in symbolic computations. *AFIPS Conf. Proc.* **27**, 413–421 (1965).
25. Evans, T. G., and Darley, D. L., DEBUG—an extension to current on-line debugging techniques. *Commun. Assoc. Computing Machinery* **8**, 321–326 (1965).
26. Fano, R., The MAC system: the computer utility approach. *IEEE Spectrum* **2**, 56–64 (1965).
27. Feldman, G., and Gilman, H., User's manual to the ODIN time sharing system, Memo. No. 23, Stanford Time-Sharing Project, Stanford Univ., Palo Alto, California, October, 1964.
28. Forgie, J. W., A time and memory sharing executive program for quick-response on-line applications. *AFIPS Conf. Proc.* **27**, 599–609 (1965).
29. Fotheringham, J., Dynamic storage allocation in the ATLAS computer. *Commun. Assoc. Computing Machinery* **4**, 435–436 (1961).
30. Fredkin, E., The time sharing of computers. *Computers Automation* **12**, 12–20 (1963).
31. Gill, S., Introduction to time-sharing, in *Introduction to Systems Programming* (P. Wegner, ed.), pp. 214–226. Academic Press, New York, 1964.
32. Glaser, E. L., and Corbato, F. J., Introduction to time-sharing. *Datamation* **10**, No. 11, 24–27 (1964).
33. Glaser, E. L., Couleur, J. F., and Oliver, G. A., System design of a computer for time sharing applications. *AFIPS Conf. Proc.* **27**, 197–202 (1965).
34. Greenberger, M., The OPS-1 manual, MAC-TR-8, M.I.T., Cambridge, Massachusetts, 1964.
35. Greenberger, M., The two sides of time-sharing. *Datamation* **11**, No. 1133–36 (1965).
36. IBM 7040/7044 Remote Computing System. I.B.M. System Reference Library No. 7040-25, form C28-6800.
37. Keller, J. M., Strum, E. C., and Yang, G. H., Remote computing—an experimental system, part II: internal design. *AFIPS Conf. Proc.* **25**, 424–431 (1964).
38. Kilburn, T., Edwards, D. B. G., Lanigan, M. J., and Sumner, F. H., One-level storage system. *IRE Trans. Electron. Computers* **EC-11**, No. 2, 223–235 (1962).
39. Kinslow, H. A., The time-sharing monitor system. *AFIPS Conf. Proc.* **26**, 443–454 (1964).
40. Kotok, A., DEC debugging tape, Memo. MIT-1 (rev.), M.I.T., Cambridge, Massachusetts, 1961.
41. Lampson, B. W., Interactive machine language programming. *AFIPS Conf. Proc.* **27**, 473–481 (1965).
42. Lichtenberger, W. W., and Pirtle, M. W., A facility for experimentation in man-machine interaction. *AFIPS Conf. Proc.* **27**, 589–598 (1965).

43. Licklider, J. C. R., Man-computer symbiosis. *IRE Trans. Human Factors Electron.* **HFE-1**, No. 1, 4–11 (1960).
44. Licklider, J. C. R., and Clark, W. E., On-line man-computer communication. *AFIPS Conf. Proc.* **21**, 113–128 (1962).
45. Lock, K., Structuring programs for multiprogram time-sharing on-line applications. *AFIPS Conf. Proc.* **27**, 457–472 (1965).
46. Lombardi, L. A., Multi-access and multi-computer systems. *Data Systems Design* **1**, No. 8, 16–24 (1964).
47. McCarthy, J., Time-sharing computer systems, in *Management and the Computer of the Future* (M. Greenberger, ed.), pp. 220–248. M.I.T. Press, Cambridge, Massachusetts, 1962.
48. McCullough, J. D., and Zurcher, F. W., A design for a multiple user multiprocessing system. *AFIPS Conf. Proc.* **27**, 611–617 (1965).
49. Martin, J., *Programming Real-Time Computer Systems*. Prentice-Hall Englewood Cliffs, New Jersey, 1965.
50. Mooers, C. N., The reactive typewriter program. *Commun. Assoc. Computing Machinery* **6**, 48 (1963).
51. Nolan, J. F., and Armenti, A. W., An experimental on-line data storage and retrieval system, Tech, Rept. 377, M.I.T. Lincoln Lab., Lexington, Massachusetts, September, 1965.
52. Opler, A., Requirements for real-time languages. *Commun. Assoc. Computing Machinery* **9**, 196–199 (1966).
53. Ossanna, J. F., Mikus, L. E., and Dunten, S. D., Communications and input/output switching in a multiplex computing system. *AFIPS Conf. Proc.* **27**, 231–241 (1965).
54. Patel, N. R., A mathematical analysis of computer time-sharing systems, M.I.T. Interim Tech. Rept. No. 20, M.I.T., Cambridge, Massachusetts, July, 1964.
55. Patrick, R. L., So you want to go on-line. *Datamation* **9**, No. 10, 25–27 (1963).
56. Prywes, N. S., Browsing in an automated library through remote access, in *Computer Augmentation of Human Reasoning* (M. Sass, ed.), pp. 105–130. Spartan, Baltimore, Maryland, 1965.
57. Prywes, N. S., and Gray, H. J., The Multilist system for real time storage and retrieval. *Inform. Process. Proc. IFIP Congr., Munich, 1962*, pp. 112–116 (1963).
58. Pyke, T. N., Jr., CORD—A time-sharing executive for a research facility, in Computer/Display Interface Study, by Computer Technology Section, Nat'l. Bur. Stds, Wash., D.C., for U.S. Army Elec. Command, TR ECOM-95829-1, July, 1966.
59. Rippy, D. E., Humphries, D. E., and Cunningham, J. A., MAGIC—A machine for automatic graphics interface to a computer. *AFIPS Conf. Proc.* **27**, 819–830 (1965).
60. Rosenberg, A., Time-sharing: a status report. *Datamation* **12**, No. 2, 66–77 (1966).
61. Saltzer, J. H., CTSS technical notes, MAC-TR-16, M.I.T., Cambridge, Massachusetts, 1965.
62. Samuel, A. L., Time-sharing on a multiconsole computer. *New Scientist* **26**, 583–587 (1965).
63. Schwartz, J. I., Observations on time-shared systems. *Proc. 20th Assoc. Computing Conf., Cleveland, 1965*, p. 525 (1965).

64. Schwartz, J. I., On-line programming. *Commun. Assoc. Computing Machinery* **7**, 199–293 (1966).
65. Schwartz, J. I., The SDC time-sharing system. *Datamation* **10**, No. 11, Pt. 1, 28–31; No. 12, Pt. 2, 51–55 (1964).
66. Schwartz, J. I., Coffman, C., and Weissman, C., A general-purpose time-sharing system. *AFIPS Conf. Proc.* **25**, 397–411 (1964).
67. Shaw, J. C., Joss: A designers view of an experimental on-line computing system. *AFIPS Conf. Proc.* **26**, 455–464 (1964).
68. Shaw, J. C., Joss: experience with an experimental computing service for users at remote typewriter consoles, Rept. No. P–3149, Rand Corp., Santa Monica, California, May, 1965.
69. Shaw, J. C., The Joss system. *Datamation* **10**, No. 11, 32–36 (1964).
70. Sherr, A. L., An analysis of time-shared computer systems, MAC-TR-18, M.I.T., Cambridge, Massachusetts, June, 1965.
71. Shortell, A. V., Jr., On-line programming. *Datamation* **11**, 29–30 (1965).
72. Simmons, R. F., Answering English questions by computer: a survey. *Commun. Assoc. Computing Machinery* **8**, 53–69 (1965).
73. Strachey, C., Time sharing in large fast computers. *First Int. Conf. on Inform. Proc., Paris, 1959*, pp. 1–12, Butterworth, June (1959).
74. Teager, H. M., and McCarthy, J., Time-shared program testing. *Assoc. Computing Machinery Natl. Meeting, 1959*, pp. 121–122, August (1959).
75. Time-Sharing System Scorecard. Computer Research Corp., Belmont, Massachusetts, Fall, 1965.
76. Vazsony, A., An on-line management system using English language. *AFIPS Conf. Proc.* **19**, 17–37 (1961).
77. Vyssotsky, V. A., Corbato, F. J., and Graham, R. M., Structure of the MULTICS supervisor. *AFIPS Conf. Proc.* **27**, 203–212 (1965).
78. Weizenbaum, J., ELIZA—A computer program for the study of natural language communication between man and machine. *Commun. Assoc. Computing Machinery* **9**, 36–45, (1966).
79. Weizenbaum, J., OPL-1: An open-ended programming within CTSS, MAC-TR-7, M.I.T., Cambridge, Massachusetts, April, 1964.
80. Wilkes, M. V., Slave memories and dynamic storage allocation. *IEEE Trans. Electron. Computers* **EC-14**, No. 2, 270–271 (1965).
81. Winett, J. M., On-line documentation of the compatible time-sharing system, Rept. 387, M.I.T. Lincoln Lab., Lexington, Massachusetts, May, 1965.
82. Woods, W. E., Time sharing and the small computer. *Computer Design* **5**, 10–12 (1966).

Formula Manipulation by Computer

JEAN E. SAMMET

IBM Corporation
Cambridge, Massachusetts

1. Introduction	47
1.1 Definition of Formula Manipulation	47
1.2 Importance of Formula Manipulation	49
1.3 Approach to Discussion of Formula Manipulation	51
2. Technical Issues in Formula Manipulation	51
2.1 General Purpose System Versus Individual Capabilities	52
2.2 Level of Language and System	52
2.3 Level of Capability and Type of User	54
2.4 General Capabilities	55
2.5 Specific Capabilities	64
2.6 Factors in Implementation	72
3. Technical Issues as Applied to FORMAC	78
3.1 General Purpose System	79
3.2 High Level Language	79
3.3 Specific Capability Provided	80
3.4 General Capabilities of FORMAC	80
3.5 Specific Capabilities in FORMAC	86
3.6 Implementation Techniques in FORMAC	92
4. Applications	95
4.1 Methods of Classification	95
4.2 Specific Applications	97
References	99

1. Introduction

1.1 Definition of Formula Manipulation

It has become almost standard in the computing industry to use words in a fashion which is quite different from any literal interpretation of them. A prime example of this occurs in the phrase *formula manipulation* which is used to cover a wide variety of activities, most of which have little or nothing to do with the actual manipulation of *formulas* as such.

In normal mathematical connotations, a formula is apt to be something of the form $y = ax^2 + bx + c$, while in physics one has formulas such as $e = mc^2$ and $E/I = r_i + r_e$. Note that in most—but not all—cases, the formula is stated with one side consisting of a single variable. However, considered within the framework of computer terminology, the phrase *formula manipulation* has been generally applied to the use of a computer to manipulate mathematical expressions in a formal fashion. Thus, for example, the use of a computer to ascertain that the derivative of x^3 is $3x^2$ is a simple but very common example of formula manipulation. The ability to expand the expression $(a + b + c + d)^4$ is another example of formula manipulation, assuming of course that a, b, c, and d remain as variables and do not have numerical values substituted for them. From an historical point of view, it should be remembered that FORTRAN stands for *Fo*rmula *Tra*nslator. This is literally true, in the sense that the compiler accepts a particular type of formula and translates this into machine code to evaluate one side of the formula. Stated another way, the class of formulas which can be accepted by FORTRAN or any other numeric compiler is limited to cases in which a single variable appears on the left-hand side. In all practicality, it is not so much a formula which is being written, but rather the assignment of the value obtained from the right-hand side, to the variable shown on the left-hand side, of the equal sign. This is, of course, equivalent to evaluating the formula.

It is important to distinguish between formula manipulation as being used in this article and a number of related terms such as *list processing*, *string processing*, and *symbol manipulation*. It is not the purpose of this article to give rigorous and acceptable definitions of these terms, but it is essential to contrast them with the phrase *formula manipulation*, so that there is no doubt as to what is meant.

The phrase *list processing* normally refers to the particular technique of storing information in a computer in a noncontiguous fashion, with pointers from each piece of data to the next. List processing is a technique which is vital in doing formula manipulation, as will be seen in Section 2.6. *String handling* (or *string processing*) is a term generally applied to operations that one wants to perform on a string of characters. These operations may be such things as insertions, deletions, and replacements of characters or sets of characters. Since a formula is obviously a string of characters, formula manipulation may involve a type of string processing. However, we are concerned about formula manipulation at the user's level. In other words, the user is concerned with manipulating expressions which appear, and the fact that these expressions are strings of characters which must be handled that way internally is not of prime concern to him. The term *symbol manipulation* is probably even more ambiguous than the terms *list processing* or *string manipulation*. *Symbol manipulation* is used to mean a variety of things: It has been used in the same sense as string processing, namely, the handling of a sequence of characters where the characters are each handled individually rather than as a meaningful whole; it is often used as a synonym for formula manipulation, since obviously the component parts of a formula or a mathematical expression are in fact symbols; it has been used to mean "nonnumerical" computation; and finally, it has sometimes been used to apply to any manipulations (other than arithmetic) done on a computer. This article uses the term *symbol manipulation* to refer to the handling of information in a computer where the symbols may be single characters or large sequences of characters.

For the purposes of this article, the term *formula manipulation* will mean the use of a computer to operate on mathematical expressions in which not all the variables are replaced by numbers, and in which some meaningful mathematical operation is to be done. Examples of the type of operations involved are differentiation, substitution, integration, deletion of a portion of an expression, etc.

1.2 Importance of Formula Manipulation

The primary motivation for the initial development of digital computers was to solve numerical problems. This is generally conceded to be true, in spite of the fact that the first UNIVAC was delivered to the U.S. Bureau of the Census whose problems by current standards would be considered inherently data processing problems. Because of this tendency for the use of a computer to solve numerical problems, there has been a major shift in emphasis in the technology of applied mathematics. Prior to the existence of digital computers, numerical analysis was a very lightly taught subject. People who had problems in applied mathematics to solve either used analytic techniques or simply did not solve the problems. Thus, courses in differential equations taught in most colleges would include a great many techniques for finding the formal solution to the differential equation if it existed, but seldom was anything said about how to find the solution numerically. This tendency was not quite so strong in the consideration of integration, where a few simple techniques were usually taught for getting the area under a curve in numerical fashion if the function was not integrable.

The first known use of a computer to do what can reasonably be called formal mathematics or formula manipulation was the differentiation programs written independently by Kahramanian [29] and Nolan [40] in 1953. There seems to have been no real appreciation of the very significant step that was taken at that time. No further development occurred for many years, and the area of numerical analysis has continued to flourish. There is nothing wrong with this, except that many students now graduating are unaware of the fact that there are analytic techniques which are important in the solution of some kinds of problems. It is hoped that the existence of the systems mentioned in this article will stimulate a return to the use of analytic methods.

For some unknown reason, there appears to have been a long gap in which little or no work was done in this area. However, starting around 1959, the tide began to turn and since then there has been an ever-increasing amount of work either described in the public literature, or in internal reports, or simply under development. An annotated descriptor-based bibliography containing about 300 items covering the field of nonnumerical mathematics has been prepared by the author [45]. Another indication of the importance of the area was the successful and well-attended ACM Symposium on Symbolic and Algebraic Manipulation held in Washington, D.C., in March 1966. The proceedings of the meeting appear in the August 1966 issue of the Communications of the ACM. Some—but not all—of the papers are cited in this article, which was written long before the meeting. It is because of the growing importance of the subject that it is being discussed here.

It may not be clear to the reader why a computer is needed for doing work in this area. Some of the applications discussed in Section 4 could not be done at all—meaning that they might take 30 man-years—without the use of a computer. In other cases, the amount of mechanical algebra that needs to be done is extremely tedious and as susceptible to human error as are numerical calculations. There are cases in which problems involving manipulation of mathematical expressions have been done by hand and checked two or three times, and then found to be wrong when the work was redone on a computer. Any reader who seriously doubts this, should try expanding $(a + b + c + d + e)^5$ in the elementary way. It will depend on the individual whether the patience, the pencil, or the eraser will wear out first in this relatively simple task. Other problems involve formulas which spread over many pages. Even finding the second derivative with respect to H of an expression as harmless looking as

$$\frac{(H - 1 + D^{1/2})^2}{D^{1/2}},$$

where $D = 1 - 2HZ + H^2$ takes several hours if attempted by "brute force." Since a computer can be used to relieve human beings of tedious tasks in other fields, it is perfectly reasonable and natural that a computer should also be applied to the field of straightforward and repetitive mathematics; this permits people to concentrate on the more creative aspects of the work. Illustrations of general problems which involve very laborious manipulations include the solution of differential equations, generation of series with hundreds or thousands of terms, inversion of matrices with symbolic entries, etc.

1.3 Approach to Discussion of Formula Manipulation

There are a number of ways in which the subject of formula manipulation could be described and discussed. One would be to give a straightforward survey of all the work which has been done in this area, system by system or category by category. This was done by the author in [46]. It was felt that a more interesting approach would be to describe the fundamental issues involved, with references to particular systems which exemplify points made, and then follow this with a description of a particular system, following the outline of the more general discussion. Section 2 provides a discussion of the main issues in a formula manipulation system, both from language and implementation points of view. (A very short but much more recent discussion of these issues is given by the author in [47].) Section 3 discusses a particular large-scale system—namely, FORMAC—primarily in the light of the general considerations discussed in Section 2. Finally, Section 4 discusses a number of applications that have been developed using a variety of systems.

It should be pointed out that the documents cited are those considered most applicable to the points being made in the text and/or reasonably accessible to a person interested in pursuing the subject further. There are a number of other documents pertaining to this material which are in existence but which are not given in the list of references. All those known to the author are included in the annotated bibliography [45].

2. Technical Issues in Formula Manipulation

In considering the general subject of formula manipulation, there are a number of technical issues which are either critical to the success of a system, or at least determine the scope of a subroutine, program, or large system. There are a number of other issues which might be called design points, in the sense that the people about to embark on the creation of routines to do nonnumerical manipulation must reach a conclusion on how they are to handle these issues.

Among the points to be considered under this major section heading are the question of a general purpose system versus individual capabilities, the question of level of language and system, the issue of the level of capability and type of user, and a long list of capabilities that one must at least consider providing. Finally, there is a discussion of some of the factors involved in implementing such a system.

2.1 General Purpose System Versus Individual Capabilities

The first major issue which must be faced in considering formula manipulation is whether the designers wish to develop a general purpose system, or whether there is a need only for a series of individual capabilities.

A general purpose system can be described as one which is useful for solving a wide class of problems in a number of ways rather than dealing with a single area such as differentiation.

It seems reasonably clear that if an organization or a group of people are concerned with only one particular facet of formula manipulation, then they presumably would not have an interest in developing other aspects. However, as will probably be seen later—even if indirectly—it is sometimes extremely difficult to separate out one particular facet of formula manipulation and say that this can be handled independently. Even the area of formal differentiation, which seems to lend itself to individual handling more than any other, does not really stand alone. If one performs differentiation one must immediately be concerned about what type of simplification is to be done, how the output is to be produced, and how expressions are to be evaluated if that is needed.

Other capabilities which one might want to consider for individual handling include automatic simplification, integration, polynomial handling, factoring, pattern matching, etc. Of this partial list, only the polynomial manipulation even begins to lend itself reasonably to a meaningful abstraction without too much concern about the other issues. Thus, it seems reasonable to suppose that there should be more interest in a general purpose system than in specific routines, although the history of developments in this area does not support this conclusion. The general purpose system has the normal disadvantage that it may be less well suited for any single item mentioned above, but is a better way of dealing with the set of all these capabilities.

2.2 Level of Language and System

In the design of a general purpose system, one must be concerned with the level of language to be used for representing the manipulations involved. Furthermore, if these manipulations are to be part of a system capable of doing numerical work as well, then there must be a decision on the type of numerical system to use, as well as the way in which the integration within the system takes place. Finally, it is necessary to determine how much flexibility and of what kind is to be provided. Each of these points is defined and discussed in the next section.

2.2.1 Independence versus Embedding

A major issue is the question of whether one wants to develop a specific language just to handle formula manipulation, rather than embedding within an existing language at some level.

The ALGY system [2] is an illustration of the development of a specific individual language to handle formula manipulation. It might be true—although it seems unlikely—that extending this concept to develop a general purpose language just for formula manipulation would be a worthwhile endeavor. However, it is the view of the author that very much of what one wants to do in the general area of formula manipulation involves numerical capability, loop control, and input-output. All these items are of necessity provided in any higher level language. The advantage to developing an individual language, of course, is that it can be tailor-made for the specific needs, without restrictions and constraints imposed by a language which was really developed for other purposes. The advantages of using an existing language are that (1) one can benefit from the extensive results already obtained in language design, user training, and possibly implementations, and (2) it reduces the needless diversity of languages in the programming field.

2.2.2 Assembly Program versus Compiler

The primary issue here—of associating the formula manipulation with an assembly program or a compiler—really belongs outside the area of formula manipulation. On the basis of experience to date with both ALPAK [9, 10] and FORMAC [5, 19, 43], it seems clear that formula manipulation capabilities (although limited to polynomials in the ALPAK case) can be provided with both an assembly program and a compiler in a fairly natural way. The advantages and disadvantages are more those pertaining to the "assembly program versus compiler" issue rather than to any primary factor in formula manipulation. It should be pointed out, however, that if one uses a compiler, then one has the option of handling the matter either with subroutine calls or by adding to the basic language which the compiler is handling. In general, using a compiler will reduce programming labor and using an assembly language will allow (but not guarantee) better object code.

2.2.3 Subroutine Calls versus Specific Language

Assuming that the formula manipulation facility is "embedded" in another system (rather than being independent), then one of the issues in considering the level of language is the determination of whether a specific language should be provided for the formula manipulation capabilities, or whether there should merely be a set of subroutine calls. (If the formula manipulations are attached to an assembly program, then there is no real choice, except for the possible use of macros.) ALPAK and SYMBOLANG [32] are examples of using subroutines with an assembly program and a compiler, respectively.

The primary advantage to the use of a specific language is the ease of writing, documenting, etc., a program. In addition, if properly done, the formula language can be inserted within the framework of a higher level language in a very natural manner so that no major distinction need be made between the numerical and nonnumerical capabilities. This latter concept is a great advantage since an appropriate combination widens the scope of potential use.

The primary disadvantage to using a specific language (rather than subroutine calls) is that it does provide restrictions in terms of the capabilities that are being given to the user as the basic package. Thus, by providing only a series of subroutine calls, one avoids problems of language syntax and embedding into a larger system. This factor is also related to the issue of flexibility versus specific capability which is discussed later. The main point of concern here is with the syntax of the calls versus the somewhat more natural language.

2.3 Level of Capability and Type of User

In considering the development of a formula manipulation system, one must be concerned with the type of user. On this latter point will depend, to a large extent, the philosophy that is adopted with regard to providing a high level but very specific capability versus developing primitive tools from which one can build up any desired capability. To be more specific, both LISP [37] and Formula ALGOL [41] take the approach that the user should be given tools sufficiently basic so that he can develop his own specific capabilities such as differentiation, integration, simplification, and expansion. Again, the argument here is a long-standing one that is almost independent of formula manipulation. We know that one of the fundamental differences between an assembly program and a compiler is the fact that while the former provides much more flexibility, it also requires much more work. The compiler provides a specific language which is likely to be good for the purposes for which it was designed, but not for much else. That is, if one wants to go beyond the bounds of the specific compiler language, one often has to resort to assembly language. This is not necessarily bad, but must be understood as being a significant factor. As will be seen, the basic language components supplied in FORMAC are things that could conceivably be built up from the basic elements of LISP, although with a tremendous effort on the part of the LISP programmer. Similarly, the approach being taken to Formula ALGOL assumes that the user will want to develop his own tailor-made routines; therefore, the designers of that system feel the important thing is to supply the user with the basic elements of the language which are needed by him to build up specific capabilities.

2.4 General Capabilities

In this section a few general capabilities will be mentioned and discussed. The criteria used in selecting this list were to include those things which are significant factors in examining the whole area of formula manipulation. In some cases the decision whether to include an item in this section or in Section 2.5 is fairly arbitrary; the primary distinction is to try and include in Section 2.5 only those items which could be considered as independent routines, and which could be replaced by others without making drastic changes in the fundamental philosophy of the system.

The capabilities listed here are things which a user might want, and are independent of implementation techniques; some of the latter are mentioned here where appropriate, but the bulk of the discussion is in Section 2.6. Where appropriate, references to work which has implemented these capabilities are included here.

2.4.1 Types of Expressions Handled

In considering the types of expressions to be handled on the computer in a formal way, there are three main possibilities: polynomials (and rational functions as a simple extension), more general expressions, and formulas (where both the formulas and expressions include trigonometric and logarithmic functions). These subdivisions are not mutually exclusive, since polynomials can be included in either of the other two. However, even though other categories could be used, experience has shown that these are the most common.

It is not at all surprising that the majority of routines written today (aside from differentiation of general expressions) handle polynomials. Polynomials by their very nature lend themselves to being handled by numerical representation and computations, even though their basic motivation is nonnumerical.

A polynomial can be represented internally by a sequence of numbers, which stand for the exponents of the variables involved and the coefficients of each term. Thus the polynomial $3x^2y - 4xy^2 + 2x$ could be represented by the triples $(3, 2, 1)$, $(-4, 1, 2)$, $(2, 1, 0)$. There are a number of schemes which have been developed to handle these representations efficiently; the schemes obviously depend on whether one deals with polynomials of a single variable or with many variables, with whether one is going to allow other than integer coefficients, and a host of other similar factors. However, even if one considers the most complicated polynomial situation, one can still store the entire polynomial as some type of sequence of numbers, and can deal with the numbers as such. The arithmetic capabilities and the simplification can be handled in a very straightforward manner. To add two polynomials one need only find the corresponding terms and add the coefficients. Thus if one wanted to add the polynomial $2x^2y + 4xy + 3x$, to the polynomial shown above, one would first represent the second polynomial as $(2, 2, 1), (4, 1, 1), (3, 1, 0)$. Then after matching up the second and third numbers in each triple, the first numbers in the triple would be added, yielding $(5, 2, 1), (4, 1, 1), (-4, 1, 2), (5, 1, 0)$ which is translated back to the algebraic form $5x^2y + 4xy - 4xy^2 + 5x$. This is not meant to imply that all polynomial manipulation systems are trivial; on the contrary certain of the capabilities that appear, e.g., in ALPAK, such as the greatest common divisor algorithm, are quite complicated. However, it must be emphasized that the ability to handle essentially numerical representations of an abstract quantity usually reduces by many orders of magnitudes the difficulties involved.

If one now wishes to handle expressions that may include trigonometric and logarithmic expressions, and powers and roots of rational functions, then one is faced with the decisions as to whether to handle general expressions as such or whether to manipulate formulas.

The distinction is significant and relates primarily to the naming problem. In one case, there is a single item (called an expression) which can be named and manipulated. In the other case, there are two items with a relation between them, and the naming problem is more severe.

As will be seen somewhat later, the name FORMAC is somewhat deceiving because the acronym stands for *Fo*rmula *Ma*nipulation *C*ompiler, whereas in reality what are being manipulated are expressions and not formulas. It does seem at this point in time that the ability to handle expressions rather than formulas provides somewhat more generality, although much more awkwardness when one wants to actually deal with formulas. There are two devices that can be used to permit a general expression handling system to deal with a formula. One is to subtract one side from the other and give a name to the result which can then be assumed equal to zero. A second way is to give names to each side of the equations and refer to them that way. (Note that this is essentially done when formulas are the basic entity, because the reference is usually made to the "LHS of formula xyz" or to the "RHS of formula xyz.") The advantage to changing equations into pairs of expressions with different names is the flexibility in dealing separately with the two halves; alternatively, this is a disadvantage in the sense of requiring more work. Thus to perform the same operation on both sides of an equation would require two steps rather than one. The one specific disadvantage to dealing with formulas is the need to keep the left- and right-hand side separate in the mind of the user, which may be impossible if the system changes them around internally at all. The only system which appears to manipulate formulas as such is MATHLAB [16]. There is insufficient experience to indicate the relative advantages of these two schemes.

2.4.2 Types of Arithmetic

In doing formula manipulation, just as in doing any type of straight numerical calculations, it is clear that one needs floating point arithmetic. One may also need double precision quite often, since in generating formulas people tend to create coefficients which are extremely large. Furthermore, lack of accuracy may be intolerable in problems of this kind, whereas it can be permitted in problems involving numerical approximations. However, the use of floating point and double precision are factors which are not particularly unique to formula manipulation although they may need to be emphasized more in this area. The main item that requires special consideration because of formula manipulation is the question of precise arithmetic.

Frequently the phrase *precise arithmetic* is used to mean *integer arithmetic*. What is needed for formula manipulation, however, is precise handling of fractions. Most FORTRAN systems right now have the characteristic that if one adds $\frac{1}{3}$ and $\frac{1}{3}$ in fixed point, the result is zero because the system provides truncation of each individual term. On the other hand, if one adds $\frac{1}{3}$ to $\frac{1}{3}$ in floating point, one will get 0.6666 . . . 7 with as many places of accuracy as the machine will provide (even up to double precision). Unfortunately, neither of these capabilities serves the real purpose needed in formula manipulation. It is characteristic of many problems that expressions are generated in which terms have coefficients that go up in a periodic pattern such as $\frac{5}{8}$, $\frac{6}{9}$, $\frac{7}{10}$, or $I/N!$ where I and N are parameters in a series expansion. To produce the floating point equivalents of these fractions would defeat the entire purpose, since few people would be able to look at such an expression and its floating point coefficients and determine what the actual pattern is that caused this particular series to be generated. For example, if one looked at the expression $x + 0.1666667x^3 + 0.075x^5 + 0.044642x^7$ it would be impossible to tell from where it came without trying to get the rational equivalent of the decimal fractions shown. Even represented in the form

$$x + \frac{x^3}{6} + \frac{3x^5}{40} + \frac{15x^7}{336}$$

it is hard to tell that this represents the expression

$$x + \frac{1}{2}\frac{x^3}{3} + \frac{1 \cdot 3}{2 \cdot 4}\frac{x^5}{5} + \frac{1 \cdot 3 \cdot 5}{2 \cdot 4 \cdot 6}\frac{x^7}{7},$$

which happens to be the first three terms of the series for *arcsin x*. This type of illustration shows the need for being able to at least do rational arithmetic. By rational arithmetic we mean that the addition of the fractions $a/b + c/d$ will yield as an answer the quotient of two numbers, namely, $(ad + bc)/bd$, or in a numerical case $\frac{1}{7} + \frac{4}{5}$ yields $\frac{33}{35}$ and not its decimal equivalent 0.94285. Furthermore, it is essential that any routine which does this rational arithmetic must have the capability of reducing fractions to lowest terms, preferably before they have a chance to exceed the machine capacity. For example, if $\frac{3}{4} + \frac{3}{4}$ is not reduced to $\frac{3}{2}$ and is carried around as $\frac{6}{4}$, it is clear that just a few calculations will overflow the word size of the machine.

The ideal type of arithmetic to be done is a variable precision rational arithmetic, in which the user can specify the degree of precision he wishes to have done for him in a particular problem. Routines to do this —although in a numerical environment—are described by Brown and Leagus [*11*].

2.4.3 Simplification

There is undoubtedly no other subject in the whole area of formula manipulation which causes as much controversy and confusion as the subject of simplification. A description of some of the basic problems in the concepts is given by Tobey *et al.* in [*53*]. A particular point made there is the significant distinction between "simplification" and "intelligibility." Almost anyone would say that the expression "$x^2 - 4x + 3$" was in a simpler form than the equivalent expression "$x^2 - 4x + 4 - 1$." On the other hand, the second version of this might be considered more intelligible to the user, because he might be able to factor the expression most easily by recognizing it as being the difference of two squares and rewriting it in the form $((x - 2) - 1)((x - 2) + 1)$ which he can then reduce to $(x - 3)(x - 1)$.

The one thing that most people—although surprisingly enough, not all—can agree on with regard to simplification is that the *user* must determine to a large extent what he considers the simpler of several forms. However, opinions differ, and not everyone agrees on how much can or should be done automatically by the system. Most people would agree that a system ought to do appropriate manipulations on zeros and ones, although there are some who would argue that it may be meaningful to the user to know that he has something of the form $A \cdot 0$ and it should not be thrown away. By doing "appropriate manipulations" with zeros and ones we simply mean that the following transformations are always made:

$$A + 0 \to A$$
$$A \cdot 0 \to 0$$
$$A \cdot 1 \to A$$
$$A^0 \to 1$$
$$A^1 \to A$$
$$1^A \to 1$$

The author has little sympathy for the view of keeping zeros and ones around even when doing abstract mathematics on a computer, and no sympathy at all if one is trying to do large amounts of tedious algebraic manipulations.

Probably the easiest way to disclose the dilemma that must be faced in trying to design an automatic simplification capability is to ask the reader whether something of the form $ab + ac$ is simpler than the form $a(b + c)$. Almost everyone to whom this question is posed hesitates and eventually comes up with the conclusion that "it sort of depends." The view on which of those two things is simpler depends very much on the context in which they are being used, and it is almost impossible to expect a system to decide this automatically. One criterion that could be used, of course, is the absolute reduction of the number of symbols in the expression; i.e., any expression that has fewer symbols than another is considered to be simpler. A disadvantage of this viewpoint is that the internal representation of any expression may be such that the system would end up with a different criterion than the user would expect simply by looking at the expression. Another fault of this criterion is that sheer reduction in the number of symbols is not necessarily desirable. If the purpose of a particular manipulation is to produce $a^3 + 3a^2b + 3ab^2 + b^3$, then the user would be frustrated to find that the system has "automatically simplified" this to the shorter expression $(a + b)^3$.

A still more difficult problem is to decide how far to carry the manipulation and combining of like terms and factors. It seems that no matter what the system designers decide to do, this is not what the users want. Thus, a system which reduces

$$\frac{(x-1)^2}{x-1}$$

to $x-1$ may or may not be making the user happier. However, the alternate approach which states that the user should always code up his own type of simplification seems to be untenable in any large-scale *practical* system, although perhaps feasible in a completely experimental environment. This view of both permitting and requiring the user to prepare his own simplification routines is held by the designers of Formula ALGOL. They will combine constants and eliminate zeros and ones appropriately, but they do nothing else automatically.

The advantages of allowing the system to combine like terms and factors and to make other transformations for automatic simplification are the following: The expressions are reduced in size which, of course, saves valuable storage space; the expressions can be put into a standard form and this knowledge can be used elsewhere in the system; the algorithms to perform other manipulations can take advantage of the fact that the expressions are in a standard, and simplified, form; and, finally, any routine coded by the user to do simplification will probably be much less efficient than if built into the system.

The disadvantages of providing this type of automatic simplification are: The automatic simplification routine itself takes time and space that the user may not be able to spare; the simplification done by the system may remove valuable information such as the fact that the expression $x-1$ really was the result of simplifying the fraction

$$\frac{(x-1)^2}{x-1}.$$

Again, as with other issues in this area there is insufficient evidence to draw final conclusions, except that experience with FORMAC seems to indicate that the advantages of providing automatic simplification are significant in terms of time and space. Some less ambitious programs are described by Hart [22] and Wooldridge [59], and a scheme based on hash coding is described by Martin in [38].

2.4.4 Pattern Matching

Pattern matching is another one of the subjects like simplification on which one could say a great deal. In this context, a pattern is a string of characters which might not be contiguous, and might even leave some option as to the exact characteristics of some of the elements of the string. However, before very much can be done about defining an intelligent pattern matching capability, it is essential that the objectives of it be well defined. For example, does one simply want to be able to find anything of the form $sin^2 x + cos^2 x$ where x can be any expression, or does one want to find much more subtle patterns? This is somewhat tied up with the problem of matching expressions, because in the pattern searching one often wants things which are similar but not quite the same. Thus, in the ultimate, this problem is analogous to the factoring and integration problems in the sense that finding arbitrary patterns under arbitrary conditions requires a fantastic mechanism, whereas finding more limited types of patterns is a more manageable case.

The amount of work which has been done in this area is relatively limited, although some reasonable starts have been made. A simple pattern matching capability appears in Formula ALGOL [41]. The system can search for a pattern and take action based on the findings. For example, it can search an expression for an occurrence of sin^2 (*formula*), where *formula* can be arbitrary, and it can extract the *formula* and use it in a search for cos^2 (*formula*). It can also search for a pattern of the form sin^2 (*formula*) $+ cos^2$ (*formula*), *but* there will be no guarantee that these two formulae will be the same. Therefore, further testing would need to be done before the expression could be replaced by 1 (if that were desired). There is currently no way to require that the two "formulas" be the same before the pattern match is deemed successful.

The type of pattern matching which is needed in formula manipulation systems is exemplified by the capabilities existent in COMIT [13] and SNOBOL [17], although nothing along these lines has really been done as far as is known to the author. The capabilities which are inherent in a syntax-directed compiler also provide much of the mechanism which is needed in pattern matching. A very limited example of this is shown by Schorr [48]. Here, a Backus normal form specification of the expressions to be differentiated is used and then extended to provide more flexibility.

2.4.5 Complex Numbers

The role of complex numbers in formula manipulation differs somewhat from that in numerical calculations. In the latter, one can obviously represent the complex number as an ordered pair and write subroutines to perform all the desired manipulations on these. In the case of formula manipulation, one wants the routines to be included in the system, and this in turn would require that a specific variable (presumably called I or some equivalent) be recognizable to the system so that all appropriate things can be done automatically. Thus, one really wants to be able to carry around something of the form $A + BI$ and operate on that with recognition of the properties of I, rather than handling the expression as an ordered pair. Obviously one can write the routines, but this is far more awkward and much less desirable, and, in fact, much worse than the comparable situation for numerical work. Nobody has yet done anything along these lines.

2.4.6 Man-Machine Interaction

The current importance of time-sharing, remote consoles and the phrase *man-machine interaction* give rise to much talk about the place of this concept in the manipulation of mathematical expressions. There are some who say that one can do good work only with such a capability; this will be disproved later in the detailed discussion of FORMAC. However, it is important to make the point that the type of man-machine interaction that is being discussed here is different from, and indeed goes beyond, that which is useful in ordinary programming. Thus, if one has a system which does "batch" formula manipulation and which is under a time-sharing system, then there are certain advantages which accrue to this, e.g., ease of debugging, ease of changing the programs, rapid turnaround, etc. All these apply equally well to FORTRAN, COBOL, and formula manipulation. However, there are certain factors which go far beyond this which are unique to the formula manipulation area.

There are a number of cases in which people are doing algebraic and analytic manipulation in which they cannot proceed more than one or two steps at a time until they see the results of these calculations. For example, if one is taking the derivative of a reasonably complicated expression, it is probably not possible to predict the form of the derivative. Thus, one does not know whether there will be several layers of fractions or whether the numerator will come out in factored form, or if so in what types of factors, or whether the denominator will, in fact, disappear, etc. In a sufficiently complicated case, one cannot even predict what variables will appear in the final result, since some of them may be canceled. In fact, the whole result might be zero without the user realizing it until he sees the answer. Thus, there is a whole class of problems in which one needs the ability to see the results of previous calculations before one can decide on the next step to be taken. This does not apply very much in numerical calculation, because one is not normally concerned with the specific value of a number prior to the final answer; in fact, if one is, tests for it can be made, but there is more likely to be concern with a range of values. That is, if the number is between certain limits one may wish to take certain action, and there is usually a reasonable number of ranges which can be split off and written down for testing ahead of time.

The point is that while one may have a little difficulty in predicting the outcome of a numerical calculation, he can have much more difficulty predicting the outcome of an algebraic manipulation because the symbols have a richer meaning and there can be much more diversity in the outcome of the manipulations.

One other facet of the man-machine interaction situation has to do with the actual physical form of the input and the output. Input of mathematical expressions from a typewriter and output on a typewriter or high-speed printer tend to obscure the form of the expression and therefore significantly hinders the analyst in the work he is doing. The use of a display device for output and light pen or similar device for input will alleviate this situation enormously. This point will also be discussed in Section 2.5.4.

There are several systems which have attempted to provide an on-line formula manipulation capability. Although the systems were either unfinished or have had very little use, it is worth describing briefly what they attempt to do.

The Magic Paper system of Clapp and Kain [12] was developed for the PDD-1. It uses a scope for both input and output and also permits input and output through typewriter and paper tape. The user can label equations, substitute, replace underlined symbols, remove equations, evaluate functions, and generate graphs. Some numerical operations are also permitted.

A system by Dunten [15] was developed to run under MIT's Compatible Time Sharing System. The input language for the former is similar to that of FORTRAN, and a notation for differentiation is included. Substitution and evaluation can be done, as can certain simplification and equation solving.

Some very interesting work has been done by Martin [39] in preparing input-output for display on the PDP-6. He has written a program in LISP which assigns complicated meanings to a series of simple light pen motions and accepts expressions which have been stored internally and which are to be displayed.

One of the most recent developments in this area is the MATHLAB system [16] which runs on the IBM 7030 (STRETCH). It can simplify, substitute, differentiate, solve equations, do a little integration, expand, and factor monomials. Since the system uses only the typewriter and not a scope, it presumably suffers from the limitation of the former with regard to difficulty of putting expressions in and reading the results.

A subset of FORMAC was made to run under MIT's CTSS, and is discussed briefly in Section 3.4.6.

2.5 Specific Capabilities

In the previous section there was a discussion of a number of general features which are significant in any formula manipulation system. This section concerns itself with specific capabilities which might be included in such a system. The primary difference between the items in this section and those in Section 2.4 is that the former issues pervade the entire system, whereas the capabilities discussed in this section are fairly independent. Thus, one can include or exclude such things as differentiation, integration, factoring, polynomial manipulation, etc., without affecting the over-all system design. The capabilities for input/output are needed, but their exact design and that of the editing does not require major interaction with other capabilities. Expression comparison can be handled to any degree of capability desired independently of the other features. The only item in this section which is somewhat questionable in terms of its lack of major interaction with other portions of the system is the "unraveling" discussed in Section 2.5.6. The decision to place it here is based on the realization that changes in this will affect the results of a particular computation only at intermediate stages, but the answers must be the same.

The above remarks should not be interpreted as meaning that anything in the above list can be handled in a manner which is completely independent of the over-all system. This section concerns itself with capabilities which enhance a system if present, but whose exact design can be changed without having a major effect elsewhere.

2.5.1 Differentiation

The use of the computer to do formal differentiation is both very old and very new. It is old because work was done in 1953 on UNIVAC and on Whirlwind by Kahrimanian and Nolan, respectively, and described by Kahrimanian [29] and Nolan [40]. The author feels that should they get the credit for first realizing that a computer can be used to do something in the area of formal mathematics. Differentiation is a relatively new topic, in the sense that people keep writing specific routines to do this on a computer. Furthermore, it has become so common that it is often used as a class exercise. Differentiation routines have been written in almost any language that one cares to mention; in particular, in assembly languages, in LISP, in COMIT, and although there is not yet a specific illustration of the use of either SLIP or SNOBOL to do this, there probably will be by the time this article appears. There are two reasons why differentiation has received so much attention. One is the fact that it is a very well defined problem and relatively easy to do on a computer. In fact, of the major capabilities needed, only polynomial manipulation seems to be any easier or any more popular. The second reason for the importance of differentiation is its practical applicability. Most problems in applied mathematics and in engineering require differentiation at some stage. Thus the combination of the tediousness of the operation done by hand plus its relative ease of programming has made differentiation one of the two most widely implemented facilities in the area of formula manipulation. This is proved by the existence of the following references whose routines have been either written or described: [*3, 21, 29, 35, 40, 48*]. The reader is cautioned that not all of these papers are of equal value, and only those considered to have particular significance are cited elsewhere in the text.

One of the major items in considering a differentiation routine is how much simplification of the result is done. This particular issue has to be spread into two subsidiary parts, the first having to do with the handling of terms and factors involving zeros and ones, and the second involving combining of like terms and factors. Most people writing differentiation routines will do the appropriate things with zeros and ones. This means that $A \cdot 0 \to 0$, $A + 0 \to A$, $A \cdot 1 \to A$, etc. as in Section 2.4.3 above. Indeterminate forms (e.g., 0^0, $0/0$, $1/0$) will be handled in whatever arbitrary way the authors deem best. However, the trickier and more interesting problems involve combining like terms and like factors; thus if the result of a complicated differentiation is something of the form $2y + 3x - 4y$, the question of whether this gets reduced to $2x - 2y$ is a very complicated one. Such general simplification is far from easy, and was discussed in more detail in Section 2.4.3. With regard to methods of implementing differentiation, most people tend to handle it by essentially distributing the differentiation operator down to the simplest expression on which the differentiation can be performed. This usually means a constant, a single variable, or a function such as sine. In the process of doing this distribution, the rules for differentiating products, quotients, etc., are used. Other methods of differentiating involve the use of tables or some kind of standard pattern matching. One of the interesting features to look for in a differentiation system is the ability to handle implicit and/or dependence differentiation. By the former is meant the ability to find dz/dx if specific functions f_1 and f_2 are given such that $z = f_1(y)$ and $y = f_2(x)$. By "dependence" differentiation is meant the ability to find dz/dx when $z = f_1(x,y)$ and $y = f_2(x)$, where f_1 is a well-defined function but f_2 is not given; i.e., all that is known is that y is some function of x but the form of function is not known. In such a case, dz/dx should contain dy/dx. Both of these situations arise quite frequently.

2.5.2 Integration

Integration is the opposite of differentiation in many ways.

It is a well-known fact learned in freshman calculus that one can formally differentiate almost any expression, while such a statement is definitely not true for integration. Integration of polynomials is quite trivial; integration of an arbitrary function is quite difficult. Thus, it is not surprising that there has been almost no work done in this area, the only major exception being the SAINT system by Slagle [51], which currently stands as a monument to the handling of integration on a digital computer. In this program he employs heuristic techniques to perform integration; the program does quite well on an MIT freshman calculus examination. Slagle has tried to handle a very wide class of functions and as a result sometimes runs out of time or space in trying to do the integration. In [16] Manove has developed a program which seems to work well for a class of functions somewhere reasonably between polynomials and Slagle's work.

2.5.3 Factoring

The situation with factoring is quite analogous to that of integration, with the exception that no one has done anything in factoring to compare with the work done by Slagle in SAINT. It was pointed out earlier that the integration of polynomials is quite trivial; similarly, the factoring of an expression with regard to a single variable or its powers is quite trivial. One can even find the highest common monomial factor automatically without too much difficulty. Furthermore, one can easily write routines to find the linear factor corresponding to rational roots of any polynomial in one variable with rational coefficients; this latter will of necessity tend to be inefficient but can at least be done. However, the ability to factor an arbitrary expression with an arbitrary number of variables is something that has not yet been implemented.

2.5.4 Input/Output and Editing

It is obvious that one needs reasonable means for getting expressions in and out of the computer. It turns out that it is also very desirable to permit expressions to be brought in at object time to be manipulated in the program, just as one brings in numbers at object time for action by a program. (This latter has profound effects on the methods of implementing expression representation, which is discussed in Section 2.6.1.)

In considering the problems of input and output, we are constrained by the equipment which is available. As long as we restrict ourselves to the main media, namely keypunch or typewriter for input, and high-speed printer for output, we are absolutely prevented from inserting two-dimensional input, and must work awfully hard to achieve it on output. Thus the normal mathematical expression

$$\frac{x_1 y^2 \sin y_2{}^3 + y_2 x_3 x_4{}^3}{x_2{}^4 y^3 + (x_1 + y_2)^{4+x_1}}$$

must be keypunched in a linear form so that it will look like (X(1)*Y**2*SIN(Y(2))**3 + Y(2)*X(3)*X(4)**3)/(X(2)**4*Y**3 + (X(1) + Y(2))**(4 + X(1))), which is almost incomprehensible without a lot of practice, and very susceptible to error even with a lot of practice. Unfortunately, the situation on output is just about as bad, because very little has been done to make the output more readable. One worthwhile attempt in this direction was made by Wactlar and Barnett [55] who developed routines to permit the use of a Photon to print mathematical expressions after they had been generated on a computer. Other work in the numerical area involves the use of special typewriters for input and output, as done in the systems described by Klerer and May [31] and Wells [57]. However this suffers from the disadvantage of requiring the special equipment; what is really needed is some good work on transcribing expressions into a readable form using a high-speed printer.

Since there are clear (and high) limitations as to what can be done with a keypunch as input and a high-speed printer as output, a really adequate solution will have to come from good display equipment. Much work needs to be done in this area, although a good start has been made in the work of Martin [39] which was referred to in Section 2.4.6.

2.5.5 Expression Comparison

Just as in the case of comparing numerical quantities, one often wants to compare mathematical expressions to determine whether or not they are the same. In the case of numbers, when one uses the phrase, *the same*, he usually has in mind a particular tolerance. That is, if two numbers differ by less than some preassigned value then they would be considered the same. This same philosophy can be made to apply in the formula manipulation situation, except that it is compounded by the fact that there are many numbers involved—not just one—and furthermore, there are many forms of the expression involved. Taking the last point first, the expressions $(a + b)^2$ and $a^2 + 2ab + b^2$ are certainly equivalent mathematically, but they are not identical. So the first point which must be determined is whether or not the user wants mathematical equivalence, or whether he requires identity. If the latter, the testing is simple, but he may not get the results he expects unless the system has a standard canonical form into which all expressions are put. If the expressions are left the way the user wrote them, things which really are identical up to associativity and/or commutativity may not test as equivalent. If one then wants to consider the mathematical equivalence, it is not a solved problem as to whether all legal mathematical expressions can be compared with the correct result; in this case, a test which said they were the same would undoubtedly be correct (unless the algorithm was designed wrong). However, a test which said two expressions were not equivalent might simply be a reflection of the inability of the algorithm to determine equivalence in every case.

After having considered the question of equivalence of the expressions, more or less independently of the coefficients involved, one must then return to the actual numerical situation. Suppose that we now have the expressions $x + y$ and $0.999999999x + 0.9995y$, and we are concerned with their equality. One thing which might be done would be to specify a tolerance that each coefficient must satisfy. In this particular case, if the tolerance were 0.000001 the expressions would not match, whereas if it were 0.001 then they would. In other words, if the difference in the coefficients of matching terms is within the preassigned tolerance then the expressions will be said to match. Unfortunately, one gets involved in this case with questions of precision which might be different from tolerance, and the issues become truly numerical rather than nonnumerical. One of the advantages to the use of rational arithmetic is that it helps prevent problems of this kind from arising. However, there are important circumstances where approximations in the manipulation of formulas are inevitable. In circuit calculations, for example, it often happens that almost all of the terms are smaller than the principal terms by a factor of 10^{12} or 10^{24} and must be ignored if the expression is to be comprehensible.

2.5.6 Automatic Substitution or Unraveling

A very interesting but not necessarily obvious point can best be illustrated by the following: Suppose we have an expression $A + B$ which is named C (i.e., $C = A + B$). Suppose we now create another expression which is $C + A$ and give it the name D (i.e., $D = C + A$). Then, the real question is whether D remains in the form $C + A$, or whether it is reduced or "unraveled" to the form $A + B + A$ which hopefully then would be simplified to the form $2A + B$ (i.e., is $D = 2A + B$ or is $D = C + A$?). This is a problem which clearly does not arise in the numerical situation since one always wants to substitute the numerical value. This concept, which has been defined only by example, is sometimes called *unraveling* or *automatic substitution*. The issue is to decide whether or not the system should do this automatically or allow the user to control it.

In attempting to consider the wishes of the potential users, let us examine the arguments on each side, i.e., for and against this unraveling. In the example cited above, one can argue that the user is simply using the intermediate variable C as a convenience in building a more complicated expression which he is naming D, and on that basis he wishes to have everything reduced to the lowest level of variable possible; i.e., he wishes everything unraveled. On the other hand, one can say that he is not at all concerned about the internal form of the expression D until he is ready to handle the output; on that basis he wishes the expression to remain actually in the form $C + A$. In viewing the first of these alternatives, there is a significant question which always arises. Consider the following statements:

$C = A + B$

$D = C + A$

$C = 3A + B$

$E = C + B$

then what expressions do D and E represent?

The easiest way out of this is to argue on logical grounds that one does not want to change D just because it contains C as some kind of a subconstituent, and therefore changes to C will not affect the value of D. This viewpoint is upheld by a comparison of the numerical situation in which A and B might be numbers; in that case C and D will be numbers and there will be no question about the value of D. If, after having assigned a value to D, we then reassign a different value to C, no one would propose that we go back and change the value of D. This same argument can, and should, appropriately be used in the non-numerical case, namely, that the value of D does not change because C did. Then, however, we must carry records of two values of C—the old one (i.e., $A + B$) which went into D and the new one (i.e., $3A + B$) which went into E. One way out of this dilemma is to always unravel down to the lowest possible level of variable. One of the arguments for this constant unraveling is that any intermediate results that the users see will be meaningful to him; normally when he is doing algebraic manipulation of this kind, he really does mean the unraveling to take place.

In the few cases in which he does not want the automatic substitution to take place, he can normally achieve this by a change of variables;

e.g., instead of saying $D = C + A$, he could say $D = C1 + A$ and carry the expression around in that form as long as he wants. At the point in the program where he really wishes to have this unraveling take place, he could substitute for $C1$ the expression named by C, and get the effect of the unraveling. It takes much more effort to do the converse, which gives added impetus to the argument for performing the automatic unraveling. That is, if automatic unraveling is not provided, and the user wishes it to take place after every step, there must be a specific command to permit this. It seems that the number of cases in which one wants to prevent the unraveling is significantly smaller than those in which one wants the unraveling to take place.

The primary disadvantages to the unraveling are the time it takes to keep doing it, and the amount of space required. One might argue that the user has no interest in these intermediate results and does not care about the exact form of any expressions except the ones he prints out, but experience with FORMAC tends to negate this view.

2.5.7 Polynomial Manipulation

In Section 2.4.1 there was a discussion of the types of expressions which a system was designed to handle, and specific mention was made of polynomials. It is worth mentioning this capability specifically under this section, because of its great importance, ease of handling, and numerical means of implementation. As pointed out earlier, almost all polynomial systems operate on numbers rather than on symbols; this gives them tremendous added efficiency. Although no really adequate comparisons of this type have been made, any system designed to handle only polynomials will outperform a system designed to handle any general expression in the area of time and space. General purpose programs to handle polynomials are described in [9, 10, 23, 30, 42, 58]. Applications which involve only the use of polynomials are also in [1, 9, 23, 28].

A reasonable extension of polynomial manipulation which can still be handled by essentially numerical processes is the manipulation of rational functions, as done in ALPAK. In this case, one usually needs some type of routine to find the greatest common divisor of two polynomials, and a good method of doing this exists in ALPAK.

It is possible to consider including polynomials as a special case within a more general system, but this has not yet been tried. Presumably it should be possible to gain considerable added efficiency, but there are obviously severe implementation problems unless the concept of handling both polynomials and general expressions is designed in from the start.

2.5.8 Other Facilities

There are a number of facilities which should be available to the user at a command level, if the choice of the philosophies discussed in Section 2.3 is to provide the user with the capabilities rather than making him create his own. There are obviously a number of ways of handling these capabilities, and this discussion will simply point out some of the more fundamental ones with an indication of the choices involved.

A fundamental requirement is the facility for substituting for a variable, or preferably for an expression; in the latter case, some pattern matching is required and it can be either very trivial or very powerful. The item substituted should be either another variable, an expression, or a number. In the latter case, the result will be a numerical quantity, and this is the means for evaluating an expression. One of the design choices is to decide whether the replacements are to be serial or parallel; in other words, if there is a sequence of pairs indicating the substitution to take place, then either the replacements can all be made simultaneously, or they can be made for the first pair first, then for the second pair, etc. For example, in the expression

$$x^2 + 2xyk + y$$

suppose we wish to replace x by $a + y$ and replace y by $a + b$. In such a case, if the substitution is made in parallel, the result will be

$$(a + y)^2 + 2(a + y)(a + b)k + a + b,$$

whereas if the replacement is made sequentially from left to right the result will be

$$(a + a + b)^2 + 2(a + a + b)(a + b)k + a + b.$$

There is no particular merit to one or the other of these options; their value depends on the particular situation involved.

Finally, there should be a means of separating expressions into component parts, and/or finding out whether specific variables or expressions appear in an expression and/or finding the ith component in an expression. These capabilities are all useful in trying to write a program to find out about the form of an expression when the user may know very little about it. Thus the user may wish to find out whether his expression is the product of factors, a rational function in a particular variable, or involves trigonometric functions, etc. He needs the tools to permit him to write a program to determine the form of his expression.

2.6 Factors in Implementation

As is natural with all programs, there is a constant interaction between the external and internal specifications of a formula manipulation system. In Sections 2.1 through 2.5 we saw many of the external characteristics of such systems. In this section we will consider many of the factors which are significant in the implementation of such external specifications. Because there is always a constant interaction between various component parts of the implementation, and because there are really more factors to be considered here, this section cannot hope to cover all alternatives. What has been done is to select those features considered most critical and try to show their importance.

It will be found in reading this section, that the issue of storage allocation and storage saving will crop up constantly, both directly and indirectly. This is inherent in the type of problem that is being considered. It is unfortunately true of the types of problems for which one wants such computer-based systems that their size is usually completely unpredictable. Even worse than that, sizes of results tend to go up exponentially, not linearly. Thus an iteration which gets to case N on a particular size memory, may get only to case $N+1$ or case $N+2$ if the memory size is doubled. Part of the reason for this is the way in which intermediate results are generated; in extreme cases the final result of a problem may be a single integer, which certainly does not take much room. Unfortunately, in order to produce that trivial size result, it may be necessary to generate expressions which take many, many thousands of words of computer memory. It is important to recognize that this differs significantly from the problem in numerical computation, where the value of the intermediate results usually does not affect storage requirements very much. Another significant difference between numerical computations and those involving formula manipulation is that the primary storage problem in the former is the program itself, whereas in the latter it is more likely to be the data, i.e., the expressions. In the numerical case, if all the tables of data and results which are needed can fit in memory along with the program, then there is no storage problem, because the storage requirements from the beginning of the problem to the end can be fixed. (It may not be possible to fit a problem on the computer, but once the program is written and compiled, one *knows* this; one does not run out of space once the computation has started.) Unfortunately, in the case of manipulating formulas, even if the system itself does not take much room, the program and the data all do. Thus, the expressions can grow to enormous size, seemingly without much provocation. Consequently, people who are involved with systems of this kind talk about the storage problem far more than they talk about running time. The latter becomes significant only as a secondary feature; in the numerical case, it becomes the critical issue. This should not be interpreted to mean that time is irrelevant, or that poor programming does not cost a great deal. On the contrary, a poor algorithm in the nonnumerical case may cost proportionately more time than in the numerical case.

The significant factors which will be considered here are expression representation, storage allocation, free list handling, and use of external storage.

2.6.1 Expression Representation

One of the significant factors to be determined in considering the implementation of any type of formula manipulation system is the way in which expressions will be represented. This is a very different point from how their storage is to be allocated, which will be discussed in the next section, although obviously the design must consider both these factors simultaneously. By *expression representation* is meant the way in which the input expression is converted into a string (which may or may not be the same internally as it was externally) and, of course, converted back out again. As indicated earlier, the case of polynomials is a much simpler problem than when general expressions are permitted. Most of the problems in the representation for the polynomials have to do with the most efficient way to store numbers. The problem can be limited to this because a polynomial by definition has a fixed form, and the only major factor is how many variables are permitted. The representation is always in terms of numbers for the coefficients and for the exponents of the variables. The latter do not appear in the representation. The issues center around the questions of whether several exponents will be packed per word, whether the coefficients follow or precede the exponents, whether exponents for all variables—even the missing ones—will be shown, or whether there will be some other type of key to indicate which exponent goes with which variable, etc. (See also the discussion in Section 2.4.1.)

When one wants to represent nonpolynomial expressions, one of the first choices to be faced is whether to keep the expression in infix form or to convert to Polish (i.e., parenthesis-free) notation. Whether the latter is prefix or suffix does not matter too much. The reason for using Polish notation is that so much of the manipulation that one wants to do requires knowledge of the precedence of operators. For example, in differentiation, in simplification, in expansion of expressions, it is always necessary to know what the leading operator is and what are the expressions which follow it. For reasons of efficiency in storage and in scanning expressions, most systems use a Polish representation internally. The use of addition and multiplication as a so-called *variary* (rather than binary) operator is the "Cambridge Polish" developed by the LISP group and first described by McCarthy *et al.* [36].[1] It is important to understand the advantages and disadvantages of this method. If addition is kept as a binary operator, then $N - 1$ plus signs are needed to add N elements. Thus to add the 5 variables a, b, c, d, e, the notation would be $++++$ABCDE. The advantage to this is that it is possible to preserve the exact form of the expression as it comes in; one of the disadvantages is that use cannot be made of the associative or commutative laws in developing a canonical form, and expressions which are equivalent up to associativity and commutativity will be represented differently. Conversely, the use of variary operators requires the assumption of the associative law. In this case, using a delimiter which will be designated as $\#$ for this example, we have the following representation for the addition of the five variables shown above: $+$ABCDE$\#$. Similarly, the delimiter Polish form for $(a - b)(a + b)$ is $* + A - B \# + AB \# \#$ where $-$ is a unary operator (and thus applies only to the B). For most practical tedious manipulations, the assumption of associativity and commutativity is an irrelevant factor; only in certain types of more abstract mathematics does this become significant.

A subsidiary question to the use of the variary Polish is the question of whether one uses a count to indicate the number of operands or a specific delimiter. In the case of LISP, the notation actually supplied this information and so the parenthesis acted as a type of delimiter. The disadvantage to using the count is that a fixed number of bits must be assigned for it; if this number is very small, then the number of operands that can follow a plus or times sign is relatively small; on the other hand, if the number of bits is relatively large, then there will seldom be that many operands and much space will be wasted. The disadvantage to the delimiter, is that any time one wants to find the end of an expression or subexpression one must scan symbol by symbol, because there is no way of detecting the end of the expression before reaching the delimiter; with a count, it is possible to skip to the end of an expression, but there must be some way to do the bookkeeping to tell where the end is relative to the size of the count at the beginning of the expression. There do not seem to be any clear-cut advantages of one of these over the other, without taking into consideration the various other factors which are discussed later.

In addition to the logical way in which the expressions will be stored

---

[1] Although the concept of allowing multiple operands for addition and multiplication was developed by the LISP group, the use of the word *variary* appears to have started with the FORMAC group.

and which has just been discussed, there is a question of how the information will be encoded, both with regard to the variables and the operators. The latter depends so much on the machine that it is virtually impossible to make any general comments. However, the issue of the representation of the names of the variables is more amenable to general discussion.

In the case of numerical calculations, the actual names of variables either do not need to appear as part of the output, or appear as special headings covered by format statements or report generators or the equivalent. In any case, however, there is no need to carry around the actual name of the variable in any real BCD form internally as long as it can be supplied for the output routine. However, the output of a general formula manipulation system of necessity consists of nothing but names (in formulas) with a few numbers. (This point does not apply to pure polynomial systems, where the fixed numerical form used internally can also be used for output.) This means that if one wants to encode the names, there must be some way of retrieving them before output to make sure the proper matches are made. This in turn requires that either the expressions have each variable represented by its BCD name, or alternatively, there must be a list of these names somewhere with a pointing mechanism to decode the name currently being referenced. This factor is independent of whether the expression is being represented in Polish or in infix.

While it is possible to keep an expression in core in an infix form with the names and operators represented in BCD form, this is so inefficient as not to warrant any consideration.

It was indicated earlier in Section 2.5.4 that it was desirable to be able to bring expressions in at object time. This has major implications for the implementation of the naming scheme, since the system may need to know the names of the variables before they are brought in.

2.6.2 Storage Allocation

It is fairly well known by now that it is characteristic of many problems in nonnumerical mathematics that they exceed the amount of storage available. That is, these problems are excellent examples of Parkinson's law rephrased to state that expressions always grow to exceed the amount of storage available. For that reason, the handling of the storage allocation is a critical factor, and a different issue than the one discussed in Section 2.6.1. It is important to recognize that the question of how the expressions are represented internally is very different from how this representation is stored.

The most important criterion in determining the method of storage allocation is the realization that the expressions change in shape and size so drastically that one is almost forced into some kind of a list structure. For example, suppose one starts to multiply $(a - b)(a + b)$. Assume this is stored in a delimiter Polish form as shown above. The result of this multiplication, in Polish again, is

$$+ \text{A} @ 2 * - \text{AB} \# * \text{BA} \# \text{B} @ 2 \#$$

where @ has been used to denote the binary operator of exponentiation. Now, if one wants to do any simplification, this would involve recognition of the fact that $* - \text{AB} \# * \text{BA} \#$ within the scope of the plus sign equaled zero; then it would be necessary to remove this from the expression, thus changing the basic size. This is a trivial example of the kind of manipulation which is involved, and which causes the sizes of the expressions to grow and shrink continuously. It is because of manipulations like this that some type of list structure is usually used in systems of this kind. This does not apply quite so much with regard to polynomials, but there, if one wishes even to allow an unlimited size of polynomials, one is forced into some kind of a list structure even if only between polynomials. That is, the elements representing any one polynomial can be completely contiguous, but since the amount of space required for one polynomial may be unknown in advance (depending on the representation), a list structure might be required to store the polynomials.

It does not seem worthwhile to go into the question of the many ways of structuring lists such as threaded lists, knotted lists, and sublists of various kinds. This is well known and described in other literature. Suffice it to say that the question of sublists does become rather tricky, particularly if one wants to use external storage, as will be discussed in a later section.

2.6.3 Free List Handling

Whenever a new expression—and hence a new list—is created, there must be some storage locations which can be used for storing it. The set of currently unused storage locations is commonly organized as a list called the *free list*. It is clear, however, that eventually this free list is used up, and therefore something must be done when more storage is needed. One possibility involves the use of some external storage media; this is discussed in Section 2.6.4. However, a first step is to return to the free list the storage locations of expressions which are no longer needed. The working-data list may contain expressions which were created temporarily in producing some expression earlier in the program, or it may contain expressions which are no longer needed by the programmer. In either case, they should be removed, and the memory locations put on the free list. There are a few well-known techniques which are in use; again, the choice of one of these or a modification of them depends on a number of factors in the over-all systems design. The best known is the "garbage collection" scheme which was introduced in LISP. In this technique, the free list is used for the creation of new expressions as long as possible, i.e., until the free list is completely empty. At that point, the garbage collection routine is automatically called into service. It examines each list to see which elements are still needed. It flags all those in active use, and then goes back and restores all the others to the free list. The currently used lists then have the flag removed, so that the next time the garbage collector is called into play it starts afresh. Under certain circumstances this is the only technique that can be used; under others it cannot be used.

Another technique is to return to the free list all expressions which are no longer needed at the time it is discovered that they are no longer needed. This can be done either by the system, the user, or both. Again, as with the garbage collector, there are some systems in which this must be done and others in which it cannot be done.

2.6.4 Use of External Storage

Since it is unfortunately true that people can easily generate expressions which exceed the size of main memory, it is extremely desirable to use external storage wherever possible, at least if one is concerned with the size of problems that can be run to completion. With the use of external storage there are two problems that must be faced. One is the use of common sublists, and the other is the size of expression which can—or must—be kept internally.

In the case of common sublists it becomes difficult to determine what to put out on the external storage because a sublist might be needed internally, and furthermore how to eliminate common sublists which eventually become unneeded by any expression at all. A great deal of bookkeeping is required to handle this. With regard to expressions which must be available internally, it becomes a matter of fundamental systems design and how individual algorithms work. For example, is the system designed so that a certain number of expressions that are being handled together must be internally available simultaneously, or must just a single expression be available, or need only part of the expression be available internally? The latter is clearly the most advantageous from the point of view of saving space, but like most other design criteria, there are advantages and disadvantages based primarily upon bookkeeping. That is, if it is not necessary to have the entire expression available while it is being worked on (e.g., by a differentiation routine), then there is a great deal of selection required to get the next portion; on the other hand, if one requires the entire expression to be available internally then this limits the size of the expression that can be handled. It is unfortunately true that in many situations an expression which would fit very nicely into main memory once it is simplified will not fit until after it has been simplified, and in the process exceeds memory—thus preventing the simplification from taking place!

2.6.5 Specific Algorithms

In implementing almost any of the capabilities discussed in Section 2.5, specific algorithms must be developed. In some cases, either it is not possible to develop algorithms or it is considered undesirable, in which case some attempt at a heuristic approach must be made. Unfortunately, there is relatively little discussion of algorithms at this level in the literature, and most of these have already been mentioned. However, it may assist the reader to give references to good descriptions of the techniques used in specific problems.

In differentiation, see Blackwell [3] and Hanson et al. [21]. For a discussion of heuristics for integration, see Slagle [51]. For a description of simplification techniques see Tobey et al. [53], and for a description of the over-all approach to the implementation of FORMAC, see Bond et al. [6], Tobey [54], and Section 3. For polynomial manipulation techniques, see references [9, 23, 30, 42].

3. Technical Issues as Applied to FORMAC

In Section 2 some of the main technical issues and implementation factors were described with references to a wide variety of systems. This discussion of many systems rather than one has the great advantage of being able to cite examples to cover almost any point, but the corresponding disadvantage of being unable to show how the union of all these issues looks in the light of one system. The purpose of this section is to match the general issues discussed in Section 2 with a concrete illustration of how they were applied in one particular system, namely, FORMAC. An over-all view is given by Sammet [44].

FORMAC (*For*mula *Ma*nipulation *C*ompiler) is an experimental system running on the 7090/94 under IBSYS-IBJOB [26, 27]. It was started in the summer of 1962 by the author (assisted by R. Tobey) with the primary objective of proving the feasibility of the concept discussed in Section 3.1. Although there were originally no plans to release the system, the desire for general feedback and the pressure from people who were interested in trying it, eventually caused a decision to make it available as an experimental system. Some comments about applications for which FORMAC has been used are given in Section 4.

3.1 General Purpose System

The basic objective of the project was to attempt to develop a general purpose but very practical system. As will be seen, certain shortcuts had to be taken in order to achieve this objective within a reasonable time period. The first decision was that FORMAC was definitely to be a general purpose system, rather than a set of individual routines each of which was designed to do one particular task. As a side commentary, it is worth noting that FORMAC was definitely designed to be practical and easy to use rather than more mathematically elegant but harder to use.

3.2 High Level Language

The most fundamental concept in FORMAC (and one of its greatest contributions) is the recognition that the formula manipulation facility should be part of a higher level language which was suitable for solving numerical mathematical problems. Only in that way could the user have the benefit of all the loop control, numerical, and input-output capabilities, as well as the other features of the normal compiler. FORTRAN was an obvious choice, and FORTRAN IV was chosen, although at the time work on FORMAC started, the latter was still under development. Another design objective was to have FORMAC run under IBSYS-IBJOB in the normal manner, in order to avoid the need for special handling.

It was decided very early to provide a definite specific language for the formula manipulation capability rather than a series of subroutine calls. Furthermore, the syntax was designed to make the additions as natural as possible and as much within the spirit of FORTRAN as was feasible for the implementation plan. It is essential to note that the conceptual language level was designed to be the same as that of FORTRAN. In other words, no attempt was made to include capabilities which were equally applicable to numerical work just because they did not happen to be in FORTRAN. For example, the question has often arisen as to why specific commands for handling matrices were not included in FORMAC; the answer to this is that such commands are not unique to formula manipulation, and since there was no attempt to add to the numerical capabilities *per se* there was no need to include them.

3.3 Specific Capability Provided

It was felt early in the design phase that the user should have available to him a fairly specific capability and definite commands to go with it. This was in contrast to the situation in which the user might have been given the more general purpose tools from which to build up his own system. In fact, this is certainly one of the fundamental ways in which FORMAC differs from LISP in concept. (LISP was the only system available for a meaningful comparison when the work on FORMAC started.) It also was felt that FORMAC should contain the most basic commands which were meaningful for manipulating expressions. Since nobody in the industry had any real experience in doing this, obviously the choices were made on the basis of the best judgment rather than experience. It should be noted that the implementation of the system involved the creation of a set of routines which might have helped the users if the system had been designed to make them available to him. That is, if the system had been planned to allow the user to get at the basic manipulating routines and the basic list processing routines, he might have been able to extend the system himself, but it was decided that this would cause more trouble in the implementation than benefit could be achieved from it.

3.4 General Capabilities of FORMAC

The details of the FORMAC language are given in increasing degrees of detail by Sammet and Bond [*43*], Bond *et al.* [*5*], and reference [*19*]. This section and the next discuss the general and specific capabilities in the 7090/94 FORMAC system in the light of the items discussed in Sections 2.4 and 2.5.

A description of how these ideas (with improvements) might be carried over into PL/I is given by Bond and Cundall [*7*]. No discussion of that subject is included here since this article was written long before that report.

3.4.1 Expressions Handled in FORMAC

FORMAC handles general expressions of the same class that FORTRAN does, and uses the same syntax. The list of FORMAC operators is shown in Table I. There are four operators which are in FORMAC but not in

TABLE I
FORMAC OPERATORS

FORTRAN (numbers)	FORMAC (expressions)
←──── $\left\{\begin{array}{cc}+ & - \\ * & / \\ ** & \end{array}\right\}$ ────→	
ALOG	FMCLOG
SIN	FMCSIN
COS	FMCCOS
EXP	FMCEXP
ATAN	FMCATN
TANH	FMCHTN
	FMCDIF (differentiation)
	FMCOMB (combinatorial)
	FMCFAC (factorial)
	FMCDFC (double factorial)

FORTRAN. These are the factorial (FMCFAC), double factorial (FMCDFC), combinatorial (FMCOMB), and differentiation (FMCDIF). The first and the third of these have the obvious meaning, and the double factorial is the same as the factorial except that the count decreases by two instead of by one. These operators permit the user to carry around such expressions as 7! in symbolic form. The differentiation is discussed in Section 3.5.1.

Any legal expression can be the operand of one of the operators. For example, such expressions as

FMCSIN(X**2*FMCSIN(Y*FMCDIF(X**4, X,1) + X*J))
X**FMCDIF(SIN(X**3),X,2)
1 + X**2 + X**3 + X**4 + X*Y + X*Y**2 + X*Y**3 + Y**4

are legal.

Polynomials are not handled separately; that is, any polynomial is represented in the same way that any other expression is represented. The third example above is an illustration of a polynomial in two variables.

It must be admitted that in spite of the acronym, FORMAC does not handle formulas directly. Since FORMAC does handle expressions, equations are handled in the manner described in Section 2.4.1, i.e., either by putting everything on one side and naming the result or by giving names to each side of the equation individually. This particular point is partially illustrated in Fig. 1, which shows the solution of a quadratic equation.

```
INPUT TO FORMAC PREPROCESSOR
 $IBFMC QUDTST  NODECK
 C            THIS PROGRAM FINDS THE ROOTS OF A QUADRATIC EQUATION WHERE
 C            THE COEFFICIENTS CAN BE EXPRESSIONS OR NUMBERS
 C            ALTHOUGH THIS WAS SET UP TO RUN CNLY 3 CASES IT COULD OBVIOUSLY
 C            BE GENERALIZED BY USING A SUBROUTINE AND READING EXPRESSIONS
 C            IN AT OBJECT TIME
       SYMARG
       ATOMIC X,Y,K
       DIMENSION CASE (3), X1(3),X2(3)
       LET CASE(1) = X**2 + 2*X*(Y+1)+ (Y+1)**2
       LET CASE(2) = 2 + X**2 - 4*X
       LET CASE (3) = 3*X**2 + K*(X+X**2+1) + 4
       N= 3
       DO 88 I = 1, N
       LET RVEXPR = EXPAND CASE (I)
 C               REMOVE PARENTHESES
       LET A = COEFF RVEXPR,X**2
       LET B = COEFF RVEXPR,X
       LET C = COEFF RVEXPR, X**0
 C               THE EXPANSIONS IN THE NEXT THREE STATEMENTS ARE
 C               DONE BECAUSE THE PARENTHESES MUST BE REMOVED TO
 C               PERMIT  MAXIMUM COLLAPSING OF EXPRESSIONS
       LET DISCRM = EXPAND B**2 - 4*A*C
       LET X1(I) = EXPAND (-B + DISCRM**(1/2))/(2*A)
       LET X2(I) = EXPAND ( -B - DISCRM**(1/2))/(2*A)
    88 CONTINUE
       FMCDMP
        STOP
        END
```

Fig. 1. Small FORMAC program.

3.4.2 Type of Arithmetic Done in FORMAC

FORMAC does not contain any direct double precision capability. The reason for not including this was the realization that it would have made the implementation much more difficult; it was also felt that this was a facility which could be omitted from the first system because it would not contribute to proving the feasibility of the basic principle.

There are a few problems whose solutions have been either hindered or prevented because of the lack of double precision.

Rational arithmetic capability was added to FORMAC after the design was frozen and the coding almost finished. It was added because it was discovered to be absolutely essential for handling the types of problems which crop up in formula manipulation. In fact, one of the first experiences and strong indications of the requirements for this capability occurred in trying to check out a problem when the system had a few basic pieces running. The answers did not agree with the hand results, and it was not clear whether the fault was in the hand solution in which the formulas were worked out for the first few cases, or in the FORMAC program which had been written in a crude form, or whether the system quite legitimately still contained too many bugs at that early stage. It was finally discovered that the fault was none of these, but rather some arithmetic errors made in converting from the normal FORTRAN scientific notation used for output to the fractional notation that was used in developing the formulas by hand. As a result of that and similar experiences on the part of other people, it was felt essential to include this capability, and it was done, although not quite as neatly as it might have been had it been designed in from the very beginning.

The rational arithmetic capability was put in as part of the automatic simplification. This was done because it is the automatic simplification routine which performs the arithmetic on coefficients, and so it is there that the rational arithmetic is needed. Some double precision calculations are done to permit larger numbers in intermediate stages which then reduce to lower terms. Further details about this are given by Tobey et al. [53].

3.4.3 Simplification in FORMAC

There is no doubt that the simplification is considered the heart of FORMAC. The approach taken was that only certain kinds of simplification should be done automatically by the system; these include appropriate handling of ones and zeros, combining of like terms and like factors, and a few other transformations involving logarithms and exponents. No attempt was made at automatic simplification of trigonometric expressions, again because this was just considered too large a task to handle in a first system. An illustration of a number of simplifications which take place is shown in Fig. 2. The automatic

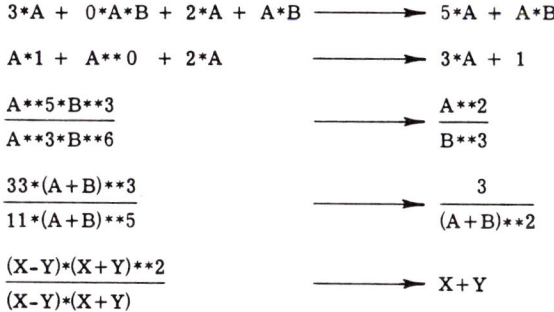

FIG. 2. Examples of Automatic Simplification.

simplification routine is executed after each command, thus preventing the growth of expressions to a size even more unwieldy than they might be normally.

As mentioned in Section 2.4.3, it was felt that the user and only the user could determine whether parentheses should be removed or expressions should be factored. To provide the user with this facility, the two commands EXPAND and COEFF were designed. The relationship of these two commands to the Automatic Simplification facility is shown in Fig. 3. The EXPAND command removes parentheses by applying the distributive and/or multinomial laws. The COEFF command

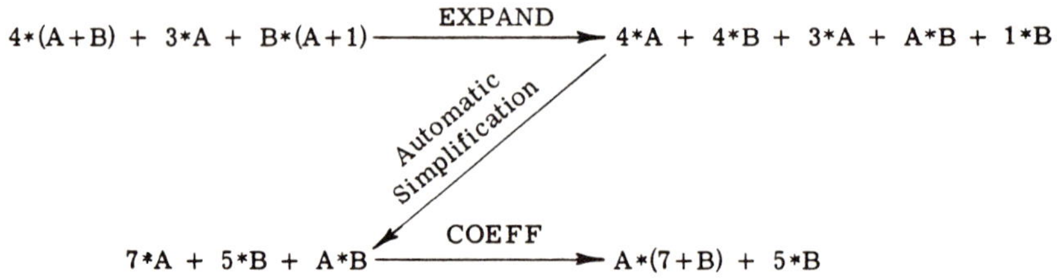

$$4*(A+B) + 3*A + B*(A+1) \xrightarrow{\text{EXPAND}} 4*A + 4*B + 3*A + A*B + 1*B$$

$$\text{Automatic Simplification} \swarrow$$

$$7*A + 5*B + A*B \xrightarrow{\text{COEFF}} A*(7+B) + 5*B$$

FIG. 3. Diagram to show relationship of EXPAND, Automatic Simplification, and COEFF.

permits the individual to find the coefficient of a particular variable or the powers of the variable. Using that command successively he can factor an expression with respect to the powers of a particular variable. It is always necessary to remove the parentheses in an expression before trying to find the coefficients of any variable.

As examples of these commands, the statements

$$\text{LET Y} = \text{EXPAND } (A - B) * (A + B)$$

$$\text{LET Z} = \text{EXPAND } (A + B)**3 *C**2$$

cause the variables Y and Z to have the following values:

$$Y = A**2 - B**2 \tag{3.1}$$

$$Z = A**2*B*C**2*3 + A*B**2*C**2*3 + A**3*C**2 + B**3*C**2 \tag{3.2}$$

There are several significant things to be noted about these few lines. First, the use of the key word LET on the left side, and the command EXPAND on the right side are the only distinguishing marks from a regular FORTRAN assignment statement. The word LET always appears on the left-hand side preceding the name of the variable; the command on the right obviously differs depending on the function to be performed.

In the case of the variable Y, the result looks quite trivial, but it is important to recognize that the actual result when the multiplication is performed contains the terms $+A*B$ and $-B*A$. It requires a great deal of work in the simplification routine to determine that these terms are the same and therefore total zero, which can then be removed from the final result.

In the case of the variable Z, the rather unusual sequence of terms and the placement of the constant at the end of the term rather than the beginning is due to the canonical form which is used internally and which is the normal (although not the only) mode of output.

If one wanted to find the coefficient of B**3 in Z, the following statement will accomplish this:

$$\text{LET ANS1} = \text{COEFF Z, B}**3$$

and the result would be
$$\text{ANS}1 = \text{C}**2$$

The main reason for describing these commands in the section on Simplification is to emphasize the point that the creation and removal of parentheses is a form of simplication, and this is under the control of the user. A detailed description of the automatic simplification concepts is given by Tobey et al. [53].

3.4.4 Pattern Matching

There is no pattern matching in FORMAC except of the most trivial kind, done by the system automatically in terms of looking for a variable for which to substitute. There is absolutely no capability of providing a general pattern matching framework within which to do manipulation. This was recognized as being important but not something to be included in the first system.

3.4.5 Complex Numbers

Complex numbers were deliberately excluded from the first version of FORMAC as being a capability that would be desirable but not essential for determining the feasibility of the basic concept. If the user needs to operate on complex numbers, he can do this by using a variable, e.g., I to denote the imaginary quantity. After every command he should then substitute -1 for I**2 and $-$I for I**3 and 1 for I**4, and do "modulo" arithmetic for higher powers of I.

3.4.6 Man-Machine Interaction

When the first concepts of FORMAC were being developed, it was recognized immediately that in the long run there would be more need for a system providing man-machine interaction than for one providing batch capability. However, in the summer of 1962, time-sharing and remote terminal equipment were not as well developed as they are today. Since we were interested in determining the validity of the basic concept—namely, including the formula manipulation facility in a regular numerical compiler—it was essential that a system be developed which would have the largest number of potential users. This automatically excluded the use of special equipment, particularly time-sharing equipment. In addition, it was felt that trying to develop a time-shared version of FORMAC initially would necessitate solving two major problems simultaneously and developing two new areas simultaneously. It was felt that this was unwise and would probably result in the failure of both. As a result, it was deliberately decided that the first system would be aimed at a class of problems in which the manipulation by hand was so tedious that a machine was required, but on the other hand sufficiently straightforward and repetitive that it could in fact be programmed without requiring interaction with the computer. This has proven to be feasible. Many of the problems that have been solved by FORMAC would not have been helped much by time sharing and would even have been hindered by some kinds of time sharing.

On the other hand, of course, there are problems which really need interaction with the computer and are very poorly suited for FORMAC, although some of them have been run successfully anyhow.

A small subset of FORMAC was made to run under MIT's time-sharing system. This was done more as an experiment than as a practical system, although it has been useful for small tasks. The features implemented included the equivalent of LET, FMCDIF, SUBST, EVAL, EXPAND, PARAM, DEPEND, AUTSIM, ERASE, plus some PRINT commands. This is described by Bleiweiss et al. [4].

3.5 Specific Capabilities in FORMAC

3.5.1 Differentiation in FORMAC

It was obvious from the beginning that a differentiation capability had to be included in FORMAC. This is simply because of the wide use of formal differentiation, as well as the large number of programs elsewhere. There were two major possibilities for handling differentiation:

(1) to make it a specific command, and
(2) to make it an operator which could be imbedded in commands.

The first alternative seemed to hold no particular advantage to the user or to the implementation, so the second was chosen as permitting the user more flexibility and the ability to get more into a single command. It is also possible to justify this decision somewhat on mathematical grounds, in the sense that differentiation really can be considered a mathematical operator just as $+$ or $\times$.

The details of the differentiation capability are given in [19], so only a brief sketch will be given here. The user can find the derivatives of any legal expression with regard to any variables, and to any degree. For example, to find the third derivative of $sin^2 (x^3 + y^3)$ with respect to x, the user writes

$$\text{LET Z} = \text{FMCDIF}(\text{SIN}(\text{X}**3 + \text{Y}**3)**2, \text{X}, 3) \tag{3.3}$$

and the result will be

X∗∗3.0∗FMCSIN(X∗∗3.0 + Y∗∗3.0)∗∗2.0∗(−108.0) + X∗∗3.0∗
FMCCOS(X∗∗3.0 + Y∗∗3.0)∗∗2.0∗108.0 + X∗∗6.0∗FMCSIN(X∗∗
3.0 + Y∗∗3.0)∗FMCCOS(X∗∗3.0 + Y∗∗3.0)∗(−216.0) + FMCSIN
(X∗∗3.0 + Y∗∗3.0)∗FMCCOS(X∗∗3.0 + Y∗∗3.0)∗12.0 (3.4)

Partial derivatives can be found by writing the variables and degrees of differentiation after the expression. Thus to find

$$\frac{\partial^5 (x^7 y^7 + x^6 y^4)}{\partial x^2 \, \partial y^3},$$

the user writes

LET ANS = FMCDIF(X∗∗7∗Y∗∗7 + X∗∗6∗Y∗∗4, X, 2, Y, 3)

and obtains the result

X∗∗4∗Y∗720 + X∗∗5∗Y∗∗4∗8820

One rather interesting feature is the use of a declaration called DEPEND, which permits functional declarations of the "dependence" differentiation which was described in Section 2.5.1. If the statement shown in (3.3) is preceded by the statement

DEPEND (Y/X) (3.5)

then the result of (3.3) and (3.5) will be

(X∗6.0 + Y∗FMCDIF(Y,(X,1))∗∗2.0∗6.0 + Y∗∗2.0∗FMCDIF(Y,(X,2))∗3.0)
∗(X∗∗2.0∗3.0 + Y∗∗2.0∗FMCDIF(Y,(X,1))∗3.0)∗FMCSIN(X∗∗3.0 + Y∗∗
3.0)∗∗2.0∗(−6.0) + (X∗6.0 + Y∗FMCDIF(Y,(X,1))∗∗2.0∗6.0 + Y∗∗2.0∗
FMCDIF(Y,(X,2))∗3.0)∗(X∗∗2.0∗3.0 + Y∗∗2.0∗FMCDIF(Y,(X,1))∗3.0)
∗FMCCOS(X∗∗3.0 + Y∗∗3.0)∗∗2.0∗6.0 + (X∗∗2.0∗3.0 + Y∗∗2.0∗FMCDIF(Y,
(X,1))∗3.0)∗∗3.0∗FMCSIN(X∗∗3.0 + Y∗∗3.0)∗FMCCOS(X∗∗3.0 + Y∗∗3.0)
∗(−8.0) + (Y∗FMCDIF(Y,(X,1))∗FMCDIF(Y,(X,2))∗18.0 + Y∗∗2.0∗
FMCDIF(Y,(X,3))∗3.0 + FMCDIF(Y,(X,1))∗∗3.0∗6.0 + 6.0)∗FMCSIN(X∗∗
3.0 + Y∗∗3.0)∗FMCCOS(X∗∗3.0 + Y∗∗3.0)∗2.0

instead of the expression shown in (3.4).

Simplification is always performed automatically on the results of the differentiation. Some further details about the implementation of the differentiation are given in [54].

3.5.2 No Integration in FORMAC

It was decided immediately that no attempt would be made to include integration because it was too difficult a task, and the prime concern was with providing the basic manipulation facilities.

3.5.3 Factoring

As indicated above, the COEFF command provides the ability to factor expressions with regard to powers of a variable. Some subroutines (written in FORMAC) for factoring expressions with rational coefficients have been developed, but aside from that the user is on his own.

3.5.4 Input-Output and Editing in FORMAC

In order to minimize the implementation effort, it was decided to use the FORTRAN input-output as much as possible. However, since the internal representation of expressions in FORMAC was completely unlike anything the user would want to see, there was a need to get to and from that encoded form. As a result, two commands—namely, ALGCON and BCDCON—were included for the sole purpose of converting to and from BCD and the internal representation. Thus BCDCON and the FORTRAN WRITE permit the output of expressions, while their input at object time is achieved through the use of READ and ALGCON.

As part of the automatic simplification, a routine called LEXICO puts all expressions into a standard order, called the canonical form. This ordering is also unlike what the user would expect, particularly since constants are placed at the end of terms. We saw in (3.2) that the results of a straightforward expansion differed considerably from what a person would normally expect to get. Because of the problem created by the need for a canonical order internally but a "human-type" order externally, a command called ORDER was specifically introduced. This command provides the user the facility of controlling the sequencing of variables within a term, places the constants at the front, and permits expressions to be arranged with regard to ascending or descending powers of the variables. As a specific illustration, if the command

$$\text{LET } z1 = \text{ORDER } z$$

were given after (3.3) and then followed by the appropriate BCDCON and WRITE commands, the expression would have the form

12.0*FMCSIN(Y**3.0 + X**3.0)*FMCCOS(Y**3.0 + X**3.0) − 108.0*X**3.0*FMCSIN(Y**3.0 + X**3.0)**2.0 + 108.0*X**3.0*FMCCOS(Y**3.0 + X**3.0)**2.0 − 216.0*X**6.0*FMCSIN(Y**3.0 + X**3.0)*FMCCOS(Y**3.0 + X**3.0)

Finally, one last command—namely, FMCDMP (standing for FORMAC DUMP)—permits the user to put out expressions. This dump command also serves as a debugging aid, because it provides much useful information about the status of the program and different variables. The

FMCDMP command is so easy to use that even though it puts information out in a very rigid format, it is often used where specific formatting of the output is not essential. Thus, to print variables X and Y, the user need only write FMCDMP(X,Y). An illustration of this command is shown in Fig. 4.

3.5.5 Expression Comparison in FORMAC

There is a MATCH command with two options, namely, MATCH ID and MATCH EQ to correspond with the matching for identity and equivalence. In regard to the latter the user may specify a tolerance which is used for each coefficient. The result of the MATCH command is a FORTRAN logical variable which takes on the value True or False depending on whether the expressions do or do not match. As a simple illustration, the statements

$$\text{LET Q} = \text{MATCH ID, (A + B)**2, A**2 + 2*A*B + B**2}$$
$$\text{LET P} = \text{MATCH EQ, (A + B)**2, A**2 + 2*A*B + B**2}$$

where P and Q are logical variables yield True for P and False for Q.

3.5.6 Unraveling in FORMAC

From a historical point of view, the issue of unraveling is probably one of the most interesting factors in the development of FORMAC. The very first set of specifications which existed, specifically did *not* include the capability of automatic unraveling; each time the user wanted to reduce an expression to its simplest component variables, he was forced to write a specific command which at that time was called UNRAVEL. The reason for the first decision was twofold: It was felt it would be easier to implement that way, and it was felt that the user would prefer to control this type of implicit substitution himself. However, it became necessary to change this decision when it was discovered that both assumptions were erroneous. First of all, it was harder to implement, and second, every problem which was written using these early specifications seemed to require unraveling every other step. While it was recognized that there was only a small sample on which to base a decision, it was still the best information available. The technique described in Section 2.5.6 could be used to block the unraveling, and so this very basic constituent in the system was changed. Experience has borne out the wisdom of this second decision.

3.5.7 No Special Polynomial Manipulation in FORMAC

As indicated in Section 3.4.1 there is no special handling of polynomials in FORMAC. They are handled just like any arbitrary expression.

90   JEAN E. SAMMET

```
FMCDMP CALLED FROM STATEMENT NUMBER   32    IN DECK 'QUDTST'

THIS IS A FORMAC DUMP OF ROUTINE 'QUDTST'.

FORTRAN VALUES
  ADDRES SYMBOL    SUBSCRIPTS    TYPE         VALUE

  03025  I                       INTG-NUMB        3

FORMAC VARIABLES
  ADDRES SYMBOL    SUBSCRIPTS    TYPE         VALUE              EXPRESSION

  03031  A                       REAL-LET     040000253331       K+3.0$
  03033  B                       REAL-LET     040000253372       K$
  03035  C                       REAL-LET     040000253414       K+4.0$
  03040  CASE         1          REAL-LET     140000253173       X*(Y+1.0)*2.0+X**2.0+(Y+1.0)**2.0$
  03041  CASE         2          REAL-LET     140000253223       X*(-4.0)+X**2.0+2.0$
  03042  CASE         3          REAL-LET     140000253241       K*(X+X**2.0+1.0)+X**2.0*3.0+4.0$
  03044  DISCRM                  REAL-LET     040000253347       K*(-28.0)+K**2.0+(-3.0)-48.0$
  03046  K                       INTG-ATOM    C00000100C000
  03050  RVEXPR                  REAL-LET     040000253330       K+K*X+K*X**2.0+X**2.0*3.0+4.0$
  03052  X                       REAL-ATOM    040000010C000
  03055  X1           1          REAL-LET     140000253416       -Y-1.0$
  03056  X1           2          REAL-LET     140000253374       3.4142135$$
  03057  X1           3          REAL-LET     140000253305       K*(K+3.0)**(-1.0)*(-5.0E-1)+(K+3.0)**(-1.0)*(K*(-28.0)+K**
                                                                 2.0*(-3.0)-48.0)**5.0E-1*5.0E-1$
  03062  X2           1          REAL-LET     140000253447       -Y-1.0$
  03063  X2           2          REAL-LET     140000253271       5.8786447E-1$
  03064  X2           3          REAL-LET     140000253452       K*(K+3.0)*(-1.0)*(-5.0E-1)+(K+3.0)**(-1.0)*(K*(-28.0)+K**
                                                                 2.0*(-3.0)-48.0)**5.CE-1*(-5.0E-1)$

  03066  Y                       REAL-ATOM    040000100000
```

FIG. 4. Results of program in Fig. 1, using FMCDMP.

3.5.8 Other Facilities in FORMAC

The other capabilities in FORMAC which have not previously been discussed come under this general heading. A complete list of all the executable commands is shown in Table II, and a list of the declarations is shown in Table III.

TABLE II
FORMAC EXECUTABLE STATEMENTS

(a) Statements yielding FORMAC variables:
  LET —construct specified expressions
  SUBST —replace variables with expressions or other variables
  EXPAND—remove parentheses
  COEFF —obtain coefficient of variable or variable raised to a power
  PART —separate expressions into terms, factors, exponents, arguments of functions, etc

(b) Statements yielding FORTRAN variables:
  EVAL —evaluate expression for numerical values of the variables
  MATCH —compare two expressions for equivalence or identity
  FIND —determine dependence relations or existence of variables
  CENSUS —count words, terms, or factors

(c) Miscellaneous statements:
  BCDCON —convert to BCD form from internal form
  ALGCON —convert to internal form from BCD form
  ORDER —specify sequencing of variables within expressions
  AUTSIM —control arithmetic done during automatic simplification
  ERASE —eliminate expressions no longer needed
  FMCDMP—symbolic dump

(d) *Plus all* FORTRAN *statements*

TABLE III
FORMAC DECLARATIVE STATEMENTS

ATOMIC —declare basic variables which represent only themselves
DEPEND—declare implicit dependence relations
PARAM —declare parametric pairs for SUBST and EVAL
SYMARG—declare subroutine arguments as FORMAC variables; flag program beginning
Plus FORTRAN *declarations*

FORMAC handles the replacement problem by providing two commands—a SUBST and an EVAL. The former provides for sequential replacement of a variable by an expression or another variable. (In this case, the expression can actually be a number, but the result remains as a FORMAC variable.) The numerical evaluation is provided through the EVAL command, which produces a FORTRAN variable as a result.

Expressions can be separated into component parts through the use of the PART command, which ascertains the main operator and separates the expression accordingly. Thus, if the expression is $ab + c$, the PART command will produce two expressions, namely, c and ab, and a code number indicating that the operator was a plus sign. Then if PART is applied again to ab, the result would be a and b, and a code number indicating multiplication. Similarly, PART applied to $sin(a + b)$ would yield $a + b$ and a code number indicating the sine.

One convenience is provided the user through the PARAM declaration. This permits the user to provide a list of pairs to be used with either SUBST or EVAL, and by naming this list the replacement is made. This saves the trouble of rewriting the list of pairs each time a call is made for the replacement, which is always caused by SUBST and EVAL.

3.6 Implementation Techniques in FORMAC

A general description of the FORMAC implementation is given in Bond et al. [6], and some specific points are discussed in [53, 54], but it is interesting to indicate some of the major points here in connection with the discussion which appeared in Section 2.6.

3.6.1 Expression Representation in FORMAC

The expression representation chosen was prefix Polish with + and * being variary operators. A delimiter is used to indicate the end of an expression. The reasons for doing this were already indicated as the pro side of the discussion in Section 2.6.1.

The names were retained by constructing a symbol table which contained the name of each variable and certain basic information about it. Each expression contained a pointer back to the symbol table so that at any time the actual name of the variable involved was available. Thus variables are actually represented by addresses in the expressions. As for the operators, they were encoded into three and five bit codes depending on the frequency of use of the operator, the less frequently used operators being represented by five bits.

3.6.2 Storage Allocation in FORMAC

For storage allocation, the method used was to store expressions in a simple list (sometimes called a chain), i.e., there are no sublists. The reason for that decision is tied up with the one to be discussed in Section 3.6.4, namely, the use of external storage. Because it was decided at the very beginning that it was essential to use the tape for external storage when free list was exceeded, it was felt that the problems of getting information to and from the tape in an efficient manner from a sublist structure were too large, and therefore the simple chain sufficed.

3.6.3 Free List Handling in FORMAC

When a new expression is created, or when more space is needed for an expression, the storage locations are obtained from the free list. Whenever a routine is finished with an expression that has been created temporarily, the storage locations occupied by the expression are returned to the free list. Thus, there is no need for garbage collection (as described in Section 2.6.3) because it is done continuously.

Some control of storage is given to the user, by providing him with an ERASE command. This permits the user to eliminate those expressions which he no longer needs and whose storage locations can thereby be returned to the free list. It should be noted that this does not eliminate the names in the symbol table; therefore, if the user happens to have a very large array which he no longer needs, the only things that he can eliminate are the actual expressions named by the elements of the array. He cannot eliminate the names of the elements of the array themselves.

3.6.4 Use of External Storage in FORMAC

As indicated in Section 3.6.2, it was decided early that it was essential to allow the use of tape for external storage. The system was designed so that whenever a routine needed space for free list it could obtain it. However, when the free list is exhausted, a routine called FMCFUL is responsible for putting on tape all expressions which are not currently being used. Thus, if a particular command involved three expressions, then all others would be dumped on tape automatically. This is something the user need not and cannot control. When these expressions are needed again by the system, they are automatically brought back from the tape. There is no provision for eliminating from the tape any unwanted or unneeded expressions; thus there is nothing analogous to the ERASE command for the tape.

The decision as to whether an entire expression needed to be in memory in order to operate on it was a very important one. It was felt that the design of the algorithms would be made very much more difficult if the restriction were not made that the expressions had to be in core. Therefore, the ground rules were laid that each algorithm could and should assume that the entire expression that it was going to work on would be in memory simultaneously. This had the net effect of simplifying enormously the design of the algorithms, but increasing the number of problems that could not be run because a single expression took up so much space that it would run out of free list. In particular, as mentioned earlier, there are cases in which an expression would fit very nicely after it was simplified, but could not be contained in memory during its creation. This was particularly true of expressions being expanded, and the reasons for this are quite obvious.

3.6.5 Specific Algorithms in FORMAC

Each executable command in FORMAC is implemented by providing a specific routine to handle it. Some of the routines obviously use common subroutines. For example, the SUBST, FIND, and COEFF commands all use a routine to match a particular variable (or limited types of expressions) to a subexpression. The EVAL command is handled by calling SUBST, and converting the final result to a FORTRAN variable.

The MATCH EQ command is handled by subtracting the two expressions being compared and expanding the result; certain transformations are then used to augment the normal action of Automatic Simplification, and if the result is zero then the expressions are equivalent. Note that in this case, the power of the MATCH EQ command lies in the number of transformations which are included; by providing more of them, the number of effective matches which can be made is increased. It was pointed out in [53] that although the Automatic Simplification routine does *not* reduce $sin^2 x + cos^2 x$ to 1, they will test as equivalent under the MATCH EQ. The reason for this is an additional transformation in MATCH which converts sine and cosine terms to their equivalent forms involving e, and this will then reduce to 1. This is not done in the Automatic Simplification routine because it was felt that the user might not always want this reduction made.

The Differentiation routine follows a procedure of distributing the differentiation operator down to the lowest node at which the differentiation can be performed. A clever "look ahead" determines which products can be ignored (i.e., not differentiated) because they involve a zero factor.

The EXPAND algorithm handles separately the cases of the distributive law and the multinomial distribution. Both are actually called from the Automatic Simplification routine, which is put into an EXPAND mode when that command is invoked. The distributive law [i.e., multiplication of two or more summands such as $(a + b + c)(d + e)$] is handled in a combinatorial fashion by forming each product; as each new term is generated, the partial result is resimplified if possible in order to avoid building up large expressions which do not fit in core but which would do so in a simplified form. The multinomial law [i.e., expansion of powers such as $(a+b+c)^6$] is handled by generating each new term from the previous one. The final result is then sent to be simplified; note that this last is definitely required, because the terms generated will initially be in such forms as A∗B and B∗A, and the Automatic Simplification routine is the one which combines these into 2∗A∗B.

The Automatic Simplification routine is described by Tobey et al. [53]. Briefly stated, it first performs on the expression a number of transformations which handle the zeros and ones and convert some of the logarithmic expressions. Then a major subroutine called LEXICO is used; this routine puts everything into a standard form, and in the process of doing this is able to determine which things can be combined, and actually does this combining. Thus, the process of putting B∗A into the standard form A∗B will automatically insure that these are recognized as being expressions which can be combined. A flag is set to indicate which subexpressions have been simplified so that this work is not repeated until the subexpression is changed.

A discussion of various other factors in the algorithm design is given in [54].

4. Applications

4.1 Methods of Classification

It is difficult, if not impossible, to discuss applications in a general way. The word *application* is used here to mean a specific problem with a specific solution; the desired result may be either numerical or symbolic (i.e., expressions), but in the former case there is a need for a large amount of formula manipulation prior to obtaining the numerical answer. In spite of the difficulties in generalizing the concepts involved, a few over-all comments can be made.

Applications can be classified in a number of ways. One is by whether or not the originators use some existing system, or whether or not they create routines of their own. Sometimes this distinction is difficult to draw, because major modifications to existing systems may cause the result to look like some special purpose system. Nevertheless, in spite of the hedging, some examples of the first kind are given in [9, 50, 52, 56], and some recent examples of the second kind are shown in [1, 20, 23, 32, 55].

Two other ways of classifying applications are by their "mathematical" as distinguished from their "application" content. In this context, the word *application* refers to the *scientific source* of the problem, e.g., physics, engineering, etc.; of course, even finer breakdowns are possible, e.g., nuclear physics, molecular physics, network analysis, etc. As an illustration of "application" areas, the following have demonstrated a need for formula manipulation systems:

- Aeroelasticity
- Astronomy
- Chemistry (theoretical)
- Economic models
- Flight simulation (missile and plane)
- Heat transfer
- High frequency vibration of quartz crystals
- Hydrodynamics
- Logical circuit design
- Meteorology
- Missile and aircraft design
- Perturbation problems of higher order
- Physics (theoretical and mathematical)
    - lens design
    - molecular physics
    - nuclear physics
- Prediction of radioactive fallout
- Reactor physics—neutron and gamma ray distributions
- Stress analysis
- War gaming

The "mathematical" areas refer to the techniques used in solving the problem. A list of mathematical areas which are known to involve a great deal of formula manipulation is the following:

- Algebraic and trigonometric expression simplification
- Analytic differentiation (ordinary and partial)
- Analytic solution of linear equations
- Boolean matrices
- Calculus of variations
- Combinatorial analysis
- Continued fractions
- Curve fitting
- Differential equations (solution by successive iterations)
- Eigenfunctions
- Elliptic functions
- Laplace and Fourier transforms
- Legendre polynomials
- Linear dependence tests on vectors
- Matrix manipulations
- Nonlinear maximum likelihood estimation
- Numerical analysis
- Quaternions
- Recurrence equations (computation of functions)
- Rewrite functions to permit integration around a singularity

Series operations (expansion of series coefficients, manipulation of polynomials, Fourier series)
Stability analysis
Symbolic determinants

Note that there is no cross connection between these two lists. Any one or more of the mathematical techniques may be used or needed in any application area.

A fourth way of categorizing applications (reverting back now to the more general usage of the term) is with respect to the generality of their solution and techniques. Some problems have interest and use outside their own domain of endeavor, while others provide information only to the workers in the very specific narrow discipline from which it arose. Most applications naturally fall into the narrow class. A few which have slightly more generality are described by Cuthill [14], Lapidus and Goldstein [32], and Tobey [52].

A fifth way of describing applications is by the breadth of mathematics which they use. A problem which involves only differentiation, only polynomial manipulation, or only general integration is significantly different—at least in concept—from a problem which might involve all three of these. There are numerous examples of the individual cases (e.g., [1, 9, 21, 33]) but no really significant illustration of a problem involving broader scope.

4.2 Specific Applications

There are a number of problems for which specific routines have been written to do formula manipulation. One of the first of these is the paper by Boys et al. [8] in 1956. They developed algebraic formulas for a large number of complicated integrals on the EDSAC. Another relatively early piece of work in this area is that of Herget and Musan [24] who performed some polynomial manipulations on a 650 to compute Bessel functions.

In more recent times, a program was written to compute the so-called e coefficients of theoretical chemistry [55]. The only programming that was needed for this was the manipulation of polynomials. This, in turn, simply reduced to array manipulation; in fact, in this problem the loop control was more complicated than the actual algebraic manipulations. On the other hand, many man-months would have been spent in getting equivalent results by hand. Using similar techniques, it was possible to generate the Newcomb operators of planetary theory [28]. Both of these applications are particularly interesting because the program output is typeset automatically by a photographic procedure using the Photon described by Gerard et al. [20].

Other applications are described by Balmer et al. [1], Fletcher and Reeves [18], and Lapidus and Goldstein [32].

Some of the applications for which ALPAK was used are (1) the distribution of zeros of Gaussian noise, (2) a study of queuing theory with and without feedback, and (3) a study of wave propagation in crystals under pressure (see [9]).

FORMAC has been used for several interesting applications. One of these was to investigate the f and g series of Lagrange; the goal was to obtain explicit expressions for the expansion coefficient in terms of a particular triplet of orbital local invariance. This is described by Sconzo et al. [50], and in more detail showing complete results by the same authors [49]. FORMAC was used to find the Christoffel symbols of the first and second kind; these have been calculated for twelve basic orthogonal coordinate systems [56].

FORMAC was used by Lederman [34] to obtain generating functions, which can be done quite easily in one case by simply expanding polynomials. As stated by Lederman: "For example, to determine the number of partitions of J having exactly I parts, no part greater than 3 and no part used more than 3 times, it is necessary to expand the generating function $(1 + ux + u^2x^2 + u^3x^3) \cdot (1 + ux^2 + u^2x^4 + u^3x^6) \cdot (1 + ux^3 + u^2x^6 + u^3x^9)$." The required FORMAC program is trivial, and is shown in [52].

Another illustration of the use of FORMAC is the work done by Cuthill [14] to derive formal solutions for boundary value and initial value problems. The program accepts as input (1) the equations (in symbolic form) to be satisfied, which includes the differential equations, equations describing auxiliary conditions such as boundary conditions, etc.; (2) a numerical description of the regions in which each of the equations are to be satisfied; and (3) sets of functions (in symbolic form) to be used in linear combinations to approximate the solution functions. From this input, the program generates an approximation to the solution of the specified problem, in terms of the specified functions, which is optimum in the least squares sense.

Other interesting FORMAC applications include the application of a general algorithm for nonlinear maximum likelihood estimation of a set of equations in observed variables with respect to given parameters, and a study of the state of stress and deformation under static and dynamic loads of an inflatable shell in the form of a rectangular plate. These applications as well as others are described in [52].

All of the applications mentioned in this section are problems which either could not have been done by hand at all, or else took so many man-months with such a high probability of error that the speed and accuracy of a computer were required in order to achieve satisfactory results.

Acknowledgments

The author wishes to express appreciation to the numerous individuals who supplied reports on which Sections 2 and 4 are based. With regard to FORMAC, as with all large systems, a great many people participated in the development of the initial system. The contributions of Mrs. E. R. Bond and Mr. R. G. Tobey were essential and of paramount importance, and the work of Messrs. M. Auslander, R. J. Evey, R. Kenney, M. Myszewski, and S. Zilles merits specific mention. Various people contributed to the unpublished algorithms described in Section 3.6.5, but the primary attribution is as follows: the MATCH was due to Mr. R. Tobey, the differentiation was originally designed by Mr. R. Tobey and improved by Mr. M. Auslander, and the final version of EXPAND was due to Mr. M. Auslander and Miss P. Cundall.

References

1. Balmer, H. A., Witmer, E. A., and Loden, W. A., A theoretical analysis and experimental study of the behavior of panels of isotropic and orthotropic material under static and dynamic loads. Aeroelastic and Structures Research Laboratory, MIT, ASRL Rept. 98-3, Lincoln Laboratory Rept. No. 71G-2, February, 1962.
2. Bernick, M. D., Callender, E. D., and Sanford, J. R., ALGY—An algebraic manipulation program. *Proc. Western Joint Comp. Conf.*, Los Angeles, May 1961, pp. 389–392.
3. Blackwell, F. W., ALMS—analytic language manipulation system. Presented at Assoc. Computing Machinery Nat. Conf., August, 1963.
4. Bleiweiss, L., Cundall, P., and Hirschkop, R., A time-shared algebraic desk calculator version of FORMAC. IBM Systems Development Division, Tech. Rept. No. TR00.1415, March, 1966.
5. Bond, E., Auslander, M., Grisoff, S., Kenney, R., Myszewski, M., Sammet, J., Tobey, R., and Zilles, S., FORMAC—An experimental formula manipulation compiler. *Proc. Assoc. Computing Machinery Nat. Conf.*, Philadelphia, August 1964, pp. K2.1-1–K2.1-11.
6. Bond, E., Auslander, M., Grisoff, S., Kenney, R., Myszewski, M., Sammet, J., Tobey, R., and Zilles, S., Implementation of FORMAC. IBM, Systems Development Div., Tech. Rept. No. TR00.1260, March, 1965.
7. Bond, E. R., and Cundall, P. A. A possible PL/I extension for mathematical symbol manipulation. IBM, Systems Development Division, Tech. Rept. No. TR00.1500, September, 1966.
8. Boys, S. F., Cook, G. B., Reeves, C. M., and Shavitt, I., Automatic fundamental calculations of molecular structure. *Nature* **178**, No. 4544 (1956).
9. Brown, W. S., The ALPAK system for non-numerical algebra on a digital computer—I: polynomials in several variables and truncated power series with polynomial coefficients. *Bell System Tech. J.* **42**, No. 5 (1963).
10. Brown, W. S., Hyde, J. P., and Tague, B. A., The ALPAK system for nonnumerical algebra on a digital computer—II: rational functions of several variables and truncated power series with rational-function coefficients. *Bell System Tech. J.* **43**, No. 2 (1964).
11. Brown, W. S., and Leagus, D. C., VPRPAK—A computer programming system for variable precision rational arithmetic. Bell Telephone Laboratories, Murray Hill, New Jersey, unpublished, 1964.

12. Clapp, L. C., and Kain, R. Y., A computer aid for symbolic mathematics. *Proc. Fall Joint Comp. Conf., Las Vegas, November, 1963* pp. 509–517. Spartan Books, Washington, D.C.
13. An introduction to COMIT programming. Research Laboratory of Electronics and the Computation Center, M.I.T., Cambridge, Massachusetts, November, 1961.
14. Cuthill, E., A FORMAC program for the solution of linear boundary and initial value problems. Presented at SICSAM Symposium, March, 1966.
15. Dunten, S. D., An algebraic manipulation program for time-shared computer consoles. B.S. thesis, M.I.T., Cambridge, Massachusetts, June, 1963.
16. Engelman, C., MATHLAB: a program for on-line machine assistance in symbolic computations. *Proc. Fall Joint Comp. Conf., Las Vegas, November, 1965* pp. 413–422. Spartan Books, Washington, D.C.
17. Farber, D. J., Griswold, R. E., and Polonsky, I. P., SNOBOL, a string manipulation language. *J. Assoc. Computing Machinery* **11**, No. 1 (1964).
18. Fletcher, R., and Reeves, C. M., A mechanization of algebraic differentiation and the automatic generation of formulae for molecular integrals of Gaussian orbitals. *Computer J.* **6**, No. 3 (1963).
19. FORMAC (Operating and User's Preliminary Reference Manual), IBM Program Information Department, Hawthorne, New York, Number 7090 R2 IBM 0016, August, 1965.
20. Gerard, J. M., Izsak, I. G., and Barnett, M. P., Mechanization of tedious algebra: the Newcomb operators of planetary theory. *Commun. Assoc. Computing Machinery* **8**, No. 1 (1965).
21. Hanson, J. W., Caviness, J. S., and Joseph, C., Analytic differentiation by computer. *Commun. Assoc. Computing Machinery* **5**, No. 6 (1962).
22. Hart, T., Simplify, Artificial Intelligence Project—Memo. 11, M.I.T., Cambridge, Massachusetts, unpublished, December, 1963.
23. Hartt, K., Some analytical procedures for computers and their applications to a class of multidimensional integrals. *J. Assoc. Computing Machinery* **11**, No. 4 (1964).
24. Herget, P., and Musen, P., The calculation of literal expansions. *Astron. J.* **64**, No. 140 (1959).
25. Hyde, J. P., The ALPAK system for non-numerical algebra on a digital computer—III: systems of linear equations and class of side relations. *Bell System Tech. J.* **43**, No. 4, Pt. 2 (1964).
26. IBM Systems Reference Library, IBM 7090/94 IBSYS Operating System, System Monitor (IBSYS), Form C28-6248.
27. IBM Systems Reference Library, IBM 7090/94 IBSYS Operating System, IBJOB Processor, Form C28-6275.
28. Izsak, I. G., Gerard, J. M., Efimba, R., and Barnett, M. P., Construction of Newcomb operators in a digital computer. Spec. Rept. No. 140, Smithsonian Astrophysical Observatory, Cambridge, Massachusetts, January, 1964.
29. Kahrimanian, H. G., Analytical differentiation by a digital computer, M.A. thesis, Temple Univ., Philadelphia, Pennsylvania, May 1953.
30. Kelley, K. R., and Wactlar, H. D., An integer and rational fraction polynomial manipulation package and a full word binary integer coefficient polynomial manipulation package. Cooperative Computing Laboratory, Tech. Note No. 21, M.I.T., Cambridge, Massachusetts (1963).
31. Klerer, M., and May, J., An experiment in a user-oriented computer system. *Commun. Assoc. Computing Machinery* **7**, No. 5 (1964).
32. Lapidus, A., and Goldstein, M., Some experiments in algebraic manipulation by computer. *Commun. Assoc. Computing Machinery* **8**, No. 8 (1965).

33. Lederman, D., An application of FORMAC to partial differentiation. TRW Space Technology Laboratories, 9851-330, June, 1965.
34. Lederman, D., Application of FORMAC to generating functions. TRW Space Technology Laboratories, 9851-331, June, 1965.
35. Maling, K., The LISP differentiation demonstration program. Artificial Intelligence Project, Memo. 10, M.I.T., unpublished, Cambridge, Massachusetts, 1959.
36. McCarthy, J., Brayton, R., Edwards, D., Fox, P., Hodes, L., Luckham, D., Maling, K., Park, D., and Russell, S., LISP I Programmer's Manual. Computation Center and Research Laboratory of Electronics, M.I.T., Cambridge, Massachusetts, March, 1960.
37. McCarthy, J., Abrahams, P., Edwards, D., Hart, T., and Levin, M., LISP 1.5 Programmer's Manual. Computation Center and Research Laboratory of Electronics, M.I.T., Cambridge, Massachusetts, August, 1962.
38. Martin, W. A., Hash coding functions of a complex variable. Artificial Intelligence Project, Project MAC Memo. MAC-M-165, M.I.T., Cambridge, Massachusetts, unpublished, June, 1964.
39. Martin, W. A., PDP-6 LISP input-output for the display. Artificial Intelligence Project, Project MAC Memo. MAC-M-242, M.I.T., unpublished, Cambridge, Massachusetts, June, 1965.
40. Nolan, J., Analytical differentiation on a digital computer. M.A. thesis, M.I.T., Cambridge, Massachusetts, May, 1963.
41. Perlis, A. J., Iturriaga, R., and Standish, T. A., A definition of formula ALGOL. Carnegie Institute of Technology, Pittsburgh, Pennsylvania, August, 1966.
42. Rom, A. R., Manipulation of algebraic expressions. *Commun. Assoc. Computing Machinery* **4**, No. 9 (1961).
43. Sammet, J. E., and Bond, E. R., Introduction to FORMAC. *IEEE Trans. Electron. Computers*, **EC-13**, No. 4 (1964).
44. Sammet, J. E., An overall view of FORMAC. IBM, Systems Development Div., Tech. Rept. TR00.1367, Dec., 1965.
45. Sammet, J. E., An annotated descriptor based bibliography on the use of computers for non-numerical mathematics. *Computing Rev.* **7**, No. 4 (1966).
46. Sammet, J. E., Survey of formula manipulation. *Commun. Assoc. Computing Machinery* **9**, No. 8 (1966).
47. Sammet, J. E., Problems and future trends in formal algebraic manipulation. IBM, Systems Development Division, Tech. Rept. No. TR00.1506-1, August 1966.
48. Schorr, H., Analytic differentiation using a syntax-directed compiler. *Computer J.* **7**, No. 4 (1965).
49. Sconzo, P., LeShack, A. R., and Tobey, R., Symbolic computation of f and g series by computer, IBM, Systems Development Div., Tech. Rept. TR00.1262, March, 1965.
50. Sconzo, P., LeShack, A. R., and Tobey, R. G., Symbolic computation of f and g series by computer. *Astron. J.* **70**, No. 4 (1965).
51. Slagle, J. R., A heuristic program that solves symbolic integration problems in freshman calculus. *J. Assoc. Computing Machinery* **10**, No. 4 (1963).
52. Tobey, R. G., Eliminating monotonous mathematics with FORMAC. *Commun. Assoc. Computing Machinery* **9**, No. 10 (1966).
53. Tobey, R. G., Bobrow, R. J., and Zilles, S. N., Automatic simplification in FORMAC, *Proc. Fall Joint Comp. Conf., Las Vegas, November 1965* pp. 37–52. Spartan Books, Washington, D.C.

54. Tobey, R. G., Experience with FORMAC algorithm design. *Commun. Assoc. Computing Machinery*, **9**, No. 8 (1966).
55. Wactlar, H. D., and Barnett, M. P., Mechanization of tedious algebra—the e coefficients of theoretical chemistry. *Commun. Assoc. Computing Machinery* **7**, No. 12 (1964).
56. Walton, J. J., Formula manipulation code for the calculation of Christoffel symbols. University of California, Lawrence Radiation Laboratory, Livermore, California, UCRL-14177, May, 1965.
57. Wells, M. B., MADCAP: a scientific compiler for a displayed formula textbook language. *Commun. Assoc. Computing Machinery* **4**, No. 1 (1961).
58. Williams, L. H., Algebra of polynomials in several variables for a digital computer. *J. Assoc. Computing Machinery* **9**, No. 1 (1962).
59. Wooldridge, D., An algebraic SIMPLIFY program in LISP. Artificial Intelligence Project, Stanford Univ., Stanford, California, Memo. No. 11, 1963.

Standards for Computers and Information Processing

T. B. STEEL, JR.

System Development Corporation
Santa Monica, California

> *'Tis all one as if they should make the standard for the measure we call a "foot" a Chancellor's foot; what an uncertain measure this would be! One Chancellor has a long foot, another a short foot, a third an indifferent foot.*
>
> Table Talk, John Selden

1. Introductory Comments 103
2. The History of Standardization 104
3. Modern Industrial Standardization 109
   3.1 American Standards Association 109
   3.2 International Standardization Activity 115
   3.3 Standardization in Information Processing 127
   3.4 Programming Languages Standardization 140
4. Summary 151
   References 151

1. Introductory Comments

The subject of standards and standardization is a frequent topic of casual conversation on the part of information processing scientists. Regrettably, it is far too infrequently the focus of serious attention in the working-day discussion of computer professionals. No other topic that is professionally relevant is as apt to induce disinterest, boredom, and apathy. The author's personal hypothesis for explaining this phenomenon rests on two premises:

(1) the pervasive willingness to "Let George do it," and
(2) the apparent complexity of the procedures leading to standardization.

One can easily sympathize with the attitude that it is irrelevant to the user to determine the algorithm that defines the meter so long as he is provided with a meter stick. The metaphysics, logic, and economics of standardization are studies that are unlikely to interest more than a small fraction of the experts in any discipline. Given this *a priori* antipathy to the subject, it follows that complex, legalistic, and superficially absurd procedures provide a sufficient barrier to deter even the conscientious.

This paper attempts to accomplish three objectives. First, through a discussion of the history of standardization and its influence on society the author hopes to arouse at least a fleeting fascination for the subject in the mind of the reader. Second, a comprehensive description of current practice in information processing standardization may dispel the fog surrounding the procedures. Finally, the author feels that an understanding of the pervasiveness of standardization actions engenders an appreciation of their significance and importance.

After a brief discussion of the long history of standardization, essentially coextensive with the history of the human race, the principal agencies affecting modern industrial standardization in the United States will be described. They are the American Standards Association[1] (ASA) and the International Organization for Standardization (ISO). Following this, the article will turn to a detailed discussion of the current status of standardization in the field of computers and information processing, an activity that had its formal beginnings in 1960.

There are many topics suitable for standardization consideration by the information processing community and all of them currently under scrutiny will be discussed at least briefly. The topic that will be given major attention is that of programming languages standardization. There are two reasons for this choice. First, this topic is as good as any for illustration of the process, and it is the one with which the author is most familiar. Second, and equally important, programming languages are far and away the most complicated entities ever considered in the industrial standardization business.

2. The History of Standardization

The earliest example of standardization predates man. The call systems of various species of primates certainly qualify as standardized items as they constitute agreements, accidentally arrived at but agreements nonetheless, among social beings over conventions to regulate behavior.

[1] *Note added in proof:* In September 1966 the American Standards Association ceased to exist. The functions, personnel, and organization of ASA were taken over by a newly created, federally chartered organization called the United States of America Standards Institutue. In deference to our Canadian and Latin American neighbors, all American Standards are now retitled "United States of America Standards." Otherwise, procedures remain the same. *Sic transit gloria mundi.*

The protohominids living in East Africa twenty million years ago, ancestors of the great apes and man, almost certainly had a call system similar to that of the modern gibbon [1]. A call system is not a language and does not imply the power of speech. Essentially, a call system is a repertory of perhaps a dozen distinct vocal calls, each being the appropriate vocal response (or the vocal component of a more elaborate response) to some biologically important and recurrent situation. Examples of such situations include discovery of food, desire for company, sexual interest, detection of danger, pain, etc.

The elements of a call system are mutually exclusive. When confronted by some specific situation the animal can only respond with *one* of the calls or with silence. It is the nature of a call system, distinguishing it from a language, that it has no provision for signals that have some features of one call and some features of another. When faced with both food and danger at the same time, one or the other situation must take precedence. In a language, one can produce utterances never heard before by making appropriate combinations; not so in a call system. Further differences between call systems and languages include the facts that

(1) calls are not *displaced*, and
(2) distinctions between calls are global.

Languages exhibit displacement in the sense that one can speak of things out of sight. Calls, on the other hand, are evoked only by the actual situation, and further, the animal makes his call at the spot and does not go home to report. The second difference refers to the existence in languages of *duality of patterning*. Languages have elements, e.g., phonemes, which have no meaning in themselves but combine into complex structures to carry meaning. No such factoring can be found in call systems.

Whether call systems can be said to constitute the earliest example of accidental and unconscious standardization depends largely on the issue of the extent to which an animal acquires utility of a call system genetically or through learning and tradition. In the case of a language, the detailed conventions are clearly learned through mimicry and example, although the ability to learn and the drive to do so are genetic [2]. Call systems are probably transmitted between generations largely through genetic means, but tradition also appears to have some role. It is not crucial to understanding modern industrial standardization, obviously, but the fact that the question even comes up is an indication of the antiquity and social importance of standardization. Man would not be man without standardization.

The slow development of true language from protohominid call systems is a complex and largely speculative subject [3, 4]. Beginning with elementary call blending and aided by the onset of verbal play, the basic elements of language developed. The survival advantages of language enhanced the chances of its appearing. There is little question that true language had developed by Palaeolithic times, and a language cannot exist without standardization at some level.

With the rise of urban civilizations in the fourth millenium B.C., script and written language came into existence, and with them the need for even more stringent standardization of language [5]. It is not pertinent to the present subject to follow the development of natural language in detail.

It is clear that the development of early languages was accidental, unconscious, and the process unrecognized. The notion that vocal and written communication between men is essentially arbitrary and conventional is a quite modern idea. The evidence suggests that the first recognized set of conventions was the collection of arbitrary agreements on weights and measures [6]. Indeed, even today it is weights and measures that come to most people's minds when they hear the word *standards* outside the context of law, morals, and ethics.

Consider what is meant by the word *dimension*, a word whose etymology involves the notion of measuring (cf. the Latin *dimensio*, a measuring). In attempting to describe the dimensions of almost anything, one refers to a unit of some scale, either explicitly or implicitly. Children are taught in school that it is an error to say that the line is "two long." It must be two inches, two centimeters, two feet, or some such description. Of course, when one says that Peter Snell ran the mile in 3:54.4, only a pair of numbers is exhibited, but the temporal units of minutes and seconds are presumed to be understood.

In this matter the question of standardization is crucial, and modern man tends to take it for granted. While it is recognized that several systems are in use, the relationship between different systems is exact. An inch is 2.54 centimeters everywhere. The technological society of the twentieth century could not function if such relationships were not maintained. More primitive systems were based on convenience rather than scientific precision.

It should be noted that much of what was said in the previous paragraph is, *strictly speaking*, in error. It is only recently that the units of the English system have been *defined* in terms of the metric system in such a way as to make exact statements possible. The tale of how this was accomplished is too long to go into here, but the fact that the relationship between the inch and centimeter could change as late as the 1950's should give cause for thought about facile assumptions on what constitutes an adequate standard.

Before the introduction of the metric system in Europe, in the course of the nineteenth century, not only did every nation have its own standards of weights and measures, more or less unrelated to those of any other nation, but the principal cities of any one country often had standards of their own, quite different from those of any other cities of their own people. It was quite usual for a city to possess a standard of commercial weight for bulky merchandise and another of troy weight for gold and silver—sometimes, indeed, two troy standards, one for gold and one for silver. Then, in linear measures there would be a foot unit for building and land measure, another and larger measure for woolen and linen cloths, and still another measure for silk fabrics, the two latter measures being known as the "ell," "aune," etc., and being direct descendants of one or another of the various cubits of the ancient civilizations of the Middle East.

When the criterion of a good scale is convenience—by no means an unacceptable criterion—the scale will, in all likelihood, seem crude and primitive. One must take care, however, to avoid judging everything in terms of modern, sophisticated notions of what is effective. The primitive craftsman is almost forced to use units that are, in some sense, natural. Thus are derived the palm, span, cubit (forearm), yard (nose to fingertip), and fathom (arm-span). Provided the same individual makes all the measurements, the results are quite good enough for trades such as carpentry and slingshot ballistics. Even in today's over-tooled society, these measurements are quicker to make and are often adequate. The author has recently seen an expert cabinet maker using finger widths to mark departures from plumb while constructing bookcases. The resultant bookcases are level within the eye's ability to judge a standard carpenter's spirit level.

These remarks on the apparent adequacy of crude measurements should not be taken as implying that carefully designed standards are not vital. Quite to the contrary, as will be seen below, it is the existence of exact industrial standards that permits the complexity of modern society. What is important to note here is that the criteria for adequacy of standards must be carefully chosen. Millisecond accuracy in time measurement and micron accuracy in distance measurement would have had no meaning or utility to the craftsmen of the Fourth Dynasty in Egypt (*ca.* 2500 B.C.). There is, perhaps, an unconscious recognition of this point in the attention being paid to criteria for the standardization of programming languages.

The requirements of construction engineering and military science forced the ancient civilizations into moderately well-defined standards of weights and measures. Perhaps the best indication of the accuracy of ancient and medieval standards can be obtained from an examination of the variation of measures separated in time and space [7]. The Egyptians of the Fourth Dynasty showed variations of 1 part in 350 in different buildings of the same age. Over the several centuries of the Roman Empire, the Roman foot varied on the average by 1 part in 400 about the mean. In Egypt over several thousand years the cubit lengthened by 1 part in 170. The Italian mile has lengthened by 1 part in 100 since Roman times, and the English foot by 1 part in 300 during the last four centuries.

Standards of weight have been less accurate than standards of length. The Roman libra varied by 1 part in 50 over the history of the Roman Empire, and Byzantine standards of weight varied by as much as 1 part in 35.

By the Middle Ages the need for certain manufacturing standards arose, largely to prevent merchants from cheating by adulterating products [8]. This was only a minor effort, however, and largely unsuccessful. The real driving force behind standardization was the growth of science in the seventeenth and eighteenth centuries and the industrial revolution in the eighteenth and nineteenth centuries.

As early as the seventeenth century the concept of scientific standards for weights and measures was suggested. The astronomer, Jean Picard, was among the leaders in advocating this action. Picard proposed to take, as a standard of distance, the length of a pendulum with a beat of exactly one second at sea level and 45° latitude. Even this proposal, of course, was dependent on a prior standard for time. *In principle* a standard for time is easy to construct. It is a consequence of the astronomical phenomena—such as the diurnal cycle—which force themselves upon everyone. In practice it is a nontrivial task not entirely resolved today.

Suggestions for the creation of scientific standards were given practical shape during the French Revolution. The National Assembly, in 1790, appointed a committee to consider the suitability of various proposals for fundamental standards. Thus was born the first standardization committee although, as will be seen below, far from the last. This committee initiated another first in standardization, often copied today, by not reporting until five years later (1795) with a set of proposals for weights and measures based on the meter (which was not itself defined by the committee until 1799). The metric system became compulsory by law in France in 1801 and, of course, has been adopted by many countries since. The vicissitudes of the metric system in its combat with the English system of units is a superb illustration of the problem of the introduction of sensible standards that conflict with vested interest and inertia. Information processing, despite its youth, is not free from this affliction.

The need for standardization of processes in connection with the development of precision instruments, machine tools, and mass production is too obvious to belabor. By the beginning of the twentieth century it had become apparent that much besides weights and measures needed to be standardized in some formal way. The nineteenth century's experience with nonstandard railroad tracks was proof enough.

This sketch of standardization in history does not do justice to the subject. Those interested in standardization as a process and socioeconomic force would do well to delve deeper into the historical background. In order to explicate the current status of information processing standardization activity, the author, with considerable regret, has foreborne to elaborate on the interaction between social gain and standards efforts. There is room for dozens of doctoral theses in history, economics, and philosophy on the effect of standardization (or lack thereof) on human institutions. The literature is extremely meager in scholarly journals, and it is even worse in the popular press. A search of the last five years of the *Readers' Guide to Periodical Literature* turned up only three articles even remotely about standards, and each was concerned with a detail.

3. Modern Industrial Standardization

American industry spends approximately one billion dollars each year on standardization, which contributes to the convenience, safety, and efficiency of everyone. Standards for light bulb sockets, screw threads, and the colors of traffic lights have obvious virtues, being designed for purposes of safety, definition, or interchangeability.

Official standards come into existence through recognized procedures of development and approval by various major standards organizations both national and international [9]. Allied to the major organizations are standards groups from the various industrial and trade associations and professional societies. The first standards organizations were established around 1900, and their contribution to industry and government has grown more or less in proportion to the growth of the whole economy.

3.1 American Standards Association

The American Standards Association (ASA) is, currently, *the* national standards body in the United States. It is a privately supported, nonprofit organization which acts as a national clearinghouse and coordinating agency for voluntary industrial standardization in the United States. An *American Standard* is a standard approved and published by ASA.

The American Standards Association began in 1918 when five American engineering societies formed a national organization to coordinate the development of national standards. The founding societies were the American Institute of Electrical Engineers, the American Society of Mechanical Engineers, the American Society of Civil Engineers, the American Society of Mining and Metallurgical Engineers, and the American Society for Testing Materials. They founded the American Engineering Standards Committee, the forerunner of the American Standards Association. Three departments of the federal government—Commerce, War, and Navy—joined the five societies and became founding members.

In 1928, this American Engineering Standards Committee was fundamentally reorganized and was renamed the American Standards Association. Twenty years later, in 1948, ASA was incorporated as a nonprofit corporation under the laws of the State of New York with a board of directors responsible for policy, administration, and financial matters. The Standards Council, representing all member bodies, was established to supervise all technical activities and to determine the over-all standards policy.

The American Standards Association is now a national federation of almost 150 technical societies and trade associations (either members or associate members). In addition there are about 2200 company members. The organization operates on an annual budget of approximately $2,000,000. Approximately 10,000 scientists, engineers, government officials, and representatives of various national organizations (trade associations and professional societies) participate in the various ASA projects and this number increases daily.

The American Standards Association has recognized more than 2500 national standards as American Standards; this figure is also increasing. Some 450 standards projects are currently active. Despite this, there is considerable (and, in the main, justified) criticism that ASA is far too conservative in its efforts.

The main functions of ASA are the following:

(1) to provide systematic means for developing American Standards,
(2) to promote the development and use of national standards in the United States,
(3) to approve standards as American Standards provided they are accepted by a consensus of all national groups substantially concerned with their scope and provisions,
(4) to coordinate standardization activities,
(5) to serve as a clearinghouse for information on American and foreign standards, and

(6) to represent American interests in international standardization work.

The American Standards Association has created sixteen formal boards, called *Standards Boards*, to review proposed American Standards and rule, from a nontechnical, administrative viewpoint, on the acceptability of proposals. These Standards Boards are listed in Table I.

TABLE I
ASA STANDARDS BOARDS

Acoustical	Materials and Testing
Chemical Industry	Mechanical
Construction	Mining
Consumer Goods	Miscellaneous
Electrical	Nuclear
Graphic	Packaging and Handling
Highway Traffic	Photographic
Information Processing Systems	Safety

Sitting atop these Standards Boards in the ASA hierarchy, as noted above, is the Standards Council, made up of representatives for each of the member groups (the trade associations and technical societies). This Council serves largely as a judicial review board, its most important functions being as follows:

(1) approval of the initiation of a standards project that has sufficiently broad national support,
(2) approval of the scope of a standards project,
(3) approval of the membership of standards committees to insure individual competence and adequate, balanced representation of all groups substantially concerned with the project,
(4) approval, as American Standards, of proposed standards that meet ASA requirements, and
(5) monitoring of the periodic review of all American Standards by those concerned to determine whether the standards should be reaffirmed, revised, or withdrawn.

There are three basic methods by which American Standards are created through ASA. They are the General Acceptance Method, the Existing Standards Method, and the Sectional Committee Method. The General Acceptance Method is employed in those cases where the issue is simple, the proposals straightforward, and the result not expected to cause controversy. Under this method a general conference of concerned groups is called, and agreement is hammered out. The agreement to standardize the inch as *exactly* 2.54 centimeters is an example of an American Standard created by this General Acceptance Method.

The Existing Standards Method is exactly what its name implies. Any organization can submit an existing standard of its own to ASA for approval as an American Standard, without going through any of the other channels for the creation of an American Standard. The American Standards Association will give approval, *pro forma*, if certain conditions are met. First, the standard must be truly national in scope and recognition. Second, proof must be submitted to and accepted by ASA that those organizations and individuals substantially concerned with the scope and provisions of the standard have already accepted it. Third, the standard must not conflict in any way with other standards in the field.

Many of the standards of the American Society for Testing and Materials, for example, have been approved as American Standards by the Existing Standards Method. As one of many instances of the application of the Existing Standards Method, the American Standard "A1.1-1965, Portland Cement, Specifications for" was determined in this way [*10*]. Indeed, approximately one-third of all American Standards have been created in this manner.

The final method for establishment of American Standards, the Sectional Committee Method, is the one of most interest in the computer and information processing field, as all information processing standards have been, and are being, developed by this method. It consists of the formation of a committee to develop one or more appropriate standards under an assigned scope. The committee is composed of representatives accredited for the specific purpose by those organized groups directly concerned with the project. Where appropriate, the committee may also contain companies and particularly qualified individuals.

The special utility of the Sectional Committee Method lies in its advance provision for proper representation so that a consensus will be assured and self-evident when the members have approved their work. It is required by ASA that membership in Sectional Committees be representative of all national groups and organizations concerned with the standards project in question.

A member of a Sectional Committee, acting as a representative of his organization, has certain responsibilities as follows:

(1) He is responsible to the general public for the technical and economic consequences of the standard which he helps to develop.

(2) He has a duty to act on the committee in accordance with the policies of the organization he represents, to keep his organization informed, and to consult with his organization when necessary.

(3) He is expected to conduct the standards work for which he is

responsible with administrative orderliness, competence, and reasonable promptness.

While the above credo sounds a bit pious, something like it is essential to sensible standardization.

The Sectional Committee may, and indeed, usually must, delegate the technical work to subcommittees. A subcommittee member functions as an individual rather than as an official representative of his organization, in contrast to a committee member. This is a point often overlooked, even within the standardization community.

The administration of a Sectional Committee is handled by a sponsor, usually a trade association. The sponsor has the following responsibilities:

(1) to organize the Sectional Committee,
(2) to ensure that the work is carried out continuously and effectively,
(3) to provide the necessary administrative services,
(4) to keep ASA informed on the progress of the work, and
(5) to submit standards to the ASA for approval, accompanied by the sponsor's technical evaluation.

The main work of a Sectional Committee is to explore the views of all its members fully and to compromise and blend these views into a resultant form that represents a sound solution to the problem at hand, acceptable (at least grudgingly) to all. This is accomplished by careful execution of formal procedures.

The formal steps for the development and approval of an American Standard by a Sectional Committee are given in ASA's document entitled, "The Organization and Work of Sectional Committees" [11]. The "Summary of Administrative Steps," section 9.15, is as follows:

"*9.15 Summary of Administrative Steps*
1. Committee meets, plans its work, and appoints subcommittees to draft the various sections of the proposed standard or standards.
2. Each subcommittee obtains suggestions:
   a. From its own members.
   b. From members of the committee.
   c. From outside sources—existing standards, research papers, etc.
3. Draft prepared and circulated to subcommittee members.
4. Discussion by correspondence or in meetings until agreement is reached on draft in subcommittee.
5. Draft circulated to committee and in some cases to a selected list of organizations and individuals not on the committee.
6. Draft discussed and acted upon by committee by correspondence or in meetings:
   a. Coordinated with other subcommittee reports, or
   b. Amended by committee, or
   c. Referred back to subcommittee for amendment.

7. Process continued until agreement on draft standard is reached by committee.
8. Draft standard published for criticism in one or more trade or technical journals, or circulated to industrial and technical groups.
9. Criticisms sifted by committee and final draft standard agreed upon.
10. Final letter ballot of the committee taken on the proposed standard.
11. Proposed standard, together with a record of the vote of each member of the committee, submitted by the chairman of the committee to the sponsor for approval and submission to ASA. In the case of autonomous committees, proposed standard submitted directly to ASA.
12. Proposed standard, together with the necessary exhibits and its own recommendations submitted by the sponsor to ASA.
13. Endorsing sponsor secured by ASA prior to ASA approval of a standard prepared by an autonomous committee.
14. Standard approved by ASA.
15. Standard published by the sponsor or the ASA."

Following approval of a proposal as an American Standard, its use is to be promoted as described [11], section 12.2, as follows:

"*12.2 Promotion of the Use of Standards*
It is an obligation of the Association and of the sponsor to promote the use of each American Standard, bringing it to the attention of the groups to whom it should be of value."

In addition, following publication of an American Standard, committee members are expected to be helpful in promoting the adoption of the standard by industry. For example, they are expected to make a formal report to the organizations they represent, see that adequate reference to the standard is made in the publications of their organizations, and use their personal influence to promote general knowledge and understanding of the standard.

The Sectional Committee Method of establishing American Standards has been elaborated at some length because of its relevance to standardization in the field of computers and information processing. The ASA Sectional Committees concerned with this field will be discussed in considerable detail in Section 3.3 below.

In the discussion of these three methods of establishing American Standards, it is important to note that the national ASA does not develop or write standards. What ASA *does* do is provide a systematic means for insuring the development of standards and exercise a judicial, and fundamentally political, function in safeguarding the principles under which American Standards are developed.

The American Standards Association operates under two fundamental principles:

(1) Organizations or groups substantially concerned with the subject matter of a standard, whether members of ASA or not, have an inherent right to have their views fully considered in the development and approval of an American Standard.

(2) An American Standard can be initiated and approved only if a consensus exists of all groups who are substantially concerned with the scope and provisions of the standard.

All American Standards are, clearly, voluntarily arrived at and are available for voluntary use. As observed above, they are reviewed on a regular basis, at least once every five years, and as a result are either reaffirmed, revised, or withdrawn. An approved American Standard has no mandatory implications. No one is compelled, under the law, to adhere to its provisions. However, American Standards can be, and frequently are, adopted by governmental agencies or other organizations for mandatory application in the appropriate context. When this happens, of course, they have legal status and noncompliance implies violation of the law. Despite this possibility of legal responsibility, court action in this area has been extremely rare.

Further details on ASA activity generally may be found in reference [*12*].

3.2 International Standardization Activity

The two principal international standardization groups related to information processing are the International Organization for Standardization (ISO) and its affiliated organization, the International Electrotechnical Commission (IEC). Both organizations are concerned exclusively with standardization and are officially recognized by the United Nations through liaison status as the appropriate bodies for the development of international standards. The full scope of ISO will not be discussed, for to do so would take this essay too far afield.

A third international organization of importance to information processing is the International Telecommunication Union (ITU). This organization includes, among others, the International Telegraph and Telephone Consultive Committee (CCITT). The ITU is also recognized by the United Nations.

Data processing manufacturers in Europe are represented by the European Computer Manufacturers Association (ECMA). This organization works with ISO and IEC. The specific aim of ECMA is to cooperate with national and international organizations in the development and promulgation of data processing standards.

Formal international standardization activity began, surprisingly late, with the founding of the International Federation of National Standardizing Associations (ISA) in 1926. This Association was dissolved at the time of World War II, but its work was eventually continued and extended by its successor, ISO.

The International Organization for Standardization (ISO) was organized in 1946, and consists of the national standards bodies of 55 countries. Final authority for the ISO is vested in its General Assembly, which is composed of delegates of the member countries and meets at least triennially. The administration of ISO is in the hands of a Council, which appoints a General Secretary to administer the General Secretariat housed in Geneva. The selection of Geneva for these headquarters is largely due to the historical position of that city as an international *and neutral* site.

Since ASA is the national standards body in the United States, it serves as the United States member of ISO. In this capacity, ASA acts in behalf of the interests of the United States and coordinates all American participation in ISO technical activities.

An approved standard, generated by an ISO Technical Committee and approved by the Council, is called an ISO Recommendation. The ISO Recommendations are developed and used on a voluntary basis only. Nevertheless, experience shows that these Recommendations are promptly recognized in the international community and generally used in international trade. At present, approximately 400 ISO Recommendations have been approved, and over 300 draft Recommendations are currently in process.

The official objectives of ISO are as follows:

(1) to promote the development of standards in the world with a view to facilitating international exchange of goods and services and to developing mutual cooperation in the sphere of intellectual, scientific, technological, and economic activity;

(2) to facilitate coordination and unification of national standards and to issue necessary recommendations to member bodies for this purpose;

(3) to set up International Standards, provided, in each case, no member body dissents;

(4) to encourage and facilitate, as occasion demands, the development of new standards having common requirements for use in the national or international sphere;

(5) to arrange for exchange of information regarding work of its member bodies and of its Technical Committees; and

(6) to cooperate with other international organizations interested in related matters, particularly by undertaking at their request studies relating to standardization projects.

The ISO Technical Committee concerned with information processing standards is TC 97—Computers and Information Processing—established in 1961 at a joint meeting of ISO and IEC. This committee is the international counterpart of ASA's X3 Committee (cf. Section 3.3

below). Many countries in addition to the United States have national organizations corresponding to X3 and TC 97.

The scope of TC 97 is standardization of the terminology, problem definition, programming languages, communication characteristics, and physical (i.e., nonelectrical) characteristics of computers and information processing devices, equipment, and systems. The Secretariat for TC 97 is currently held by the United States.

The members of TC 97 are as listed in Table II.

TABLE II
ISO TC 97

	Members (Participating)	
Belgium	Italy	Sweden
Canada	Japan	Switzerland
Czechoslovakia	Netherlands	United Kingdom
France	Poland	United States
Germany	Spain	U.S.S.R.
	Members (Observer)	
Australia	Greece	Norway
Austria	Hungary	Pakistan
Burma	Iran	Portugal
Chile	Ireland	Republic of South Africa
Columbia	Israel	Rumania
Denmark	New Zealand	Yugoslavia

In addition to the Secretariat, TC 97 consists of eight Subcommittees. The organization of TC 97 is shown in Fig. 1. The titles, scopes, and countries holding the Secretariats of the Subcommittees are as follows:

SC1—Vocabulary

SCOPE: Provision of a multilingual glossary for information processing systems and related subjects covered in the general scope of ISO/TC 97 and, where appropriate, abbreviations and letter symbols.

SECRETARIAT: Netherlands

SC2—Character Sets and Coding

SCOPE: Standardization of character sets, character meanings, the grouping of character sets into information, coded representation, and the identification of it for the interchange of information between data processing systems and associated equipments; also, preparation of reports on the problems related to analog devices.

SECRETARIAT: France

SC3—Character Recognition

SCOPE: Standardization of input-output character forms for the interchange of information between data processing equipments and

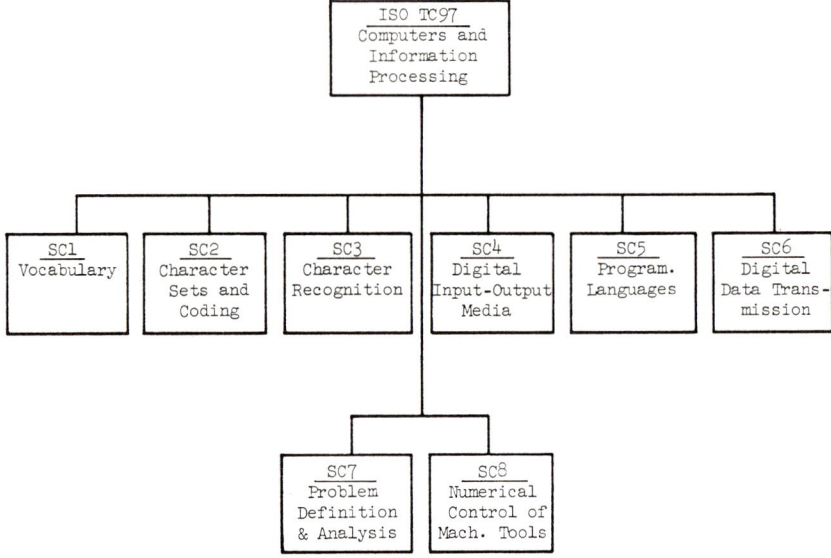

FIG. 1. International Organization for Standardization TC 97 Subcommittees.

associated equipments utilizing only humanly legible printed character sets, i.e., character recognition.

SECRETARIAT: United States

SC4—Digital Input-Output Media

SCOPE: Standardization of those physical characteristics of input-output media which are required for the interchange of information between data processing systems and systems of associated equipment.

SECRETARIAT: Italy

SC5—Programming Languages

SCOPE: Standardization and specification of common programming languages of broad utility, with provision for revision, expansion, and strengthening and for the definition and approval of test problems.

SECRETARIAT: United States

SC6—Digital Data Transmission

SCOPE: Determination and definition of the system parameters governing the operational action and reaction between communication systems and digital data generating and receiving systems.

SECRETARIAT: United States

SC7—Problem Definition and Analysis

SCOPE: Processing of appropriate standards on problem definition and analysis which assure a complete and valid description of information processing problem requirements, and the most appropriate means and plans to meet them; consideration of means, format, context, and other techniques by which the foregoing may be described. In particular, the areas of methodology, data representation, and flow-chart symbology are pertinent to the problem of achieving a systematic means of preparing the required information for analysis.

SECRETARIAT: Netherlands

SC8—Numerical Control of Machine Tools
SCOPE: (still to be established)
SECRETARIAT: France

The ISO Technical Committee concerned with office machines is ISO TC 95. This is the international counterpart of ASA's X4 Committee (cf. Section 3.3 below). Other countries also have national standards organizations corresponding to X4 and TC 95. The current TC 95 projects include draft proposals on key top and printed symbols for adding machines, typewriter keyboard arrangements, and basic paper layouts.

The term *International Standard* exists at present only as a generic term because to establish one requires *unanimity*, impossible in today's world. Standards which have been approved by majority vote in ISO are known as *ISO Recommendations*.

A draft ISO Recommendation is a proposed standard developed and accorded a majority vote by an ISO Technical Committee. It is circulated to all ISO member countries for acceptance. When approved by a majority of the ISO member countries, it becomes an ISO Recommendation. As is true of American Standards, the use of international standards is voluntary. Nevertheless, ISO Recommendations are being used to an increasing extent because of their fairly rapid adoption as national standards by the various ISO members.

The development work on international standards is done by Technical Committees using a prescribed procedure. In order to initiate an ISO project, a proposal must be made by a member country. The proposal is then circulated to all other member countries to determine the extent of international interest. A minimum of five members is necessary to start an ISO standards project and, if sufficient interest is shown, a Technical Committee is formed to develop an ISO Recommendation.

One participating member, normally the proposing country, is appointed as the Secretariat of the Technical Committee. The Secretariat is responsible for outlining a program of work and for circulating it to other members for consideration and approval. The Secretariat supports all the administrative functions of the committee, and international meetings of the committee members are called, as necessary, by the

Secretariat. Decisions of the committee are made solely by majority vote, and the final vote is always by letter ballot.

One difference between ISO and ASA methods of approval of a proposed standard is the voting method. All voting in ISO Technical Committees is done on a majority (one country—one vote) basis only, while ASA approval of a proposed standard is done by a consensus method.

The procedural steps of an ISO Technical Committee are as follows [*13*]:

(1) A first Draft Proposal on an agreed item of work is prepared by the Technical Committee Secretariat.

(2) The Draft Proposal, with an explanatory report, is distributed to the participating members of the Technical Committee for consideration and comment.

(3) Comments are considered, and if necessary, a second Draft Proposal is prepared and the procedure repeated until the proposal is approved by letter ballot by a majority of the participating members.

(4) A Draft Proposal approved by a majority of the committee becomes a Draft ISO Recommendation and is sent with an explanatory report to the ISO General Secretariat.

(5) The General Secretariat distributes the Draft ISO Recommendation to all ISO member bodies with a ballot for reply within five months.

(6) The member bodies vote by indicating:
    (a) approval of the Draft as presented (editorial comments may be appended),
    (b) disapproval of the Draft for technical reasons set forth (acceptance of these technical reasons will change the vote to approval), and
    (c) abstention from voting [if 60% of the total of (a) and (b) approve, the Draft is accepted].

(7) A second Draft ISO Recommendation is prepared, if necessary, and this entire procedure is repeated until the Draft is approved by 60% of the members voting.

(8) Upon approval, the Draft ISO Recommendation with a Final Report is referred by the General Secretariat to the ISO Council, which determines whether or not it should be accepted as an ISO Recommendation.

As noted, ASA, as the national standards body in the United States, serves as the United States member in ISO. In this capacity, ASA acts for and in behalf of the United States' interests concerned with the subjects under consideration and coordinates all American participation in the ISO technical activities.

STANDARDS FOR COMPUTERS AND INFORMATION PROCESSING

The ASA function in international standardization, as with the *national* program for the development and approval of American Standards, is the coordination of all viewpoints and the statement of formal opinion, based on a national consensus. Thus, the same ASA principles and procedures apply to the processing of ISO projects in the United States as apply to the development and approval of American Standards.

The ISO items which are treated by ASA are of three major types:

(1) desirability of new projects and participation therein,
(2) agreement with drafts under development in Technical Committees of which the USA is a Participating Member, and
(3) acceptance of Draft ISO Recommendations as a Member Body of ISO.

As ISO Recommendations are being used increasingly in international trade, it is important that the United States' interests be actively represented in the formulation and acceptance of these standards. The American Standards Association has full knowledge of the work being done and is communicating this information to appropriate American groups. Under ASA auspices, the United States' viewpoint is being carefully presented on each project. These facts are significant, as American companies are directly affected by ISO Recommendations in world trade.

The International Electrotechnical Commission (IEC) is the international group concerned with standardization in the electrical and electronics field. It was organized in 1904, and in 1947 affiliated with the ISO, although as an autonomous and financially independent body. At the moment, 38 nations are members of IEC. The administration of IEC is carried out by a council with a secretariat again located in Geneva. Viewpoints representing the United States are developed by the United States National Committee (USNC), a part of ASA.

The IEC Technical Committee working in the data processing field is TC 53—Computers and Information Processing—which began its work in 1961. The scope of TC 53 is to prepare international recommendations for standardization of the electrical characteristics of computers and information processing devices and systems, including such devices as process control computers and machine-tool control computers.

Originally TC 53 had four subcommittees. Two of these have recently been disbanded, however, and their work reassigned to TC 97 subcommittees. The current organization of TC 53 is shown in Fig. 2. The titles and scopes of the two remaining subcommittees are as follows:

SC53B—Digital Data Transmission

SCOPE: Standardization of electrical characteristics of the interfaces

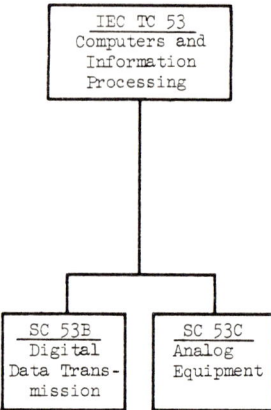

Fig. 2. International Electrotechnical Commission TC 53 Subcommittees.

between data transmission equipments, computers or ancillary equipments, and such other electrical characteristics as may be necessary to enable equipments to be interchanged.

SC53C—Analog Equipments for Information Processing Systems
SCOPE: Standardization of electrical characteristics of the analog interfaces between analog equipments, information processing systems using digital techniques, and such other electrical characteristics as may be necessary to enable equipments to be interchanged.

The International Telecommunications Union (ITU) is concerned with standards in the field of telephone, telegraph, and broadcast communications. One important body of this union is the International Telegraph and Telephone Consultive Committee (CCITT). This committee has the responsibility for data transmission standards, a matter of considerable importance to information processing. The interests of the United States in this area are represented, curiously, by the Department of State. State has delegated this responsibility, somewhat less curiously, to the International Division of the Federal Communications Commission. Of particular importance to information processing is Study Group A—Data Transmission—established in 1959. This group deals primarily with communications codes and other aspects of data transmission.

The functional organization of ITU and CCITT is shown in Fig. 3. Unlike the standards promulgated by the other standards organizations described in this paper, which are voluntary, the CCITT recommendations are *mandatory* in nature although the details of enforcement are unclear.

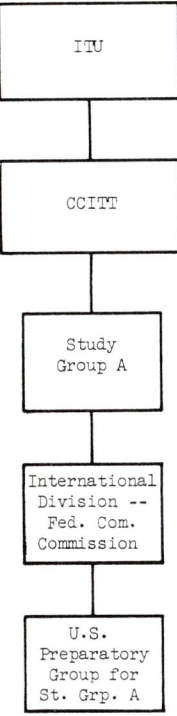

Fig. 3. International Telecommunications Union and International Telegraph and Telephone Consultive Committee functional organization.

The European Computer Manufacturers Association (ECMA) was officially organized in 1961. It, too, is headquartered in Geneva. The members of ECMA are those companies who manufacture and market data processing machines in Europe. Many companies normally thought of as American are members of ECMA.

The aims of ECMA are to study and develop, in cooperation with the appropriate national and international organizations, methods and procedures to facilitate and standardize the use of information processing systems and to promulgate sundry standards applicable to the functional design and use of data processing equipment.

Standards developed by ECMA are voluntary in application. Approved ECMA standards are universally available and are intended to be drafts for consideration by ISO, where, presumably the users' views will be considered and the final standards approved. The *user* has no direct input to ECMA.

The work of ECMA is accomplished by Technical Committees. The organization of these committees is shown in Fig. 4. The scopes of the committees are as follows:

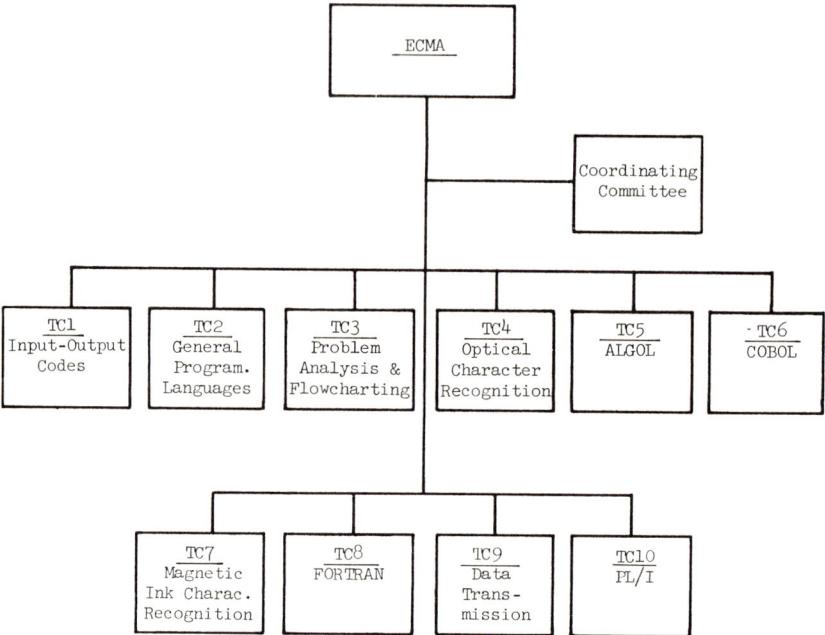

Fig. 4. European Computer Manufacturers Association Technical Committees.

TC1—Input and Output Codes
SCOPE: Definition of common character sets and their coded representation suitable to input-output media and data transmission in order to facilitate interchange of information between data processing equipment.

TC2—General Programming Languages (now disbanded)
SCOPE: Conduct of a survey of basic development in the field of programming techniques, and definition of the desirable characteristics of programming languages with a view to establishing programming languages with wide applicability and to facilitating compatibility between them.

TC3—Problem Analysis and Flow Charting
SCOPE: Definition of a common diagrammatic and symbolic representation of problems and their solutions with computer systems.

TC4—Optical Character Recognition
SCOPE: Definition of a minimum number of character sets legible both to humans and to machines; specification of fonts, parameters, measurements, and tolerances; definition of document specification.

TC5—ALGOL

SCOPE: Examination of the present position of ALGOL and determination of the extent to which it would be possible for ECMA members to use ALGOL, as defined in the 1960 report, as a standard.

TC6—COBOL

SCOPE: Definition of a common interpretation of COBOL 61 which will take into account specific European requirements, in order that ECMA members may realize in practice, to the greatest possible extent, the aims expressed in the COBOL 61 report.

TC7—Magnetic Ink Character Recognition (MICR)

SCOPE: Drafting of working specifications for applications of CMC7 and E13B, taking European requirements into account.

TC8—FORTRAN

SCOPE: Consideration of the ISO and ASA working papers on FORTRAN and subsequent documents to insure that European requirements are taken into account in order that ECMA members can realize and practice the highest possible degree of interchange of FORTRAN programs.

TC9—Data Transmission

SCOPE: Definition of common parameters which will facilitate communication within and between data processing systems using transmission links; preparation of coordinated viewpoints covering those requirements which are of common interest to both the European computer manufacturers and the telecommunications services.

TC10—PL/I

SCOPE: Study of the language PL/I and reporting on its suitability as the basis of an ECMA standard.

The ECMA's heavy emphasis on programming languages should be noted.

The International Federation for Information Processing (IFIP) is the international professional society concerned with all aspects of the information processing sciences. It does not work directly in the field of standards, but where standards affect general information processing considerations, IFIP has an interest.

The International Federation for Information Processing came into existence, officially, in 1960, and its current membership consists of 24 technical societies from 24 member countries. The United States' member is the American Federation of Information Processing Societies (AFIPS).

The aims of IFIP are as follows:

(1) to sponsor international conferences and symposia on information processing, including mathematical and engineering aspects;
(2) to establish international committees to undertake special tasks falling within the spheres of action of the member societies; and
(3) to advance the interests of member societies in international cooperation in the field of information processing.

It has established three technical committees and two working groups. The organization of the IFIP committees is shown in Fig. 5.

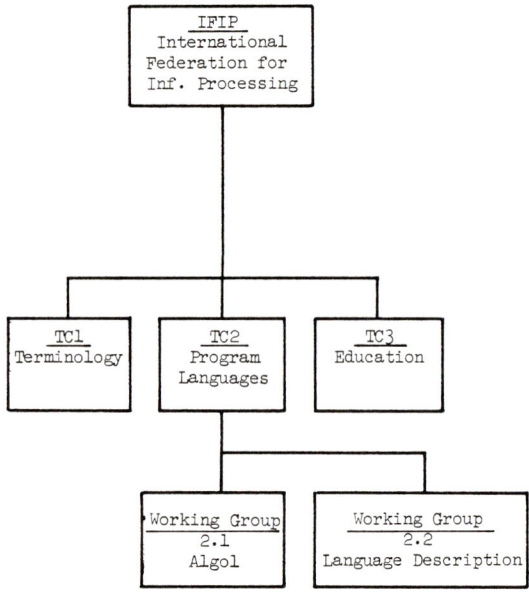

FIG. 5. International Federation for Information Processing Technical Committees.

The scopes of the committees are as follows:

IFIP TC1—Terminology

The scope of this committee is the establishment of terminology of digital computers and data processing devices, equipment, media, and systems. Its objective is to promote the exchange of information leading to the compilation of a multilingual glossary for information processing systems and related subjects.

STANDARDS FOR COMPUTERS AND INFORMATION PROCESSING   127

IFIP TC2—Programming Languages

The goal of this committee is to promote the development, specification and refinement of common programming languages, with provision for future revision, expansion, and improvement.

IFIP TC2—Working Group 2.1, ALGOL

This group has approved a revised ALGOL 60 as an official IFIP language and submitted it to ISO. It is now working on an improved ALGOL language (ALGOL 66).

IFIP TC2—Working Group 2.2, Programming Language Description

This group (currently being established) will survey techniques for formal language description (cf. Section 3.4 below).

IFIP TC3—Education

The objectives of this committee are to establish comprehensive training programs and suggested curricula for the education of technical people from all over the world who are in fields in which the computer can make a significant contribution. Another function is to generate material to acquaint the lay public with the computer and its impact on various aspects of society.

3.3 Standardization in Information Processing

In the information processing field, standards are currently in the early phase of development. These standards concern programming languages, media (i.e., punched cards, perforated tape, magnetic tape), data transmission, codes, data elements, flow charts, vocabulary, and character shapes for machine recognition.

Within ASA it is the Information Processing Systems Standards Board (one of ASA's sixteen Standards Boards) that monitors standardization activity in the field of information processing. The Information Processing Systems Standards Board (IPSSB) came into existence in 1963. This board processes standards in the field of information processing and handles the administrative review of the X3, X4, X6, and Z39 (Library Work and Documentation) Sectional Committees. Further it is anticipated that Sectional C85 (Terminology in the Field of Automatic Control) will be assigned eventually to IPSSB.

The 15 organizational members of IPSSB are responsible for matters such as:

(1) reviewing the personnel of Sectional Committees,
(2) approving scopes and sponsors of Sectional Committees,
(3) periodically reviewing the progress of work,
(4) suggesting new areas of work to be initiated,

(5) receiving finished work from Sectional Committees with tally of votes and history,
(6) harmonizing conflicts within industry, and
(7) recommending whether a proposal should be declared an American Standard.

The ASA group working directly in the area of information processing standards is ASA Sectional Committee X3—Computers and Information Processing—which was formed in 1960. It is sponsored by the Data Processing Group of the Business Equipment Manufacturers Association (BEMA). There are at present 36 organizations holding membership in

TABLE III
ASA SECTIONAL COMMITTEE X3 MEMBERSHIP

Producer

Addressograph Multigraph Corp.
Bunker Ramo Corp.
Burroughs Corp.
Farrington Electronics, Inc.
Friden, Inc.
General Electric Co. EDPD
Honeywell EDPD
IBM Corp.
Monroe International, Inc.
Moore Business Forms, Inc.
National Cash Register Co.

Olivetti-Underwood Corp.
Pitney Bowes, Inc.
Radio Corp. of America EDPD
UNIVAC Division of Sperry Rand Corp.
Royal Typewriter Co., Inc., Div. of Litton Industries
SCM Corp.
The Standard Register Co.
UARCO, Inc.
Xerox Corp.

Consumer

Air Transport Assoc.
American Bankers Assoc.
American Gas Assoc. and Edison Electric Institute
American Petroleum Institute
Association of American Railroads
Council of State Governments

Department of Defense
General Services Administration
Insurance Accounting and Statistical Assoc.
National Retail Merchants Assoc.
Life Office Management Assoc.
National Machine Tool Builders Assoc.

General Interest

Administrative Management Soc.
Association for Computing Machinery
Data Processing Management Assoc.
Electronic Industries Assoc.
Engineers Joint Council
Industrial Communications Assoc.

Institute of Electrical and Electronic Engrs.
Joint Users Group
National Bureau of Standards
Systems and Procedures Assoc.
Telephone Group
ASA X4 Sectional Committee on Office Machines

X3, divided into three groups—Producer, Consumer, and General Interest. Through 12 representatives, selected from its group of members, BEMA represents the producers (manufacturers) in X3, and the 12 votes of this group represent BEMA's position. The present membership of X3 is shown in Table III.

The current scope of X3 is the standardization of the terminology, problem description, programming languages, and communication characteristics (cf. Note 1) as well as the physical (i.e., nonelectrical) characteristics (cf. Note 2) of computers and data processing devices, equipment, and systems (cf. Note 3). At present, the IPSSB is reviewing the scope of the X3 Sectional Committee for possible revision.

- Note 1: This includes the standardization of symbology, coded character sets and representations, input-output media and formats, and character recognition.
- Note 2: This includes standardization of both logical and structural characteristics.
- Note 3: This includes process control systems.

At present, there are seven subcommittees operating under the direction of X3. Their titles and scopes are as follows:

X3.1—Optical Character Recognition

SCOPE: Printed input and output to data processing systems for interchange of information between data processing and associated equipment. Humanly legible printed character sets, e.g., character recognition.

X3.2—Codes and Input-Output

SCOPE: Standardization of coded character sets (cf. Note 1) and input-output for information processing systems (cf. Note 2) and the interchange of information between systems and equipment, including code representations, recording formats (cf. Note 3), input-output media (cf. Note 4) and equipment (cf. Note 5). The scope of the X3.2 Subcommittee is presently under consideration for possible reorganization and revision.

- Note 1: This includes machine-sensible coded characters.
- Note 2: This includes process control systems.
- Note 3: This includes such formats and format indicators as are required to define data fields, records, program instructions, etc.
- Note 4: This includes the physical, electrical, and logical properties of media (other than OCR, MICR, and transmission systems).
- Note 5: This includes those aspects of input-output equipment required for interchange of media between systems and equipment.

X3.3—Data Transmission

SCOPE: Determination and definition of the operational characteristics governing the performance of digital data generating and receiving systems combined with communication systems.

X3.4—Common Programming Languages

SCOPE: Standardization of common program languages of broad utility through standard methods of specification with provision for revision, expansion, and improvement, and for definition and approval of test problems.

X3.5—Terminology and Glossary

SCOPE: (a) Coordination with and recommendation to the other subcommittees of ASA X3 in the establishment of definitions required for their proposed standards; (b) recommendation to X3 of a general glossary of data processing terms including communications.

X3.6—Problem Definition and Analysis

SCOPE: Information processing problem definition and analysis standards to provide a systematic means of studying information processing problems, of documenting, and of preparing the required information for analysis.

X3.7—Magnetic Ink Character Recognition

SCOPE: (a) Development of standards for MICR; (b) resolution of problems which may arise in industry and the market place involving the manufacturers and printers.

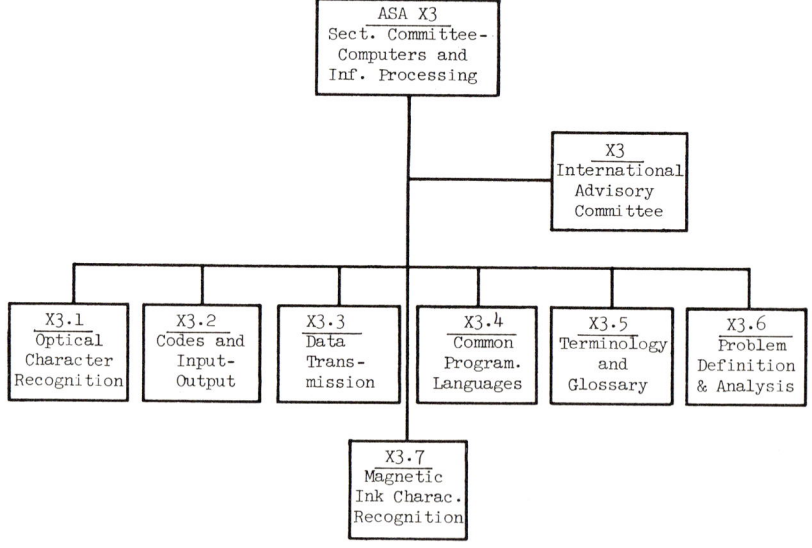

FIG. 6. American Standards Association X3 Subcommittees.

In addition to the X3 Subcommittees, there is an X3 International Advisory Committee. The purpose of this group is to coordinate United States' activity with that of the International Organization for Standardization (ISO) and its corresponding Technical Committee on Computers and Information Processing, ISO TC 97. The organization of X3, its Subcommittees, and their Working Groups, is shown in Figs. 6 to 13.

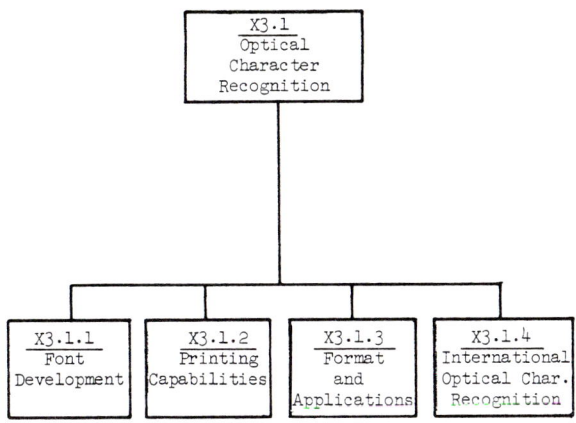

Fig. 7. The X3.1 Working Groups.

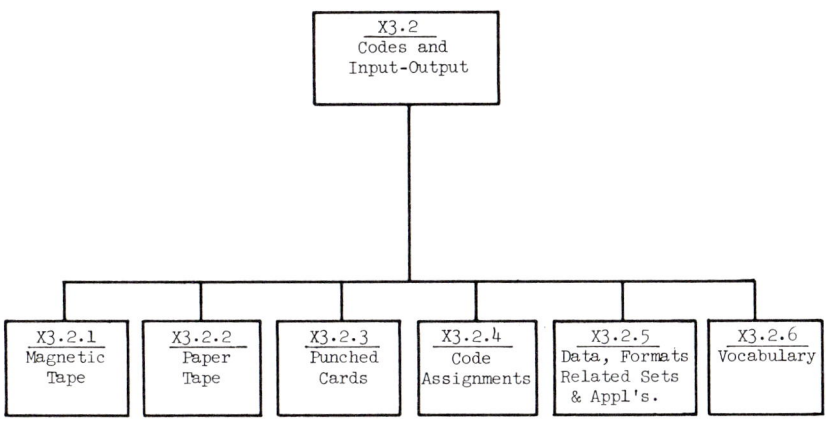

Fig. 8. The X3.2 Working Groups.

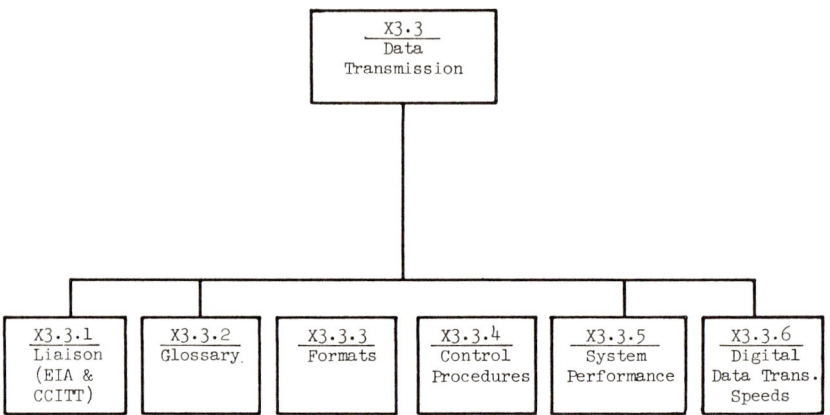

Fig. 9. The X3.3 Working Groups.

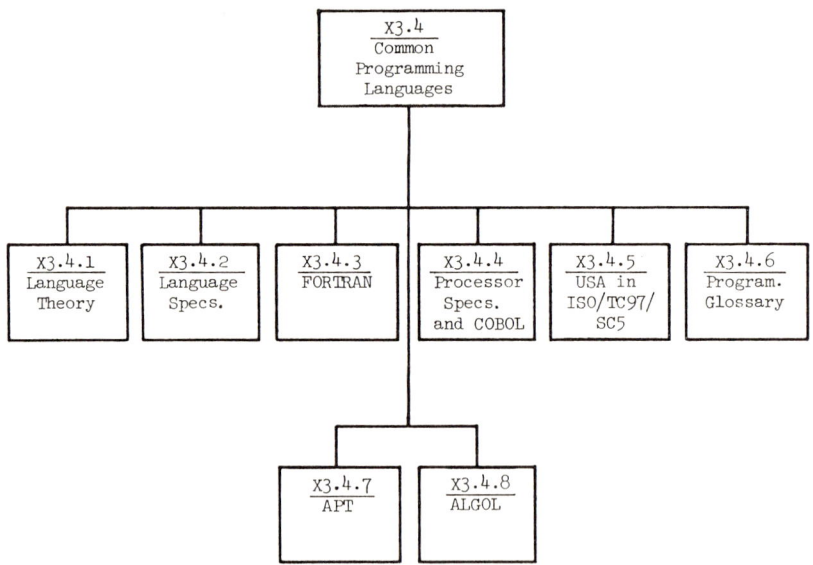

Fig. 10. The X3.4 Working Groups.

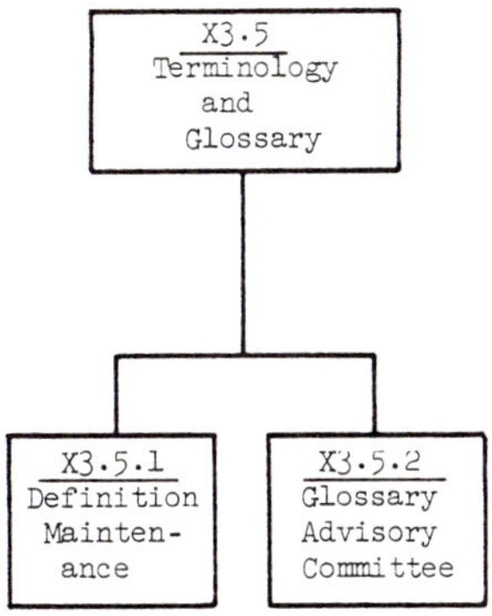

STANDARDS FOR COMPUTERS AND INFORMATION PROCESSING

FIG. 11. The X3.5 Working Groups.

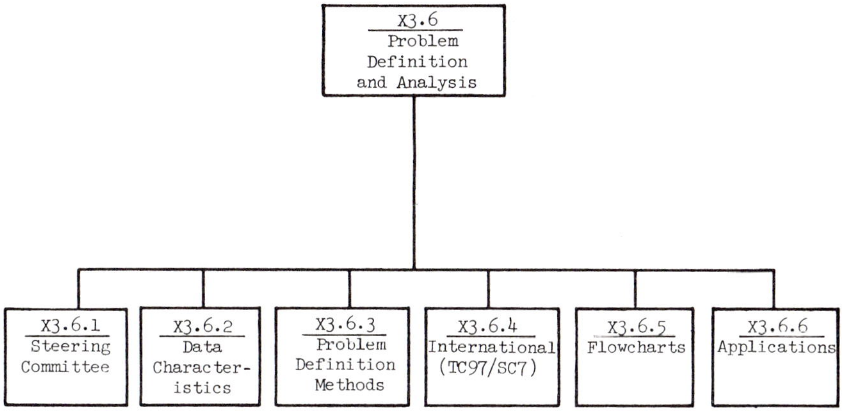

FIG. 12. The X3.6 Working Groups.

FIG. 13. The X3.7 Working Groups.

Another group working in the general field of data processing is ASA Sectional Committee X4, Office Machines. This committee, formed in 1962, is sponsored by the Office Machines Group of BEMA. Its membership is analogous to that of X3, having a Producers Group, a Users Group, and a General Interest Group. The X4 Sectional Committee membership in addition to the manufacturers is shown in Table IV for comparison with that of X3.

TABLE IV
ASA SECTIONAL COMMITTEE X4 MEMBERSHIP (NONMANUFACTURERS)

User and general interest	
American Institute of Electrical & Electronic Engrs.	National Office Management Assoc.
American Petroleum Institute	National Records Management Council
American Soc. of Mechanical Engrs.	National Retail Merchants Assoc.
Association of Consulting Management Engrs., Inc.	National Secretaries Assoc.
	Systems & Procedures Assoc.
	Telephone Group
	United Business Education Assoc.
General Services Administration	ASA X3 Sectional Committee on Computers and Information Processing
Insurance-Accounting-Statistical Assoc.	

The scope of the X4 Committee concerns the standardization of terminology and definitions of functions of office machines. The ASA Information Processing Systems Standards Board is currently reviewing the scope of Sectional Committee X4 for possible revision in parallel with its review of the scope of X3.

The organization of X4 is shown in Fig. 14.

To date there have been five approved American Standards in the Office Machines area resulting from the work of X4 and its Subcommittees. The approved American Standards are:

(1) X4.1–1963, Reaffirmation of the Sheet Sizes (for newsprint, forms, stationery, etc.).

(2) X4.2–1963, Card Size Designation (5 by 3 in. file and index cards, etc.).

(3) X4.3–1964, Definition of Cash Register.

(4) X4.4–1964, Definition of Calculating Machine.

(5) X4.5–1965, Definition of Accounting Machines.

There are a large number of standards projects in process in the X4 Subcommittees. Among those soon to become proposed American Standards are a 10-key keyboard for adding machines and a correspondence keyboard for typewriters.

STANDARDS FOR COMPUTERS AND INFORMATION PROCESSING

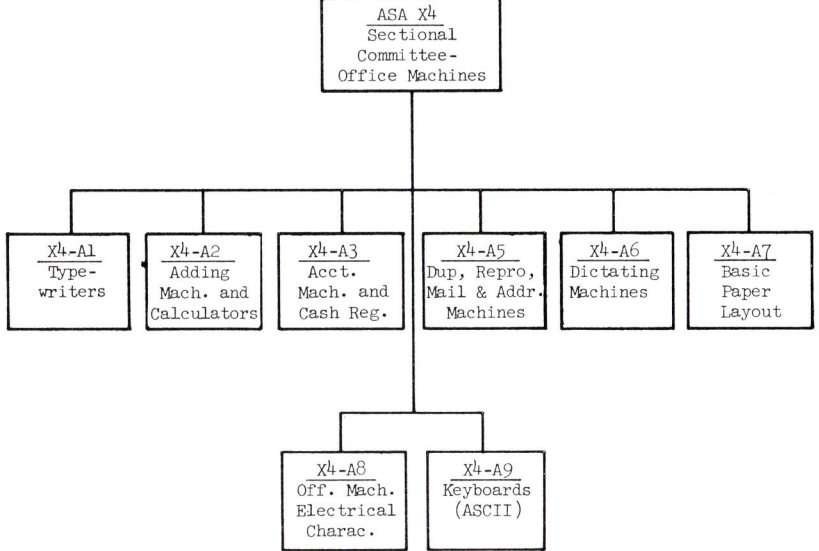

Fig. 14. American Standards Association X4 Subcommittees.

As in the case of X3, BEMA represents the interests of manufacturers in X4. The BEMA votes are held by an equal number of BEMA member companies, which are selected periodically for this purpose from the BEMA/OMG member companies. Table V lists the BEMA/OMG member companies.

TABLE V
ASA X4 PRODUCER GROUP MEMBERSHIP

Addressograph Multigraph Corp.
American Automatic Typewriter Co.
Burroughs Corp.
A. B. Dick Co.
Dictaphone Corp.
Dura Business Machines, Inc.
Thomas A. Edison Industries of McGraw-Edison Co.
Farrington Electronics, Inc.
Friden, Inc.
The Gray Manufacturing Co.
IBM Corp.
Monroe International, Inc., Div. of Litton Industries
Moore Business Forms, Inc.
National Cash Register Co.
Olivetti-Underwood Corp.
Pitney Bowes, Inc.
Recordak Corp.
Remington Rand Div. of Sperry Rand Corp.
Royal Typewriter Co., Inc.
SCM Corp.
The Standard Register Co.
UARCO, Inc.
Victor Comptometer Corp.
Xerox Corp.

Another group working in the data processing area is ASA Sectional Committee X6, Computers and Related Equipment. This Committee is concerned with the electrical and electronic characteristics of data processing equipment and is sponsored by the Electronic Industries Association (EIA).

The Scope of this Committee, along with those of X3 and X4, is currently under review by the ASA Information Processing Systems Standards Board for possible revision.

The Electronic Industries Association (EIA) is a national organization of electronic manufacturers in the United States and is an industrial member of ASA. The Electronic Industries Association began in 1924 as the Radio Manufacturers Association and has since undergone several changes of name, the present name having been adopted in 1957. Among the various objectives of EIA are the development of technical standards in the electronics area and participation in national and international standardization in the electronics industry. To pursue these aims, EIA has established two committees as part of the Industrial Electronics Panel; TR30 and TR31.

The TR30 Committee, Data Transmission Systems and Equipment, is responsible for developing data transmission system requirements and definitions and for developing standards for the characteristics of interface facilities. The TR31 Committee, Numerical Control Systems and Equipment, is responsible for the formulation of standards for numerical control systems and equipment including those for machine tool control and covers codes and formats as well as related electronic areas.

Since the participants of EIA committees are interested in the details of data processing media such as punched cards, perforated tape, magnetic tape, and data transmission, there has necessarily been a close liaison with the BEMA-sponsored activities on these subjects. Members from both organizations often meet jointly on these items.

The Electronics Industries Association has set up many other committees relating to data processing equipment. These pertain primarily to electrical and physical characteristics of components, such as semiconductors, tubes, microelectronics, reliability, and military requirements. As noted above, EIA also sponsors the ASA X6 Sectional Committee, Computers and Related Equipment.

The original trade association for the business equipment industry was organized in 1916 and was known as the Office Equipment Manufacturers Institute. In 1961 the name was changed to the Business Equipment Manufacturers Association, partially due to changing times and partially to make its initials an easier acronym to pronounce.

The Business Equipment Manufacturers Association is organized into three groups:

(1) the Data Processing Group,
(2) the Office Machine Group, and
(3) the Office Furniture Manufacturers Group.

The functional structure of BEMA is shown in Fig. 15.

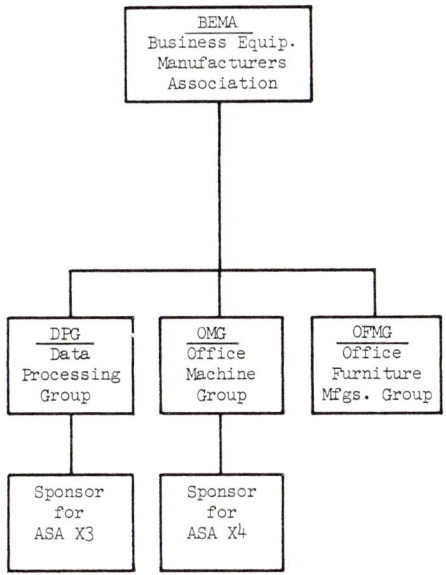

FIG. 15. Business Equipment Manufacturers Association functional organization.

Among the duties of a Sectional Committee sponsor, such as BEMA, is to recommend a proposed standard, which has been approved by the Sectional Committee, to ASA for approval. It is BEMA's policy that any standard so recommended as an American Standard shall be purely voluntary, nondiscriminatory, and relate only to those areas of systems or machines where standardization is clearly in the interests of the public, the affected user groups including the U.S. Government as well as the manufacturers of such equipment (another pious but essential position).

Many American professional societies also work in the area of information processing standards. The national professional society for the data processing community in the United States is the American Federation of Information Processing Societies (AFIPS), organized in 1961. This organization participates in standards work through its member organizations, which are the Association for Computing Machinery (ACM) and the Institute of Electrical and Electronic Engineers (IEEE).

Other professional societies are represented in standards work through membership in the General Interest Groups of ASA's X3 and X4 Committees. Still other societies have established standards committees to work in areas of specific interest. Examples of user groups that have established standards committees are SHARE, GUIDE, CO-OP, and COMMON.

To conclude this discussion of information processing standards in general, there is given below a status report on the existing American Standards and proposed American Standards, together with a survey of the present activity of the various X3 Subcommittees (except X3.4, which is considered in some detail in Section 3.4 below).

At the present time there are twelve American Standards in the field of computers and information processing, one of which (X3.5) is undergoing revision. American Standards are designated, in the case of those developed by the Sectional Committee Method, by a decimal serial, signifying the order in which the standard arose, which is attached to the designation of the Sectional Committee itself. This designation has nothing to do with the subcommittee originating the proposal, a matter that is sometimes confusing. The approved American Standards (as of April 15, 1966) are as follows:

(1) American Standard Signaling Speeds for Data Transmission, X3.1–1962, approved August 8, 1962;
(2) American Standard Print Specifications for Magnetic Ink Character Recognition, X3.2–1963, approved November 7, 1963;
(3) American Standard Bank Check Specification for Magnetic Ink Character Recognition, X3.3–1963, approved November 7, 1963;
(4) American Standard Code for Information Interchange, X3.4–1965, approved December 28, 1965;
(5) American Standard Flow Chart Symbols for Information Processing, X3.5–1965, approved July 9, 1965;
(6) American Standard Perforated Tape Code for Information Interchange, X3.6–1965, approved July 9, 1965;
(7) American Standard Interchange Perforated Tape Variable Block Format for Positioning and Straight Cut Numerically Controlled Machine Tools, X3.7–1965, approved July 9, 1965;
(8) American Standard Interchangeable Perforated Tape Block Format for Contouring and Contouring/Positioning Numerically Controlled Machine Tools, X3.8–1965, approved July 9, 1965;
(9) American Standard FORTRAN, X3.9–1966, approved March 7, 1966;
(10) American Standard Basic FORTRAN, X3.10–1966, approved March 7, 1966;

(11) American Standard Specification for General Purpose Paper Cards for Information Processing, X3.11–1966, approved March 7, 1966; and
(12) American Standard Vocabulary for Information Processing, X3.12–1966, approved April 13, 1966.

It would appear on the surface that American Standard X3.4 was approved later than American Standards X3.5, X3.6, X3.7, and X3.8. This is the result of a *revision*. American Standard X3.4 was originally approved as X3.4–1963 on June 17, 1963. It was subsequently revised, and the revision was approved on December 28, 1965. The original number was retained, however. This will also happen to American Standard X3.5.

As of April 15, 1966, there were five proposed American Standards in process at ASA—"in process" in the sense that they had been approved by X3 and submitted to the IPSSB for approval and forwarding to the Standards Council for final approval and publication. These proposed American Standards are:

(1) pAS (proposed American Standard) Recorded Magnetic Tape (200 CPI, NRZI),
(2) pAS Character Set for Optical Character Recognition,
(3) pAS for Parallel Signaling Speeds for Data Transmission,
(4) pAS for Bit Sequencing of the ASCII in Serial-by-Bit Data Transmission, and
(5) pAS for Character Structure and Character Parity Sense in Serial-by-Bit Data Communication in the ASCII.

Finally, as of April 15, 1966, there were five proposed American Standards under consideration for vote by X3. They are:

(1) pAS for One-Inch Perforated Paper Tape for Information Interchange,
(2) pAS Recorded Magnetic Tape (800 CPI, NRZI),
(3) pAS Twelve-Row Punched Card Code for Information Interchange,
(4) pAS 11/16 in. Perforated Tape for Information Interchange, and
(5) Revised pAS for Take-up Reels for One-Inch Perforated Tape for Information Interchange.

The reader should not be misled by this chronicling of an apparently steady march of proposed standards through the system to final approval as American Standards. It does not imply that everything that is proposed goes through eventually. Although much work and coordination is done at the Subcommittee level to insure, as fully as is humanly possible, that everyone concerned will be satisfied, several of the present American Standards had a very rocky road on their way to becoming American Standards, and at least one of the proposed American Standards seems headed for oblivion. It is the author's prediction that by the time this paper is in print, pAS Twelve-Row Punched Card Code for Information Interchange will have been sent back to Subcommittee and altered beyond all recognition. The current proposal calls for a punched card code that would make obsolete all existing punched cards containing alphabetic information. It seems unlikely that this defect will be sufficiently outweighed by certain minor technical advantages possessed by the proposal to permit its adoption.

A brief survey of the activities of the various X3 Subcommittees shows the following status: X3.1 is primarily concerned with coordinating work with ISO TC 97 SC 3 on optical character recognition, having forwarded a proposed American Standard in the area; X3.2 is quite active and attempting to develop standards on a 1600-CPI magnetic tape, standards for the location and dimensions of holes in punched cards, the positioning of printed characters on punched paper tape and, very significantly, the representation of ASCII (American Standard Code for Information Interchange) in 8-bit environments; X3.3 is working on control procedures, system performance, error control, and transmission speeds in the area of data transmission standards; X3.5 is considering new terms and definitions for inclusion in an updated version of the American Standard Vocabulary for Information Processing; X3.6 is preparing a revision to the American Standard Flow Chart Symbols to bring the standard into direct conformity with ISO proposals; and X3.7 is preparing several suggestions for additions to a forthcoming revision of the American Banking Association MICR Specifications. As noted, X3.4 is discussed in some detail below.

3.4 Programming Languages Standardization

As noted above, programming languages for digital computers represent the most complex entities for which standardization has ever been attempted. Two points can be made to bring the complexity of programming languages into clear focus. First, there is no agreed method for describing programming languages fully, and second, there is no known method for determining whether a particular instance of a language processor (a compiler) does or does not, in fact, implement a standard.

Consider the problem of describing a programming language. The only method known today that will guarantee to describe a programming language fully is the exhibition of a compiler for that language. This might be satisfactory except for the detail that there is no way of telling whether *another* compiler, perhaps for a different computer, implements the same language. This whole problem of description of programming languages was the subject of a Working Conference on Formal Language Description Languages, held in Vienna in 1964 under the sponsorship of Technical Committee 2 of the International Federation for Information Processing [*14*]. One incidental outcome of this meeting was a decision by IFIP TC 2 to establish a Working Group (WG 2.2) to study the problem. The description of programming languages is clearly still a serious scientific problem with no solution usable by standardization bodies in view.

What has been done so far in this area is to describe programming languages in words, supplemented by mathematical and logical notation and symbolism where feasible, and *hope for the best*. In addition, some work has been done on developing test problems that will, at least partially, insure that implementations meet the standard. From a purely scientific viewpoint, the members of the various working groups concerned with programming language standardization really ought to report to their parent committees that their assigned task is impossible without a major prior effort by the technical community; and that this prior effort would have to produce an *effective* procedure for describing the languages that are of concern. There are two reasons for not making such a report, aside from the usual human desire not to talk oneself out of a job. First, it is clear that approximate, halfway standards are better than none. The present chaos in programming languages is so bad that it is often compared to the Tower of Babel, and any help is worth having. Second, many of the problems of describing programming languages tread very close to problems of mathematical unsolvability (in the strict sense of *impossible*, not just undone); it may turn out that some programming languages are really not fully describable.

Much of this complexity went unrecognized in 1960 when Sectional Committee X3 and its Subcommittee X3.4 on Common Programming Languages were formed. Late in 1960, X3.4 was established and proceeded to organize itself into four Working Groups: X3.4.1, Language Structure: X3.4.2, Goal-Oriented Languages; X3.4.3, Implementation-Oriented Languages; and X3.4.4, Processor Methodology.

Essentially, X3.4.1 was concerned with the problem of language description, and its charter has remained the same to the present day. It has not done a great deal on the surface, which is not surprising in view of the difficulties attached to the problem it faces. The Working Group has, however, in addition to generating several technical papers, helped sponsor a Working Conference on Mechanical Language Structures, held in Princeton in August 1963 [*15*]. One difficulty with X3.4.1

is the fact that its members are drawn largely from the academic world, and there are difficulties with funding for travel to meetings.

The concern of the original X3.4.2 was with the kinds of languages now known as problem-oriented languages (such as report generators) in which a *problem to be solved* is stated. The attendant processor is supposed to determine the algorithm for actual solution and generate the code to effect that solution. The original X3.4.2 could never figure out what it was supposed to do, and eventually it evaporated. The present X3.4.2 has only an accidental relationship to the old one.

The original X3.4.3 was in a little better shape. It was to be concerned with the languages known as procedure-oriented languages (such as FORTRAN) in which the *algorithm to solve a problem* is stated. The attendant processor has only to implement the algorithm. As will be seen below, this Working Group eventually came to be concerned only with FORTRAN.

The original plan for Working Group X3.4.4 was for it to deal with those problems that had to do with processors, such as establishing test problems. This remains one of its functions today, although with the subsequent addition of COBOL to X3.4.4's responsibilities, the test case generation activity has become limited to COBOL processor testing.

In May 1961, ISO TC 97 held an organizing meeting in Geneva with the objective of establishing appropriate working groups and determining their scopes and programs of work. With this meeting, international activity in standardization for computers and information processing had its beginnings, and it became necessary for X3 to name representatives to the various ISO TC 97 Working Groups (later to become Subcommittees). Logically, X3.4 drew the assignment for liaison with, and participation in, TC 97 Working Group E—Programming Languages—(Working Group E eventually became Subcommittee 5, and is so called today). This was a particularly serious responsibility, as the United States was assigned the Secretariat for WG E and, thus, had to do more than simply look out for the interests of the United States. To meet this responsibility a new Working Group, X3.4.5, was formed under X3.4; Working Group X3.4.5 still retains the Secretariat role in Subcommittee 5.

On May 17, 1962, recognizing that the X3.4 structure was not satisfactory, X3.4 reorganized itself into approximately its present form. Although X3.4.1 remained essentially unaltered, X3.4.2 was given the task of monitoring the programming language world to uncover candidates for potential standardization and to develop criteria for

(1) admission to consideration for standardization, and
(2) adequacy of proposed language standards.

Specific responsibility was given X3.4.3 for developing a standard for the FORTRAN language. In addition to its immediate concern for processors, X3.4.4 was assigned COBOL, while X3.4.5 retained its international liaison role. Finally, X3.4.6 was created to serve as the programming language liaison with the vocabulary activity in X3.5 and IFIP TC 1.

In a report such as this it is not possible to treat in detail all of the activities of X3.4 and its various Working Groups. The discussion that follows concentrates on the standardization efforts mounted for three specific languages: ALGOL, FORTRAN, and COBOL. Brief mention will then be made of X3.4.2's work in APT (later pursued by X3.4.7), in PL/I (just under way) and in criteria development. It will not be possible to do more than observe here that X3.4.5 undertook the United States' responsibility for the difficult task of surveying programming languages and their implementations for ISO TC 97 SC 5, that X3.4.6 has labored hard (and generally in vain) to provide guidance to X3.5 in the area of programming language vocabulary, and that all X3.4 Working Groups, as well as the Subcommittee itself, have been deeply involved in interaction with X3.2 and its Working Groups in treating the question of the programming language implications of standard codes and character sets (also generally in vain).

The history of efforts to develop an ALGOL standard is complex and confusing, and this description will cover only its highlights, emphasizing the United States' activity and positions.

ALGOL originated through an international committee and, in its own way, is a tribute to the efficacy of international scientific cooperation. The history of ALGOL, however, is largely one of European enthusiasm and United States' disinterest. While the reasons for this are irrelevant in this discussion, the fact is paramount. It is essential to an understanding of the ALGOL situation to discuss it from the point of view of ISO, rather than from the point of view of ASA. In the case of ALGOL the impetus was international and the reaction national. Quite the reverse situation occurred with respect to FORTRAN, as will be seen below.

The principal parties interested in ALGOL at the international level are IFIP WG 2.1, ECMA TC 5, and ISO TC 97 SC 5 (originally WG E). The interest of IFIP is primarily in technical development, rather than in standardization, at least in the formal sense understood by ISO, and WG 2.1 was established by IFIP with the former end in view. On the other hand, ECMA and ISO have formal standardization as their sole concern.

As noted above, in May 1961, ISO TC 97 (and with it WG E) held an organizing meeting in Geneva. Although the programming languages survey was the major activity planned by WG E initially, WG E recognized that ALGOL standardization would become a prominent feature of its work. In March 1962 there was a programming languages symposium in Rome, which had as one of its by-products the determination by a gathering of experts that five ambiguities existed in the published definition of ALGOL 60; IFIP WG 2.1 undertook to correct this deficiency. In June 1962, X3.4 took its first real cognizance of this situation by passing a resolution worded as follows: "Resolved that ISO TC 97 WG E invite IFIP TC 2 to submit to ISO a specification of ALGOL for consideration as an international standard." Quickly following, X3.4.2 produced a document suggesting specific resolutions for the five ambiguities noted at the Rome meeting, and in order to formalize its work with ALGOL, X3.4.2 established an ad hoc Task Group, X3.4.2A, with the specific responsibility for ALGOL.

At the Munich meeting of IFIP WG 2.1 in September 1962, specific resolutions of the issues raised in Rome were generated. The resulting language, ALGOL 60 (with clarifications) was submitted to the IFIP Council for approval as the official IFIP ALGOL language. The council granted approval, although the language as proposed was without input-output and there was no proposal for language subsets. Part of the rationale for this position can be found in the argument then raging over whether ALGOL was intended as a *programming* language to be implemented or as a *publication* language for the communication of algorithms to people. While this argument has not yet been fully resolved, it is clear that the standardization community looks upon ALGOL as a programming language.

Following X3.4's directive and with the cooperation of X3.4.2, X3.4.5 established the United States' position on ALGOL and transmitted it for consideration at WG E's October 1962 meeting in Paris. This position was articulated in Document ISO/TC 97/WG E(USA 19)80, the specific recommendations being as follows:

A. ISO/TC 97/WG E should be concerned with ALGOL 60 (IFIP) as a potential programming language standard, and not merely as a publication language.
B. ALGOL 60 (IFIP) should not be considered acceptable as a Proposed Standard Programming Language without provision for or resolution of the following:
  1. Input/output facility should be provided and explicitly defined in the language. IFIP/WG 2.1 should be asked to resolve such technical requirements and propose their solution. Suggestions should be submitted to WG 2.1.
  2. A standard subset should be defined by IFIP/WG 2.1 and included in the proposed ALGOL Standard documentation in the manner that 2.1 feels is appropriate....
  3. WG E should request that the five problem areas of ALGOL 60 (Rome) should be resolved by IFIP/WG 2.1....

C. A means should be provided to determine whether or not an implementation satisfies the standard.
  1. It is, therefore, suggested that WG E provide a set of test programs, with a description of their behavior, to be included as part of any standard ALGOL, or ISO Recommendation. Such test programs should fall into at least two classes: those which exercise the features of ALGOL 60 (Rome), and those which exercise only the features of the official subset. It is recognized that the successful execution of such test programs is a necessary but not sufficient condition that the language implemented satisfies the standard.
  2. It is further recommended that WG E limit its language measuring activity to the provision of test programs. It should in particular refuse to comment as to whether any given processor qualifies in accordance with any ISO standard or recommendation.
D. The relationship between WG E and IFIP/WG 2.1 should be such that WG E as a standards processing authority will normally refer all technical or developmental problems and proposed solutions re ALGOL to IFIP/WG 2.1. WG E should not customarily take the initiative in language development.

Document 80 has been quoted *in extenso* because, in addition to expressing the United States' position at the Paris ISO meeting, it still represents United States' sentiment even though the official position has changed owing to the exigencies of compromise and politics.

At the Paris ISO meeting, WG E adopted the essence of Document 80 with the exception of Section C on test problems. At the same time the Netherlands submitted the IFIP ALGOL 60 (without subsets or input-output) as a candidate for international standardization. It was agreed to defer consideration of this matter until the next meeting of WG E.

In January 1963 the question of "dual" or conflicting standards was raised by X3.4 because standardization efforts were going on for both FORTRAN and ALGOL, ostensibly languages intended for the same purpose—scientific computing. The American Standards Association frowns on conflicting standards, but in this case agreed that a standard FORTRAN and a standard ALGOL were both acceptable in the absence of agreement on what a standard language ought to be. On March 7, 1963, X3.4 explicated this position with the following resolution: "It is premature to adopt any available language as a standard programming language of broad utility. However, useful purposes will be served by specifying ASA standard versions of certain artificial languages, e.g., ALGOL, FORTRAN and COBOL." With this statement the groundwork was laid for X3.4's subsequent work, which has been largely devoted to attaining standards in the three languages mentioned, as well as to beginning work on two others that came to the Committee's attention subsequently.

On April 26, 1963, X3.4 took a further position with respect to ALGOL—a position it maintains today—namely, that X3.4 first work toward attaining an international (ISO) standard ALGOL and *subsequently* work toward attaining an American (ASA) Standard ALGOL.

On June 5, 1963, at the ISO TC 97 WG E meeting in Berlin, WG E took up the question of consideration of IFIP ALGOL as a candidate for standardization. It was unanimously agreed that the submission of IFIP to date, while a significant contribution, was incomplete, and that further action should await input-output specifications and subset definitions. This was consistent with the United States' position as outlined in Document 80. Later in the year IFIP WG 2.1 began efforts to comply with this request and informally circulated a tentative subset proposal and a set of six input-output primitives. The European Computer Manufacturers' Association took exception to the subset and the Association for Computing Machinery in the United States took exception to the input-output. Each group generated proposals of its own in the respective areas.

In February 1964, X3.4 established, upon recommendation by X3.4.2, two new Working Groups, one of which, X3.4.8, was a reconstitution of X3.4.2A at a higher and more formal level. At the same time X3.4 went on record as endorsing the ACM input-output proposal as a part of any ISO ALGOL standard. It should be noted that the ACM proposal was in addition to, and superimposed upon, the IFIP input-output primitives; it was not a substitution.

At several points in the past few years the destinies of ALGOL, COBOL, and FORTRAN standardization have intertwined. The dual standard problem has already been mentioned. A further issue has been the order of priority for the various efforts. On April 20, 1964, X3.4 established its policy on this matter through the following resolution:

Recognizing that, of those programming languages which are current candidates for standardization, FORTRAN and COBOL are the predominant languages in use in the US, and that the use of ALGOL is predominant outside the US, X3.4 reaffirms its intention to vigorously pursue the promotion of:

    a. A national ASA and an international ISO standard for FORTRAN and any desirable subsets thereof,

    b. A national ASA and an international ISO standard for COBOL, and any desirable subsets thereof,

    c. An international ISO and *then* a national ASA standard for ALGOL and any desirable subsets thereof,

such that none is considered to the exclusion or preferment of one over another at the international or national level. In particular, at this time, no particular or general action in pursuing either FORTRAN or ALGOL shall be designed to be, or be interpreted as, a preferment of one over another at the international level. [author's italics]

At the New York meeting of ISO TC 97 SC 5 in May 1964 (SC 5 having now replaced WG E) it was agreed that the IFIP WG 2.1 ALGOL proposal be used as the basis for preparation of an ISO Draft Proposal on

ALGOL. It was further agreed that in the Draft Proposal a *unique* subset of ALGOL should be recognized. At that time there was no commitment as to which subset (IFIP or ECMA) should be chosen. The United States, and thereby X3.4.8, was requested to prepare the ACM input-output recommendations in the form of a part of the Draft Proposal on ALGOL.

During the next twelve months all of the committees concerned worked diligently to prepare the relevant documents and all was in order by the required four months prior to the next ISO TC 97 meeting. On May 21, 1965, X3.4 formally registered its approval of the documents pertinent to ALGOL, thereby recommending to the United States' delegation to ISO TC 97 in a positive manner.

On September 10, 1965, at the ISO TC 97 SC 5 meeting in Copenhagen, definitive action was taken on the Draft Proposal on ALGOL. The IFIP ALGOL was adopted together with *three* levels of subsets; ECMA, IFIP with recursion, and IFIP without recursion. This was, of course, a departure from the United States' position that it preferred a *unique* subset. The documents acted upon included both the IFIP and the ACM input-output proposals; ISO TC 97 was requested to expedite action, and SC 5 appointed an editing committee to assist in preparing a first draft for an ISO Recommendation.

At the time of this writing (April 1966) the editing committee has completed its work, and it remains only for AFNOR (the French standardization agency) to complete the required translation of the draft ISO Recommendation into French.[2] Then the long cycle of formal approval can begin.

At the commencement of this account the author asserted that only the highlights of the ALGOL story would be given. Let the reader be assured that this policy was, in fact, followed, despite the length of the story.

On May 17, 1962, by resolution, X3.4 established Working Group X3.4.3 to develop American Standard FORTRAN proposals as part of the general reorganization of X3.4. On that date X3.4 resolved that:

X3.4 form a FORTRAN Working Group, to be known as X3.4.3-FORTRAN, with the scope:

To develop proposed standards of FORTRAN language.

Organization: Shall contain a Policy Committee and a Technical Committee. The Policy Committee will be responsible to X3.4 for the Working Group's mission being accomplished. It will determine general policy, such as language content, and direct the Technical Committee.

Policy Committee Membership. Will be determined by the X3.4 Steering Committee subject to written guidelines which may be amended later and including the following:

[2]*Note added in proof:* The translation is not completely satisfactory as of November 1966.

a. For each FORTRAN implementation in active development or use, one sponsor voting representative and one user voting representative are authorized.
b. A representative who is inactive may be dropped.
c. Associate members, not entitled to vote but entitled to participate in discussion, are authorized.

Technical Committee. Will develop proposed standards of FORTRAN language under the Policy Committee direction. The Technical Committee will conduct investigations and make reports to the Policy Committee.

On June 25, 1962, invitations to an organizational meeting of X3.4.3 were sent to manufacturers and user groups interested in participating in the development of FORTRAN standards, and the first meeting was held August 13–14, 1962. It was decided by X3.4.3 to proceed because it determined that

(1) FORTRAN standardization was needed, and
(2) a sufficiently wide representation of interested persons was participating.

A resolution on objectives was adopted unanimously on August 14 1962:

The objective of the X3.4.3 Working Group of ASA is to produce a document or documents which will define the ASA Standard or Standards for the FORTRAN language. The resulting standard language will be clearly and recognizably related to that language, with its variations, which has been called FORTRAN in the past. The criteria used to consider and evaluate various language elements will include (not in order of importance):
a. Ease of use by humans,
b. Compatibility with past FORTRAN use,
c. Scope of application,
d. Potential for extension,
e. Facility of implementation, i.e., compilation and execution efficiency.

The FORTRAN standard will facilitate machine-to-machine transfer of programs written in ASA Standard FORTRAN. The Standard will serve as a reference document both for users who wish to achieve this objective and for manufacturers whose programming products will make it possible. The content and method of presentation of the standard will recognize this purpose.

It was the consensus of the group that

(1) there was definite interest in developing a standard corresponding to what is popularly known as FORTRAN IV, and
(2) there was interest in developing for small and intermediate computers a FORTRAN standard near the power of FORTRAN II, suitably modified to be compatible with the associated FORTRAN IV.

Accordingly, two Technical Committees, designated X3.4.3-IV and X3.4.3-II, respectively, were established to create drafts. Most of the detailed work in developing drafts has been done by technical committees.

The X3.4.3-II Technical Committee completed and approved a draft in May 1963. A Technical Fact-Finding Committee was appointed and reported in August 1964 on a comparison of the X3.4.3-II approved draft and an approved working draft of the X3.4.3-IV Technical Committee. This brought to light stylistic, terminological, and content differences and conflicts. In April 1964, the X3.4.3-IV Technical Committee completed a draft of FORTRAN. In June 1964, X3.4.3 received and compared the two drafts. It then

(1) resolved conflicts in content, and
(2) resolved the conflicting style and terminology.

This was accomplished by recasting the X3.4.3-II document to reflect the style of the X3.4.3-IV document while retaining the original content. To reduce confusion, X3.4.3 decided to call the languages Basic FORTRAN and FORTRAN.

These documents were submitted to X3 and approved for publication. They appeared in the October 1964 issue of the *Communications of the ACM* and, after the long process of approval, review, and further approval, were finally granted official status as American Standards X3.9 and X3.10 on March 7, 1966.

While this national activity on FORTRAN was taking place, there was a parallel effort in ISO. Naturally, ISO TC 97 SC 5 looked to the United States for developmental work in FORTRAN, as they had looked to IFIP for ALGOL. Details of the international activity in FORTRAN are, in many respects, similar to those in ALGOL and do not bear repeating. At the Copenhagen meeting of ISO TC 97 SC 5, actions similar to those regarding ALGOL were taken, and at the time of this writing, international FORTRAN standardization is in precisely the same position as international ALGOL standardization—waiting on the French. Thus, one of X3.4's basic precepts is being fulfilled.

In response to X3's expressed interest in process control languages, X3.4.2 established on February 20, 1964, a Task Force, X3.4.2B, with the charge of examining APT and other languages for process control. In February 1964, X3.4.2B became a Working Group in its own right, designated X3.4.7. It has had no problem yet with international complications, but it has had to deal with a situation in which part of a system involved in its effort (APT) is proprietary and subject to the disclosure rules of one company. This had, necessarily, slowed its work and made its task far more difficult than it might otherwise have been.

Because of a need to coordinate with the original COBOL group, the

Committee on Data Systems Languages (CODASYL), X3.4.4 has also had problems. It has taken a slightly different approach from other X3.4 Working Groups in the development of COBOL standards. It started with a basic COBOL and defined additional functional modules as independent entities which may be added to the basic standard. In conjunction with this work, the development of test procedures to determine whether a given processor correctly implements the given functional modules has been proceeding in parallel. Also, X3.4.4 has assumed the task of informing the world about its progress toward COBOL standardization through the publication of a bulletin, formally known as the *X3.4 COBOL Information Bulletin* in deference to the wishes of CODASYL.

Because a large number of COBOL processors were in existence at the time X3.4.4 began its work, one of the most important efforts of the Working Group has been its feature availability study. The draft COBOL standard now in preparation is based largely on the determination, through this study, of what existing COBOL really is. Another phase of this work has been the development of test programs that determine whether a given processor *really* has given features, independent of what the manual says. It is one of the failures of X3.4 that this clearly desirable activity has not been extended to other languages.

At the time of this writing, X3.4.4's major effort is to assure that the working documents embodying proposed COBOL standards will meet the required publication schedules so that COBOL can be taken up as the major topic at the next ISO TC 97 SC 5 meeting, probably to be held in May 1967 in Moscow.

Among the major past efforts of X3.4 not already discussed is the criteria development activity of X3.4.2. Specifically, X3.4.2 generated a set of criteria for the suitability of a document as a proposed draft standard, as follows:

"(a) The format must follow ASA rules.

(b) The definition of the language must be clear, precise, and self-consistent.

The use of rigorous metalanguage, algorithms, diagrams, etc., is preferred, but concise natural language may be acceptable. Any combination of techniques may be used to enhance clarity.

Usage of these techniques should be compatible with related standards in the field: e.g., if flow-charts are used for explication, the symbology should be that of the ASA flow-chart standard.

(c) The description of the language must provide sufficient information such that any program written in the language is capable of one and only one interpretation. A program violating any rule of the language is not a 'program written in the language.'

(d) Some appendices giving design considerations, possible subsets, ASCII representation, hardware and media representations, specific criteria, etc., are required when appropriate. Discussions of this nature are in general preferred as appendices rather than as part of the standard.

Devices such as an index and a table of contents are recommended where they will facilitate the use of the document."

In addition to serving as a guide to other Working Groups in generating documents, these criteria have been directly applied to the FORTRAN documents prior to publication; they will, undoubtedly, also be applied to other proposed draft standard documents as they appear.

Current activity in X3.4, in addition to pursuing the work on ALGOL, APT, and COBOL and maintaining continued liaison with other standardization activities that impinge on programming languages, is concerned with the language PL/I. In a fashion similar to the cases of ALGOL and APT, X3.4.2 has established a Task Force, X3.4.2C, with the charter to study PL/I for consideration as a possible candidate for standardization. This Task Force began its work in April 1966.

4. Summary

There are, perhaps, a thousand individuals actively concerned with standardization in the computer and information processing field, and their employers are spending several million dollars annually to support this activity. One might well ask if twelve standards in the six years of work is worth the effort. The answer is "probably not," and this hesitation would turn into a certainty if the next six years produced only a dozen more standards. The process should accelerate rapidly, however, and, just possibly, the next half decade should see real and useful progress toward the creation of systematic standards to replace the chaotic situation now prevalant, particularly in the programming languages area.

At any rate, it is clear that we must try.

REFERENCES

1. Hockett, C. F., and Archer, R., The human revolution, *Am. Scientist* **52**, 70–92 (1964).
2. Dobzhansky, T., *Mankind Evolving*. Yale Univ. Press, New Haven, Connecticut, 1962.
3. Jesperson, O., *Language. Its Nature, Development and Origin*. Allen & Unwin, London, 1922.

4. Sommerfelt, A., Speech and language, in *A History of Technology*, (C. Singer, E. J. Holmyard, and A. R. Hall, eds.), Vol. I, pp. 85–109. Oxford Univ. Press, London and New York, 1954.
5. Hooke, S. H., Recording and writing, in *A History of Technology* (C. Singer, E. J. Holmyard, and A. R. Hall, eds.), Vol. I, pp. 744–773. Oxford Univ. Press, London and New York, 1954.
6. Skinner, F. G., Measures and weights, in *A History of Technology* (C. Singer, E. J. Holmyard, and A. R. Hall, eds.) Vol. I, pp. 774–784. Oxford Univ. Press, London and New York, 1954.
7. Petrie, W. M. F., Weights and measures, ancient historical, in *The Encyclopedia Brittanica*, 11th ed., Vol. XXVIII, pp. 480–488, Encyclopedia Brittanica, New York, 1911.
8. Salzman, L. F., *English Industries of the Middle Ages*. Oxford Univ. Press (Clarendon), London and New York, 1921.
9. Gorn, S. (ed.), Structures of standards-processing organizations in the computer area. *Commun. Assoc. Computing Machinery* **6**, 294–305 (1963).
10. American Standards Association, Inc., *1966 ASA Catalog*. American Standards Assoc., New York, 1966.
11. American Standards Association, *The Organization and Work of Sectional Committees*, 6th ed. ASA PR 27. American Standards Assoc., New York, 1960.
12. Melnitsky, B., *Profiting from Industrial Standardization*. Conover-Mast Publ., New York, 1953.
13. ISO General Secretariat, Directives for the Technical Work of ISO. ISO/DIR CGS-19, 1963.
14. Steel, T. B. (ed.), *Formal Language Description Languages for Computer Programming*. North-Holland Publ., Amsterdam, 1966.
15. Proceedings of a working conference on mechanical language structures. *Commun. Assoc. Computing Machinery* **7**, 51–136 (1964):

Syntactic Analysis of Natural Language

NAOMI SAGER

Institute for Computer Research
in the Humanities
New York University
New York

1. Linguistic Basis for Computations 153
   1.1 Immediate Constituent Analysis 154
   1.2 String Analysis 154
   1.3 Left-to-Right Scanning and Predictive Analysis 155
   1.4 Transformational Analysis 156
   1.5 Other Methods 156
2. A Procedure for Left-to-Right String Decomposition of Sentences . 157
   2.1 Word-by-Word Formulation of String Structure 157
   2.2 Indirectly Defined Strings: *wh* and *C* 160
   2.3 Restrictions 162
   2.4 Syntactic Ambiguity 163
3. The String Program 163
   3.1 General Description 166
   3.2 Restrictions 168
   3.3 Special Processes 170
   3.4 Treatment of Syntactic Ambiguity 175
   3.5 Output 178
   3.6 Discussion 183
   References 186

1. Linguistic Basis for Computations

Writers of programs for handling natural language material, whether for mechanical translation, automatic indexing, or other purposes, have learned (sometimes the hard way) that without grammatical analysis their efforts at processing language data reach an early limit. Thus, persons whose original goals may have been far afield find themselves concerned with automatic syntactic analysis, and, as they become further acquainted with the problem, with different grammatical theories, since no piecemeal assemblage of grammatical rules will suffice for treating the coherent and productive, yet complex and detailed, mechanism of language.

The main styles of grammatical description can by now each be associated with an existing program or program-in-the-making.

However, not all discussion of the computability of language has been related to program development; for example, papers [2, 37] treat the application of the notion of grammatical categories—familiar from the Polish logicians—to language word classes, paralleling what linguists had already been doing, i.e., defining word classes on syntactic grounds. The notion of grammatical categories was related by Hiż to an early form of linguistic string analysis [26] and to transformational analysis [24].

1.1 Immediate Constituent Analysis

Several discussions and programs are based on immediate constituent analysis (ICA), or developments therefrom [21–23, 27, 43, 44]. ICA is similar to the method of parsing and traditional methods of syntactic analysis, which segment a sentence into parts (e.g., noun phrase and verb phrase) and these in turn into smaller parts, and so on. It was formulated by Leonard Bloomfield and others [3, 17, 51], and has been formalized under the name phrase-structure analysis by Chomsky [9]. A formal theory of grouping as a basis for ICA is given by Hiż [25].

The weak equivalence of several other types of grammars used by syntactic programs (e.g., dependency grammar of Hays and projective grammar of Lecerf [38]) to an immediate constituent grammar is shown by Gross [13]. Despite progress in this line of program development, there is not as yet an efficient IC analyzer which covers the bulk of English grammar, provides a reasonably small number of analyses per sentence and is not limited as to the length of sentences it analyzes. This is partly due to certain inherent difficulties of constituent analysis for computational purposes.

1.2 String Analysis

These deficiencies do not exist in linguistic string analysis [18]. The main relevance of string analysis for computational purposes is that it overcomes the problem of discontinuity in a natural way and provides a framework for introducing further linguistic refinements without adding appreciably to the bulk or complexity of the grammar. These features are both due to the fact that the linguistic string is the least segment of a sentence with respect to which grammatical restrictions can be stated. For example, a current string analysis program [45], using several hundred rules (in this case, strings and restrictions) would require the addition of several hundred restrictions framed on the existing strings, in order to refine it by the main transformational subclasses. If we consider a program without a string framework, the leading program, the Harvard Predictive Analyzer [34, 35, 40] using currently several thousand rules, is estimated by Kuno [33] to require an order of magnitude increase in the number of grammar rules in order to achieve a considerable refinement.

A program using an early form of string analysis ran successfully on the Univac I at the University of Pennsylvania in 1959 [20]. The Univac program incorporated the main constructions of English grammar, not all in equal detail, and obtained one preferred analysis of a sentence. It was utilized for the syntactic part of one of the earliest question-answering programs (Baseball) [12]. Using string analysis, it was shown [46] that the fully nested structure of English made possible the utilization of a push-down store technique in a left-to-right word-by-word analysis of a sentence, to produce all syntactic analysis of the sentence in a single scan. The left-to-right procedure for string analysis, as programmed for the 7094, obtains all analyses of a typical sentence (of a scientific text) in about 5 seconds. These number 1–5 per sentence, given the convention (which can be lifted) that permanent predictable ambiguities which can be read off existing outputs are not printed. Most often, the first analysis is the one that expresses the author's intended meaning. Another string program [7], which uses a canceling and cycling automaton form of string grammar [15], is in use for analyzing narrative medical text.

1.3 Left-to-Right Scanning and Predictive Analysis

The left-to-right approach was used in an essential way in predictive analysis, developed by Ida Rhodes in the National Bureau of Standards program for syntactic analysis of Russian [1, 41, 42]. Since 1961, a push-down technique has been combined with predictive analysis in the Harvard program for syntactic analysis of English (HPA). The HPA goes beyond the limitations of IC programs by using a set of rules each of which specifies a structure up to the end of that structure (from the point at which the rule applies) and places each structure in respect to the analysis of the sentence up to the point at which the rule is used. This enables the HPA to insert material nested inside of a structure while keeping track of the still expected residue of the structure.

During this time, in the field of compiler writing, the single-scan left-to-right approach to scanning an input string of a formal language, and other syntax-oriented approaches, began appearing in the literature [6, 28, 29]. Recent developments suggest that syntax-oriented compilers may be developed to accept languages having essential natural language mechanisms.

1.4 Transformational Analysis

There remains the linguistic method of transformations [8, 9, 16, 19] which, while not easily computable, provides a much subtler analysis and brings together on syntactic grounds semantically equivalent or related sentences. Joshi [30–32] has designed an algorithm (machine independent) for transformational decomposition, and is writing a substantial portion of a transformational grammar of English in a form suitable for the algorithm. His procedure is entirely based on some rather basic and quite general properties of transformations and does not depend on any prior analysis, such as immediate constituent, or string analysis, above. Several programs in the specifically generative style of transformations [10] have been constructed. Matthew's method [39] was to analyze by synthesizing sentence strings from transformational rules, though the program did not reach a practical working stage. Walker and associates [49, 50] are constructing a transformational program as part of an information retrieval system. As yet this program covers only certain portions of English, but it is to be hoped that the system will be extended. There exist related studies around the problem of the computability of generative structures and transformations. Among these we might mention Yngve's treatment of discontinuous elements [14, 53].

1.5 Other Methods

In the work on natural language, there are still only a few programs which attempt to incorporate a substantial portion of the grammar of the language. A number of existing programs (not mentioned here) make one or another simplification of the problem. As an example of a program which includes a large-scale computer grammar of a language quite different from English we note the work at Berkeley on Chinese [11], which is related to methods of Lamb [36]. Reference should also be made to COMIT, a programming language designed for syntactic treatment of natural language [52]. Several survey articles have appeared: Simmons [48], on question-answer programs, though some idea of the full linguistic complexity of questions may be obtained from Bolinger [5]; Bobrow [4], a general survey of computer programs for syntactic analysis of English.

The remaining two sections of this paper describe in greater detail the left-to-right procedure for string analysis of sentences (Section 2) and the computer program based on it which is now in operation (Section 3). The description emphasizes the means of handling such essential features of language structure as detailed subclass restrictions, coordinate and comparative conjunctions, and syntactic ambiguity. The program was developed as part of the National Science Foundation Transformations and Discourse Analysis Project at the University of Pennsylvania.

2. A Procedure for Left-to-Right String Decomposition of Sentences[1]

2.1 Word-by-Word Formulation of String Structure

The procedure described in this section is based on an axiomatic formulation of linguistic string theory which presents, in terms of particular syntactic categories for words of the language (e.g. N noun, tV tensed verb), a set of elementary strings of word categories and rules for combining the elementary strings to form sentences. An example of an elementary string is $N\ tV$ (*Power corrupts*). Recognizing the structure of a sentence will mean decomposing the sentence into elementary strings of the language, each elementary string being defined as a sentence, or as entering at a stated point of another elementary string in a sentence.[2] The procedure calls upon the strings and restrictions (described below) of a particular language but is itself independent of the particular grammatical material used. One is able to change details of the grammar without altering the program structure. One might even expect that such a program would be usable for other languages by changing the entire grammatical content, i.e., the list of strings and restrictions.

The strings are groupable into classes based on how and where they can be inserted into other strings. If $\xi = X_1 \cdots X_n$ is a string, X ranging over category symbols, the following classes of strings are defined:

l_X Left adjuncts of X: adjoined to a string ξ to the left of X in ξ, or to the left of an l_X adjoined to ξ in this manner.

r_X Right adjuncts of X: adjoined to a string ξ to the right of X in ξ, or to the right of an r_X adjoined to ξ in this manner.

n_X Replacement strings of X: adjoined to a string ξ replacing X in ξ.

s_ξ Sentence adjuncts of the string ξ, adjoined to ξ at any inter-element point or to the left of X_1 or to the right of X_n, or

---

[1]Talk presented at the National Science Foundation Seminar on Documentation Research, Washington, D.C., March 6, 1962.

[2]We use the term "elementary string in a sentence" to designate the sequence of words in a sentence which correspond to an elementary string of word categories (string of the grammar). Henceforth "string" is to mean "elementary string" unless otherwise indicated.

c_ξ to the right of an s_ξ which has been adjoined to ξ in one of these manners.

c_ξ Conjunctional strings of ξ, conjoined to the right of X_i in ξ $(1 \leq i \leq n)$ or to the right of a c_ξ conjoined in this manner.

z Center strings, not adjoined to any string.

There are various restrictions on the repetition and the order of various members of the classes of adjuncts.

Roughly speaking, a center string is the skeleton of a sentence and the adjuncts are modifiers. An example of a left adjunct of N is the adjective *green* in *the green blackboard*. A right adjunct of N is the clause *whom we met* in *the man whom we met*. A replacement string of N is, for instance, *what he said* in the sentence *What he said was interesting*. The same sentence with a noun instead of a noun-replacement string might be *The lecture was interesting*. Examples of sentence adjuncts are: *in general, at this time, since he left*. The C-strings, which will be described below, have coordinating conjunctions at their head. An example is *but left* in *He was here but left*. Examples of center strings are *He understood* and also *We wondered whether he understood*.[3]

The words of the language are assigned to one or more word categories on the basis of their grammatical properties in the language as a whole; e.g., *the* has the one assignment T (article); *move* has three alternative assignments, N (noun) /tV (tensed verb) /V (untensed verb). Therefore, to the sequence of the words of a sentence there corresponds a family of one or more sequences of categories, one per word. We call each such sequence of categories a representation of the given sentence. The theory now asserts that every sentence in the language has at least one representation which is identical to a string in class z, or to one upon which there have been carried out adjunctions, replacements, or conjunctions, as provided in the above definitions.

In the terms of the string-class definitions above, we can now define an analysis of a sentence. We will say that a sentence representation is analyzed if we can assign every symbol in that sentence representation to some elementary string, either a center string, or an adjunct or replacement string inserted according to the operation of the string-class definitions. Each analyzed sentence representation is a different

---

[3] In this formulation of string grammar, the occurrence in a sentence of a subject or object which does not consist of a word category with its adjuncts is treated as the result of N-replacement; e.g., *I know that he was there* from *I know N* (*I know something*). This treatment is problematic for the few verbs which do not occur with an N object, e.g., *wonder*: *I wonder whether he was there*, ∄ *I wonder something*. This difficulty does not arise if the elementary strings are allowed to have strings as elements, e.g., Σ for subject strings, Ω for object strings, yielding an assertion center string $\Sigma t V \Omega$ (t = tense). This is the approach adopted in the machine grammar.

syntactic analysis of the sentence whose successive words belong, respectively, to the successive categories of the analyzed sentence representation.

To set the stage for recognizing the structure of a sentence, we observe the following, as a direct consequence of the above: For a given sentence, there exists at least one sentence representation such that, if we proceed from left to right through a sentence, each successive word belongs to a category which is either the continuation of an unfinished string, or is the beginning of a new string permitted at that point in the sentence representation by the string-class definitions.

We start out by requiring the occurrence of a center string, since the theory asserts that every sentence has a center string. To illustrate, suppose that the grammar contains only a single center string, $N\,tV\,N$, and a single adjunction class r_N containing a single string $P\,N$.

Grammar:
$$N\,tV\,N \in z$$
$$P\,N \in r_N$$

Suppose the sentence to be analyzed is

Cars without brakes cause accidents.
$\quad N \quad\quad P \quad\quad N/tV \;\; N/tV/V \quad N$

The first symbol N of the required center string $N\,tV\,N$ matches the first sentence symbol N. The sentence word *cars* is thereby analyzed as the first element of the center string. [In a richer grammar the symbol N might be the beginning of some other string permitted in the sentence-initial position; in that case, there would be a second analysis at this point.] The second sentence word does not have a classification which matches the current (second) symbol of the center string. However, it does have a classification P which is the first symbol of a string $P\,N$ permitted at this point as a right adjunct of N. Accepting this analysis of the second sentence word, the program inserts in the list of requirements the string $P\,N$ (with P already satisfied) and pushes down the remaining requirements of the center string, to return to them when the $P\,N$ string is finished. We proceed in the same way for the $P\,N$ string as for its host, the $N\,tV\,N$ string; i.e., we ask at each word position: Does one of the category assignments of the current sentence word match the current symbol of the string in progress? If it does, we advance in that string. If it does not, we ask: Is it the beginning of some string which is permitted at this point? If so, we begin a similar process at the next level by inserting the remaining symbols of the string into the list of requirements already established.

The procedure produces an analysis of a sentence if, by accepting one match at each position, it reaches the end of the sentence with no requirement unsatisfied. Since n matches at the ith position means that we have n potential analyses of the sentence which are identical up to the ith position but different from i and on, we can obtain all analyses of the sentence either by carrying different analyses in parallel or by stacking alternative analyses at each branch point and following them through in some prescribed order. In the example sentence, the string $P\,N$ (*without brakes*) is the only interruption in the $N\,tV\,N$ center string (*cars cause accidents*), and there is only one analysis.

2.2 Indirectly Defined Strings: *wh* and C [4]

Two classes of strings require additional description. The first of these, the class of *wh* strings (relative clauses), has members which are identical (except for the prefixed *wh* word) with a large number of already defined strings, in all but one (or two) symbol position(s) of the string. It is therefore convenient to obtain these strings in the process of computation by an operation (called "omission") on strings already defined. The operation of omission consists of skipping one required N (or $P\,N$) from a string ξ or from certain adjuncts of ξ. For example, from the center string $N_1\,tV\,N_2$ (*The man wrote the book*) two *wh* strings can be obtained by omitting, respectively, N_1 and N_2: *wh* $tV\,N_2$ (*who wrote the book*) and *wh* $N_1\,tV$ (*which the man wrote*). When the *wh* string adjoins a host N, the omitted N can be identified with the host N; e.g. the *wh* string from which N_1 was omitted adjoins N_1 (*the man who wrote the book*). The omission operation may also be applied to N in certain adjunct strings, mainly $P\,N$. For example, from $N_1\,tV\,N_2\,P\,N_3$ (*The author chose the title of the book*) in which $N_1\,tV\,N_2$ (*The author chose the title*) is the center string and $P\,N_3$ (*of the book*) is an adjunct of N_2 (*title*), we can form three *wh* strings which can adjoin N_3: (1) *wh* $N_1\,tV\,N_2\,P$ ((*the book*) *which the author chose the title of*), omitting N_3; (2) P *wh* $N_1\,tV\,N_2$ ((*the book*) *of which the author chose the title*), omitting $P\,N_3$; and (3) $N_2\,P$ *wh* $N_1\,tV$ ((*the book,*) *the title of which the author chose*), omitting N_2 with its adjunct $P\,N_3$.

Another class of strings which is best defined by an operation is the class of C strings headed by coordinate conjuctions *and*, *or*, *but*, etc. If listed, this class would contain all of the strings of the grammar, plus virtually all parts of all strings (each preceded by C), which makes a very large class. But at any point in a sentence the choice of C string

---

[4]To justify going into some linguistic detail here, we note that the procedure would not function without a considerable organization of the linguistic data.

must be made from a limited subset of C strings, depending on which strings precede C in the analyzed portion of the sentence.

One way to define these C strings is as follows: if α and β are strings in class x, then $\alpha\, C\, \beta$ is a C equivalence and the portion $C\,\beta$ is a C string. For example, let x be the class of center strings, with α the assertion center and β the question. $\alpha\, C\, \beta$ gives us such sentences as *It is a fact and who can deny it*. Or let $x =$ the right adjuncts of N; an example is *the delegates elected but not receiving the requisite majority of the votes*. When $\alpha = \beta$ (that is, when the same string ξ appears on both sides of the C equivalence), shortened forms $\xi_1\, C\, \xi_2'$ and $\xi_1'\, C\, \xi_2$ may occur, where ξ' is structurally identical to ξ except that certain elements present in ξ are absent in ξ'; but the first element of ξ_1 is never absent. For example, *I came and I went* has a shortened form *I came and went*, and *to formulate the question and to answer the question* has a shortened form *to formulate and to answer the question*. The elements which are absent in ξ' can be shown to be zero occurrences of the words which satisfy the corresponding elements of ξ. Shortened forms $\xi_1'\, C\, \xi_2'$ can also be obtained by the above rule: *to formulate and answer the question*. An operation similar to omission can be defined in order to obtain C strings with zeroed elements; and, if desired, the zeroed words can be filled in: *I came and (I) went*.

Alternatively, the shortened forms can be defined without reference to the zeroed elements. The most frequent case is one in which the zeroed elements in a C equivalence $\xi_1\, C\, \xi_2$ form an unbroken sequence around C from a point a in ξ_1 to a point b (determined by a) in ξ_2. This includes sequences with zeroing only in ξ_1 or only in ξ_2 or with no zeroing at all. The C strings in this case can be defined as follows: Let $\xi = X_1 \cdots X_n$. If a conjunction C appears following X_l in an occurrence of ξ in a sentence ($1 \leq l \leq n$), then the string headed by C which can interrupt ξ at this point is any one of the following:

$$CX_l;\quad CX_{l-1}X_l;\quad CX_{l-2}X_{l-1}X_l;\quad \cdots;\quad CX_1 \cdots X_l$$

For example, let $\xi = to\; V\; \Omega$ (*to repeat the question*). In a sentence which begins *To repeat the question and answer* $\cdots$, $l = 3$, and corresponding to $C\, X_l$ we have *to* $V\, \Omega\, C\, \Omega$ in which *question* and *answer* are both seen as N. Another analysis (corresponding to $C\, X_{l-1}\, X_l$) of the word sequence is *to* $V_1\, \Omega_1\, C\, V_2\, \Omega_2$ in which *answer* is taken as a verb, with $\Omega_2 = 0$. For the same ξ, an example of $C\, X_l$ where $l = 2$ would be *to* $V\, C\, V\, \Omega$ (*to formulate and answer the question*).

There are also cases in which the zeroed elements are final or interior portions of ξ_2. The C strings in these cases always appear after the complete ξ_1 and can be characterized in respect to the structure of ξ_1.

The main C strings of this type are listed here for $\xi_1 = \Sigma\, t\, V\, \Omega$, in which Σ = subject, V = untensed verb, t = a tense suffix or auxiliary (including forms of *have, be, do*), and Ω = object.

$\Sigma\, t\, V\, \Omega$	C	Σ		*He laughed and she also.*
$\Sigma\, t\, V\, \Omega$	C	Σ	t	*He laughed but she didn't.*
$\Sigma\, t\, V\, \Omega$	C	Σ	Ω	*He chose a rose and she a poppy.*
$\Sigma\, t\, V\, \Omega$	C		t	*He should have gone but didn't.* also *but hasn't, but couldn't.*
$\Sigma\, t\, V\, \Omega$	C		$\overline{D}$	*He left and fast.* ($\overline{D}$ = a subset of verb and sentence adjuncts)

2.3 Restrictions

A string is a sequence of word categories, but not every combination of words drawn from the respective categories makes a satisfactory string occurrence in a sentence. Sometimes only words having related grammatical properties are acceptable in the same string, or in adjoined strings. We define subcategories to express these grammatical properties. Then particular strings will carry restrictions as to the subcategories of words which can occur together as elements in the same string or of related strings. For example, the fact that a plural noun cannot occur as the subject of a singular verb constitutes a restriction on the $N\, tV\, N$ center string. Restrictions could be entirely eliminated if we were willing to increase the number of categories and strings by a very large amount. For example, instead of the restriction on subject-verb agreement as to number, we could list every string to which this restriction applies, writing the string once in its singular and once in its plural form. However, in so doing we would not only double the number of these strings and increase the number of categories but we would mask the relationship between the strings of each pair.

The machinery for applying restrictions in a recognition program is based on the observation that restrictions operate within a particular scope: (1) either within some string ξ, or (2) between some element of a string ξ and the head of φ where φ is an adjunct of ξ or a replacement string inserted into ξ, or (3) between the heads of two φ adjoined to the same ξ and related to each other in one of a few specified ways. Thus in the recognition procedure it becomes a relatively simple matter to locate the arguments of a restriction. One moves from a particular symbol to one of the members of its adjunct classes (or vice versa) or to one of the other elements of the given string, or among related adjuncts of the given string.

2.4 Syntactic Ambiguity

Syntactic ambiguities stem from several sources: from multiply classified words, like *increase* which can be a noun or a verb, and also from the possibility of the same symbol sequence resulting from different applications of the string-class definitions. For example, in the sentence *People wearing hats is unusual*, the segment *people wearing hats* can be assigned to only one string, a noun-replacement string agreeing with the singular verb *is*. In the sentence *People wearing hats are unusual* the same segment is assigned to different strings, as a plural noun (*people*) with a right adjunct (*wearing hats*) where the plural noun agrees with the plural verb *are*. The sentence *People wearing hats can be unusual* is ambiguous. Since the verb *can be* does not distinguish number, both above assignments of the segment *people wearing hats* are grammatical. [One might think that *people wearing hats* can also be taken as a compound noun, like *feather bearing hats*. This requires accepting *hats wear people* as grammatical.]

We distinguish temporary ambiguities which arise in the course of computation but are resolved when the entire sentence is analyzed, from permanent ambiguities, i.e., more than one syntactic analysis of the sentence. In the course of analyzing the sentence *People wearing hats is unusual*, a temporary ambiguity exists after the first three words have been analyzed (in two ways). This ambiguity is resolved when the word *is* comes on the scene. When one proceeds from left to right, some of the temporary ambiguities are resolved in situ, because the context built up on the left leaves no room for particular choices of word categories or syntactic structures at a given point in the analysis. Further assistance in resolving ambiguities is provided by restrictions. Certain nouns, for example, must be preceded by an article or possessive when they are singular in subject position; e.g., we may have *Book ends are needed*; *The book ends happily*, but not *Book ends happily*. Hence the application of the restriction on these nouns, say, after the first word of the sentence *Book ends are needed* eliminates one analysis immediately (the one which would take *book* as subject and *ends* as verb).

3. The String Program

This section describes the common features of two computer programs which employ the procedure of Section 2 [*45*]. The first, written in IPL V, has been in operation since the fall of 1964, and the second, written in FAP for the 7094, since December 1965.[5]

---

[5] The IPL V program was written by James Morris and the FAP program by Carol Raze.

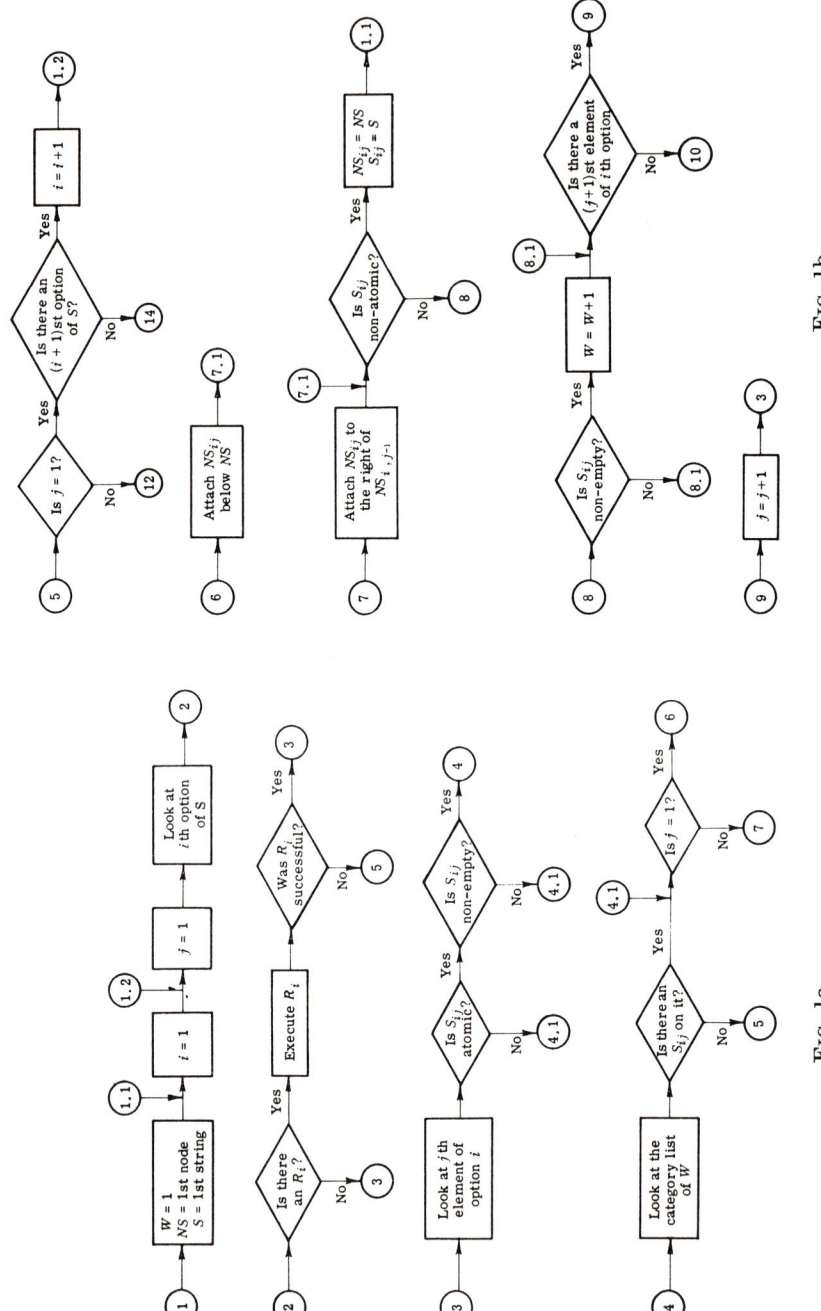

Fig. 1a

Fig. 1b

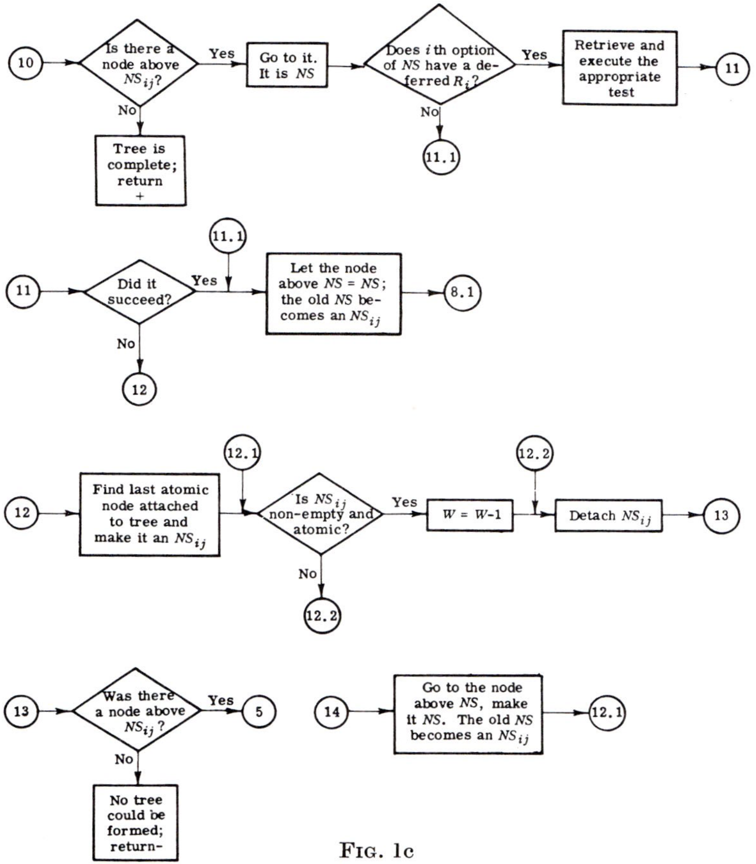

SYNTACTIC ANALYSIS OF NATURAL LANGUAGE

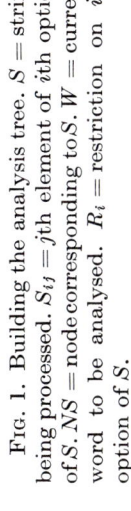

FIG. 1. Building the analysis tree. S = string being processed. S_{ij} = jth element of ith option of S. NS = node corresponding to S. W = current word to be analysed. R_i = restriction on ith option of S.

FIG. 1c

3.1 General Description

The analysis routine of the program is a fairly general language-independent processor which when supplied a grammar (coherent set of definitions) and an input string (sentence) to parse, proceeds from the beginning to the end of the sentence trying to analyze the sentence as a case of some chain of substitutions contained in the definitions. At each decision point, it takes the first available option, backing up to try successive options either because the chosen path fails or in order to obtain alternative analyses after the first successful analysis. The record of the analysis is kept (internally) in the form of a tree. The steps in building the analysis tree in the FAP program are shown in Fig. 1.[6]

The grammar is entered into the machine as a set of definitions of "grammar strings." A grammar string S is defined to be S_1 *or* S_2 *or* $\cdots$ *or* S_n; S_i is defined to be S_{i1} *and* S_{i2} *and* $\cdots$ *and* S_{im}; S_{ij} is a string similar to S. The S_i's are called the options of S, and the S_{ij}'s the elements of S_i. A chain of substitutions terminates when the S_{ij}'s are atomic, i.e., word-category symbols. [An elementary linguistic string in the sense of Section 2 thus corresponds to an option of a grammar string as defined here.] The machine representation of a grammar string is shown in Fig. 2. What mainly distinguishes the definitions from other formal language specifications are:

(1) The content of the definitions: Each definition represents a linguistic string or set of strings, so that there is a one-to-one correspondence between the linguists' string grammar and the set of definitions accepted by the program.

(2) The restrictions: Associated with each definition is a restriction list which contains tests corresponding to the linguistic restrictions associated with the given string or set of strings. The restrictions (tests) are written in a special language of basic routines. Despite the fact that restrictions can be looked upon theoretically as abbreviations for families of unrestricted strings, it would be cumbersome (though not impossible) [47] to write a string grammar of a natural language without them, especially if some degree of refinement is desired.

---

[6]Figures 1 and 2 are taken from Carol Raze, The FAP String Analysis Program, in [45]. The tree structure in the FAP program differs from the illustrated trees of Fig. 3–5 (which use the IPL V form) in that a node NS in the FAP tree contains 2 pointers which point, respectively, to the left sibling, or if NS is left-most, to the parent node, and to the right sibling if there is one. The node NS (representing the grammar string S) also has a grammar pointer to the string S in the grammar.

The List of S

Head of S (1st word)	a	b	c	d	e	f	g	h	i	j	k	m	S (Name of string)
2nd word	p	n	\multicolumn{10}{l	}{Address of restriction on S_1}	Address of S_1

. . . .

$(n+1)$-st word	p	n	Address of restriction on S_n	Address of S_n

The List of S_i

1st word	a	n		Address of S_{i1}
2nd word	p	n		Address of S_{i2}

. . . .

m-th word	p	n		Address of S_{im}

Fig. 2. Machine representation of a string S. S is defined to be S_1 or S_2 or $\cdots S_n$. S_i is defined to be S_{i1} and S_{i2} and $\cdots S_{im}$, S_{ij} is a string similar to S. The alphabetical symbols represent fields. Letters c through m are fields consisting of one bit reserved for string properties and are found only in the head of a string. If a certain property is present the bit in the appropriate field will be set to one(1). The first two fields of a word in any list (a, b and p, n) are necessary for the program. The fields represent:

a Always 0—signals the beginning of a list
b Always 1—signal for a head
c Atomic property (if present, the string has only a head)
d Empty atomic (null of adjunct sets)
e Special empty atomic (null of omission and zeroing)
f Transparent
g Save
h Freeze
i Recursive
j Min-word
k Special process
m Repetitive property
n Always 0—signal for a nonhead
p Always 1—signal for the middle of a list

(3) Special process definitions: Various words in the language (e.g., coordinate and comparative conjunctions, comma, parentheses) are marked "special," where special means that a word carries its own grammar definition as part of its dictionary entry. When a special word

becomes the current sentence word the dictionary-carried definition is inserted into the current string in a prescribed position. Thus certain structures (headed by special words) need not be predicted by the otherwise deterministic procedure; they are allowed to interrupt anywhere and carry their own definitions. These definitions may call on strings in the grammar, or alternatively the strings can be composed at run-time using an R1-specify restriction (described below). The definition for *and*, for example, carries an R1 restriction which retrieves a portion of the analysis tree constructed prior to the appearance of *and*, and constructs a set of strings in isomorphic correspondence to the retrieved structure, i.e., carries out what was called structural repetition in the preceding description of conjunctions.

3.2 Restrictions

In the program, a restriction is a test which must be executed successfully before a particular sequence of sentence words can be accepted as an instance of the grammatical entity (definition) which carries the restriction. Thus all restrictions are basically wellformedness tests. In practice, however, it is possible to perform some of these tests before any attempt is made to determine whether the definition in question can be satisfied starting with the current sentence word. In addition, therefore, to the wellformedness tests proper (R2 in the set of restriction types below) which are performed after a definition φ is associated with particular words in the sentence, there are specialized restriction types (R1, R3–R7) which are executed before φ is attempted:

R1 (specify)	Replaces the given definition of φ with one obtained by executing the R1 test.
R2 (wellformedness)	Checks that the instance of φ just constucted meets detailed wellformedness tests.
R3 (disqualify)	Disallows a particular value (option) of φ which it will be impossible to satisfy with the words in the given sentence, or in the analysis thusfar constructed.
R4 (omission)	Accepts the null element of omission as value of φ in an omitting *wh* string, or the null element of zeroing in a conjunctional string which allows zeroing.
R5 (SP scope)	Tests whether a special node φ (corresponding to a special process definition) may be tried on the next higher level of the analysis tree.

SYNTACTIC ANALYSIS OF NATURAL LANGUAGE 169

R6 (SP insert) Tests whether a special node φ may be inserted at the present point in the current string.

R7 (category check) Disqualifies φ if the current sentence word is not in a word category which can begin φ.

All restrictions are composed from a basic vocabulary of restriction routines. These are mainly divided into logical tests and routines for moving about the analysis tree (location routines). An important feature of the location routines is "transparency," a device which was introduced to compensate for certain discrepancies between the linguistic string grammar and its machine representation. For example, in the interests of computational simplicity, appearances of X in string definitions are replaced by $\bar{X}$, where $\bar{X} = l_X \, X \, r_X$, and l_X and r_X are allowed to take on the value zero. As a result of this convention, the analysis tree contains nodes which are not mentioned in the linguistic description of the same structures and interfere with a simple statement of restrictions as relations among elements of the same string or of host-adjunct pairs. To overcome this obstacle, various routines which search the analysis tree "see" only the essential linguistic nodes; other nodes are passed through in the course of the search as though they were transparent. [The nodes which are to be considered transparent are specified by the user.]

To illustrate, suppose the simple grammar of Section 1 were to be entered into the machine as the following definitions:

z_1 (center) $= \bar{N}_1 \, tV \, \bar{N}_2$ [subscript indicates position in string]

$\bar{X} = l_X \, X \, r_X$ [for $X = N, tV, P$]

$l_X = l_{tV} = r_{tV} = l_P = r_P = 0$ [i.e., all adjunct sets except r_N are empty]

$r_N = PN$ string or 0 [i.e., r_N has as value a PN string or zero]

PN string $= \bar{P} \, \bar{N}$

Transparent nodes: $\bar{X}, r_X, l_X$ [for $X = N, tV, P$]

The analysis tree corresponding to the string analysis of the sentence *Cars without brakes cause accidents* would be as shown in Fig. 3. In the course of checking *cars* against *cause* for agreement in number, the restriction routines will pass through the transparent nodes $\overline{tV}$ and $\bar{N}_1$.

Transparency is also used in preparing the output because the tree representation somewhat obscures the fact that a sentence has been decomposed into elementary strings. The string character of the analysis is restored in the output display by causing the print routine to

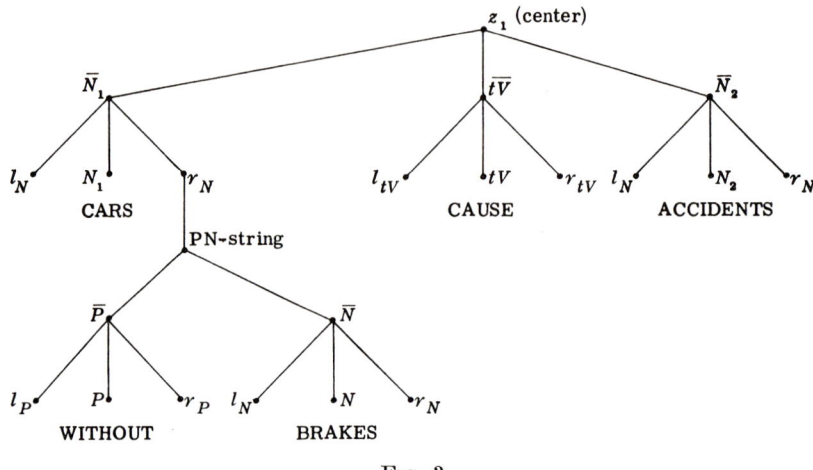

Fig. 3

ignore transparent nodes. Each nontransparent nonatomic node (i.e., each linguistic string) is assigned a numbered line of output on which is written the values of nontransparent nodes which appear under it in the tree: For an atom, the value is a sentence word; for a linguistic string, the value is the number of the output line on which the string is written. The output corresponding to the analysis tree above would be:

(1) z_1 (center) = CARS 2. CAUSE ACCIDENTS
(2) PN string = WITHOUT BRAKES

The fact that the number 2. falls to the right of *cars* indicates that the PN string on line (2) is a right adjunct of *cars*.

3.3 Special Processes

When a word marked "special" (i.e., carrying an M attribute) becomes current, the program inserts an element Mj (= the value of the M attribute for the given word) into the current string ξ at a point just following the most recently satisfied element X_l. Mj is the name of a grammar definition ($M1$ for *and*, $M2$ for *or*, etc.) and unless the insertion of Mj is disqualified by an R6 test in Mj, the various options of Mj are tried just as though Mj had been the $(l+1)$th element of ξ. If all the options of Mj fail, the program erases Mj and tries X_{l+1} in the normal manner. It also removes the "special" tag from the current word since X_{l+1} might be satisfied by this word in one of its nonspecial category assignments (e.g., *but* as adverb rather than conjunction in *They found but one*); in this case the program continues from this point as usual.

However, if the program finds itself at the end of the current string without having used up the special word, it restores the "special" tag to the word and ascends one level in the tree (unless blocked by an R5 test). It then repeats the whole process at the new level, beginning with the insertion of an Mj node at the current point in the string at that level. If all efforts (special and nonspecial) fail, the program backs up to the previous sentence word, as it would normally on failure.

This scheme is especially apt for conjunctions. For example, suppose the sentence in Fig. 3 were interrupted by a conjunctional string after the word *brakes*. Figure 4 shows two alternative ways in which the string *and headlights* could be attached to the analysis tree. The program would first conjoin *and headlights* to the deeper string (*without brakes*); it would later obtain the second analysis in which *and headlights* is conjoined to a string (*cars cause accidents*) higher in the tree.

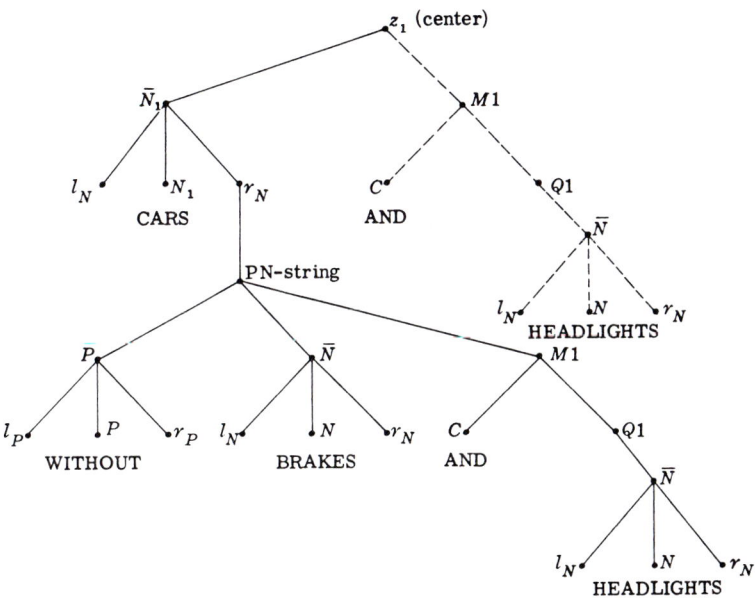

Fig. 4

3.3.1 Coordinate Conjunctions: and, or, but

The Mj definitions for coordinate conjunctions all contain an option $C\ Q1$, where the content of $Q1$ is specified by an R1 restriction as follows: Given that Mj has been inserted following X_l in ξ, the options of $Q1$ are:

$$X_l;\quad X_{l-1}X_l;\quad X_{l-2}X_{l-1}X_l;\quad \cdots;\quad X_1 \cdots X_{l-1}X_l.$$

That is, the restriction carries out the "structural repetition" of Section 1. In Fig. 4, the first option X_l of $Q1$ is used in both conjoinings shown.

While a gross string analysis of conjunctional sequences need not take account of the existence of zeroed elements, the identifying and supplying of zeroed elements in (or just before) conjunctional strings facilitates applying to a conjunctional string $C\xi_2$ the restrictions housed in the string ξ_1, which apply as well to ξ_2. For example, in the sentence *She likes toys and animals too*, the analysis which would have animals liking toys too (similar in form to *She likes toys and he too*) is ruled out by the restriction as to subject-verb agreement in number applied to the complete ξ_2: $\not\exists$ *She likes toys and animals likes toys too*.

An analogous situation exists in the *wh* strings to which the operation of omission has been applied. Here, too, it is often useful to redirect a restriction from a null element (here the omitted element of an adjunct *wh* string) to the appropriate element of the host string. For example, in sentence 5 of the sample text, the program checks *was* (line 7) against *porosity* (line 2) for agreement in number.

3.3.2 Scope-Marked Conjunctions: Either···or, neither···nor, both···and

In terms of the operation of structural repetition by which conjunctional strings are obtained, the words *either* (as part of *either-or*), *neither* (as part of *neither-nor*) and *both* (as part of *both-and*) can be seen to mark the point in the host string beyond which elements cannot be "repeated" in the conjunctional string, e.g., $\exists$ *John wrote a paper and Mary corrected it*, $\exists$ *John both wrote and corrected a paper*, $\not\exists$ *John both wrote and Mary corrected a paper*. That is, a pair $C'\cdots C$ (e.g., *either $\cdots$ or*) marks off a structure X (a string or string segment) which also appears following C in the sentence: $C'\ X\ C\ X$. Since X is the expected structure when C' occurs, it is possible to define a special process, initiated by C', which inserts the string $C'\ X\ C$ at the interrupt point; when the $C'\ X\ C$ string is satisfied, the program reverts to its normal operation and finds an X as it expected before the interruption. The tree in Fig. 5 illustrates the result of this process. Here C (*or*) is a nonspecial element, because it is not an independent string head, but part of $C'\ X\ C$.

3.3.3 Comma

The comma is troublesome because in some of its uses it is a required string element (e.g., in conjunctional sequences of the form $X, X\ and\ X$)

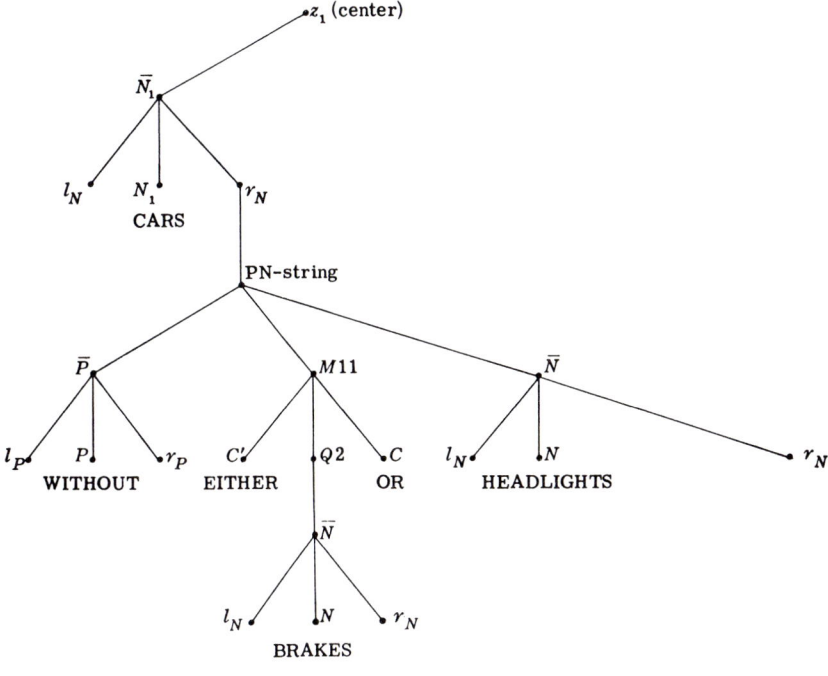

Fig. 5

while in other uses it is punctuational and as such not entirely subject to grammatical description. In order to proceed, we assume that if a given comma does not analyze as a conjunction ($Q1$ option with various restrictions), then it is all right to accept the comma as punctuation. The words following the comma must then be analyzed by the ordinary grammar. In addition, particular strings which either should or should not be set off by punctuation commas carry their own restrictions to this effect, e.g., *The children asleep, they* ···

3.3.4 Comparative Conjunctions: –er ··· than, as ··· as

The comparative forms in English are particularly rich structurally and one way to handle them is to see their resemblance to strings and processes already defined. Accordingly, the special process definition which is initiated by *than* (when preceded by *more, less* or X-er; $X =$ adjective, a few adverbs) or by *as* (when preceded by adverbial *as*) contains several options:

(1) Conjunctional. Compare, for example,

apples and oranges	more apples than oranges
People will buy the book and read it.	More people will buy the book than read it.
	People will more (often) buy a book than read it.
	but ∄ People buy more books than read them.

With a few restrictions which depend on the placing of the comparative marker in the host string, the large body of comparative strings can be obtained using the same set of strings ($Q1$) as are generated in the conjunctional special process.

(2) *wh* like. There exists in the grammar a *wh* string with omission which adjoins a whole sentence, e.g., *The crowd dispersed quietly, which they had not expected*. When the ultimate verb in this string is such as can occur with *that S* as its object (S = sentence), there is a similar comparative string:

| *The crowd dispersed quietly, which they had not expected.* | *The crowd dispersed more quietly than they had expected.* |

The *wh* string which adjoins an N also has a comparative analog:

| *The boxes which we asked for have arrived.* | *More boxes than we asked for have arrived.* |

Than and *as* can therefore be placed in the same class as *which* (as heading the same strings) and handled by the ordinary grammar, with the restriction that *than* and *as* each be preceded in the sentence by the appropriate comparative marker, and with certain restrictions on the strings headed by *than* and *as* vs. *which*. There is also a shortened form of the passive strings of this type (headed only by the comparative string heads); e.g., *More people than expected were there, The crowd dispersed more quietly than expected*, etc.

(3) N *is* A strings. As a right adjunct of N, a comparative marked adjective behaves (in string terms) as though it were preceded not by N alone but by N *is* A (A = adjective), from which the various $Q1$ strings can be obtained:

Someone smarter than I could solve the problem.
Someone smarter than I am could solve the problem.
Someone smarter than I am patient could solve the problem.

(4) Inverted assertion: $\Sigma\, t\, V\, \Omega\, C\, t\, \Sigma$. This option covers the comparative strings in which the subject is permuted with W, *have*, *be*, or *do*. For example, (from a text):

> *Mammals have generally been conceded to possess a much wider "plasticity" and "adaptability" of coordination than do amphibians.*

(5) Special zeroing, for small adverb subclasses: *more beautiful than ever, more people than ever*.

3.4 Treatment of Syntactic Ambiguity

3.4.1 Saving Reusable Portions of the Analysis

Even an ambiguous sentence is ambiguous only in certain respects. It is likely, then, that two (or more) syntactic analyses of a given sentence will be identical in their analysis over some portion or portions of the sentence. It would be wasteful to recompute such portions for each analysis. Also, in the course of obtaining an analysis, numerous false paths are tried; i.e., the first m words of an n-word sentence may be subject to an analysis which is later found not to fit in an analysis of the entire n-word sequence. In this case, too, it would be wasteful to recompute common portions of the various paths. The string analysis programs therefore are equipped with a device called "saving" by which computed instances of certain strings (substructures of the analysis tree) are copied before being dismantled. These substructures are then available for reuse as "plug-in" units in other analyses or paths.

A structure which contains no restriction that examines the context outside that structure is called *autonomous*, and can be saved and used in any context which calls for such a structure—subject, of course, to any further restrictions imposed by the new context. The grammar writer can minimize computer time by making as many strings as possible autonomous; but it should be noted that this aim conflicts with the desire to house restrictions as low in the tree structure as possible, so that non-wellformed sequences will be discarded soon after their construction. To make it possible to save a particular instance φ of a nonautonomous structure, when this is justified, the program keeps track of the paths followed in executing restrictions during the construction of φ; and (in the IPL program) φ is saved only if no restriction path extended beyond φ (to a node not in the substructure of φ). Making use of this possibility, many restrictions are in the form of an implication in which the if-clause checks for some feature which separates the autonomous from the nonautonomous cases. The FAP program also saves that portion of a nonautonomous φ which was constructed before a restriction path extended beyond φ.[7]

3.4.2 Permanent Predictable Ambiguities

By far the largest number of alternative analyses are of the type in which the breakdown of the sentence into elementary strings in the various analyses is the same but the string assignment is different. The most frequent situations are these:

(1) Alternative analyses due to nesting vs. repeatability: The operation of adjoining, say, a right-adjunct of N to a particular N is repeatable (*a man from Philadelphia whom I met*). In many cases, such as in a sequence of $P\,N$'s in r_N: $N_1\,P\,N_2\,P\,N_3\cdots$, the second adjunct can adjoin either N_1 (repeatability) or N_2 (nesting): *the house of my friend in Philadelphia* $\cdots$.

(2) Same string in different adjunct sets which enter at the same point: Again to use the example of a $P\,N$ string, the $P\,N$ string is a member of the sets r_N, r_V, and s.a. (sentence adjuncts). There are certain points in a sentence at which two or all three of these sets can enter; e.g., all three can enter after the object, when the object is N:

r_N: *He opened the box with the blue cover.*
$r V$:   *He opened the box with interest.*
s.a.:   *He opened the box with time to spare.*

In some cases, we can resolve the ambiguity by bringing a restriction to bear; e.g., for $P\,N$ in r_V, *of* is not an acceptable value of P.

Until we can establish subclasses that will give us better discrimination, we have permanent predictable ambiguities in these situations, on which it seemed unrewarding to spend computer time. Where there are alternative analyses due to repeatability vs. nesting, the program chooses the analysis due to nesting. Where strings in r_N, r_V, and *s.a.* overlap, the program assigns the common string to the first adjunct set having permission to enter in the given situation.[8]

---

[7] This technique of partial saving is described more fully in Carol Raze, "User's Manual for the FAP String Program," in preparation.

[8] It should be emphasized that not printing the permanent predictable ambiguities is not a solution to the problem of obtaining the intended (preferred) analysis; this lies in more refined subclasses and other constraints which may be drawn from the textual context. Nevertheless, at this stage of research, there is a considerable practical gain in being able to suppress ambiguities selectively.

The min-word test, which accomplishes this assignment, is based on a simple observation: If in the course of back-tracking through an n-word sentence in order to obtain an alternative analysis, the program has reached back as far as the mth word ($m \leq n$) and no further (i.e., it has destroyed the given analysis for words m through n), then in starting forward from this point any attempt to construct an adjunct string α_i beginning with word m will only result in an ambiguity if any previous analysis contains α_i as an adjunct string beginning with word m. The program keeps a record of the current value of "the min-word" (m in the above observation). There also exists a "suppress list" containing the names of the strings $\alpha_1, \alpha_2, \cdots$, etc., which we do not wish to have the program shift from one adjunct slot to another in order to obtain different analyses. After each analysis, the program scans the entire analysis tree comparing the name of each node with the names of the strings on the suppress list and in case of equality attaches the attribute pair N_i, N_j to the first word subsumed under the node in question; $N_i = \alpha_i$, the name of the string at that node, $N_j = $ the first node above N_i, which in the machine representation of the grammar is the name of the adjunct set from which α_i was taken in this analysis (if α_i is occurring as an adjunct). The following R3-restriction on each α_i prevents the program from taking α_i as an adjunct somewhere else in the tree: Not all the tests (a), (b), and (c) are true: (a) There has already been at least one successful analysis; (b) the current word is the min-word; (c) N_i, N_j appear as an attribute pair of the current word.

3.4.3 Freezing Grouped Segments

While the min-word test deals with the external relations of the strings obtained in a decomposition of a sentence, the freeze test concerns their internal structure. If it can be established that the words of an already computed structure φ have no other possible segmentation in the given sentence, then in undoing an analysis it is justified for the program to treat φ as though it were a single word or a "frozen" block of words. The freeze test is executed when the program is about to dismantle a computed structure φ in the course of back-tracking. If the test succeeds, the program skips back over all the words subsumed by φ and continues its back-tracking from there; i.e., it detaches the node φ (with all its substructures) from the analysis tree as a unit.

As an example, consider the distinguished segment $l_N N$ (N with its left adjuncts). If the sentence word satisfying N (the "core value" of $l_N N$) is the type of noun which requires a preceding article or possessive, then except under statable conditions the sequence of words which stretches from a preceding article or possessive up to and including the noun in question cannot be differently segmented.[9] Thus in the sentence

A 10–40 per cent w/r sucrose density gradient was prepared according to the method of B. and L

the word sequence *a 10–40 per cent w/r sucrose density gradient*, as an instance of $l_N\ N$, can be "frozen." The freeze test is only applied after one analysis of the sentence has already been obtained.

3.5 Output

As illustrated in Section 2.2, in an analysis of a sentence each component linguistic string is assigned a numbered line of output on which are printed the words of the string in the sentence. If an element in a string S_1 is itself a string S_2, then the number of the output line of S_2 appears in the element position of S_2 in S_1. Sentence adjunct strings are preceded by an asterisk, *, to distinguish them from all other adjuncts, which are positionally indicated: If a right (left) adjunct string S_2

04 Ferrous Extraction and Refining

M04--24522. THE EFFECT OF CALCIUM CARBONATE ON THE REDUCIBILITY OF IRON-OXIDE AGGLOMERATES. P.K. Strangway and H.U. Ross. Can Met Quart, v 4, no 1, Jan-Mar. 1965, p 97-111.
    Briquettes, consisting of pure ferric oxide and ferric oxide with 1, 2, 5 and 10% calcium carbonate, were sintered at 1200 C. They were then reduced by hydrogen in a loss-in-weight furnace at temperatures ranging from 600 to 1000 C. It was found that calcium carbonate increased the reducibility in all instances. At low reduction temperatures, the effect was more pronounced as the calcium carbonate content increased. This, in turn, corresponded to a greater initial porosity which was developed during sintering. At higher reduction temperatures, however, this effect was more pronounced for briquettes with small calcium carbonate additions. In this instance, the porosity which was developed during reduction became more important than that which was developed during sintering. 22 ref. (AA)

FIG. 6

[9]The statable exceptions mentioned above involve reanalyzing the N as a left adjunct of N, e.g., as part of a compound noun or compound adjective.

adjoins an element E of S_1, the number of the output line of S_2 is printed to the right (left) of E in S_1.

Figures 7–14 contain the computer outputs for the sentences of the metallurgy abstract shown in Fig. 6. The second parse of Sentence 4 (Fig. 11), if it exists at all for this choice of words for the strings in question, would have to be construed as something like: *The effect was more pronounced as (measured by) the increased calcium carbonate content.* A more detailed form of output, giving the grammatical names of every string element, is shown in Fig. 11.

```
SENTENCE   1. BRIQUETTES , CONSISTING OF PURE FERRIC OXIDE AND FERRIC
              OXIDE WITH 1 , 2 , 5 AND 10 PERCENT CALCIUM CARBONATE , WERE
              SINTERED AT 1200 CEGREES CENTIGRADE .

      PARSE      01
 1.  SENTENCE            =                   2.   .

 2.  C1 ASSERTION        =          BRIQUETTES ,  3.      WERE      SINTERED   4.

 3.  VING +              = CONSISTING     OF  5.  OXIDE AND   6.

 4.  C20 P N             =          AT        7.  DEGREES 10.

 5.  L-A OF N            =                   PURE FERRIC

 6.  CONJ STG            = 11. OXIDE 12.

 7.  L-A OF N            =          1200

10.  ADJ IN R-N          = CENTIGRADE

11.  L-A OF N            =                   FERRIC

12.  C20 P N             =          WITH     13. CARBONATE ,

13.  L-A OF N            =                    1 , 14. PERCENT        CALCIUM

14.  CONJ STG            = 2   , 15.

15.  CONJ STG            = 5   AND 16.

16.  CONJ STG            = 10
NO MORE PARSES
```

FIG. 7

SENTENCE 2. THEY WERE THEN REDUCED BY HYDROGEN IN A LOSS-IN-WEIGHT FURNACE
           AT TEMPERATURES RANGING FROM 600 TO 1000 DEGREES CENTIGRADE

```
        PARSE       01
   1. SENTENCE         =                2.

   2. C1 ASSERTION     =     THEY        WERE • 3.    REDUCED   4.

   3. ADVERB           = THEN

   4. C20 P N          =        BY         HYDROGEN   5.

   5. C20 P N          =        IN        6. FURNACE  7.

   6. L-A OF N         = A              LOSS-IN-WEIGHT

   7. C20 P N          =       AT        TEMPERATURES 10.

  10. VING +           = RANGING    FROM 11. DEGREES 12.

  11. L-A OF N         =         600 TO 13.

  12. ADJ IN R-N       = CENTIGRADE

  13. CONJ STG         = 1000

  NO MORE PARSES
```

FIG. 8

SENTENCE 3. IT WAS FOUND THAT CALCIUM CARBONATE INCREASED THE REDUCIBILITY
            IN ALL INSTANCES .
```
        PARSE       01
   1. SENTENCE         =             2.

   2. C1 ASSERTION     =     IT       WAS     3.

   3. C132 VEN 0-PASS  = FOUND    THAT   4.

   4. C1 ASSERTION     =     5. CARBONATE    INCREASED    6. REDUCIBILITY   • 7.

   5. L-A OF N         =                                 CALCIUM

   6. L-A OF N         = THE

   7. C20 P N          =     IN       10. INSTANCES

  10. L-A OF N         =        ALL
  NO MORE PARSES
```
FIG. 9

SYNTACTIC ANALYSIS OF NATURAL LANGUAGE   181

```
SENTENCE  4. AT LOW REDUCTION TEMPERATURES , THE EFFECT WAS MORE PRONOUNCED
          AS THE CALCIUM CARBONATE CONTENT INCREASED .
     PARSE    01
 1. SENTENCE           =              2.

 2. C1 ASSERTION       = * 3.   4. EFFECT    WAS    5. PRONOUNCED    * 6.

 3. C20 P N            =      AT           7. TEMPERATURES ,

 4. L-A OF N           = THE

 5. ADVERB             = MORE

 6. C161 CS1 C         =      AS  10.

 7. L-A OF N           =                 LOW              REDUCTION

10. C1 ASSERTION       =    11. CONTENT    INCREASED

11. L-A OF N           = THE                           CALCIUM CARBONATE
```
Fig. 10

```
SENTENCE  4. AT LOW REDUCTION TEMPERATURES , THE EFFECT WAS MORE PRONOUNCED
          AS THE CALCIUM CARBONATE CONTENT INCREASED .
     PARSE    02
 1. SENTENCE           = INTRODUCER CENTER END MARK
                              2.

 2. C1 ASSERTION       = *      SUBJECT   * VERB  * OBJECT        R-V  *
                         * 3.   4. EFFECT    WAS    5. PRONOUNCED    * 6.

 3. C20 P N            = L-P PREPOSITION   N
                              AT           7. TEMPERATURES ,

 4. L-A OF N           = ARTICLE QUANTIFIER ADJECTIVE TYPE NS NOUN
                         THE

 5. ADVERB             = ADVERB
                         MORE

 6. C160 CS0 O-BE      = L-CS CS0 OBJ-BE            *
                              AS  10. CONTENT 11.

 7. L-A OF N           = ARTICLE QUANTIFIER ADJECTIVE TYPE NS NOUN
                                                 LOW              REDUCTION

10. L-A OF N           = ARTICLE QUANTIFIER ADJECTIVE TYPE NS NOUN
                         THE                           CALCIUM CARBONATE

11. C132 VEN O-PASS    = VEN       * PASSIVE-O R-V  *
                         INCREASED

NO MORE PARSES
```
Fig. 11

SENTENCE 5. THIS , IN TURN , CORRESPONDED TO A GREATER INITIAL POROSITY
         WHICH WAS DEVELOPED DURING SINTERING .
     PARSE   01
  1. SENTENCE   =   2.   .

  2. C1 ASSERTION   =   3.   * 4. CORRESPONDED   TO 5. POROSITY 6.

  3. L-A OF N   = THIS ,

  4. C20 P N   =   IN   TURN ,

  5. L-A OF N   = A   GREATER INITIAL

  6. C85 WH STG   = WHICH 7.

  7. C1 ASSERTION   =   ( )   WAS   DEVELOPED   *10.

 10. C164 CS4 SN   =   DURING SINTERING
NO MORE PARSES

FIG. 12

SENTENCE 6. AT HIGHER REDUCTION TEMPERATURES , HOWEVER , THIS EFFECT
         WAS MORE PRONOUNCED FOR BRIQUETTES WITH SMALL CALCIUM CARBONATE
         ADDITIONS .
     PARSE   01
  1. SENTENCE   =   2.   .

  2. C1 ASSERTION   = * 3. HOWEVER ,   4. EFFECT   WAS   5. PRONOUNCED 6.

  3. C20 P N   =   AT   7. TEMPERATURES ,

  4. L-A OF N   = THIS

  5. ADVERB   = MORE

  6. C20 P N   =   FOR   BRIQUETTES 10.

  7. L-A OF N   =   HIGHER   REDUCTION

 10. C20 P N   =   WITH   11. ADDITIONS

 11. L-A OF N   =   SMALL   CALCIUM CARBONATE
NO MORE PARSES

FIG. 13

```
SENTENCE  7.  IN THIS INSTANCE , THE POROSITY WHICH WAS DEVELOPED DURING
              REDUCTION BECAME MORE IMPORTANT THAN THAT WHICH WAS DEVELOPED
              DURING SINTERING .

        PARSE        01
  1.  SENTENCE            =              2.       THAN  3.     .

  2.  C1 ASSERTION        = * 4.     5. POROSITY  6.     BECAME      7. IMPORTANT

  3.  CONJ STG            = 10.

  4.  C20 P N             =           IN          11. INSTANCE ,

  5.  L-A OF N            = THE

  6.  C85 WH STG          = WHICH 12.

  7.  ADVERB              = MORE

 10.  C1 ASSERTION        =           13.  14.    ( BECAME )    ( IMPORTANT )

 11.  L-A OF N            = THIS

 12.  C1 ASSERTION        =           ( )         WAS       DEVELOPED 15.

 13.  L-A OF N            = THAT

 14.  C85 WH STG          = WHICH 16.

 15.  C20 P N             =           DURING      REDUCTION

 16.  C1 ASSERTION        =           ( )         WAS       DEVELOPED  *17.

 17.  C164 CS4 SN         =           DURING SINTERING

   NO MORE PARSES                     FIG. 14
```

3.6 Discussion

3.6.1 Natural Form for Discontinuous Entities

The method of immediate constituent analysis is powerful up to a certain point because to a very large extent the modifiers of a word will be found next to it in the sentence. However, it has two drawbacks: One, there are cases of modifiers which are at a distance from the word they modify, e.g., adverbs at a distance from their verb, as in *Softly she tiptoed out of the room*; or a relative clause at a distance from its noun, as in *An explanation is here offerea which is adequate for all the cases above*. Two, more seriously, there are a great many grammatical dependences between words which are in different constituents, as in number agreement between the subject noun and its verb, or the requirement for an anticipatory *it* subject in sentences like *It is surprising that he was there* where *that he was there* requires that the subject be *it*.

The problem of dependence at a distance as in the above examples is also of interest for computational work because no limit can be specified for the distance between the words or clauses which participate in the dependence: e.g., *It might perhaps begin to seem to · · · to become surprising to John and Mary and Jim and · · · and Jack that she was there*. This problem exists when the sentence is taken as constructed from words or constituents. However, there is one segmentation of sentences in which the problem of dependences at a distance does not arise. This is the segmentation of each sentence into a center string and adjunct strings. Every grammatical dependence in a sentence occurs between parts of a string or between an adjunct and the string to which it is adjoined.[10] For example, the number agreement is between the subject and verb of a string, e.g., between *explanation* and *is* in the center string *An explanation is here offered* in the sentence *An explanation is here offered which is adequate for the cases above*; and *which is adequate for all the cases above* may indeed be at a distance from *explanation*, which it modifies, but is adjoined to the string *An explanation is here offered*, of which *explanation* is a part. This string analysis can be carried out in a regular way on all sentences of a language, and because it is a form of grammatical analysis in which no dependences are at a distance, it is particularly convenient for syntactic computation.

3.6.2 Computational Economy of Strings

By recognizing a word (as member of a word class) in the sentence as being a word in a string in that sentence, word-by-word string analysis can use rules for string succession in sentences, instead of rules for word class or constituent succession in sentences. The number of grammatical strings which is adequate for describing the great bulk of the sentences of English is about 125, grouped into about 15 classes, and the only combination rules in string analysis are those that state which class of strings enters strings of some class of strings at some point of the (latter) string. Hence the number of rules for string expectation is

[10] A special case is a relation between a pair of adjuncts adjoined to the same string. An extreme case of this is the zeroing after *don't* in *People who smoke distrust people who don't* where *who smoke* and *who don't* is a system of two adjuncts adjoined to *People distrust people*.

quite small (about 150 rules, i.e., strings and string class definitions, plus about 150 restrictions in the present computer grammar).

By using strings we also get a framework for expressing restrictions, which can be formulated in respect to a string. The value, to a grammar or analyzer, of having a system in respect to which restrictions can be stated lies in the following: Natural language notoriously has a vast amount of detail and many at least apparent exceptions to every rule. This has not precluded the formulation of precise and detailed grammars of languages. The reason is that the variety of structures in a language are grouped into sets of structures which have a family resemblance plus various specific differences for various subsets of words. With regard to the exceptions, the great bulk of them can be shown to be extensions of a rule to some words beyond the range for which the rule had been defined. For this reason it is most efficient to recognize genera of structures and specific differences (for specific words or word subclasses) within each genus. Using a grammar whose elements are strings grouped into classes makes it possible to state general rules about whole classes of strings, restrictions upon these rules to account for differences in particular strings, and finally, if we wish, further restrictions to account for stylistic and near-idiomatic forms involving very small classes of words. Using string analysis, considerable refinement is thus possible without an undue increase in the number of rules.

3.6.3 Relation to Transformations

Transformational analysis decomposes each given sentence into one or more elementary (kernel) sentences and unary or binary transformational operations upon these. The elementary sentences are assertions, and the given sentence can be looked upon as being transformationally composed from these elementary assertions. The strings into which a given sentence is decomposed by string theory can to a large extent be identified with the elementary sentences of that sentence under transformational theory.

In most cases the relation is direct; e.g., in most cases, the center string is the main kernel sentence of the given sentence, and very many adjuncts can be filled out to the corresponding kernel sentence merely by adding to the adjunct a distinguished word from the string to which the adjunct has been adjoined; which word this is can be recognized directly from the form of the string. For example, in *An explanation* ··· *which is adequate* ··· the string *which is adequate* can be filled out to a connective *wh* plus *An explanation is adequate* (these being the transformation and the kernel sentence under transformational analysis).

In other cases the relation between string and transformational decompositions is more complicated. However, here too, the more detailed relations discovered by transformational analysis apply within string-related segments of the sentence. Some of these relations can be incorporated as refinements of the string grammar, but others remain beyond the reach of a practicable string program. However, this does not mean that the string output for the sentences containing these transformational relations is incorrect, but that it misses connections of the given sentence to other sentences of the language.

ACKNOWLEDGMENTS

The string grammar of English used by both programs was tested by Morris Salkoff and the author at the Courant Institute of Mathematical Sciences, New York University. We wish to thank C.I.M.S. for the hospitality of the computer center and for useful advice concerning the structure and preparation of the FAP program. Some of the design of the FAP program was suggested by analogy with methods used in the NU-SPEAK list processing language developed at C.I.M.S. by Professor J. Schwartz.

The author wishes to thank Morris Salkoff for helpful criticism of this manuscript.

REFERENCES

1. Alt., F. L., and Rhodes, I., The hindsight technique in machine translation of natural languages. *J. Res. Nat. Bur. Std.* **B66**, No. 2, 47–51 (1962).
2. Bar-Hillel, Y., A quasi-arithmetical notation for syntactic description. *Language* **29**, No. 1, 47–48 (1953).
3. Bloomfield, L., *Language*. Holt, New York, 1933.
4. Bobrow, D. G., Syntactic analysis of English by computer—a survey. *AFIPS Conf. Proc.*, Spartan, Baltimore, Vol. 24, pp. 265–387 (1963).
5. Bolinger, D. L., *Interrogative Structures of American English*, Publ. of the American Dialect Society, No. 28. Univ. of Alabama Press, University, Alabama, 1957.
6. Brooker, R. A., and Morris, D., An assembly program for a phrase structure language. *Computer J.* **3**, No. 3, 168–174 (1960).
7. Bross, I., A syntactic formula for English sentences: Application to scientific narrative, Ms., Roswell Park Memorial Inst., Buffalo, New York, 1965.
8. Chomsky, N., A transformational approach to syntax. *Proc. 3rd Texas Conf. Probl. Linguistic Anal. English, 1958*, pp. 124–58, Univ. of Texas, Austin, Texas (1962).
9. Chomsky, N., *Syntactic Structures*. Mouton, The Hague, 1957.
10. Chomsky, N., Three models for the description of language. *IRE, Trans. Inform. Theory* **2**, 113–124 (1956).
11. Dougherty, Ching-Yi, and Martin, S. E., Chinese syntactic rules for machine translation, Project for Machine Translation, Univ. of California, Berkeley, California, 1964.
12. Green, B. F., Jr., Wolf, A. K., Chomsky, C., and Laughery, K., Baseball: An automatic question answering, in *Computers and Thought* (E. A. Figenbaum and J. Feldman, eds.), pp. 207–216. McGraw-Hill, New York, 1963.
13. Gross, M., On the equivalence of models of language used in the fields of mechanical translation and information retrieval. Paper presented at the

NATO Advanced Study Institute on Automatic Translation of Languages, Venice, July 1962.
14. Harman, G. H., and Yngve, V. H., Generative grammars without transformation rules. MIT TLEQPR No. 68, Mass. Inst. Technol., Cambridge, Mass., 1962.
15. Harris, Z. S., A cycling cancellation-automaton for sentence well-formedness. *Bull. Intern. Computation Centre* 5, 75–100 (1966).
16. Harris, Z. S., Co-occurrence and transformation in linguistic structure. *Language* 33, 283–340 (1957).
17. Harris, Z. S., *Methods in Structural Linguistics*. Univ. of Chicago Press, Chicago, Illinois, 1951.
18. Harris, Z. S., *String Analysis of Sentence Structure*, Papers on Formal Linguistics, No. 1. Mouton, The Hague, 1962.
19. Harris, Z. S., Transformational theory. *Language* 41, 363–401 (1965).
20. Harris, Z. S., et al., *Transformations and Discourse Analysis Papers (T.D.A.P.)* Nos. 15–19. Dept. Linguistics, Univ. of Pennsylvania, 1959.
21. Hays, D. G., Basic principles and technical variation in sentence-structure determination, RAND Paper 1984, Rand Corp., 1960.
22. Hays, D. G., Automatic language-data processing, in *Computer Applications in the Behavioral Sciences* (H. Borko, ed.), pp. 394–421. Prentice-Hall, Englewood Cliffs, New Jersey, 1962.
23. Hays, D. G., Grouping and dependency theories, RAND Paper 1910, Rand Corp., 1960.
24. Hiż, H., Congrammaticality, batteries of transformations and grammatical categories. *Proc. Symp. Appl. Math.* 12, 43–50 (1964).
25. Hiż, H., Steps toward grammatical recognition. *Intern. Conf. Std. Common Language Machine Searching Transl., Cleveland, 1959*, pp. 811–822 (1959).
26. Hiż, H., Syntactic completion analysis and theories of grammatical categories, *T.D.A.P.* No. 21, Univ. of Pennsylvania, 1959.
27. Hockett, C. F., The quantification of functional load, RAND Paper 2338, Rand Corp., 1961.
28. Ingerman, P. Z., *A Syntax-Oriented Translator*. Academic Press, New York, 1966.
29. Irons, E. T., and Feurzlig, W., Comments on the implementation of recursive procedures and blocks. *Comm. ACM* 4, No. 1, 65–69 (1961).
30. Joshi, A. K., A procedure for a transformational decomposition of English sentences, *T.D.A.P.* No. 42, Univ. of Pennsylvania, 1962.
31. Joshi, A. K., String representation of transformations and a decomposition procedure, Part I, *T.D.A.P.*, Univ. of Pennsylvania, Dec. 1965.
32. Joshi, A. K., Transformational analysis by Computer. Paper presented at National Institutes of Health Seminar in Computational Linguistics, Oct. 6–7, 1966.
33. Kuno, S., Automatic syntactic analysis. Paper presented at N. I. H. Seminar on Computational Linguistics, Oct. 6–7, 1966.
34. Kuno, S., and Oettinger, A. G., Multiple-path syntactic analyser, in *Information Processing 1962*, pp. 306–312. North-Holland Publ., Amsterdam, 1963.
35. Kuno, S., The predictive analyzer and a path elimination technique. *Comm. ACM* 8, 453–462 (1965).
36. Lamb, S. M., On alternation, transformation, realization, and stratification, Monograph Series on Language and Linguistics, No. 17, pp. 105–22. Georgetown Univ., 1964, Inst. of Languages and Linguistics.

37. Lambek, J., The mathematics of sentence structure. *Am. Math. Monthly.* **65**, 154–170 (1958).
38. Lecerf, Y., Une représentation algébrique de la structure des phrases dans diverses langues naturelles. *Compt. Rend.* **252**, No. 2, 232 (1961).
39. Matthews, G. H., Analysis by synthesis of sentences in a natural language. *1st Intern. Conf. Machine Transl. Appl. Language Anal., Teddington, England, 1961* (1961).
40. Oettinger, A. G., *et al.*, Mathematical linguistics and automatic translation, Rep. No. NSF–9, Vol. 2, Cambridge, Mass., 1963.
41. Rhodes, I., Hindsight in predictive syntactic analysis. *Natl. Bur. Std. (U.S.) Rep.* **7034** (1960).
42. Rhodes, I., A new approach to the mechanical syntactic analysis of Russian, Mechanical Translation Group, U.S. Dep. of Commerce, Appl. Math. Div. *Nat. Bur. Std. (U.S.), Rep.* **6595** (1959).
43. Robinson, J., PARSE: A system for automatic parsing of English, RM–4654–PR, RAND Corp., Santa Monica, California, 1965.
44. Robinson, J., Preliminary codes and rules for the automatic parsing of English, RM3339–PR, RAND Corp., Santa Monica, California, Dec. 1962.
45. Sager, N., Morris, J., Salkoff, M., and Raze, C., Report on the string analysis programs, NSF Transformations Project, Dept. of Linguistics, Univ. of Pennsylvania, March 1966.
46. Sager, N., Procedure for left-to-right recognition of sentence structure, *T.D.A.P.* No. 27, Univ. of Pennsylvania, 1960.
47. Salkoff, M., A string grammar of English in Backus normal form, String Project, Inst. for Computer Research in the Humanities, New York University, in preparation.
48. Simmons, R. E., Answering English questions by computer: A survey. *Comm. ACM* **8**, No. 1, 53–70 (1965).
49. Walker, D. E., and Bartlett, J. M., The structure of languages for man and computer: Problems in formalization. Paper presented at the First Congress on the Information Sciences, 1962.
50. Walker, D. E., *et al.*, English Preprocessor Manual, Language processing techniques sub-department, Information Sciences Dept., The Mitre Corp., Bedford, Mass., 1964.
51. Wells, R., Immediate constituents. *Language* **23**, 81–117 (1947).
52. Yngve, V. H., *COMIT Programmer's Reference Manual.* M.I.T. Press, Cambridge, Mass., 1962.
53. Yngve, V. H., A model and a hypothesis for language structure. *Proc. Am. Phil. Soc.* **104**, No. 5, 444 (1960).
54. Yngve, V. H., Random generation of English sentences. *1st Intern. Conf. Machine Transl. Appl. Language Anal., Teddington, England, 1961* (1961).

Programming Languages and Computers: A Unified Metatheory

R. NARASIMHAN

Computer Group
Tata Institute of Fundamental Research
Bombay, India

1. Introduction 189
   1.1 Motivation for a Metatheory 189
   1.2 Scope of the Present Work 191
   1.3 Relation to Other Works 193
   1.4 An Outline of the Structure of the Article 194
2. Simple Computation Processes 196
   2.1 Introduction 196
   2.2 Simple Programming Languages: Computation on Basic Flow Charts 196
   2.3 Simple Programming Languages: Computations on General Flow Charts 202
   2.4 Simple Computer Languages and Programs 207
   2.5 The Translation Problem 211
   2.6 A Structure for Translators 214
3. Hierarchical Computation Processes 217
   3.1 The Need for Extending the Scope of the Metatheory . . 217
   3.2 Hierarchical Programming Languages 219
4. Relevance of the Approach to the Design of Computing Systems . 225
   4.1 Specifying a Computational Language 225
   4.2 Natural Languages and Computational Languages . . . 229
   4.3 Syntax, Semantics, and Systems 231
   4.4 The ALGOL Report 233
   4.5 Language Design and System Design 238
5. Concluding Remarks 240
   References 244

1. Introduction

1.1 Motivation for a Metatheory

1.1.1 The primary objective of this article is to give a formal description of the notion of a computation carried out on a computer and do this in such a way that certain practical problems of central importance that arise in computing activity can be stated and studied rigorously within this formalism. More specifically, the attempt is to formulate a metatheory of computation that could deal with computation in a programming language and computation in a computer within an integrated framework. Problems of a clearly pragmatic nature that enter into the design and use of efficient programming languages and computers should be within the scope of such a metatheory if it could be adequately developed.[1]

1.1.2 Much work has been done in recent years in describing and studying the behavior of finite state machines (or finite automata), on the one hand, and Turing machines (or potentially infinite automata) on the other. But it has become disconcertingly clear to those who are concerned with what might be termed the pragmatics of the design and utilization of computing machines that the results of these studies have little relevance to the problems they have to contend with. The reasons for this are evident and have been pointed out by others. Briefly, these reasons could be summarized by saying that the pragmatics of computing machines have to do with their structural and functional aspects *as systems* and not, primarily, either with their finiteness or their universality. Thus, problems that are naturally formulated and solved within the framework of models whose principal preoccupation is with either the finiteness of finite automata or the universality of universal Turing machines are not the kinds of problems that arise when computing machines are viewed, and have to be dealt with, as systems. It is this, the formulation of a metatheory of computation that takes explicit account of the fact that computers are really computational systems, that is the principal aim of this article.

1.1.3 The close connection, from the systems viewpoint, between computers and computational or programming languages[2] can be seen as follows. In a real-life context, one starts with a certain large class

---

[1]The need for a pragmatically motivated theory of computation has been voiced by several workers interested in the design of efficient programming languages and translators. A good idea of the prevailing views can be had, for example, from reference [22] and the discussions reported there. By far the most substantial work, to date, in this area has been done by McCarthy [*14, 15*]. It will be seen that concerning aims there is almost complete agreement between his work and that presented here. There are also similarities between some of the details of his theory and that described here. The basic approaches, however, are quite dissimilar. In Section 1.2 this question is considered in greater detail.

[2]Throughout this article, we use the terms *programming language* and *computational language* as coequivalent. See Section 4.1 for further remarks concerning this.

of problems with input-output specifications more or less well defined. The totality of algorithms which is relevant to these problems form the set of sentences of the computational language whose design is sought. To design this language its various components must be specified.[3] And this one should like to do so that in some well-defined sense two criteria are satisfied.

(1) The language must be problem-oriented. That is, the sentences of the language must mirror, in a natural way, the problems they are set up to solve. This means that minor variations in problem specifications should result in minor variations in the sentences that describe them. The variables of the problem should be identical to or, at least, should immediately correspond to the variables of the sentential forms. Procedures that relate variables in the problem area must have easily definable correspondence to structural entities of the language relating the corresponding variables in it, etc. The language must be, in other words, problem-oriented in as many of its levels as possible, if not in all its levels.

(2) The language must be so defined that the design of a computer language and of a translator for translating the input sentences can be done readily and effectively. The problem-oriented language should be such that it is easy to define a computer whose machine language is *well matched* to the former.

Notice that this concept of "well matchedness" refers to all aspects of the specification of the two languages including the computation processes implicit in them. Clearly, in order to be able to cope with this problem, we need a metatheory in which the notions: programming language, computer language, computation in a programming language, computation in a computer language, equivalence between two computations one specified in the former language and the other in the latter, translators which preserve this equivalence, etc., can be described and dealt with coherently. This will be our principal endeavor in this article.

1.2 Scope of the Present Work

1.2.1 Traditionally, only one major problem area has engaged the attention of both programming language and computer system designers. This

---

[3]In Section 4 the connection between language design and system design is dealt with in considerable detail. The notion of a computational language and the specification of its components are discussed from a more general point of view there. Readers not immediately interested in the technical aspects of computation theory may find it profitable to read Section 4 after Section 1, and either skip Sections 2 and 3 completely or return to them subsequently.

is the class of algorithms associated with numerical analysis.[4] However, in recent years, several other problem areas have begun to attract increasing attention. Some of them are picture processing, game playing (or, more generally, problem solving), information retrieval, etc. By now, there is general agreement among all concerned that a language designed specifically for numerical analysis is quite inefficient in coping with problem specifications arising in these other areas. Attempts have been made, with more or less success, to tackle each of these problem areas independently and to work out the structures of programming languages suited to each case.

The scope of the present paper may be outlined in this context as follows:

(1) We shall recognize the existence of a wide diversity of problem areas and the need for problem-oriented languages well matched to each of these.

(2) We shall seek to set up a framework within which efficient design (in the sense defined earlier) of such languages can be undertaken in a uniform manner.

(3) We shall also seek to relate this language design at each stage in a natural way to the design of computer systems that are capable of carrying out the algorithms specified using these problem-oriented languages.

There are, however, other important aspects of computer systems design with which this paper does not directly concern itself. It may be worthwhile to make a few remarks about these.

1.2.2 Many characteristic design problems arise when a large computer system is formed out of the interconnection of several more or less autonomous computers each with its own computational language and well-defined input-output behavior. The principal design considerations of such systems are connected with: (1) the data rates of the several processors and the interfacing of their information transfer (i.e., the data interface), (2) the communication interface for command transfer (i.e., the language interface), and (3) the formulation and implementation of the administrative hierarchy among the processors. Some well-known examples of systems of this kind are man-machine real-time systems, time-sharing console systems, and multiprocessor systems.

---

[4]Probably the most systematically specified programming language for this problem area is ALGOL. However, the computation process defined by ALGOL is very ill-matched to the classical von Neumann type of computers. FORTRAN is a much better matched language in this respect. ALGOL is considered critically from the viewpoint of this paper in Section 4.4.

Of the three problems enumerated above, the first is clearly not a language problem, while the second clearly is. The third is connected with the global structure of the process and its logical and engineering aspects. It should be possible to extend the results of this article and make them applicable to the language interface in the situation described above. However, we shall not here concern ourselves with this possibility any further but limit our attention to the design of systems comprising programming languages, translators, and computers, for a diversity of problem areas.

1.2.3 Before going on to a discussion of the special approach to this problem taken in this article, it is perhaps useful to consider briefly attempts that have been made by other workers in this field to construct a metatheory of computation with approximately the same aims in view. This should help one to have a proper perspective on the work presented here and to evaluate it adequately.

1.3 Relation to Other Works

1.3.1 Two aspects of specification of programming languages are particularly emphasized in this article. The first is concerned with what has sometimes been referred to as the semiotics of such languages. The second has to do with the descriptive structure of these languages: that they consist of descriptions of a set of primitive processes and a recursive system of rules for generating descriptions of other processes in terms of these primitives. These two aspects have been individually commented upon by other workers on a variety of occasions. The author will briefly consider some of these observations in this section and point out their relevance to the approach taken in this article.

1.3.2 Concerning the semiotics of programming languages, perhaps Gorn [5, 6], more than anyone else, has argued consistently and vigorously that a complete specification of a programming language must, by definition, include a specification of a processor—idealized, if you will—for that language. It is impossible to separate a language from its interpreting machine. Similar views regarding programming languages have been expressed by Samelson [23], Burks [2], Dijkstra [4], Woodger [26], and others.

The approach adopted in this article is completely in consonance with all these views. Actually, one contribution of the present work may be thought of as the specification of an explicit structure to the processor that underlies the definition of a programming language. This structure is specified in a uniform manner for all programming languages, including computer languages as special cases. Thus, one is able to talk about problem specifications in two different programming languages in terms of a common model for processors. This, then, allows one to introduce the notions "equivalence between computations," "translation of a computation given in one language to an equivalent computation in a second language," etc., in a pragmatically significant way.

1.3.3 The standard form for the specification of programming languages introduced in this paper has similarities to the models introduced by McCarthy [*14, 15*] and Landin [*11, 12*]. They are all based on the use of a certain set of primitive functions and predicates as atoms and recursive schemes for constructing and using other functions and predicates in terms of these. McCarthy has also introduced the concept of a flow chart in a way analogous to ours, although this construct does not play any significant role in his formalism. His description of a computation process in terms of the succession of values assumed by a state vector is very similar to our description in terms of the assigned set.

These similarities in detail notwithstanding, the global aspects of McCarthy's metatheory and that presented here are completely different. The principal reason for this is that his preoccupations are still essentially recursive-function-theoretic (see in this connection, the review of McCarthy's original paper by Nerode [*20*]). And for reasons outlined earlier, his formalism suffers from the same kinds of inadequacies as the Turing machine formalism. Pragmatically important problems such as the design of programming languages appropriate for given problem areas, design of computer systems well matched to given programming languages, and defining efficient structures for translators are capable of being adequately handled only within a model that assigns similar structures to programming languages and computer languages both globally and locally.

1.3.4 The particular definition of a flow chart as a labeled, directed, graph given here, although arrived at independently, seems to have been, except for minor differences, originally introduced by Kaluznin [*7*]. His principal aim was to attempt a classification of recursive functions on the basis of the complexity of their defining graphs. In a subsequent paper on *graphschemata*, Peter has proved the essential hopelessness of such attempts [*21*].

1.4 An Outline of the Structure of the Article

1.4.1 The approach adopted here may be briefly summarized as follows. We first introduce a certain standard form for the specification of programming languages. A programming language L is specified by first defining a set of primitives consisting of a set of names, a set of basic functions, a set of basic predicates, a set of selection operators, and a set of attributes. Next, a class of general flow charts is defined over these primitives. This is the class of sentences of L. Finally, a computation process is defined over sets of general flow charts.

The computation process specified in a programming language L defines a uniform procedure for effecting particular computations in L. This procedure is finitely describable and, hence, is equivalent to a machine with a finite control which, with possibly unbounded memory, realizes these computations acting on appropriate inputs.

By restricting our consideration to such machines which, however, have only a finite memory, we arrive at the notion of a computer[5] which realizes specific computations described in a computer language.

Given a programming language L and a computer language C, one can now introduce the concept of equivalence—equivalence in a certain, well-defined finite sense—between a computation in L and a computation in C. A translator $E(L, C)$, then, is a finite device which translates the input specifications for computations in L to inputs for the computer C to realize equivalent computations.

1.4.2 In this article, we study in some detail two classes of programming languages referred to, respectively, as simple computational or programming languages and hierarchical computational or programming languages. It will turn out later that the former are precisely the analogs—in the sense of finite equivalence discussed above—of the classical von Neumann type of computers. In contrast to these, hierarchical computational languages, like ALGOL, for example, require special software control features before computations defined in them could be realized on a von Neumann type of computer.

Section 2 is devoted to a consideration of simple programming languages and simple computer languages. A simple computational process is defined over single flow charts in L, a simple programming language. A simple computer is one that is capable of realizing simple computational processes. The notion of a program for such a computer C, that is (finitely) equivalent to a given flow chart in L, can now be precisely defined, and, hence, the notion of a translator $E(L, C)$ that translates flow charts in L to equivalent programs in C. Section 2 concludes with a description of a structure for such a translator.

---

[5]The term *computer* here refers to the total system which could consist partly of hardware and partly of software. We shall, in this article, denote by the same symbol, a computer and a computer language. Completely specifying a computer system is equivalent to completely specifying a computer language. See Section 2.4 for further comments.

In Section 3, a hierarchical computation process is introduced as a process defined over sets of flow charts of a hierarchical programming language satisfying certain completeness conditions. The translation problem as applied to hierarchical computations and simple computers is then formulated and we make some general remarks concerning the construction of such translators.

Section 4 is of a more general nature. The relevance to other linguistics issues, of our approach to language design, e.g., to the study of natural languages, is discussed there. The ALGOL report is critically analyzed from the viewpoint of the metatheory described in this article. It is further shown that current issues concerning the syntax and semantics of programming languages, and the relationship between the two, are more coherently formulated and studied within the specification schema for computational languages outlined in this section. The section concludes with a discussion of the main issues involved in language design and system design.

The main ideas of the article and the approach to programming language design exemplified herein are summarized in Section 5.

2. Simple Computation Processes

2.1 Introduction

Simple computation processes are (semantic) computations defined over the sentences of simple programming languages. A simple computer is a finite state device that realizes (in a certain finite sense, to be made precise later) such simple computations. The input language of a simple computer—that is, the language in which the intended computations are specified—is a simple computer language.

In this section, all the above notions are formally defined and the translation problem for simple computations is precisely formulated. This would then enable us to specify a structure for such translators.

The two main theorems of the section state that all functions definable by sentences of a simple programming language are partial recursive. The converse is also true. There exists a simple programming language such that all number theoretic partial recursive functions are definable by sentences of this language.

2.2 Simple Programming Languages: Computation on Basic Flow Charts

2.2.1 The specification of a simple programming language consists in specifying three components, viz.,

(i) a set of primitives comprising a set of names, a set of basic functions, a set of basic predicates, a set of selection operators, and a set of attributes;
(ii) a set of general flow charts; and
(iii) a computation process defined over single general flow charts.

The set of general flow charts is the set of sentences of the language. A general flow chart, however, is defined in terms of a special class of flow charts called the basic flow charts. The computation process is actually defined over basic flow charts. Since, by definition, general flow charts are reducible (by substitution methods defined precisely later on) to basic flow charts, the computation process is extended to general flow charts in an obvious manner.

In this section we define the primitives, the basic flow charts, and the computation over basic flow charts. Consideration of general flow charts and the extension of the computation process to them will be taken up in Section 2.3.

2.2.2 Let L be a simple programming language. The primitives of L are the following five sets satisfying the conditions stated below:

(1) a denumerably infinite set V of names;
(2) a finite set $F = \{F_0, F_1, \ldots, F_n\}$ of basic functions;
(3) a finite set $P = \{P_1, P_2, \ldots, P_m\}$ of basic predicates;
(4) a finite set $S = \{S_1, S_2, \ldots, S_p\}$ of selection operators; and
(5) a finite set $A = \{A_1, A_2, \ldots, A_q\}$ of attributes.

The conditions to be satisfied by the primitives are of two kinds which may be roughly termed *syntactic* and *semantic*. The syntactic conditions are the following:

(1) The elements of V are constructed from a finite alphabet by a given set of generation rules.

(2) Each basic function has the form $F_i(X_i; Y_i)$, where F_i is the name of the function and

$$X_i = \{X_i(1), X_i(2), \ldots, X_i(a_i)\},$$
$$Y_i = \{Y_i(1), Y_i(2), \ldots, Y_i(b_i)\},$$

are the input and output argument sets, respectively, of F_i.

(3) Each basic predicate has the form $P_i(Z_i)$ where P_i is the name of the predicate and $Z_i = \{Z_i(1), Z_i(2), \ldots, Z_i(c_i)\}$ is the input argument set of Z_i.

(4) Each selection operator has the form $S_i(W_i; B)$, where S_i is the name of the selection operator, and $W_i = \{W_i(1), W_i(2), \ldots, W_i(d_i)\}$

is called the selection parameter set of S_i and B is a set referred to as the structured operand of S_i.

(5) With each member of the input/output argument sets of $\{F_i\}$ and $\{P_i\}$ is associated a specific set of attributes from A called the set of admissible attributes for that argument of that basic function or basic predicate.

(6) With each member of the selection parameter sets of $\{S_i\}$ and with each structured operand is associated a specific set of attributes from A, called the set of admissible attributes for that selection parameter or structured operand of that selection operator.

(7) Each attribute A_i of the set A has associated with it a finite set of attribute values as its range.

(8) Here, F_0 is a special function called the null function whose input and output argument sets are both empty.

Before enumerating the semantic conditions we have to introduce methods for converting the function, predicate, and selection operator forms described above into labels. This we do as follows.

In a basic function form $F_i(X_i(1), \ldots, X_i(a_i); Y_i(1), \ldots, Y_i(b_i))$ replace each of the arguments by a specific name from V. Now, each of these names has a set of admissible attributes associated with it, viz., the admissible set associated with the argument that the name has replaced. By an attribute assignment to such a name we shall mean the assignment of a particular value (from its range) to each of its admissible attributes.

Let us refer to such a name with a specific attribute assignment as a *bound name*.

The first semantic condition is:

(1) There exists a well-defined value space for each bound name.

We shall use the generic term *constant* to denote a fixed value from the value space of some bound name.

A designation label is obtained from a selection operator form by replacing each of its selection parameters by a bound name or constant, and its structured operand by a bound name.

A basic function label (basic predicate label) is obtained from a basic function form (basic predicate form) by replacing each of its input arguments (input arguments) by a bound name, or a designation label, or a constant,[6] and each of its output arguments by a bound name or a designation label.

The other semantic conditions may now be stated as follows:

---

[6]It is implied, of course, here as well as in the case of designation labels, that the constant belongs to the value space of a bound name that it replaces.

(2) For every assignment of a value from the respective value spaces to each of the bound names in the selection parameter set of a designation label, there results the selection of a bound name belonging to the value space of the bound name identifying the structured operand.

We shall refer to this as the evaluation of the designation label with the given assignment of selection parameter values.

(For terminological convenience, let us refer to a bound name selected by a designation label according to the above schema as an indirect bound name. All other bound names will be called direct bound names.)

(3) For every assignment of a value from the respective value spaces to each of the bound names in the input set of a basic function label, and to the bound names in the designation labels, if any, in its output set, there results an assignment of a value from the respective value spaces to each of the direct and indirect bound names in the output set of the label.

We shall refer to this as the evaluation of the basic function label with the given assignment of input values.

(4) For every assignment of a value from the respective value spaces to each of the bound names in a basic predicate label, there results a truth value, true or false.

We shall refer to this as the evaluation of the basic predicate label with the given assignment of input values.

Note that in the implementation of any specific programming language, explicit notational conventions have to be adopted to make clear, unambiguously, in each occurrence of a bound name in a label, its name as well as its particular attribute assignment. For the purpose of the metatheory that we are developing now, it turns out to be unnecessary to go into these details. Hence, we shall not consider them any more in this article. It is important to bear in mind, however, that knowledge of a bound name implies knowledge of its name as well as its attribute assignment. The importance of this will become clear when we discuss the structures of translators later on.

2.2.3 A basic flow chart $g(U_0, U_1; L)$ defined over the primitives (V, F, P, S, A) of a simple programming language L is a finite, directed, connected, labeled graph satisfying the following conditions:

(1) There are at most two branches leaving every vertex. If a vertex has no outgoing branch, it is called a terminal vertex. If it has exactly two outgoing branches, it is called a decision vertex.

(2) Every branch has a basic function label associated with it.

(3) Every decision vertex has a basic predicate label associated with it. Of its two outgoing branches, one has the Boolean label "1" (corresponding to the truth value, true) assigned to it, and the other, the Boolean label "0" (corresponding to the truth value, false.)

(4) A terminal vertex may or may not be labeled. If it is labeled, it has a basic predicate label.

(5) There is a unique vertex, designated as the initial vertex, which does not have any incoming branches.

(6) Let $V(g)$ denote the set of bound names occurring in all the branch and vertex labels of g. There are two sets $U_0 \subseteq V(g)$ and $U_1 \subseteq V(g)$ called, respectively, the input and output sets of g. Either or both of these sets may be empty.

2.2.4 Given a basic flow chart $g(U_0, U_1; L)$ and a set of bound names $U \subseteq V(g)$, by an assignment to U, we shall mean an assignment of a value from its respective value space to each of the elements of U.

We now wish to define a simple computation over a basic flow chart g, as a certain well-defined process which generates a sequence of assignments to sets $U \subseteq V(g)$. We shall use the following terminology in this context. At any stage in the computation process, by the assigned set we shall mean the set $U \subseteq V(g)$ whose elements have been assigned values at least once up to that stage. By the current value of the assigned set U, we shall mean the last assigned value of each element in U at that stage.

With these preliminaries, we can now define a simple computation over a basic flow chart $g(U_0, U_1; L)$, with a given initial assignment to U_0, as the following process:

(1) Begin with the initial vertex of g and the initial assigned set U_0.
(2) Having arrived at a vertex of g with some assigned set $U \subseteq V(g)$,
   (a) If the vertex is terminal and unlabeled, stop. If the vertex is terminal and labeled, evaluate the label and then stop.
   (b) If the vertex has exactly one outgoing branch, select this branch and (i) evaluate the basic function label associated with the selected branch using the current values of the assigned set U. This results in an assigned set U' where $U \subseteq U' \subseteq V(g)$. Go to (2) with the vertex on which this branch terminates and the assigned set U'.
   (c) If the vertex is a decision vertex, evaluate the basic predicate label associated with it using the current values of the assigned set U. This results in a truth value, true or false. Select the outgoing branch which has the Boolean label corresponding to this truth value and go to (b(i)).

2.2.5 A simple computation over a basic flow chart for a given initial assignment is well defined if, and only if, the following conditions are satisfied:

(1) Whenever a basic function label or a basic predicate label is to be evaluated, all the bound names in its input set and the bound names in the designation labels, if any, in its output set belong to the assigned set at that stage.

(2) The indirect bound names selected by the designation labels using the current values of the assigned set satisfy the obvious compatibility conditions as regards their attribute assignments.

(3) The computation terminates.

(4) The assigned set at termination includes the output set of the basic flow chart.

It follows from well-known results of recursive function theory that there exists no uniform procedure to determine whether a simple computation over a given basic flow chart and an initial assignment is well defined or not.

2.2.6 Consider now the special class of basic flow charts with terminal vertices either all labeled or all unlabeled. It is clear that by incorporating additional branches (if necessary) in the graphs and labeling each such added branch with the null function label F_0 the first set of flow charts can be brought to a standard form having a single unlabeled terminal vertex. The second set, similarly, can be brought to a standard form having two unlabeled terminal vertices. All incoming branches into one of these would have the Boolean label 1 (in addition to function label F_0), and all incoming branches into the other would have the Boolean label 0 (in addition to the function label F_0). We shall refer to the first terminal vertex as the 1-output vertex and to the second as the 0-output vertex, of the flow chart.

Let $g(U_0, U_1; L)$ be a basic flow chart in standard form with a single terminal vertex. Whenever a computation over g is well defined, we obtain a correspondence between an assignment to U_0 and an assignment to U_1. Denote this partial function by $f_g(U_0, U_1)$. We shall refer to f_g as the function represented (or, equivalently, specified) by the flow chart g.

Analogously, in case the basic flow chart is in standard form with two terminal vertices, it represents a partial predicate $p_g(U_0)$.

We shall refer to such functions and predicates as computable[7] functions and computable predicates in L.

---

[7]Strictly speaking, they are partial computable in L. Since this should be clear from the context, we shall omit the locution and simply refer to them as computable henceforth.

2.3 Simple Programming Languages: Computations on General Flow Charts

2.3.1 So far, we have restricted ourselves to basic flow charts in a simple programming language L. We now wish to extend the class of flow charts in L by allowing functions and predicates other than those basic in L to occur as labels in them. But we wish to do this in a certain constructive manner so that computations over these general flow charts can still be effectively defined in terms of functions and predicates basic in L.

Our procedure will be to define first the class of formal functions and formal predicates in L by means of a certain explicit construction procedure starting from the class of basic flow charts in standard form as explained in Section 2.2.6. We shall then introduce a reduction procedure based on substitution of one flow chart in another. It would follow from our construction procedure that formal functions and formal predicates can be reduced, in a finite number of steps, to basic flow charts in the standard form for functions and predicates, respectively. Thus, whenever computations based on these reduced flow charts are well defined, these flow charts represent functions and predicates computable in L in the sense explained in Section 2.2.6.

The class of general flow charts in L is now defined making use of formal functions and formal predicates in a manner exactly analogous to the class of basic flow charts which are defined making use of basic functions and basic predicates. A general flow chart, according to the above definition, is reducible again to a basic flow chart by repeated substitution and the resulting flow chart is unique up to the bound names occurring in it. Thus, the extension of a simple computation process to general flow charts becomes quite straightforward. It is defined as the computation over the basic flow chart to which the general flow chart can be reduced.

In the remainder of this Section we shall develop the details of this procedure.

2.3.2 Let L be a simple programming language with primitives $\{V, F, P, S, A\}$. Without loss in generality, let us assume that the names of the basic functions, predicates, and selection operators all belong to V.

By the phrase "a permissible attribute assignment in L" let us refer to an attribute assignment that is permissible for some element of the argument set (input, output, selection parameter, or structured operand) of a basic function, or a basic predicate, or a selection operator in L.

By a formal bound name in L, we shall mean a name in V with a permissible attribute assignment in L. Note that by our first semantic

PROGRAMMING LANGUAGES AND COMPUTERS: A UNIFIED METATHEORY

condition every formal bound name in L has a well-defined value space associated with it. Hence, we can also carry over the notion of constants to apply to these formal bound names and speak about a "constant in L" meaning a fixed value from the value space of some formal bound name in L.

Making use of formal bound names, we can now define the concept of formal labels in L as follows:

$d(W_1, \ldots, W_n; B)$ is a formal designation label in L provided $n \geq 1$, $\{W_i\}$ are formal bound names or constants in L, B is a formal bound name in L, and d is a name in V. The name of this formal designation label is called d.

$f(X_1, \ldots, X_k; Y_1, \ldots, Y_j)$ is a formal function label in L provided $k, j \geq 1$, $\{X_i\}$ are formal bound names, formal designation labels, or constants in L, $\{Y_i\}$ are formal bound names or formal designation labels in L, and f is a name in V. The name of this formal function label is called f.

$p(Z_1, \ldots, Z_m)$ is a formal predicate label in L provided $m \geq 1$, $\{Z_i\}$ are formal bound names, formal designation labels, or constants in L, and p is a name in V. The name of this formal predicate label is called p.

Let F^* denote the set of all formal function labels in L, and P^* the set of all formal predicate labels in L. It is clear that the set of basic function labels in L and the set of basic predicate labels in L are contained in the set F^* and P^*, respectively. We now define the notion of a formal flow chart in L as follows.

A formal flow chart in L is a finite, directed, connected, labeled, graph satisfying all the conditions given in Section 2.2.3 for basic flow charts except that now each branch label is in F^* and each vertex label in P^*.

We can now talk about formal flow charts being in standard form whenever their graphs, with terminal vertices either all labeled or all unlabeled, have been converted to graphs with a single unlabeled terminal vertex, or two unlabeled terminal vertices with the use of additional branches labeled with F_0 in the manner described in Section 2.2.6. We shall refer to formal flow charts as function graphs in case they are in standard form with a single unlabeled terminal vertex, and as predicate graphs, if they are in standard form with two unlabeled terminal vertices (identified as the 1-output vertex and 0-output vertex, respectively, as described earlier).

We shall identify particular function graphs and predicate graphs by means of distinct names belonging to V.

We are now in a position to define formal functions and formal predicates in L which, as described in Section 2.3.1, would then allow us to extend the simple computation process to flow charts other than basic flow charts in L.

Formal functions (formal predicates) in L are defined inductively as follows:

(1) A function graph (predicate graph) in L is a formal function (formal predicate) in L provided the formal function and formal predicate labels that occur as branch and vertex labels, respectively, in it are all basic function and basic predicate labels in L, respectively.

(2) A function graph (predicate graph) in L is a formal function (formal predicate) in L provided
   (i) the names of formal function and formal predicate labels that occur as branch and vertex labels, respectively, in it are those of formal functions and formal predicates, respectively, already defined in L, and
   (ii) for each such branch and vertex label, an explicit 1 : 1 correspondence is given between the set of bound names and constants occurring in it and the set of bound names occurring in the input-output set of the function graph and predicate graph, respectively, identified by the name of that label.

(3) Nothing is a formal function (formal predicate) in L unless its being so follows from (1) and (2) above.

2.3.3 Given a formal function f in L, let f_1 be the name of some branch label occurring in it that is not a basic function label. Then there is a straightforward procedure for replacing that branch in f by the function graph identified by f_1. We shall refer to this as the replacement of the branch label f_1. The procedure is as follows:

(1) In the function graph identified by f_1, replace the bound names that occur in its input-output set by the bound names and the constants that occur in the branch label f_1 using the explicit correspondence given (see definition in Section 2.3.2). This name or constant substitution is to be done systematically, wherever the original names appear in the branch and vertex labels of the function graph f_1.

(2) Having done this, consider the set of local names of the function graph f_1, i.e., the set of bound names occurring in the labels of the graph other than those mentioned in its input-output set. Change each of these names that also occur in the function graph f to new names from V to avoid such clash of names. Again, this name substitution[8] is to be done systematically wherever it occurs in f_1.

[8]Notice that only the name part of the bound name is substituted for; the attribute assignment remains unaltered. One can give a mechanical procedure for replacement of these names one by one systematically. We do not go into the details here since it should be fairly obvious how this could be done. An analogous name-changing procedure is introduced in Section 3.2.6, in connection with hierarchical computations. It is easily seen that the technique described there would apply here also with suitable modifications.

(3) The function graph f_1 so modified is substituted for the branch labeled by f_1 in the formal function f as shown in Fig. 1.

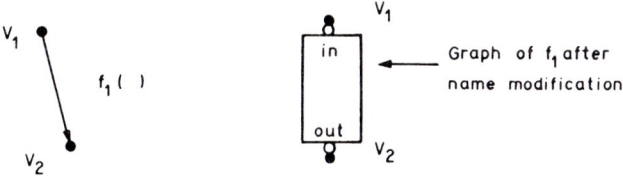

FIG. 1. Replacement of the branch label $f_1(\ )$ by the function graph identified by f_1.

Analogously, one can define the replacement of a vertex label p_1 in f, that is not a basic predicate label, by the predicate graph identified by p_1. The procedure for modification of names is identical. The modified graph is substituted for the vertex labeled by p_1 in f as shown in Fig. 2.

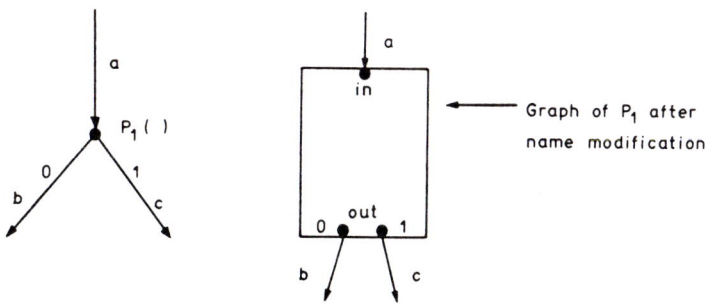

FIG. 2. Replacement of the vertex label $p_1(\ )$ by the predicate graph identified by p_1.

Clearly, all the above apply equally well to replacement of branch labels and vertex labels in a formal predicate p in L.

Replacement of a branch label or a vertex label in a formal function (formal predicate) leaves it a formal function (formal predicate) with the same input-output set as before. This fact is readily verified.

Thus, given a formal function f (formal predicate p) in L, we can replace the branch and vertex labels occurring in it which are not basic function and predicate labels, respectively, one by one. Clearly, the structure of the resulting graph is independent of the order in which this replacement is carried out. It is also readily verified by induction that this procedure can be iterated and, in a finite number of steps, the original formal function f (formal predicate p) reduced to a basic flow chart in L in the standard form with one unlabeled terminal vertex (two unlabeled terminal vertices). The reduced basic flow chart is unique up to the name part of the local bound names occurring in it. Its input-output set (input set) is identical to that of the original formal function f (formal predicate p). Hence, whenever a simple computation over this basic flow chart is well defined, the formal function f (formal predicate p) represents a computable function f (computable predicate p) in L.

2.3.4 A general flow chart in L is a formal flow chart in L, the names of whose branch and vertex labels are all names of formal functions and formal predicates in L, respectively, with an explicit 1:1 correspondence given between the set of bound names and constants occurring in the labels and the set of bound names occurring in the input-output set of the function graph and predicate graph, respectively, identified by the names of the labels.

From the discussion in Section 2.3.3, it follows that a general flow chart in L can be reduced, in a finite number of steps, to a basic flow chart in L with the same input-output set, and the reduced graph is unique up to the name part of the local bound names occurring in it. A simple computation on a general flow chart is now defined as being equal to the simple computation on the basic flow chart to which it can be reduced.

The set of general flow charts in L is the set of sentences in L. The connection between general flow charts in L, and formal functions and formal predicates in L, should be clear. A formal function in L is a general flow chart in L that is in standard form with a single unlabeled terminal vertex. Similarly, a formal predicate in L is a general flow chart in L that is in standard form with two unlabeled terminal vertices (identified as the 1-output vertex and 0-output vertex, as described earlier in Section 2.2.6).

Concerning these general flow charts the following two main theorems can be proved. We shall merely state the theorems here without proof. The proofs are quite straightforward although somewhat tedious. For details, see the work by Peter [21] referred to earlier in this article, and also a report by Basu [1a], where similar theorems (with minor differences in the definition of a flow chart) are proved.

Theorem 1: Given a simple programming language L with primitives $\{V, F, P, S, A\}$, functions and predicates computable in L are partial recursive with $\{F\}$, $\{P\}$, and $\{S\}$ as the initial functions.

Theorem 2: There exists a simple programming language L with primitives $\{V, F, P, S, A\}$, such that all number-theoretic partial recursive functions are computable in L.

2.4 Simple Computer Languages and Programs

2.4.1 In Sections 2.2 and 2.3, we have considered in some detail a standard model for simple programming languages. In terms of the primitives of such a language, we defined the notion of basic flow charts and a simple computation process over basic flow charts. As outlined in Section 1, our primary objective is threefold: (1) to introduce a standard model for programming languages and argue the adequacy of the model for the design of languages well matched to a diversity of problem areas, (2) to introduce a standard model for computer languages, and (3) to consider the translation problem between programming languages and computer languages in a uniform manner.

The two main theorems of the last section prove the adequacy of our programming language model from a purely computation-theoretic point of view. Arguments concerning the adequacy of the model for the design of problem-oriented languages will be taken up in Section 4, where the entire problem is considered from a more general standpoint. In this section, our concern will be to develop a standard model for computer languages. Keeping in mind the last aspect of our main objective, we shall attempt to develop a model for computer languages that is structurally as similar as possible to that developed earlier for programming languages.

Except for two main differences—concerned with the finiteness and homogeneity of attributes of the value spaces (see Section 2.5.1)—it will be seen from the development below that the two models are almost identical. Since we have already spent considerable time in discussing in detail the model for programming languages, we shall restrict ourselves to a description here of only those aspects where the second model differs from the first one.

2.4.2 Specification of a simple computer language C consists in specifying

(1) a set of primitives $\{R, D, I, J\}$ satisfying certain conditions to be stated presently, where R is a finite set of registers, D is a finite set of address operators, I is a finite set of instruction types, and J is a finite set of jump types;
(2) a set of programs p in C over these primitives; and
(3) a simple computation process over these programs.

The details of these specifications will now be considered in the order enumerated above.

The primitives of C satisfy the following conditions[9]:

(1) $R = \{R_1, R_2, \ldots, R_q\}$ is a finite set of registers. Each register R_i has a finite set of states $\{R_i(1), \ldots, R_i(r_i)\}$ associated with it, which we shall refer to as the range of R_i.

(2) $D = \{D_1, \ldots, D_t\}$ is a finite set of address operators. Each D_i has the form:

$$D_i(W_i(1), \ldots, W_i(d_i); B),$$

where $W_i(k)$ is the kth input variable of D_i and takes on values from a given fixed range $S(D_i; k) \subseteq R$; B, the output variable of D_i, is a given fixed set of registers $S(D_i, \text{out}) \subseteq R$.

Each such address operator form can be converted into an address label by assigning a fixed value from its range to each of its input variables, i.e., by replacing each input variable by the name of a specific register from its admissible range. Now, for every assignment of states from their respective ranges to the input arguments, the address label selects a register from the fixed output set of registers associated with that address operator, i.e., the label computes the *name* of a register belonging to a certain, given, fixed set of registers.[10]

Let us, for terminological convenience, refer to a register so selected by an address label as an indirectly named register. All other registers will be called directly named.

(3) $I = \{I_0, I_1, \ldots, I_m\}$ is a finite set of instruction types. Each I_j has the form:

$$I_j(x_j(1), \ldots, x_j(a_j); y_j(1), \ldots, y_j(b_j)),$$

where,

$$x_j(k) \in S_0(j; k) \subseteq R, \quad 1 \leq k \leq a_j$$

$$y_j(k) \in S_1(j; k) \subseteq R, \quad 1 \leq k \leq b_j \ ;$$

$S_0(j; k)$ is called the range of the kth input variable of I_j, and $S_1(j; k)$ is called the range of the kth output variable of I_j.

An instruction type can be converted into an instruction by replacing each of its input and output variables by either a register name belonging to the range of that variable or by an address label such that the output set of the label is included in the range of that variable.

[9]In describing the conditions to be satisfied by the primitives, we shall not attempt to deal separately with syntax and semantics as we did in the case of programming languages. This distinction should be clear from our statements below; in any case, as we shall see in Section 4, this distinction is somewhat arbitrary.

[10]Note that in the case of specific address operators this computation might depend on the *names* of certain of the input registers and not on their states. See Section 2.4.3 for some examples.

Now for every assignment of states, from its respective range, to each register directly named in the input set of an instruction, and to each register named in the input set of each address label occurring in the instruction, the instruction assigns a specific state, from its respective range, to each of the directly and indirectly named register in its output set.

(4) I_0 is a special instruction type whose input and output sets are both empty.

(5) $J = \{J_1, \ldots, J_n\}$ is a finite set of jump types. Each J_i has the form:

$$J_i(Z_i(1), \ldots, Z_i(c_i)),$$

where,

$$Z_i(k) \in S_2(i; k) \subseteq R, \qquad 1 \leq k \leq c_i;$$

$S_2(i; k)$ is called the range of the kth input variable of J_i. A jump type can be converted into a jump condition by replacing each of its input variable by either a register name belonging to the range of that variable, or by an address label such that the output set of the label is included in the range of that variable.

Now, for every assignment of states, from its respective range, to each register directly named in the input set of the jump condition, and to each register named in the input set of each of the address labels occurring in the jump condition, the jump condition assumes one of the truth values, true or false.

2.4.3 It should be clear that the primitives of a simple computer language as defined above are completely general and do not presuppose in any way particular physical realizations of the elements, registers, etc., which enter into the definition. The definition, nevertheless, takes into account the structure of computer languages as they are known at present. Perhaps it is worthwhile to consider a few examples to illustrate this.

The set R of registers includes arithmetic and index registers, main and temporary storage locations, locations for individual characters if operations on characters are available, control indicators like overflow indicators, etc.

Writing M to represent the class of main memory locations, A the class of accumulators, and Q the class of index registers, we shall consider a few examples.

A single address modification scheme could correspond to an address operator of the form

$$D_1(W_1, W_2; B)$$

where $W_1 \in M$, $W_2 \in Q$, $B \subseteq M$. Thus, the address label $D_1(17, 8; M)$, would refer to the memory location obtained by modifying the memory location name (i.e., address) 17 by the contents of the index register named 8.

An address modification scheme $D_2(W_1, W_2; B)$, where $W_1 \in A$, $W_2 \in Q$, $B \subseteq M$ could, for example, give rise to an address label $D_2(7, 8; M)$ meaning: the memory location obtained by modifying the contents of the accumulator named 7 by the contents of the index register named 8, etc.

A typical single address instruction would be

$$\text{CLEAR ADD } (D_1(17, 8; M); 3), \quad \text{with} \quad 3 \in A,$$

meaning: Clear add the contents of $D_1(17, 8; M)$ to the accumulator named 3. Here, $D_1(17, 8; M)$ identifies the memory location described earlier.

The "do-nothing" instruction is referred to by I_0.

A typical jump condition would be $OVJ(7)$ with $7 \in A$, meaning: jump on overflow in the accumulator named 7.

The reason for the jump condition having a single argument will become clear when we discuss the structure of a program in Section 2.4.4.

It is important to bear in mind that, in our model, the program, at execution time, stays external to the "computer" that is actually involved in the computation. The program is in the form of a directed, connected, labeled graph, and the control unit of the computer reads the labels as directed by the computation process and carries out the computation steps. The program itself does not change during execution. We could think of the program as being on a tape, for example, after linearization. It could also remain in a reserved part of the main memory. This is the case in actual present-day computers. But it must be emphasized that this fact is irrelevant to the computation process. The process itself only refers to the labeled graph. How this graph is represented either inside or outside the computer at execution time is based on aspects of computer design not directly connected with computer language design and usage.

2.4.4 Given a computer language C with primitives $\{R, D, I, J\}$, a program p in C is a finite, connected, directed, labeled graph defined in a manner exactly analogous to that of a basic flow chart g in a simple programming language L (see Section 2.2.3).

The branch labels are instructions in C and the vertex labels are jump conditions in C. Let the set of all registers directly named in the labels of p be $R(p)$. Two sets W_0, W_1, contained in $R(p)$ are specified as the input and output sets, respectively, of p. Either or both of these sets may be empty.

An assignment to a set of registers $R_1 \subseteq R$ is an assignment of a particular state, from its range, to each one of the registers included in R_1. The notions "assigned set," "the current value of the assigned set" can now be defined in a manner exactly analogous to the definitions in the case of simple programming languages (see Section 2.2.4 for details).

A simple computation over a program $p(W_0, W_1; C)$ and an assignment to W_0, called the initial assignment to p, is a process which, again, is defined exactly analogously to a simple computation process over a basic flow chart $g(U_0, U_1; L)$ (see Section 2.2.4 for details).

Again in a manner exactly analogous to that given in Section 2.2.5 for basic flow charts, one can specify when a computation over a program $p(W_0, W_1; C)$ is well defined.

Henceforth, we shall refer to the finite state device which carries out computations over programs $p(W_0, W_1; C)$, in a simple computer language C, as a simple computer and denote it also by the same symbol C. This should cause no confusion. It should be evident from the definitions in this section, that a simple computer is an almost exact analog of the classical von Neumann type of computer.

2.5 The Translation Problem

2.5.1 As pointed out in the beginning of the last section, the model that has been introduced for computer languages differs from that introduced earlier for programming languages only in two respects. In a computer language, there are only finitely many names—or registers—which can assume only finitely many values—or states—and these states are not further distinguished in terms of any other attributes. Except for these differences, a computer language is in fact a programming language.[11] As is well known, with a suitable set of instruction and jump types, a computer language C is also a universal programming language. The exact meaning of this is as follows: Given any simple programming language L and a basic flow chart g in L, then for each computation based on g one can realize an equivalent computation based on a program p in C. The two computations are equivalent in a certain finite sense to be made precise presently. It is also well known that if one

---

[11]This may sound like a truism but its implications are far reaching. For example, it would imply that any model for programming languages, by fixing certain of its parameters or features, should be reducible in a natural way to a model for computer languages. There is no indication, so far as the author knows, of this realization in any published literature.

allows the computer to be potentially infinite, then the two computations become strictly equivalent.

From the point of view of utilization of a given computer, or of the design of a computer for a set of programming languages, it is the study of this translation problem—that is, going from a g in L to an equivalent p in C—that is of maximum interest. In the rest of this section, we shall be concerned with this problem.

To this end, we shall first define the notion of a program that is equivalent to a basic flow chart and, under certain assumptions, show how to construct such a program given a basic flow chart. In the next section, we shall consider the structure of a translator that converts general flow charts in a given programming language into equivalent programs in a given computer language.

2.5.2 The equivalence—what was termed above as finite equivalence—between a basic flow chart in L and a program in C is based on the concept of memory allocation. We shall consider this first.

Consider a simple programming language L with primitives $\{V, F, P, S, A\}$ and a basic flow chart g in L. Let the set of bound names and constants occurring in g be $V(g)$. Let C be a simple computer language with primitives $\{R, D, I, J\}$.

A memory allocation function M, $M = M(g, C)$, defines a mapping of $V(g)$ into R. This mapping is, in general, a one-to-many mapping as described below:

Let $M(v) = A$, where $v \in V(g)$, $A \subseteq R$. And let

$$A = \{R_A(1), \ldots, R_A(r_a)\}$$

where the ordering of the set of registers is given and fixed as part of the memory allocation mapping.

Denote by $T = R_A(1) \times R_A(2) \times, \ldots, \times R_A(r_A)$ the Cartesian product of the set of states of the $R_A(i)$.

The mapping M, then, maps on each element $t \in T$ a distinct value $v(k)$ of the bound name v. Considering some fixed ordering, say, the lexicographic one, of the elements t of T, we shall say that t_k represents the kth value $v(k)$ of v. The set $\{v(1), \ldots, v(s)\}$, where s is the power of the set T, is the set of values of v represented in C under the memory allocation $M(v) = A \subseteq R$.

If v is a constant, then, of course, it is mapped on to some fixed element t_1 of T.

2.5.3 For a given basic flow chart g in L and a computer language C, we shall now define what we mean by programs in C that correspond to the basic function and predicate labels that occur in g. We shall refer to these as program segments. Next, assuming the existence of these program segments, we shall give a systematic procedure for connecting them together to form a program $p(g)$ that corresponds to g.

Let the primitives of L and C be as given in Section 2.5.2. Assume that some memory allocation function M is given and kept fixed in the rest of the discussion that follows.

Let $F_i(U_0(i), U_1(i))$; $F_i \in F$; $U_0(i), U_1(i) \subseteq V(g)$ be some branch label occurring in g. We shall say that a program p in C corresponds to this branch label in g under the memory allocation function M provided the following hold:

(1) p is in standard form with a single unlabeled terminal vertex.

(2) $p = p(M(U_0(i)), M(U_1(i)))$, i.e., $M(U_0(i))$ and $M(U_1(i))$ are the input and output sets, respectively, of p.

(3) When restricted to the values of the elements of $U_0(i)$ and $U_1(i)$ represented in C,

$$F_i(U_0(i), U_1(i)) = p(M(U_0(i)), M(U_1(i)))$$

under the correspondence defined by M.

In other words, the output assignments resulting from evaluating the branch label with given input assignments correspond, under M, to the output assignments resulting from computing the program p with corresponding (under M) input assignments. And this is to hold for all input assignments obtained with values of the elements of $U_0(i)$ represented in C under M.

(4) Consider the instructions and jump conditions that occur as labels in p. If R_k is any register included in the input or output set of any of these labels, and $R_k \in M(V(g))$, then $R_k \in M(U_0(i)) \cup M(U_1(i))$.

Analogously, we define for predicate labels. Let $P_i(U(i))$; $P_i \in P$, $U(i) \subseteq V(g)$ be some vertex label occurring in g. We shall say a program p in C corresponds to this vertex label under the memory allocation function M provided the following hold:

(1) p is in standard form with two unlabeled terminal vertices: a 1-output vertex and a 0-output vertex.

(2) $p = p(M(U(i)))$.

(3) When restricted to the values of the elements of $U(i)$ represented in C,

$$P_i(U(i)) = p(M(U(i)))$$

under the correspondence defined by M.

(4) Consider the instructions and jump conditions occurring as labels in p. If R_k is any register included in the input or output set of any of these labels, and if $R_k \in M(V(g))$, then $R_k \in M(U(i))$.

2.5.4 It should be evident that the program segments satisfying the conditions given above are precisely the analogs of formal functions and formal predicates suitably name-modified for replacing given branch labels and vertex labels, respectively, in a general flow chart as defined in Section 2.3.3.

Assume now that, given a basic flow chart $g(U_0, U_1)$ in L, the program segments that correspond to all its branch and vertex labels under some fixed memory allocation M are available. One can now define the replacement of the labels in g by their corresponding program segments exactly as done in Section 2.3.3. When all the labels in G have been replaced, it is easy to verify that the resulting directed, connected, labeled graph is the program $p(M(U_0), M(U_1))$ in C. This program is equivalent to the given flow chart in the following sense: When restricted to the set of values represented in C of the elements of U_0 and U_1,

$$g(U_0, U_1) = p(M(U_0), M(U_1))$$

under the correspondence defined by M, when considered as mappings between sets of assignments.

2.5.5 The procedure outlined above is a procedure for translation by substitution. The substitution scheme works in an analogous manner both while going from a general flow chart in L to its equivalent basic flow chart in L, and while going from a basic flow chart in L to its equivalent program in C. The underlying significance is this: The relationship between a general flow chart and its corresponding basic flow chart in L is similar to that between a basic flow chart in L and its corresponding program in C. The correspondence in the former case is direct. The correspondence in the latter case is indirect through the memory allocation function.

2.6 A Structure for Translators

2.6.1 In the last section, we gave a certain constructive procedure to go from a flow chart g, to its equivalent program $p(g; M)$, assuming the existence of a memory allocation function M and the various program segments that correspond under the mapping M to the branch and vertex labels in g. Clearly, for a given computer C and a flow chart g, there must exist constraints on admissible memory allocations such that the necessary program segments can be realized. In this section, we shall consider briefly the basic aspects of this translation problem.

2.6.2 A translator $E = E(L, C)$, for a simple programming language L and a simple computer C, is a finite device which, given any general flow chart g in L, translates it into an equivalent program $p(g; M)$ under some memory allocation M.

Discussions in Section 2.3 and 2.5 suggest a uniform structure for such a translator. The translator consists of two components: an analyzer E_A and an assembler E_S.

The input to E_A is the general flow chart g in L, to be translated, and a reduction set[12] for each one of the labels occurring in g. Its output is the reduced form of g as a basic flow chart in L. Denote this by g*.

The assembler E_S uses a dictionary $D(L, C)$. This dictionary must contain the following information:

(1) For the set of attributes in L, for each possible value space that could be associated with a bound name in L, the dictionary must specify admissible memory allocations for that bound name.

(2) For each selection operator in L, the dictionary must specify a program schema for C such that the following holds: Given a corresponding designation label in L, under any admissible memory allocation for the bound names and the constants occurring in the designation label, the program schema should be convertible into a (program, address label) pair such that the address label evaluated at the termination of the program selects a register that corresponds, under the given memory allocation, to the bound name selected by the designation label. And this should hold for any initial assignment to the designation label permissible under the memory allocation.

(3) For each basic function (basic predicate) in L, the dictionary must specify a program schema for C such that the following holds: Given a corresponding basic function label (basic predicate label) in L, under any admissible memory allocation of the bound names and constants occurring in the label, the program schema should be convertible into a program segment that corresponds to that basic function label (basic predicate label) under the memory allocation mapping chosen.

Using this dictionary D, the assembler can now convert the reduced flow chart $g*$ into its equivalent program $p(g*; M)$ after first making some admissible memory allocation M for all the bound names and constants occurring in $g*$.

2.6.3 The principal problem is to show that such a dictionary can be constructed given a simple programming language L and a simple

---

[12] A reduction set for a label is the complete set of formal functions and formal predicates in L using which, by appropriate name changing and repeated substitutions (as explained in Section 2.3), the label could be reduced to its corresponding basic flow chart in standard form. Clearly, these have to be specified as part of the input specification for the flow chart g.

computer C, and to show, furthermore, that it can be used in the manner described above. We shall not go into detail here since the actual construction of such a dictionary is intimately dependent on the details of the structures of L and C. At the level of the discussion here, we could only prove the sufficiency of such a dictionary for the translation problem. The proof of this should be quite evident.

It is perhaps worth pointing out that the particular method of using the dictionary for memory allocation and translation outlined above presupposes the availability of a sufficiently large primary memory in C relative to the size of the flow chart g^* to be translated. When this condition is not met, not only does constructing a memory allocation function become complex but also the computation process itself has to be partitioned into subprocesses and carried out with the help of a "supervisor." This corresponds to the so-called "overlay" schemes. This, then, is no longer a simple computation process and the model we have been studying so far is not capable of coping with this. Such computation processes, however, can be subsumed under the class of hierarchical computations which we shall study in the next section.

2.6.4 In concluding this section on simple computation processes, we shall make a few comments on the relevance of the translation procedure described to the procedures actually used in writing translators for real-life computers.

(1) Note that everything said so far applies, *mutatis mutandis*, if we consider the translation between two simple programming languages L and L_1. Thus, keeping one of the languages, say, L_1, and a computer C fixed, we can try to realize $E(L, C)$ for any L as follows:

$$E(L, C) = E(L, L_1) + E(L_1, C).$$

Recall that in going from a programming language L to a computer language C, two major operations have to be performed simultaneously. First, one must find an admissible memory allocation function, and next, using this one must construct the program segments. Where there is much discrepancy between the primitives of L and those of C, both of these operations are bound to be complicated.

In the two-stage translation procedure indicated above, one could attempt to get around some of this complication by the following ruse. The intermediate language L_1 could be set up so that its primitives overlap partly those of L and partly those of C. In the standard methods used, L_1 is the symbolic assembly language of the computer C. And it is designed such that in going from L to L_1, the memory allocation function is close to an identity mapping but the program segments in

L_1 are generated in detail. In going from L_1 to C, the memory allocation is done in detail while the program segments carry over with minimal alterations.

(2) The major problem concerning translators is the problem of constructing them. A translator has to be incorporated as a program in some computer and so has to be made available in the language of that computer.

Now, for a fixed programming language L, consider the task of constructing translators $E(L, C_i)$ for various computers C_i in their respective computer languages. It would be of considerable advantage if one could restrict oneself to writing these in some standard programming language and get their computer versions generated automatically. For a programming language L with a sufficiently rich set of primitives, this problem can be solved formally as follows:

Let C_1 be a computer and let $E(L, C_1)$ be given as a program for C_1. Denote this program by $p(E(L, C_1); C_1)$. Now to construct $p(E(L, C_2); C_2)$ for some other computer C_2 we can adopt the following procedure. Construct $g(E(L, C_2); L)$ which represents the flow chart in L of the translator $E(L, C_2)$. This can be translated using $p(E(L, C_1); C_1)$ to yield $p(E(L, C_2); C_1)$, i.e., the translator $E(L, C_2)$ in the computer language C_1. Using *this* now, one can again translate $g(E(L, C_2; L)$ and so obtain $p(E(L, C_2); C_2)$ which is the required translator in the computer language C_2.

The technique outlined above is the one described in reference [24] where JOVIAL is used as the programming language L.

3. Hierarchical Computation Processes

3.1 The Need for Extending the Scope of the Metatheory

3.1.1 In the last section, we defined a simple computation as a certain process to be carried out over single general flow charts of a simple programming language L. The process itself was actually defined only over basic flow charts in L. The extension of this process to general flow charts became possible because a general flow chart, by definition, was reducible to a basic flow chart leaving the input-output sets invariant. The possibility of this reduction depended critically on the fact that our constructive definition for general flow charts explicitly excluded the occurrence of a label in a flow chart that referred to itself, or of the occurrence of two labels in two different flow charts which mutually referred to each other. The main consequence of this restriction is that recursive procedures, as they are normally understood in computer programming terminology, are outside the scope of simple programming languages.

A second major deficiency in a metatheory of computation that is restricted to simple computational processes is that within it, we cannot describe the use of closed subroutines in computations. The reduction technique that was outlined earlier to go from a general flow chart to a basic flow chart was, in effect, nothing but a systematization of the use of open subroutines. For obvious reasons, a metatheory that cannot permit the use of subroutines as closed subroutines does not have much pragmatic significance.

Third, we have already seen that this requirement to define the entire computation in terms of a single flow chart precludes the possibility of partitioning a given computation into several subcomputations and carrying them out one by one at execution time. It is clear again, that a model for computation that is limited in this way is not of very great value from the practical point of view.

In this section, we shall describe an extension to the simple computation model we have been dealing with so far, which would be free from all these deficiencies. This extension is called a hierarchical computation process and is defined over a set of flow charts instead of a single flow chart. The actual details of the process are, thus, set up to take into account not merely the evaluation of function and predicate labels occurring in a given flow chart, but going from one flow chart, at some intermediate stage, to another flow chart, or to a sequence of flow charts, and returning to the original point and continuing with the computation there. It will be seen that a model that admits of this facility should be sufficiently powerful to encompass recursive procedures, closed subroutines, overlay techniques, and similar computational innovations that are responsible for the power and flexibility of modern computer systems.

Before starting on a detailed description of a hierarchical computation process, it must be emphasized that, in contrast to the case of simple computations, there is a whole family of hierarchical computation processes that could be described. The individual processes would all have the common feature that they are defined on sets of flow charts rather than on single flow charts. And, hence, as we shall see later on, they would all require the use of a "supervisor" of some sort for being realized on a simple computer. For the rest, the individual processes might differ significantly in their details; for example, in their initialization procedures in going from one flow chart to another, in their terminal procedures on leaving a flow chart, and in the types of substitutions for the arguments allowed. However, clearly, these differences in detail have peripheral significance only in comparison to the basic distinction that exists between simple and hierarchical computations.

Since the main aim in this section is to examine the essential ways in which the two computation processes differ, and also to identify certain characteristics that are common to all hierarchical computation processes, we shall content ourselves with studying one particular model for hierarchical computation languages. The motivations for some of our definitions would become clear if one keeps in mind the aim stated above.

3.2 Hierarchical Programming Languages

3.2.1 We shall describe in this section one specific model for hierarchical programming languages in terms of the three components of such a language: the set of primitives; the set of sentences, a sentence in this case consisting of a collection of general flow charts satisfying a certain completeness condition; and the computation process over a sentence.

The structure of a hierarchical programming language is thus exactly similar to that of a simple programming language. Only in this case, our construction procedure for general flow charts would be devised so that the deficiencies enumerated in Section 3.1 would be avoided. It will be seen later that the particular manner in which we define the hierarchical computation process is intimately connected with this construction procedure for the flow charts in the language.

3.2.2 Let L be a hierarchical programming language. The primitives of L are the five sets $\{V, F, P, S, A\}$, exactly identical to the primitives as defined for a simple programming language. Each set satisfies the same syntactic and semantic conditions as enumerated in Section 2.2.2. Thus the notions "designation label," "basic function label," and "basic predicate label" in L are defined exactly identically to the definitions given in Section 2.2.2.

We shall make the same assumption as at the start of Section 2.3.2 and introduce the terms "formal bound name in L," "constant in L," and "formal designation label in L" in exactly the same way as we did in that section. Using these notions we shall redefine "formal function (predicate) label in L" as described below.

A formal function label in L and a formal predicate label in L are defined recursively as follows:

(1a) $f(X_1, \ldots, X_j; Y_1, \ldots, Y_k)$ is a formal function label in L provided: $j, k \geq 1$; $\{X_i\}$ are formal bound names, formal designation labels, or constants in L; $\{Y_i\}$ are formal bound names or formal designation labels in L; and f is a name in V.

(1b) $p(Z_1, \ldots, Z_m)$ is a formal predicate label in L provided: $m \geq 1$,

$\{Z_i\}$ are formal bound names, formal designation labels, or constants in L; and p is a name in V.

(2a) $f(X_1, \ldots, X_j; Y_1, \ldots, Y_k)$ is a formal function label in L provided: $j, k \geq 1$; $\{X_i\}$ are formal bound names, or formal designation labels, or constants, *or formal function labels* in L; $\{Y_i\}$ are formal bound names or formal designation labels in L; and f is a name in V.

(2b) $p(Z_1, \ldots, Z_m)$ is a formal predicate label in L provided: $m \geq 1$; $\{Z_i\}$ are formal bound names, formal designation labels, constants, *or formal function labels* in L; and p is a name in V.

(3) Nothing is a formal function label or a formal predicate label unless its being so follows from (1) and (2) above.

3.2.3 Let F^*, P^* be the set of all formal function labels and formal predicate labels in L, respectively.

A formal flow chart in L is a finite, directed, connected, labeled graph defined in a way exactly similar to a basic flow chart in Section 2.2.3 except that now each branch label is in F^* and each vertex label in P^*.

With this definition of a formal flow chart, we can introduce the concept of flow charts being in standard form exactly as we did in Section 2.3.2. Following the terminology introduced there, we shall refer to a formal flow chart in L as a function graph in case it is in standard form with a single unlabeled terminal vertex, and as a predicate graph in case it is in standard form with two unlabeled terminal vertices (identified as the 1-output vertex and the 0-output vertex, as described earlier).

Again, as before, we shall identify specific function graphs and predicate graphs in L by means of distinct names belonging to V.

3.2.4 We now define formal functions (formal predictaes) in L as follows:

A function graph (predicate graph) in L is a formal function (formal predicate) in L provided the following hold:

(i) Each branch label $f(X_1, \ldots, X_j; Y_1, \ldots, Y_k)$ is a formal function label in L with the property that its name f, as well as the names of all formal function labels occurring in this branch label, identify specific function graphs in L.

(ii) Each vertex label $p(Z_1, \ldots, Z_m)$ is a formal predicate label in L with the property that its name p identifies as specific predicate graph in L, and the names of all the formal function labels occurring in this vertex label identify specific function graphs in L.

(iii) For each occurrence in the branch and vertex labels of the graph of a formal function label or a formal predicate label identifying a function graph and a predicate graph, respectively, in L, an explicit 1 : 1

correspondence is given between its input-output argument sets and those of the function graph and predicate graph, respectively, it identifies.

3.2.5 A general flow chart in L is a formal flow chart in L, the names of whose branch and vertex labels are all names of formal functions and formal predicates, respectively, in L, with an explicit $1:1$ correspondence given between the bound names and constants occurring in the input-output sets of the labels and the set of bound names occurring in the input-output sets of the function graph and predicate graph, respectively, identified by the names of the labels.

A finite set of general flow charts $G = \{g_1, \ldots, g_k\}$ in L is a complete set of general flow charts provided G has the following property: Consider the set of branch and vertex labels, that are not basic function or basic predicate labels in L, occurring in the members of G; if g is the name of an element of this set, then for some unique i, $1 \leq i \leq k$, $g = g_i$.

To simplify terminology, in all of the following discussions we shall mean by a "flow chart," a "general flow chart" in L.

3.2.6 Let L be a hierarchical programming language with primitives $\{V, F, P, S, A\}$. We shall now enlarge the set of names available in L by embedding V in a set V^* by a constructive procedure as follows: to the alphabet of V we add the digits $0, 1, 2, \ldots, 9$, if they are not already present, and also add a distinct punctuation symbol $\triangle$ not identical to any of the symbols in the original alphabet. The set V^* of names consists of the union of the two sets: (1) names in V, (2) the set of names of the form $v \triangle n$, where $v \in V$, n is any finite string in the digits $0, 1, \ldots, 9$, and $\triangle$ is the special punctuation symbol described above.

Given a flow chart $g = g(U_0, U_1)$ in $L = L(V, F, P, S, A)$, we shall denote by $g^n = g^n(U_0^n, U_1^n)$, $n \geq 1$, an integer, the flow chart in $L^* = L^*(V^*, F, P, S, A)$, obtained as follows from g:

g^n is obtained from g by replacing the name part v of each bound name that occurs as an argument of any of its branch and vertex labels, by $v \triangle n$. The constants that occur in g as arguments and the names of labels (either of g or occurring in the labels of g) are left unchanged.

By U_0^n, U_1^n, we shall denote in an obvious way, the sets obtained from U_0, U_1, by the above name-changing process. These are now the input-output sets of g^n. Adopting a consistent notation, by U_0^0, U_1^0, we shall refer to U_0, U_1 (i.e., with the original names from V).

It will be seen from the definition of the hierarchical computation process given below that the set of bound names ending in Δn is precisely the one that enters into the nth level computation.

3.2.7 A hierarchical computation process is defined over a complete set of flow charts G in L and generates a sequence of assignments to sets $U^n \subseteq V^*(g^n)$, $n \geq 0$, where $V^*(g^n)$ denotes the set of bound names occurring in g^n. As in Section 2.2.4, by the assigned set of $V^*(g^n)$ at any stage in the computation process, and by the current value of the assigned set of $V^*(g^n)$, we shall refer to, respectively, the set $U^n \subseteq V^*(g^n)$ whose elements have been assigned values at least once up to that stage, and the last assigned value of each element of U^n at that stage.

With these preliminaries, we are now in a position to define a hierarchical computation process.

3.2.8 Let $G = \{g_1, \ldots, g_k\}$ be some given complete set of flow charts in a hierarchical programming language L. Let g_m, for some m, $1 \leq m \leq k$, be specified as the main flow chart of G, and let an initial assignment be given to the input set of g_m. A hierarchical computation over G with these initial conditions is the following process:

(1) Begin the 0th level computation at the initial vertex of g_m with the given initial assignment to its input set.

(2) Having arrived at a certain branch or vertex label in the nth level computation for $n \geq 0$, do either (3) or (4), whichever applies.

(3) If the current label to be evaluated is not a basic function or predicate label in L, then let it be $g_i(X_0^n, X_1^n)$, $1 \leq i \leq k$. Select its first input argument from the left which is a function label. Then do either (i) or (ii), whichever applies.

    (i) If no such argument exists, go to (2) to start the $(n+1)$st level computation with the following initial conditions: Start at the initial vertex of $g_i^{(n+1)}$ using as the initial assignment to its input set the current values of X_0^n.

    (ii) If such a first argument exists, let it be $g_j(Y_0^n, Y_1^n)$, $1 \leq j \leq k$. Then go to (2) to start the $(n+1)$st level computation with the following initial conditions:
Start at the initial vertex of $g_j^{(n+1)}$ using as the initial assignment to its input set the current values of Y_0^n.

(4) If the current label to be evaluated is a basic function or basic predicate label in L, evaluate it using the current values of its input set. Then do either (5) or (6), whichever applies.

(5) If the label just evaluated is a nonterminal branch label or a nonterminal vertex label, then select the next label (vertex or branch,

respectively) exactly as in the case of a simple computation and go to (2).

(6) If the label just evaluated is that of a terminal branch (i.e., a branch that ends on an unlabeled terminal vertex), or of a terminal vertex, then do either (i) or (ii), or (iii) below, whichever applies.

>   (i) If the current computation is at the 0th level, stop.
>   (ii) If the current level [i.e., $(n+1)$st level] computation just terminated originated from (3ii) above at the nth level, replace $g_j(Y_0^n, Y_1^n)$ by Y_1^n in that label [encountered at (3ii) at the nth level], assign the current values of W_1^{n+1} to Y_1^n, where W_1^{n+1} is the output set of the $(n+1)$st level computation, and go to (3).
>   (iii) If the current level [i.e., $(n+1)$st level] computation just terminated originated from (3i) at the nth level, then assign the current values of W_1^{n+1} to X_1^n, where W_1^{n+1} is the output set of the $(n+1)$st level computation and X_1^n is the output set of the label $g_i(X_0^n, X_1^n)$ at the nth level to compute which the $(n+1)$st level was started. Then go to (5) to continue with the nth level computation.

For a given initial condition, the result of the hierarchical computation is the set of current values, at termination, of the output set of the main flow chart.

3.2.9 Several explanatory comments should perhaps be added to supplement the description of the hierarchical computation process given above. We shall list some of these here.

(1) In making assignments from one input argument set to another [in going from the nth to the $(n+1)$st level], or from one output set to another [in returning from the $(n+1)$st to the nth level], use should be made of the explicit 1:1 correspondence between the two relevant sets as given in the definition of the flow charts.

Note that if the output set at the $(n+1)$st level is null, then so is, necessarily, that at the nth level. In this case, the truth value which is the result of the computation at the higher level is made use of in selecting the next branch at the lower level.

Our definitions of a branch label and vertex label in a flow chart in L imply, as can be readily verified, that no function label could occur with a null output set. Hence, a null output set at the termination of the computation at some level $n \geq 0$ implies, necessarily, that one has completed evaluating a predicate label. And this can, again, happen only at a vertex.

(2) From the way the hierarchical computation process is defined, it is seen that at the time of evaluation of a label, its input-output sets are bound names, constants, or designation labels, exactly as in the case of a simple computation. However, the formalism described allows one, in a hierarchical programming language, to replace a bound name or a set of bound names in the input set of a label by a bound name or a set of bound names belonging to the output set of some other label.

Clearly, for consistency, the two sets of bound names must have the same attribute assignments. But once this condition is met, the embedded labels could be arbitrary. In particular, they could belong to an entirely different computation language with its own set of primitives and computation rules but occurring as a sublanguage in the original one.

This is a standard and also a very powerful technique for embedding one language in another. Note that it is not essential that the two languages be similar. The original could be a linear language while the embedded one could be a picture (i.e., two-dimensional) language. What is important is that the name and attribute sets should overlap.

In Section 4.4, where ALGOL is considered from the point of view of our hierarchical language model, we shall see specific instances of usage of this embedding technique.

3.2.10 We shall conclude the discussion of hierarchical programming languages by considering very briefly the translation problem as it applies to these languages and simple computers.

Since a hierarchical computation, although defined over a fixed, finite set of flow charts, is actually carried out in terms of sets of flow charts $\{g_i^n\}$, $n \geq 0$, which are generated at "computation time," it is evident that such a computation process cannot be realized as a simple computation process in a simple computer. The basic reason for this is, of course, that a fixed memory allocation function cannot be defined *a priori* since argument names, which continue to be created as the computation proceeds, can only be taken into account "dynamically."

An immediate consequence of this is the following: A hierarchical computation can be realized in a simple computer only through the mediation of an auxiliary program—the so-called executive program or supervisor. Let us refer to this combination as a system S.

Since the input-output sets of a hierarchical computation are associated only with the main flow chart (which has a fixed set of names being involved in the 0th level computation), an equivalent computation—i.e., finitely equivalent, as discussed earlier—in a system S could still be defined in a manner strictly analogous to that given earlier for simple computations.

A translator for hierarchical computations would then be a function of a given programming language L and a system S. It would take as inputs complete sets of flow charts in L together with the initial conditions for specific computations, and generate as outputs appropriate inputs for the system S, such that S, acting on these inputs, could realize equivalent computations.

Because of its inherent dependence on the specifications of a system S, no uniform structure could, in general, be suggested for a translator in this case. It should, however, be clear to those familiar with the design of translators for ALGOL-like languages how the definition of a hierarchical computation process, as given here, suggests in a natural way the use of push-down stores and other control features which have recently become standard in computing activity. In Section 4.4 further related comments can be found.

4. Relevance of the Approach to the Design of Computing Systems[13]

4.1 Specifying a Computational Language

4.1.1 So far in this article, our primary concern has been to work out in detail the structure of a specific model for programming languages. This we have sought to do within a certain well-defined framework emphasizing the pragmatic aspects that enter into the design of a language that is meant to be used and "understood." In this final part, we shall try to widen the scope of the article by considering—although only in a general and somewhat tentative manner—several matters which are more or less closely related to our central problem. The main motivation in attempting this is twofold: first, to identify problem areas which have to be recognized and studied before one could hope to achieve a satisfactory theory of general language behavior, a problem of central importance to any nontrivial design of man-machine communication systems. Second, the author wishes to show that there has been—and continues to be—a good deal of confusion regarding the description and design of programming languages. Looked at from the point of view of an adequately formulated theory, several of the ostensible problems turn out to be either definitional, or circular, or pseudo-problems.

To facilitate this extension of the area of discussion, to begin with, a set of components will be outlined in terms of which a computational

---

[13]This section has been written so that it can be read as a self-contained unit independently of Sections 2 and 3 for the most part. See footnote 3 in this connection.

language must[14] be specified. In doing this the author's aim is a proposal for a framework sufficiently general so that within it, not only languages composed of linear strings, but languages composed of two-dimensional entities (such as pictures [*10, 13, 17*]) or possibly even more general languages, e.g., choreography, could be formulated.

4.1.2 Let L be a computational language. To specify L, then, the following components of L should be specified (see Section 4.1.4 for explanatory remarks concerning these components):

(1) *A vocabulary* (or *alphabet*) A is a finite set composed of two disjoint parts:
    (i) a terminal vocabulary A_T (i.e., the set of *word names*, which we shall refer to as *words*, for short), and
    (ii) a nonterminal vocabulary A_N (i.e., the set of *phrase names*, which we shall refer to as *phrases*, for short).

(2) *A grammar* G is a finite set of rewriting rules for *sentence* generation. The notions of *context* and *composition* of the elements of A must be first defined. Using these notions, a major component of G consists of a finite set of rewriting rules of the form: phrase p in context $c \rightarrow$ a given composition of specific phrases and/or words. A sentence is a composition of a finite number of words, generated in a finite number of steps by the application of the rules of G.

(3) *A structure function* F_G, based on a grammar G, is a partial function defined over the set S of sentences of L. Let s be a sentence of L, and let $F_G(s)$ be defined. Then:

$$F_G(s) = \{ F_1(s), F_2(s), \ldots, F_{r(s)}(s) \},$$

where the $\{F_i(s)\}$ are the syntactic structures assigned by G to s.

(4) *A set of attributes* P is a finite set $P = \{P_1, P_2, \ldots, P_k\}$ of partial functions defined over the words of A. Each P_i, $i = 1, \ldots, k$, has a finite range of values which we shall denote by the set: $\{P_{1i}, P_{2i} \ldots, P_{n(i)i}\}$. The attributes P_i in P for which $P_i(a)$, $a \in A_T$, is defined, are called the admissible attributes of a. An attribute assignment to a is the assignment of a particular value (from its range $\{P_{ji}\}$) to each of its admissible attributes P_i.

[14]The schema given below is of the nature of a meta-meta-model. A model for computational languages at the metatheoretic level is obtained by fixing, in a specific way, the structure of the grammar rules, the structure of the dictionary, etc. The models that we have been considering in the last two parts are metatheoretic models in this sense. "*Must* be specified" asserts thereby that the schema presented in this meta-meta-formulation is a minimum prerequisite and that in fact existing programming languages conform to this model. To substantiate this assertion, ALGOL is considered in some detail from this point of view in Section 4.4. In Section 4.2, the possible relevance of this meta-meta-framework to natural languages is considered.

(5) *A Dictionary* $D = D(P, A, G)$ is a finite dictionary which consists of two parts:
  (i) To each word $a \in A_T$, for every attribute assignment to a, D assigns a (semantic) value.
  (ii) A subset of the phrases in A is specified to be primitive. Let $\alpha \in A$ be a primitive phrase. Let $s(\alpha)$ be some composition of words (of A) derived from α by a finite number of applications of the rules of G. For each such α, the dictionary D defines an algorithm (i.e., a machine with a finite control but, possibly, potentially infinite storage, i.e., a Turing machine) to compute a (semantic) value for $s(\alpha)$ for every admissible assignment of (semantic) values to the words composing $s(\alpha)$. A nonterminating computation, let us say, computes an empty (semantic) value for $s(\alpha)$. Some or all of the (semantic) values of $s(\alpha)$ may be empty.

(6) *A (semantic) computation process* Σ_L is an algorithm defined over the sentences of L. Let s be a sentence of L and let $F_G(s)$ be defined. Let $a_1, a_2, \ldots, a_{k(s)}$ be the words occurring in s. Denote by $P(aj)$, $j = 1, 2, \ldots, k(s)$ a particular attribute assignment for aj. Then

$$\Sigma_L(F_G(s), a_1, a_2, \ldots, a_{k(s)}, P(a_1), \ldots, P(a_{k(s)}), D(P, A, G))$$

computes a (semantic) value for the sentence s, under the given attribute assignments for the $\{a_j\}$, the dictionary specification $D(P, A, G)$, and the structure function F_G based on the grammar G. In case $F_G(s)$ is multiple-valued, i.e., there are m, say, syntactic structures assigned by G to s, then Σ_L computes a (semantic) value for each value of $F_G(s)$, i.e., it computes m such values. Some, or all, of these values may be empty.

4.1.3 A *programming language*, now, is a computational language in the sense defined above. A *computer language* (i.e., the machine language of a computer) is a programming language with the restriction that all (semantic) values, either assigned by the dictionary or computed by Σ_L, are finite in range.

A *computer* is a finite state device which computes the (semantic) value of any sentence of a computer language.

4.1.4 Several explanatory remarks should perhaps be added to supplement the above, rather formal, description of a specification schema for programming languages. The author will list these remarks below pointing out, wherever relevant, the connection with the particular models for programming languages we have been studying in the earlier parts of this article.

(1) Since only finite (semantic) computation procedures are of significance, the dictionary must be finite at any stage of the computation process. This is the primary reason for requiring the vocabulary to be finite. The word names could, however, be made into a potentially infinite list by giving a finite set of generative rules for constructing word names out of a finite set of symbols.[15] In this case, the dictionary will consist of a fixed, finite part, and a variable part which must be supplied, *ad hoc*, each time a computation is to be carried out.

(2) What the author has called the grammar G (i.e., the system of rules for sentence generation) and the structure function F_G (i.e., the syntax analyser based on G) together constitute the essentials of the syntactic component of a language as normally understood. Nothing has been said about structures of grammars apart from indicating that at least one major component would be made up of context-dependent (in general, but context-free in specific cases, perhaps) rewriting rules. This much seems to be generally accepted for natural, as well as for programming, languages.

Nevertheless, it is clear that the detailed specification of grammars is a very important part of the specification of languages. And basic to this specification is the appropriate definition of the notions "context" and "composition of words."[16] In our model for programming languages, the syntax rules are implicit in the rules for the construction of flow charts (i.e., the labeled graphs) and of their branch and vertex labels. Since these formation rules are fairly trivial, the syntax analysis also turns out to be quite trivial. (See Section 4.3 and also Section 5 for further related comments.)

(3) Specifying the set of attributes is, in the author's view, an important aspect of the specification of a language. In many of the programming languages in current usage, attribute assignments do play an essential role under the term *declarations*. Nevertheless, there does not seem to be a sufficient awareness or appreciation of this fact in published studies. The central role attribute functions play in translation (specifically, in the efficient construction of storage allocation functions) should be evident to any one who has had anything to do with compiler designs.

---

[15]This procedure, which is normally adopted in the case of most programming languages, will be seen to be a special case of using sentences of one language as syntactic entities in another language. See in this connection remark (2) under hierarchical programming languages, Section 3.2.9.

[16]That explicit definitions of these notions are necessary would become clear if one considers two-dimensional languages, pictures, for example. Here, composition by concatenation is no longer as naturally defined as it is in the case of linear strings [*10, 17*]. The same is true of "context."

In general, by means of attributes one characterizes the spaces in which word names (i.e., the variables of the computation process) assume values. In ALGOL, for instance, there are effectively only two attributes: *type*, and *array bounds*. (These are discussed in greater detail in Section 4.4.) In an extended version one could, for example, add the attribute *precision* with values: single, double, triple, etc. That attributes play an important role in the efficient structuring of dictionaries has recently been emphasized, as applied to natural languages, by Katz and Fodor [8]. Their "semantic markers" are closely analogous to values of attributes as we have defined the latter.

(4) It is widely acknowledged that, in the case of a natural language, a dictionary forms an important part of the semantic component of any model for that language. It is of interest that there has been no similar explicit recognition of this fact with respect to programming languages. This is mainly due to the fact that descriptions of programming languages tend to be almost always descriptions of specific implementations of them. And no effort is made to separate out that aspect of the language embedded in the computer system in which the implementation has been done. Even ostensibly machine-independent descriptions, like the ALGOL-60 report, tend to be confused where this aspect of the description of the language is concerned.

In our programming language model, the dictionary consists of a fixed part containing the algorithms for the evaluation of the basic functions, basic predicates, and the selection operators. The variable part of the dictionary is precisely what we have been referring to as the assigned set. At each stage in the computation process, it is this part of the dictionary which is used to obtain the (semantic) values of the word names involved in that stage.

4.2 Natural Languages and Computational Languages

4.2.1 The considerations in the last section show that the central emphasis in specifying a computational language is on the specification of a procedure for the computation of semantic values of the sentences of the language. The main requirement is that this procedure be *uniform* for all sentences of the language. In providing a structure for this procedure we have made use of linguistically significant notions like grammar and dictionary. This, and the usage of the term *language* in this context, raise certain basic questions. What are the connections, if any, between natural and computational languages? What relevance could a metatheory of computational languages have to a linguistic theory of natural languages. In this section, what seems to the author to be the more important issues involved will be briefly outlined.

4.2.2 Perhaps the most articulate statement of the basic issues involved in constructing a linguistic theory of natural languages is to be found in the writings of Chomsky [3]. Briefly summarized, his argument is that there is one principal fact of language behavior to which any adequate linguistic theory must address itself. It is that a mature speaker of a language is able to produce new sentences appropriate to given situations and a mature listener is able to understand these immediately. And not only this, but the latter is able to deal more or less satisfactorily with deviant sentences.

Outlining the structure of a plausible theory that could cope with this "creative" aspect of language usage, Chomsky suggests that this linguistic competence could be explicated in terms of a system of rules called the *grammar* of a language. The grammar of a language should ideally contain three components: a central syntactic component and two interpretive components: a phonological component and a semantic component. "The grammar as a whole can . . . be regarded as, ultimately, a device for pairing phonetically represented signals with semantic interpretations, this pairing being mediated through a system of abstract structures generated by the syntactic component" [3].

4.2.3 It will be seen that, making allowances for terminological differences, a considerable amount of structural similarity exists between such a model for natural languages and the model for computational languages suggested earlier. Although much the greater part of the efforts of Chomsky and his co-workers has been devoted to working out in detail the structural aspects of the syntactic component, the little that has been done toward explicating a theory of the semantic component [9] shows that the similarity noted above is neither fortuitous nor merely superficial.

This is not surprising since in both cases the respective models are intended to function as devices that produce semantic interpretations or compute semantic values of inputs which are well-formed sentences. But there are at least two important details in which the two models are not equivalent or, at least, if equivalent, the correspondences are not apparent.

First, it is not clear, for instance, in the case of natural languages, that the procedure for semantic computation is a uniform one in the sense in which it is in the case of computational languages. In fact, it seems to the author to be plausible that natural language discourse is computational in the above sense the less "natural" it is or, in other words, the more "artificial" or rigidly conventionalized it is. It may well turn out that a major part of language behavior is computational in only a partial or "private" sense.

Second, and much more critically, what renders theory construction for natural languages so much more difficult is the absence of any clear or natural indication as to what constitutes a semantic value or interpretation of a sentence of a natural language. This difficulty does not arise in the case of computational languages since we assume the specification of the semantic values to be given as part of—in fact, the central part of—the specification of such languages.

Both these critical differences—that natural languages are computational only in a restricted or "private" sense, and that the notion "semantic value" for these languages is not well specifiable— if true, would imply certain limitations on what a metatheory for natural language behavior could hope to accomplish. Instead of being able to specify a single universal computer for a language, it could only, at best, expect to be able to delimit a family of computers having certain close structural similarities. Toward this delimitation, however, it appears quite plausible that an adequately constructed theory of computational languages would have a great relevance.

4.3 Syntax, Semantics, and Systems

4.3.1 Among designers of programming languages the concepts which have generated the greatest amount of argument are "syntax" and "semantics."[17] The points at issue may be summarized as a series of questions: Should a programming language have a syntax? If so, how should it be formulated? And how made use of? What is meant by the semantics of a programming language? What is the connection between its syntax and semantics? Should syntax be defined so that it is impossible to write a semantically meaningless program? What is meant by a semantically meaningless program? What is the relationship between the processor, the syntax and the semantics of a programming language? And so on.

In this section, some of these questions are considered in the light of the specification schema outlined in Section 4.1 and it is shown that, in an adequately formulated model of programming languages, many of these questions either do not arise or have a natural basis for resolution.

4.3.2 Note, to begin with, that the specification of a programming language L is actually the specification of a certain computation process over the sentences of L. This is the function Σ_L of Section 4.1. We have argued that Σ_L should be a function, among other things concerned with

---

[17]A not untypical summary of the prevailing views on these notions may be found in reference [25]. See, in particular, the panel discussion on "Metasyntactic and Metasemantic Languages" included therein.

the input sentence, of the structure function F_G and the dictionary specification $D(P, A, G)$. The structure function and the dictionary, in their turn, are themselves required to have certain specific functional features.

The basic idea behind all these requirements is that:

(1) We assume a certain finite number of atomic computation processes (i.e., subprocesses) as primitively given;

(2) Any particular input sentence describes a computation in terms of these atoms;

(3) The way in which these atoms should be put together to realize the intended computation is mirrored in a well-defined (i.e., uniform) manner in the way the input sentence is composed out of the names of these atoms.

4.3.3 Given such a schema for the specification of a programming language, one can now give a precise sense to the questions we started out with. At the meta-meta-level, one can ask whether there are other plausible ways of structuring descriptions, or, equivalently, specifications, of computation processes. Linguistic studies (see Section 4.2) as well as metamathematical studies, would seem to indicate a negative answer to this question. Note that the point at issue is not whether every description could be reduced to a description of this type. This, in any case, is well known to be true. Rather, it is one of being able to characterize what is a proper, or an *adequate*, description in a pragmatically given context. The main thesis of this article may be summed up by saying that such characterizations are meaningfully possible only if one approaches language design from the point of view of computer system design.

Much more fundamentally, one could ask whether computation processes describable in these specific ways are adequate models for all behavioral situations encountered in real life. The present article does not address itself to this question.

4.3.4 Accepting that Σ_L is a function of the structure function F_G and the dictionary $D(P, A, G)$, one could ask several questions at the meta-level concerning their specific roles. The argument that syntax should be abolished would, perhaps, be interpreted as the requirement that Σ_L may not depend explicitly on F_G. At the other extreme, to ask for a syntax specification such that it is impossible to formulate a semantically meaningless sentence would be equivalent to requiring that, for every sentence s, if $F_G(s)$ is defined, then so is $\Sigma_L(s)$.

It is evident from the specification schema given in Section 4.1 that there is really no clear-cut boundary between the syntax and the semantics of a programming language. As pointed out there, one could approximately look upon G and F_G as together constituting the syntactic component of the language, and P and D as together constituting the semantic component. But, intrinsically, there is little merit in this dichotomy since the dictionary itself, in its structure, must depend on the grammar. This also brings out the really fundamental point that for a given, fixed, input-output behavior of a computational system, there is a good deal of freedom in structuring the syntactic and semantic components. Each such assigned structure would give rise to a suitable definition for Σ_L. This result is well known in recursive function theory which has at least three distinct, but equivalent, models.

4.3.5 One is thus led back again to a consideration of the adequacy of a model with reference to external contexts, i.e., as a submodel embedded in larger models. Some aspects of this problem are considered in Section 4.5. But, as a preliminary step, in the next section we shall analyze critically one particular model that has generated a considerable amount of interest among language designers, namely, the ALGOL-60 formulation.

4.4 The ALGOL Report

4.4.1 Publication of the ALGOL-60 report [18] was a significant event in several aspects. The report was the outcome of a conscious effort to formulate precisely and "unambiguously" a machine-independent language for the specification of algorithms. Both in terms of the approach to the problem and the methodology used, it was a radical departure from anything attempted so far. Some, at least, of its proponents genuinely seemed to believe that the ALGOL report solved—or was almost on the point of solving—the vexing problem of the design of a universal programming language.

The controversy generated by this attitude has, quite naturally, been considerable and, at times, bitter. It is not necessary for us to review at this stage the several arguments that have been advanced for and against ALGOL.[18] What does concern us here, however, are three points:

(i) The basic motivation underlying the ALGOL report has a direct

---

[18]For a good, representative account, the interested reader may be referred to reference [25]; especially, to the several panel discussions transcribed therein. The paper by Woodger [26], included in that volume, has specific bearing on the remarks made in the rest of this section. It is recommended to those interested in getting to know ALGOL from the point of view of computer system design.

relevance to the main issues that we have been concerned with in this article.
(ii) There is general agreement on some of the contributions the report has made to the design of programming languages.
(iii) Equally, there is basic agreement on some of the deficiencies in the formulation set forth in the report.

In this section, the ALGOL formulation is considered critically with reference to the metatheory the author has been advocating, keeping in mind the three points enumerated above. We shall see that some, at least, of the controversy generated by the ALGOL report is based on a confusion in the report which is the result of not clearly distinguishing between the several aspects of the language it seeks to specify; i.e., between the grammar, the sentence structure, the dictionary, and the computation process. Some of the deficiencies of the language and, also, some of the suggestions that have been put forward for its extension will become clear when considered with reference to our model.

4.4.2 At the outset, one should clearly bear in mind the following points concerning the ALGOL formulation which, as has been remarked above, the report itself does not explicitly bring out, resulting in a confusion of the total picture.

(1) The computation process implicit in the formulation is a hierarchical computation process defined over a complete set of flow charts as described in Section 3.[19] As we saw there such a process, in general, cannot be reduced to a simple computation process. Further, features such as the use of push-down stores, the need for run-time memory allocation, the necessity for a supervisor (or a run-time compiler) to enable the execution of an ALGOL program on a simple computer, etc.—features which have given rise to a good deal of discussion subsequent to the publication of the ALGOL-60 report—are, in fact, characteristic of all hierarchical computation processes (see Sections 3.2.9 and 3.2.10 for details).

(2) Certain aspects of ALGOL are connected with the fact that an ALGOL program is generated as a linear string instead of as a graph (or a

---

[19]The computation process implicit in the ALGOL formulation is actually not identical to the hierarchical computation process described in Section 3; it is rather a variant of this process. The differences, however, are only in detail and are not of significance to the metatheoretic arguments of this section. The complete set of flow charts over which the computation process is defined, in the case of an ALGOL program, consists of a single nested system of blocks together with the procedures declared therein. The difference between this structure of a "sentence" in ALGOL and that in the hierarchical computation model is, however, an essential one and we consider this aspect in greater detail below.

set of graphs). Labels, designational expressions, statement brackets and other similar punctuations, GO TO statements, and so on, belong to this category. These do not appear in our model, and it is clear that they are not intrinsically relevant to the specification of a programming language.

(3) As formulated, ALGOL actually consists of a set of languages each with its own set of grammar, dictionary, and computation rules. These languages are interconnected in that the sentences of some occur as phrases in others. At least the languages in the accompanying tabulation should be distinguished.

Language designation	Sentence designation
$L1$	Identifier
$L2$	Number
$L3$	Simple arithmetic expression[20]
$L4$	Boolean expression
$L5$	Block or program

The reformulation of languages $L1$ to $L4$ in terms of our model for computational languages is quite straightforward as can be readily verified. We shall not attempt this task here, although it is strongly recommended as an exercise to anyone interested in obtaining an insight into the translation process involved in going from an ALGOL program to a machine language program.

It is, however, worth considering in some detail this reformulation for the language $L5$ since it would help to highlight the basic similarities and differences between our model and ALGOL.[21] In this reformulation, we shall restrict ourselves to the essential features of ALGOL and not attempt to define all its particular details. These latter do not have any direct bearing on what we are discussing right now. In any case, it

[20] The sentences of $L3$ are not "simple arithmetic expressions" as defined in ALGOL since, according to this report, a parenthesized arithmetic expression is again a simple arithmetic expression. In the reformulation given herein an arithmetic expression of ALGOL would be a formal function in the language $L5$. We do not go into these details here since the reformulation is intended for illustrative purposes only.

[21] The grammars of $L1$, $L2$, $L3$, and $L4$ are formulated as context-free (CF) grammars in the ALGOL report. This has led some to claim that ALGOL is a CF language. Although by now all such claims have been effectively refuted, the counterargument itself has not been set forth as convincingly as might have been done. It is clear that since $L1$ to $L4$ are embedded in $L5$, for ALGOL to be a CF language the grammar of $L5$ should be a CF grammar. Now, the sentences of $L5$ enumerate all computable programs, i.e., all partial recursive functions. Hence, clearly, there can exist no CF grammar for $L5$.

should be easy enough to see how these details could be introduced into the formalism.[22]

4.4.3 In the terminology[23] of our model, $L5$ effectively has one basic function F and a class of basic predicates P, which could occur as branch and vertex labels, respectively. There are two attribute functions, call them $A1$ and $A2$, with values as shown below:

$A1$: Real | Integer | Boolean
$A2$: m-tuples of the form $(\langle E \rangle : \langle E \rangle, \ldots, \langle E \rangle : \langle E \rangle)$, for $m \geq 0$, an integer; if $m = 0$, the attribute value is referred to as "scalar"; $\langle E \rangle$ denotes a formal function of the language $L5$ (see footnote 20).

It is evident that $A1$ is nothing but the attribute function, "type," of the ALGOL report; $A2$ specifies the "bound-pair list" associated with a variable. That is, a variable is either a scalar or is some component of an m-dimensional array. ALGOL allows the index bounds in each dimension to be specified in terms of arithmetic expressions. The restrictions defining the valid usage of $\langle E \rangle$, as well as its interpretation, would be incorporated in the dictionary, of course.

In the simplest case F, the assignment statement, has the form[24]:

$$F(\langle E \rangle; \langle I \rangle)$$

with the interpretation: Assign the value of $\langle E \rangle$ to $\langle I \rangle$. Again, $\langle E \rangle$ denotes a formal function of $L5$, and $\langle I \rangle$ a sentence of $L1$. The permissible attribute assignments for $\langle I \rangle$ are:

$A1$: Integer; $A2$: Scalar

or

$A1$: Real; $A2$: Scalar

or

$A1$: Boolean; $A2$: Scalar

---

[22]Thus, specifically, we shall ignore the fact that ALGOL does not restrict itself exclusively to binary branchings at all decision vertices in its flow charts.

[23]In this section we assume familiarity with the contents of Section 3.2 and freely use the terminology and concepts introduced there. Also, familiarity with the ALGOL-60 report is presupposed.

[24]Note that in ALGOL, $\langle E \rangle$ is required to be specified by writing explicitly the particular intended arithmetic expression as the input argument in the function label. In our model, one would identify the particular expression with a certain flow chart in $L5$, and then write the *name* of this flow chart as the input argument in F. This argument would then appear as $E(\langle I \rangle, \ldots, \langle I \rangle; \langle I \rangle)$. The name of the flow chart under consideration is E. The input arguments denote the actual parameters (i.e., names) to be substituted for in the evaluation of E, and the output argument is a dummy name.

The use of subscripted variables amounts to the introduction of the special class of selection operators:

$$S_m(\underbrace{\langle E \rangle, \langle E \rangle, \ldots, \langle E \rangle}_{m \text{ times}}; \langle I \rangle); \quad m = 1, 2, \ldots;$$

$\langle E \rangle$ and $\langle I \rangle$ have the same syntactic significance as before. The attribute assignments permissible for $\langle I \rangle$ now are:
  $A1$: Integer or Real or Boolean
  $A2$: m-tuple "bound-pair list" with $m = 1, 2, \ldots,;$
S_m, in an obvious way, selects the component name, as specified by the values of the $\langle E \rangle$'s, of the m-dimensional array (of names) identified by $\langle I \rangle$.

The assignment statement F can now be generalized to be of the form:

$$F[\langle E \rangle; S_m(\langle E \rangle, \ldots, \langle E \rangle; \langle I \rangle)].$$

The set of vertex labels of the flow charts of $L5$ are the sentences of the language $L4$, i.e., the Boolean expressions $\langle B \rangle$. This set is not finite. But the set of basic predicates of $L4$ is finite, viz., the "relation operators." Thus, if $\langle B \rangle$ is a Boolean expression, then the flow chart in $L5$ at the decision vertex, corresponds to the conditional statement:

$$\textit{if } \langle B \rangle \textit{ then } \ldots \textit{ else } \ldots$$

where the "..." denote arbitrary flow charts with the condition that the first flow chart (i.e., the one following *"then"*) does not start with a decision vertex.

A procedure statement is strictly the analog of our branch label and vertex label whose names identify a formal function and a formal predicate, respectively, and it is defined in a very similar way.

Neglecting the general conditional statement, the only other principal component of $L5$ is the FOR statement. As has been noted by others (see, e.g., Naur [19]), the FOR statement really represents a flow chart with a special structure. We shall not go into the details of these flow charts here, since they have no direct relevance to our main argument. However, it is perhaps worth noting that the realization of the FOR statement requires the introduction of additional basic functions, of the nature of selection functions, for the assignment of values to the controlled variable, and also additional basic predicates to test the exit condition from the FOR loop. It is quite straightforward to work out the format of these as they appear in ALGOL.

4.4.4 The deficiencies in ALGOL and the extensions that have been proposed to overcome some of these can be summarized in terms of the reformulation as follows, and they will be seen to be quite natural and rather obvious. The first extension is to include other attribute functions, analogous to $A2$, but associated with other structured operands like "string" and "list." The next logical extension is to admit a greater variety of basic functions and selection operators, and also to relax the restriction that the output arguments should be exclusively scalars.

Looked at from the system design aspect, however, there is a significant difference between the ALGOL formulation and the model presented in the earlier parts of this article. This is concerned with the input-output specifications of the subprograms out of which the main program is composed.

In our model, the input-output argument sets are explicitly associated with each formal function and each formal predicate (and, in particular, with each basic function and basic predicate). Thus, the specification of the input-output interfaces between the subprograms is explicitly built into the formalism. In ALGOL, these interfaces between the sub-blocks of a program are, in general, not explicitly defined but to be inferred contextually.[25]

While this might have the virtue of minimizing redundancy in program specification, clearly it has great deficiencies from the system design point of view. As has been remarked by several others, this makes it extremely difficult to design a complex ALGOL program in terms of independent modules with well-defined input-output features, test them separately, and then compose them together into a single program by suitable interconnection of their interfaces, i.e., by suitable identification of the input-output argument names of the several modules.

This facility, which is strictly the analog of the design of a computer system in terms of independent, functional subsystems with well-defined interface connections, is clearly a prerequisite if it is to be possible for a group of people to undertake program design as a team activity. The same is true of a computer system design and, in fact, the two activities are essentially equivalent in what they set out to accomplish.

4.5 Language Design and System Design

4.5.1 The main thesis of this article, as has been emphasized several times before, is that the design of a programming language is strictly equivalent to the design of a computing system, and a proper structure

---

[25]The *declarations* at the head of a block precisely fulfill this purpose. They specify the initialization of values intended for the names that are referred to in that block.

for the language is precisely one that brings out this equivalence in a natural way. In the last few sections, several arguments were presented to substantiate this thesis. These have been concerned with the correspondences between specific details that enter into the design of either a language or a system. In this section, we shall examine the relevance the particular model presented earlier in this article (see Section 2) has to the points made.

4.5.2 To begin with, observe that, except for the restriction to finiteness, a programming language and a computer language have identical structures in the model considered. Thus, allowing for this restriction, a computer language whose instructions, jump conditions, and address operators are the basic functions, predicates, and selection operators, respectively, of a programming language is identical to the latter. For a given programming language and a given system, then, the closer the above equivalence, the better the match between their structures. To that extent, in other words, the task of constructing a translator is simplified.

Since, in general, it would be unrealistic to expect the translator to reduce to an identity mapping, the design criteria for a system, given a language, should be to approach this ideal situation. From the considerations of Section 2, it would follow that the computer language, in this case, should be designed so that the memory allocation function as well as the structure of the dictionary is simplified. Where a single system has to match several languages, the above simplification should be sought to be optimized over the set of input languages.

Note that this optimization is the more difficult to achieve, the larger the number of different input languages. It was pointed out in the last section that a natural method of extending an input language is to increase the variety of basic functions, predicates, and attributes available in the language. A union of several input languages (keeping the computation process fixed) can always be thought of as a single extended input language. A "universal" programming language is presumably one which includes in itself all other programming languages. It is clear now that such a universal language should be either poorly matched to a large number of problem areas, or it would be such that it would be practically impossible to design a computer system well matched to it. This leads one to conclude that all attempts to formulate a universal programming language are intrinsically misguided.

4.5.3 Language design as well as system design, then, is most meaningfully handled within a more or less well-delimited problem area. Computationally, this delimitation would be done by seeking answers to the following kinds of questions: What attributes are natural characterizations of the variables of the problem area? What basic functions and predicates of these variables characterize the operations intrinsic to the problem area? What is the nature of the computation process that relates to the problem area? And, finally: What are the rules in terms of which descriptions of such a process can be given making use of the variables, functions, and predicates that have been postulated?

A little reflection would convince one that practically all existing programming languages which have been designed to cope with well-defined problem areas do, in fact, presuppose an answer to each of the questions listed above. To be sure, in many instances, the answers might have been arrived at intuitively rather than after a deliberate analysis. Our model thus provides a framework within which the design of programming languages for different problem areas could be approached in a uniform and efficient manner.

The same arguments are equally valid for the design of complex system programs. The major task here, however, is defining the nature of the computation process involved. In the case of man-machine systems, time-sharing systems, and other real-time systems, constructing system programs turn out to be so complicated an undertaking primarily because this task is undertaken without first formulating an explicit description of the process along the lines we have been considering.

5. Concluding Remarks

5.1 The principal aim in this article has been the development of a unified metatheory of programming languages and computers such that within the framework of this theory the design of problem-oriented languages for a diversity of problem areas, and computers well matched to these languages, could be attempted in a coherent and efficient manner.

To this end, in Sections 2 and 3 we considered in some detail two classes of programming languages—the simple and the hierarchical—and the computation processes associated with them. We saw that several problems of great practical significance that arise in the design and translation of efficient programming languages could be formulated and studied adequately in terms of a certain standard model for these two classes of languages and a standard model for simple computer languages. In Section 4, we widened the area of discussion by presenting a specification schema for computational languages of considerable general applicability and studied, in the light of this formulation, several issues that have recently generated a great deal of interest among those

PROGRAMMING LANGUAGES AND COMPUTERS: A UNIFIED METATHEORY

concerned with programming language design and translator construction. Specifically, we studied the ALGOL formulation from this point of view and showed that some of its characteristic features are in fact those common to all hierarchical computation processes. This study also enabled us to bring out clearly certain deficiencies, from the systems design standpoint, that are inherent in the structuring of ALGOL.

5.2 It should have become clear by now that the particular standard model for programming languages that we have been advocating is structurally very closely related to symbolic assembly languages with very general macrodefinition facilities. As pointed out earlier [see remark (1) in Section 2.6.4], in the case of assembly languages of actual computers, the functions and predicates available in the language correspond to the instruction and jump types built into the computer. The reason for this restriction was discussed there. Our model for programming languages may be thought of as a generalization, to the limit, of this basic concept.

This is perhaps the most significant difference between the approach to programming language design taken in this article and those other approaches—like ALGOL—currently in vogue, which use context-free grammars and similar grammatical models for the specification of the syntactic component of the language. It may be worth restating, at this stage, our primary reasons for rejecting the approach to programming language design preeminently exemplified by ALGOL.

The arguments advanced at great length in Section 4.4 show that several features which contribute essentially to the specificational complexity of ALGOL—like GO TO statements and a good deal of the punctuation conventions—are features which intrinsically do not have anything to do with the descriptive power of the language but only with a particular way of representing (i.e., a particular schematization of) the sentences of the language. We saw in that section that, after pruning the language down to its essentials from its descriptive standpoint, what remains of it does conform, notational conventions apart, quite closely to our model. In comparison to this reduced version, the intrinsic merits of a graph-theoretic model, with function labels explicitly incorporating the input-output sets at every level, were argued at length there.

5.3 In the early days the ALGOL report gave rise to a large volume of activity in the design of syntax-directed translators and other compiler-compiler projects. Of late, the enthusiasm for this kind of work has waned significantly. It is generally conceded now that these approaches do not offer any significant solution to the general translation problem.

The reason for the failure of these approaches should be clear when looked at from the point of view of the metatheory discussed in this article. In going from a programming language to a computer language, what one is concerned with is to realize equivalence-preserving translations in a semantic sense. Here, the language component that plays a critical role is the dictionary that relates the primitives of the two languages. For solving the general translation problem a significant requirement is the specification of uniform procedures for structuring a dictionary and standard methods for using it. It is precisely at this stage that most syntax-directed compilers and the other similar "generalized" translators take recourse to the use of symbolic assembly language, or even machine language, routines to do their work for them!

What the compiler-compilers actually accomplish is to give a uniform procedure for constructing syntax analyzers for a class of languages whose syntactic specifications use a grammatical model of a certain kind (the so-called BN form [1]). The complexity of a compiler-compiler is really a measure of the complexity of the grammatical model and has no direct bearing on its semantic translation capability. The arguments in terms of our model show that this kind of grammatical structuring of programming languages is neither necessary nor does it have any relevance to the descriptive power of these languages as applied to specific problem areas. If these arguments are valid, it would follow that the work on syntax-directed compilers and so on amount to nothing more than so many exercises in elaborate program construction.

5.4 Two problems of very great fundamental importance which have continued to remain open problems notwithstanding all the current activity on programming language specification, design, and translation, are: (1) the problem concerning the relationship between natural and computational languages, and (2) the problem concerning language learning and usage, computational as well as natural.

The relationship between natural and computational languages is clearly of basic importance if one wants to attempt the design of nontrivial man-machine information processing systems. We considered this problem somewhat tentatively in Section 4.2 and came to the conclusion that there are several aspects of language specification which have to be better formulated and understood before this problem of relationship could even be adequately stated.

The second open problem—that of language learning and usage—has more far-reaching implications. From at least one point of view, it would not be a distortion to claim that the formulation of adequate, pragmatically motivated models of language behavior is, or should be, the central aim of the so-called artificial intelligence studies. To this end, clearly, the formulation of pragmatically adequate models of programming languages which can cope intelligently with well-delimited problem areas should have immediate relevance.

The problem of structuring a program so that it functions as a good chess-playing program, for instance, one that learns from its past behavior and improves its chess-playing capabilities, could be formulated as the problem of the design of a certain computational system with a specification (or, equivalently, description) language with appropriate functions, predicates, attributes, structured operands, and dictionaries and their manipulations. Several questions naturally arise when the problem is so formulated. For example, should a picture language form an intrinsic part of this system? If so, what kind of picture language? What attributes? What functions? And so on.

Similar linguistic problems arise in the domain of picture analysis and description in general. The so-called pattern recognition problem, for example, is clearly a problem of the design of a language (in which the classes of patterns occur as sublanguages) with suitable descriptive capabilities [13, 17].

All available evidence would seem to indicate that linguistic studies—natural as well as computational—should concern themselves more and more with models for language design, learning, and usage in pragmatically significant problem situations, if such studies are to amount to something more than mere play with formalistic details.

Acknowledgments

It is a great pleasure to acknowledge the contributions made by Dr. J. Nievergelt then a graduate student at the University of Illinois to an initial version of the metatheory presented in this article. The result of this joint effort appeared as an internal report [16] of the Digital Computer Laboratory at the University of Illinois. It must be pointed out that many of the central ideas of the current version are already present in that original report. The details incorporated therein, however, are either inadequate or wholly wrong. Subsequent to the publication of the above report the author has been working on improvements to the metatheory to make it more comprehensive and less inadequate. The collaboration of Mr. S. K. Basu in all this effort has been of considerable assistance. The author is much indebted to Dr. R. A. Kirsch for giving him an opportunity to present a revised version of the metatheory in a series of lectures at the National Bureau of Standards during the summer of 1965. The version described in this paper takes into account several points that were brought up during the discussions following the lecture series. Miss F. Kotwal Mr. G. N. Phatak and Mr. V. S. Patil must also be thanked for their competent and prompt assistance in the preparation of the typed copy.

References

1. Backus, J. W., The syntax and semantics of the proposed international algebraic language of the Zurich ACM-GAMM conference., in *Inform. Process. Proc. IFIP Congr., 1959*, pp. 125–132, UNESCO, Paris (1960).
1a. Basu, S. K., On computation in programming languages, Computer Group Tech. Rept. No. 1, Tata Institute of Fundemental Research, Bombay.
2. Burks, A. W., Programming and the theory of automata, in *Computer Programming and Formal Systems* (P. Braffort and H. Hirschberg, eds.), pp. 100–117. North-Holland Publ., Amsterdam, 1963.
3. Chomsky, N., Current issues in linguistic theory, in *The Structure of Language* (J. A. Fodor and J. J. Katz, eds.), pp. 50–118. Prentice-Hall, Englewood Cliffs, New Jersey, 1964.
4. Dijkstra, E. W., An attempt to unify the constituent concepts of serial program execution, in *Symbolic Languages in Data Processing*, pp. 237–251. Gordon & Breach, New York, 1962.
5. Gorn, S., The treatment of ambiguity and paradox in mechanical languages. *Proc. Symp. Pure Math.* **5**, 201–218 (1962).
6. Gorn, S., Summary remarks. *Commun. Assoc. Computing Machinery* **7**, 133–134 (1964).
7. Kaluznin, L. A., On the algorithmisation of mathematical problems. (Russian.) *Prob. Kibernetiki* **2**, 51–67 (1959); see also Review B2071. *Math. Rev.* **24**, 335 (1962).
8. Katz, J. J., and Fodor, J. A., The structure of a semantic theory, in *The Structure of Language*. (J. A. Fodor and J. J. Katz, eds.), pp. 479–518. Prentice-Hall, Englewood Cliffs, New Jersey, 1964.
9. Katz, J. J., and Postal, P. M., *An Integrated Theory of Linguistic Descriptions*. Research Monograph No. 26. MIT Press, Cambridge, Massachusetts, 1964.
10. Kirsch, R. A., Computer interpretation of English text and picture patterns. *IEEE Trans. Electron. Computers* **EC-13**, 363–376 (1964).
11. Landin, P. J., The mechanical evaluation of expressions. *Computer J.* **6**, 308–320 (1964).
12. Landin, P. J., The next seven hundred programming languages. *Commun. Assoc. Computing Machinery* **9**, 157–166 (1966).
13. Ledley, R. S., High speed automatic analysis of biomedical pictures. *Science* **146**, 216–223 (1964).
14. McCarthy, J., A basis for a mathematical theory of computation, in *Computer Programming and Formal Systems* (P. Braffort and H. Hirschberg, eds.), pp. 33–70. North-Holland Publ., Amsterdam, 1963.
15. McCarthy, J., Towards a mathematical science of computation, *Inform. Process. Proc. IFIP Congr., Munich, 1962*, pp. 21–28. North-Holland Publ., Amsterdam (1963).
16. Narasimhan, R., and Nievergelt, J., On computation in computers and in Programming languages, Digital Computer Lab., File No. 582, Univ. of Illinois, Urbana, Illinois, Jan. 1964.
17. Narasimhan, R., Syntax directed interpretation of classes of pictures. *Commun. Assoc. Computing Machinery* **9**, 166–173 (1966).
18. Naur, P. (Ed.), Report of the algorithmic language ALGOL-60. *Commun. Assoc. Computing Machinery* **3**, 219–314 (1960).

19. Naur, P., The basic philosophy, concepts, and features of ALGOL, in *Symbolic Languages in Data Processing*, pp. 385–389. Gordon & Breach, New York, 1962.
20. Nerode, A., Review No. 5766. *Math. Rev.* **26**, 1094 (1963).
21. Peter, R., Graphschemata und Rekursive Funktionen. *Dialectica* **12**, 373–93 (1958).
22. Proceedings of a working conference on mechanical language structures. *Commun. Assoc. Computing Machinery* **7**, 51–136 (1964).
23. Samelson, K., Programming languages and their processors. *Inform. Process., Proc. IFIP Congr., Munich, 1962*, pp. 487–492. North-Holland Publ., Amsterdam (1963).
24. Schwartz, J. I., Jovial, a general algorithmic language, in *Symbolic Languages in Data Processing*, pp. 481–493. Gordon & Breach, New York, 1962.
25. *Symbolic Languages in Data Processing*. Gordon & Breach, New York, 1962.
26. Woodger, M., The description of computing processes: some observations on automatic programming and ALGOL-60, in *Symbolic Languages in Data Processing*, pp. 391–407. Gordon & Breach, New York, 1962.

Incremental Computation

The Preliminary Design of a Programming System Which Allows for Incremental Data Assimilation in Open-Ended Man-Computer Information Systems[*][†]

LIONELLO A. LOMBARDI

University of Rome
Rome, Italy

Introduction	248
1. General Concepts	250
1.1 The Problem	250
1.2 Problems Arising from Current Practice	253
1.3 The Approach Adopted Here	258
1.4 The Unified Language	260
1.5 The Organizational and Managerial Aspects: Decisions and Policies	262
1.6 Techniques Involved: On-Line Computation and List Processing	265
1.7 Where We Stand Now and What Remains to be Done . .	268
2. Syntax	270
2.1 General	270
2.2 Primitive Alphabet	270
2.3 Forms	272
2.4 Unknowns and Synthesis	274
3. Memory Organization	276
3.1 General	276
3.2 Lists	277
3.3 Aggregates in Lists	281
3.4 Free Storage List and Logical Lists	284
3.5 Embedding with an Auxiliary List	286
3.6 Mating of Braces and Conditional Forms	288

[*]The research reported herein was started while the author was associate director for systems at EURATOM in 1962. It was continued intermittently during the two academic years (1962–1964) that he spent as visiting associate professor at the MIT Sloan School of Management, where it was partly supported by the Advanced Research Project Agency under Office of Naval Research Contract Nonr-4102(01), (project MAC). The research was completed during the summer 1964 at the UCLA Western Data Processing Center, with sponsorship by the Advanced Research Project Agency under Contract SD-184, "Computer Networks and Time-Sharing." Final editing was performed in 1965, while the author was a consultant for the National Planning Institute of the United Arab Republic, and in 1966, while he was a consultant for ENEL—Ente Natzionale Energia Elettrica, Rome, Italy.

[†]Small type has been used for remarks and comments which are only of marginal interest. During preliminary reading paragraphs in small type should be skipped in order to avoid interrupting the logical sequence of the presentation.

4. Operation of the Incremental Computer 290
   4.1 The Library 290
   4.2 Evaluation by Synthesis 292
   4.3 Primitive Evaluation 299
   4.4 Infixes and Prefixes 302
   4.5 Conditional Forms and Their Threshold Policies . . . 306
   4.6 Looped Lists 309
   4.7 Recursive Functions and Discharge Lists 312
   4.8 Literal Functions 317
   4.9 Shorthands 321
   4.10 Processes in Abstract Spaces 323
Appendix: Properties of Forms 327
   A.1 Structural Proofs 327
   A.2 Levels of Forms 328
   A.3 Canonical Decomposition 331
   A.4 Substitutes 332
   References 332

Introduction

This is a research paper on the following problem: Today's computers (hereafter called *conventional computers*) were originally designed and developed for the specific purpose of efficiently executing information processes, once these are completely determined and formalized. Recently, however, emphasis of applications has been on situations where the computer should execute processes or parts thereof while these are being determined. This mode of operation, called *on-line*, is aimed at allowing the abilities of the human being and the machine to complement each other by close interaction. So far, work on the ensuing problem of enabling processors to operate on-line effectively has been focused on ingenious extensions of conventional computers, while there have been no major attempts of revising the logical foundations of their design.

Here, on the contrary, we try to answer this more far-reaching question: If we were to forget that conventional computers exist, and wanted to design a computer by having in mind capabilities for on-line operation as a primary goal, how would we design it? There is no reason *a priori* to believe that the logical design of such a computer would be basically the same as that of the conventional one. In fact, the theoretical machine or programming system, called *incremental computer*, that is discussed here as a possible answer to this question, departs from the foundations of conventional computers and programming systems. For example, its language has no instructions or statements, but *well-formed expressions* or *forms* instead. The machine does not execute programs or procedures; instead it *evaluates* forms directly.

Although the language (Section 2), design (Sections 3 and 4), and performance (Sections 1 and 4) of this incremental computer may seem offbeat, they are rooted in the results of extensive research carried out during the last decade by many independent groups in four main areas:

(1) formula translation with push-down lists as in the Bauer-Samelson [12] method,
(2) declarative computation as in LISP (see McCarthy [9] and Berkeley and Fredkin [1]),
(3) memories organized as association lists (see Newell and Tonge [10]), and
(4) real-time man-computer interaction.

Although these four areas of research had goals different from the one pursued here, this new logical design would not be possible at present without their results: The logical design of the incremental computer takes advantage of the results of these four, by and large independent, areas of research and allows us to put them into a proper perspective by utilizing them to benefit each other.

So far, the research reported herein has been conducted on a rather theoretical level. The only experimentation up to now has been the implementation in the LISP language (on the time-shared IBM 7094 of the MIT Computation Center) of a reduced version of the incremental computer, written by Dr. Bertram Raphael (see Lombardi and Raphael [8]).

Except for the first (introductory) section, where general concepts are discussed, this article has the form of a notebook which describes the language of the incremental computer (Section 2), its memory structure (Section 3), and its operation (Section 4). There may be incompleteness and inconsistency due to lack of experimentation, but the information contained here is sufficient to pinpoint many of the problems, perhaps elicit solutions more suitable than the ones proposed, and provide an initial guideline for the implementation of an incremental computer. It would be advisable that such initial implementation take place in terms of an *interpreter*, operating on a conventional machine, which accepts as language the language of the incremental computer.

Technically speaking, this article is self-contained in the sense that no previous acquaintance with information processing is required on the part of the reader (except for some nonessential side remarks). Still, the questions discussed here will be considerably more meaningful to a reader who has a direct, although not necessarily technical, grasp of the current problems arising in the information sciences. In addition, the reader who has a technical acquaintance with *list processing* techniques will be in a better position to understand the methods used here.

It should be clear that this is a report on current research, not a piece of educational literature dealing with established material. We advise the reader to skim through Section 1, where the aims, problems, and techniques of incremental computation are discussed in an informal, nontechnical (and necessarily incomplete and shallow) way. Then he should read Sections 2, 3, and 4 by skipping most technical details, referring back to Section 1 whenever it seems appropriate. Only at this state (not just after reading Section 1) will he start to grasp how incremental computation works and what it is for. At this point, if he is still interested, reading this article systematically will be in order.

At this stage the reader will also realize that the logic of the incremental computer is very simple-minded, but that the realization of an efficient incremental computer requires a considerable amount of refinement. Both of these characteristics, on the other hand, are shared with conventional computers designed in the late 1940's.

While being formed, this material was presented in the interdepartmental graduate course "Advanced Topics in Information Processing" offered at MIT and in the ten day condensed course "Man-Computer Information Systems" offered by Physical Sciences Extension and Engineering Extension at the University of California at Los Angeles, July 20–31, 1964. Excerpts from this article can be used out of context for educational purposes in specific areas. For example, the study of Section 3 and Sections 4.6 and 4.7 would give to the previously unacquainted student a good grasp of list processing techniques and pushdown lists. Similarly, the study of Sections 4.2, 4.3, 4.4, 4.8, and 4.9 would give him a good introduction to techniques similar to the ones used in compiling and interpreting programs written in artificial languages for conventional computers (e.g., conversion of infixes to Polish notation, Bauer-Samelson algorithm, etc.).

1. General Concepts

1.1 The Problem

The logical foundations of today's digital computer design are reasonably satisfactory, even in the long run, for traditional users such as physical, social, life or earth scientists, econometricians, accountants, or engineers. These users need large-scale calculations based on preplanned and well-specified algorithms. For their purposes higher arithmetic speeds and larger memories than those available today will be useful. However, such advances will mainly be in terms of faster circuitry and flexibility of compatible modular construction, which are in an advanced stage of development at present and will soon become available.

The same relatively satisfactory situation is found in the field of algebraic languages (though the implementation of some important improvements in this area is overdue). The basic technical problems relating to user-oriented terminal equipment (visual displays, light pencils, etc.), interactive compilation, immediate reaction time, and incremental transmission of information between man and machine have essentially been solved. We definitely expect that the practical consequences of the solution of these technical problems will be available in the near future. Consequently, we are approaching a state where the computation requirements of scientific users will have essentially been met.

In contrast to the above, it is clear that the present-day philosophy of information system design is far from being able to provide solutions to problems emanating from complex control needs of large-scale business enterprises, military establishments, and medical or civil organizations. The benefits expected to be derived from the successful solution of problems in these areas are potentially greater by orders of magnitude than those realized by current applications of computers. Typical among the areas of information processing troubled by this inherent inadequacy of conventional philosophies are the command and control of complex and diversified defense systems, the complementation of computer and scientist in creative thinking, and the supply of information input for quantitative analysis and management planning, control, and decision making.

The identifying property of these unsolved problems is that they involve information processes which need to undergo continuing evolution along lines which cannot be entirely predicted in advance. Under such evolutionary circumstances instability of structure and design is to be expected. Consequently, no one can have sufficient foresight or information which will allow him in a single step to predict all the implicit developments in such processes or to formalize the ultimate solution of problems emanating therefrom. The way to cope with this problem would be to design a system which provides an environmental structure where patterns of information can grow freely without necessarily depending on predetermined programs. But the survival of such an evolutionary structure is not possible with present methods.

In fact, conventional digital computers (i.e., those patterned after the classical ideas of Turing and von Neumann) require a high degree of specificity and inflexibility in the data that they can accept. The limitations ensuing from this requirement inhibit their use in *incremental data assimilation*, a process which requires data, algorithms, and machines that are adaptively growing and incrementally modifiable.

More precisely, the philosophy of conventional information system design treats all problems by freezing them into fully specified, predetermined programs on which the environment (human users, other computer systems, or stochastic interaction among relevant variables) becomes inflexibly dependent at run time. Such a philosophy cannot provide an appropriate avenue for approaching the wide class of unresolved problems. Let us see what is the origin of this situation and which steps should be taken in order to remove it.

Indeed, this situation should be no surprise, because so far information systems were designed for an entirely different purpose. The intent of their early designers was to automate the execution of procedures, once the procedures were completely determined. The basic contributions of these early designers were the concepts of "executable instructions," "program," and "stored program computer." Information systems based on this conventional philosophy of computation handle effectively only an information process which

> is *self-contained*, in the sense that its data have a completely predetermined structure, and can be reduced to an alogrithm in *final* form, after which no changes can be accommodated except those for which provision was made in advance.

Consequently, the current role of automatic information systems in defense, business, and research is mainly confined to simple routine functions such as data reduction, accounting, and lengthy arithmetic computations. Such systems cannot act as evolutionary extensions of human minds in complex, changing environments.

But the problem treated here is a different one and needs a different solution. Accordingly, we have been working on an alternative design logic for computers which incorporates some new ideas. This new design logic yields processors (called *incremental* or *open-ended* computers) which can meaningfully utilize both algorithms and data supplied in successive increments. We envision that after the assimilation of current data increments, the processor will issue indicative, although not binding, requests for new pertinent information. The open-endedness of such processors is inherent in their very foundations, that is to say, it is implicit in their basic mode of operation. In addition to preserving the usual performance of conventional computers in mathematical and business processes, such new computers open new possibilities of fruitful collaboration among separate independent machines, and between these machines and humans. Concepts such as "compilation" or "run time," which have so far been the crutches of computation practice but at the some time the brakes of computation development, will be eliminated and replaced by a unified methodology of interaction between machines and their environment.

> From the standpoint of the professional programmer, this new solution consists of a programming system which (1) never requires making any stipulations on the structure or pattern of the data (so that such structure can vary in time), (2) does

not require programs to be completely written before it can begin to execute them meaningfully (so that every program is always open to accommodate the yield of further programming work), and (3) allows for *explosion* (the opposite of *aggregation*) of sections of both program and data at any time without requiring reprogramming.

1.2 Problems Arising from Current Practice

The epitome of the problem that we are discussing is the current state of the art in computer-based system for assisting in the command and control of diversified military operations or in the management of business enterprises. The programs for such systems are naturally very large because they have to incorporate a wide variety of different options and provide for many different contingencies. With present technologies, it takes years to write such a program, and until the program is completely written and debugged it cannot be field-tested. More specifically, it certainly can be tested at any time for locating programming mistakes (grammatical or logical), but to no extent can it be evaluated before completion in order to assess the extent to which it performs the functions for which it is being written. Hence it often happens that, while a program is being developed, there are changes in the conditions which had originally motivated a need for it. The ensuing inconsistencies between the program and its current purpose cannot be immediately spotted because, as stated, the program cannot be continually field-tested during its development. And if the program is finally rejected, its shape is generally so intricate and its various components so intimately intertwined that it often becomes unrealistic to try to recuperate any substantial parts of it for further use.

These problems are particularly acute in providing digitally programmed automation support to military command and control and (to a lesser extent because of a lower pressure to go semiautomatic) to business management. The reason is that in such areas the function of a program, which generally is a strategy, always changes quickly and unpredictably: A military or business strategy, no matter how competently and previdently designed, is bound to be a losing strategy if it is not amenable to rapid updating when the environment changes (e.g., the enemy, ally, other divisions of the same army or company, or business competitor changes his behavior).

So what is being done now? A large amount of work is being devoted to writing programs which anticipate and provide for all conceivable evolutions of a strategy and have preprogrammed means of handling them. Still, only a few such evolutions will actually eventually take place, so that a large amount of planning and programming talent is being wasted. In addition, such programs grow very large, because they incorporate large sections which will never be used. Hence, frequently they are difficult to maintain and operate and require very large computer complexes to run them. Besides, no matter how much foresight the planners have, they are bound to overlook or rule out some evolutions which may occur: Thus this approach is also unsafe, because accommodating unpredicted evolutions might require rewriting the whole program, which may take a very long delay when time is critical.

Subroutining techniques are a popular palliative to this kind of difficulty. However, their beneficial effect is limited. In fact, when one modularizes his large program by breaking it down into subroutines, he makes irreversible commitments to the way such subroutines and the main program fit together. Now evolution may affect not only the single subroutines, which can always be rewritten, but also the over-all organizational structure and the interfaces between subroutines or between the main program and the subroutines. Modifications of this nature may require rewriting everything from scratch. Besides, in most cases one cannot draw much significant information (except for the trivial work of debugging) by running a subroutine out of context, with fictitious testing data.

Command and control is not the only area where such problems come about. A similar kind of difficulty is found in computer simulation modeling (e.g., over-all modeling of an aircraft, a traffic system, or a firm). There again one cannot test a model significantly until it is completely written and debugged and a substantial amount of money, effort, and time has been spent on it. Hence, by not being able to get a feedback response from the real world *while* (rather than *after*) one is writing the model, one finds it difficult to select the right features to incorporate.

These problems call for a solution in terms of *open-endedness* of the programs which are being written, and of the language in which they are being written. Now the question is: Can open-endedness be obtained by minor extensions of present techniques? The answer is: Maybe so, but only with great effort.

In fact, let us see what open-endedness should consist of in a conventional computer. Here we will refer to languages such as FORTRAN or ALGOL or PL/1, although what we are saying also holds for machine language. An open-ended program is a program with *gaps* in it, or also, in particular, an unfinished program. For example, a gap may be a missing arithmetic formula contained in another arithmetic formula. If we use the lower case character x and a mnemonic assembled in the format

$$(x, \text{MNEMONIC}) \qquad (1.1)$$

in order to identify a gap, a FORTRAN arithmetic statement might look like, for example,

$$X = \text{SOMEF } (4. \times (x, \text{ABC}) - X., \text{SQRTF}(3.)) \qquad (1.2)$$

where

$$(x, \text{ABC}) \qquad (1.3)$$

denotes a gap. That is, (1.3) stands in (1.2) for an expression which, when (1.2) is written, is not specified. Any rational expression is qualified to replace (1.3) in (1.2).

Similarly, and using analogous notations, one could introduce into the language the possibility of having gaps which stand for a whole string (of unspecified length) of statements. A third place where one may want to have the possibility for gaps is in the data, where a notation similar to (1.1) would allow for replacing sequences of constants (of unspecified length for each gap) within a "line" of input, or also strings (an unspecified number of consecutive lines). A fourth place is in the subroutining systems, by allowing for calling subroutines which are not currently in the library.

Before seeing how gaps can be compiled and executed, we have to discuss what we want to accomplish with them. First, let us examine for what reasons one may prefer to put a gap in a program or data instead of writing the piece of program or data for which the gap stands. There may be two important reasons, namely:

(1) The programmer is not in a position to specify a piece of program or data at the time when he is developing the program or data which surround it. This may occur either because he does not have the information available at the time, or writing it involves some work that he elects to postpone, or because he prefers to run the program with a gap in order to obtain a feedback on the basis of which he will get a lead about writing a piece of program or data to replace it, or because of combinations of these and many other similar reasons.

(2) The programmer decides that the gap is to be there in its own right, and to remain a gap in the output obtained from running the program. That is, he means the gap to be *a free variable* in the algorithm that he writes. Hence, the *execution* of an algorithm with gaps can be looked upon as a *compilation* of such algorithm into another one, which can eventually be *specialized* to a particular use by filling the gaps with appropriate information.

<small>These two reasons for having gaps are distinct in origin. Still, however, they happen to be amenable to identical processing. Thus, in the following sections, where gaps (principally under the new name of *unknowns*) will become one of the crucial features of the language of the incremental computer there discussed, a unique notation and unique processing pattern will be applied to them.</small>

The second kind of gaps may look confusing to the reader at this stage, but it will become clearer after discussing the question: How, and with what purposes in mind, can or should programs with gaps be run?

There are no major difficulties in compiling a program with gaps: It just requires some modifications of an available compiler. At execution time the compiled code, run on a direct-access, on-line computer, would have instructions developed by the compiler which, when the control runs into a gap, would interrupt the execution, print out the occurring gap at a terminal in order to ask the programmer sitting at such terminal to provide information to replace the gap, compile such information if it is a piece of main program, load it if it is a subroutine, or simply read it if it is data, and then resume execution.

> Such a compiler has been designed on a preliminary basis by my graduate assistants Gordon C. Everest and Lee L. Selwyn at the MIT Sloan School of Management. It would take adequate care of gaps originated in item (1) mentioned above. It would also allow one to spot gaps in subroutines and parts of the data which may have been prepared outside the control of the current user. Thus, it is felt that it would be a substantial help in programming effort by spotting gaps and drawing attention to them. This is all it would be useful for.

But more is needed. We want the system to be able to *execute*, not just compile, a program with gaps, and issue as output information which contains such gaps; i.e., functions of such gaps, whereby the latter are free variables. In this way an incomplete program could be used in order to give significant information concerning its behavior. Furthermore, one would locate all of the gaps and feel free to fill in only some of them. The programmer would be able to have the computer help him evaluate the exact role of, and relationship between, the various pieces of information in a process so that he could see the gaps of which each part of the output is a function (in particular, some gaps may turn out to be irrelevant because the program control never flows through them).

One may attempt to obtain such behavior by having the compiler produce an object code, which when it finds, for example,

$$4 + 3$$

replaces it with a 7, while when it finds

$$4 + (x, \text{ABC}) \tag{1.4}$$

leaves it as it is (that is, it leaves the operation symbolically indicated), so that (1.4) would appear in the output of the object program. Similarly, when (1.2) is found during execution, it would be left as it is and possibly delivered as output without change, except that SQRTF(3.) would be replaced by 1.732....

But let us see what happens if (1.2) occurs within a loop. At the beginning of the first pass in the loop, X may have a numerical value, say, 6. Assuming that X does not change value as a result of the execution of other statements of the loop, its value at the beginning of the second pass will be not a number, but, literally, the symbolic expression

$$\text{SOMEF } (4. \times (x, \text{ABC}) - 6., 1.732)$$

and at the beginning of the third pass

SOMEF (4. × (x, ABC) — SOMEF(4. × (x, ABC) — 6., 1.732), 1.732)

and so on. These expressions will grow out of hand and become useless. And if a control statement (e.g., IF or a computed GO TO) contains in its decision formula either a gap or a variable which, like X above, within the available limited information context cannot be computed as a number but only as a function of gaps, then the control statement could not be executed. The only thing to do would be to proceed in all directions specified by the control statement, and assign to each variable which gets recomputed a value (numerical or symbolic) which carries in some way the information that the new value holds only if the above control statement is executed in a certain way.

We have no reason to think that this is not feasible, but we certainly are not able to do it in a useful way. Anyway, it is apparent from the discussion that extensions of conventional compilation methods do not provide a sound, adequate tool for building along the lines of open-endedness. Thus we need a new basic philosophy for designing automatic information systems to deal with information processes taking place in a changing, evolutionary environment. This new approach requires departing from the ideas of Turing and von Neumann. Now the role of the machine is no longer "executing determined procedures," but rather helping in "determining procedures." Open-endedness, which was virtually absent from the Turing–von Neumann machine concept, must lie in the very foundations of the new philosophy.

The basis of the new approach is an *incremental computer* which, instead of *executing* frozen commands, *evaluates* expressions under the control of the available information context. Such evaluation must mainly consist of replacing gaps (or unknowns) with data and performing arithmetic or relational reductions. The key requirements for the incremental computer are:

(1) The extent to which an expression is evaluated is controlled by the currently available information context. The result of the evaluation is a new expression, ready to accommodate new increments of pertinent information by simply evaluating it again within a new information context.

(2) Algorithms, data, and the operation of the computer itself are all represented by *expressions* of the same kind, i.e., in a common language.

(3) This common language used in designing machines, writing programs, and encoding data is directly understandable by untrained human beings.

While the Turing–von Neumann computer is computation-oriented, the incremental computer is *interface-oriented*. Its main function is to catalyze the open-ended growth of information structures along unpredictable guidelines. Its main operation is an *incremental data assimilation* from a variable environment composed of information coming from human beings and/or other processors. (Still, the incremental computer is a universal Turing machine, and it is able to perform arithmetic computations quite efficiently.)

> The incremental computer is actually a programming system more than anything else. It is designed to be first implemented on an interpretive basis on a conventional computer, and only later to be partially or totally built in hardware (a *fixed plus variable* structure such as those being developed by G. Estrin and B. Bussel at UCLA seem the natural vehicle for the latter purpose). However, the mode of implementation does not affect the language nor the logic, so that it makes no difference whether we view the incremental computer as a computer or as a programming system.

1.3 The Approach Adopted Here

The above indicates that a substantially different frame of references has to be sought in order to design an open-ended programming system. In particular, the above discussion shows that most of the difficulties arose from the fact that conventional languages and computers are *procedural* or *time-sequenced*; i.e., their basic operation consists of executing instructions or statements and branching upon encountering some particular (*control*) instructions or statements.

Thus the basis for the new design should not rely on time sequencing. The natural alternative to time-sequenced programs is a *functional representation* of an algorithm, consisting of an expression (hereafter called *form*) having the data as domain (variables) and the results as range (values). The elemental operation of a computer programmed in this way will no longer be the *execution* of a statement or instruction, but the *evaluation* of a form.

> Now this may sound odd. In particular, it may seem unrealistic to think that this way of computing, which departs radically from the (now two decades old) foundations of all modern computers, can yield any kind of practical effectiveness. Fortunately, however, the concept is not new: It has already been used (although for rather different purposes) and has proved very successful. In particular, the LISP language allows for, but does not require, representing algorithms of any complexity functionally, exactly as specified above. Moreover, such representations turn out to be very compact to write and clear to read (at least for those who are familiar with the somewhat unusual LISP notation). Years of experience with LISP show beyond any doubt that such functional or *nonprocedural* programming is at least as practical as conventional programming (although a professional coder with conventional, time-sequenced programming methods well entrenched by his training may find it difficult to switch over, and may find LISP not too palatable at first). Thus, we will not here try to prove

further that nonprocedural programming, from a practical standpoint, is as good as or better than conventional programming. We appreciate that the nonspecialist may find it hard to believe, but all we can do for him is to refer him to people who have been using LISP, and suggest that he take a guided tour over a LISP program. But reading McCarthy [9] or Berkeley and Fredkin [1] may prove sufficient.

In its basic operation, the proposed incremental computer accepts expressions or *forms* as definitions of algorithms, fills their blanks or *unknowns* if, and only if, the pertinent values are available, replaces references or *quotations* of other forms with the respective forms themselves (again if, and only if, these forms are available), simplifies the forms by performing basic arithmetic and relational operations, and issues the results. In general, processing of a form is completed by its routing through various contexts containing different information, thus allowing the form to assimilate pertinent information from each of them. Consequently, we can view this process as a *conditional evaluation* under the control of the context.

The two parallel theories of formal logical systems and Turing machines converge in showing that all universal digital computers have the same scope of operational ability (though generally not the same power nor efficiency). More precisely, they can evaluate all *number-theoretic* or *Turing-computable* functions. It is well known that one cannot possibly design a computer which, logically speaking, is better than another one. This fact has limited, since the very beginning, the natural progress of computation science.

The incremental computer has exactly the same scope and limitations of operations as the conventional ones. That is, it can compute no more and no fewer functions. Consequently, if we look at the incremental computer as an isolated item out of any context, its unusual design would be a dry academic exercise without any practical justification. The relevant point, however, is not the class of computations that this machine *can potentially execute* in the abstract, but rather the way the computer selects by interacting with its environment the computations that it *will actually execute*, and when (in time), where (i.e., in which information context), under what stimuli, in what mode, and to what extent it will execute them. Thus it is not in the isolated computer itself, but rather in its interface with the variable environment that the new design yields a drastic difference of behavior.

The proposed design is viewed as the natural infrastructure for the gradual and adaptive formalization of the information which develops in complex organizations. Such information is reduced to a common base in the sense that both elemental and aggregate objects, as well as algorithms, are represented in the same language, namely, the language of forms. There is no formal distinction between elemental objects, aggregate objects, and algorithms. The functioning of the incremental computer is very simple because all processes are reduced to a restricted number of primitive operations on forms. Yet this simplicity should not affect the efficiency of operation.

Let us clarify somewhat by an informal example—informal, because we are not yet using the programming language of the incremental computer, described in Section 2—how the incremental computer works. Consider the expression or form

$$f_1(f_2((x, A), 3, (x, B)), f_3(5, (x, C), (x, D))) \qquad (1.5)$$

where f_1, f_2, and f_3 are functions of 2, 3, and 3 arguments, respectively, and $(x, A), (x, B), (x, C)$, and (x, D) are unknowns. When presented with (1.5), the incremental computer knows that it has to evaluate it in the context of previously accumulated information that it has available. Assume that this context provides (in the *library*) a definition, in terms of other forms, for f_1 and f_2, but not for f_3, and, in terms of data, values (which again are forms, but not necessarily constant numbers) for (x, A) and (x, D), but no clue to the value of (x, B) and (x, C). Assume further that the value of (x, D) is a form which contains an unknown (x, F), and that (x, F) has at present no assigned value. Hence, the computer will produce as value for (1.5) a new form which defines, *at the present state of its (the computer's) knowledge*, the new function of four arguments (*free variables*)

$$f_4((x, B), (x, C), f_3, (x, F)) \qquad (1.6)$$

Then it will display the definition of (1.6) and/or store it in the library for further utilization. In this way, the computer derives from (1.5) another form which is at present more meaningful than (1.5) in the sense that it is the *specialization* of (1.5) to the present particular context, which consists of the knowledge of the meaning of $f_1, f_2, (x, A)$, and (x, D). The result of such specialization is open-ended, in the sense that it is still amenable to assimilating new increments of information consisting of values for $(x, B), (x, C), f_3$, and/or (x, F). In this way the incremental computer *adapts* general forms to the particular context in which they are used.

Another way of looking at this operation is considering it as a partial *compilation* of (1.5) with the values of $f_1, f_2, (x, A)$, and (x, D) as parameters. The result of such compilation is amenable to further compilations upon assignment of values of $(x, B), (x, C), f_3$, and/or (x, F).

1.4 The Unified Language

A unique language is used for writing expressions or forms (the term *forms* is borrowed from the professional terminology of logicians), input data, and output results. (This unification of the language is also found in LISP.) This language is designed to accommodate mnemonic descriptions in natural English, of any length, of no matter what elements of the forms (e.g., constants, functions, unknowns, etc., all defined in Section 2) so that it can be directly used by human beings for programming, preparing the input, and reading the output. Still the very same language is "machine language" for the incremental computer: This computer is designed in a way to operate directly on such language.

> The importance of this last aspect lies in the fact that in this way partial results of evaluation are always directly accessible to human beings. We can conceive of and easily implement a mode of operation where, upon encountering occurrences of unknowns or functions whose value is not available within the present information context (i.e., gaps), the computer interrupts evaluation and interrogates a human being sitting at a terminal, asking him to supply such values if he can and wants to. The computer may display to him the gap along with the form in which it occurs, in order to give him clues on possible values. Then, if the human being supplies values, the computer considers them as a last minute, *on-line* addition to the present information context. Otherwise it goes ahead leaving the gap open.

This unification of the language has another implication which is worth discussing. Consider in fact the problem of designing a "higher level language" for the incremental computer. In general, the purpose of implementing a higher level language is to incorporate in a fixed piece of coded information (*compiler, generator,* or *interpreter,* in the case of conventional computers) a substantial number of features which are common to all processes of a certain class, for which the higher level language is designed (i.e., *class invariants*). Thus, while programming in the higher level language, the effort of a human being is limited to expressing those aspects of the particular process that he has in mind which identify it within that class, while the aspects common to the whole class are taken for granted, since they are provided by the system. (For a more detailed discussion of this general question of defining and designing a higher level language on the basis of class invariants see Lombardi [*4, 5, 7*].)

> A secondary purpose of higher level languages is to allow for independence of the awkward peculiarities and incompatibilities of machine languages. But this question does not come up here, because the machine language of the incremental computer is tailored in such a way as to be the same for all versions of the incremental computer, as well as directly usable by human beings.

Now in the incremental computer there are no compilers, generators, or interpreters. Still, one can provide for incorporation in the information context (the library) of features common to all processes of a certain class: He can do that by including functions in the library which are primarily (although not necessarily) meant to be used to fill gaps in expressing processes of that class. Thus one develops higher level languages which, unlike the ones of conventional computers, have exactly the same grammar as (i.e., they are structurally identical to) the basic machine language. The only difference is that when writing in the higher level language one can reduce his effort and the length of the expressions by including *quotations* of the above functions. An expression written in this way, when evaluated on a computer where the higher level language is implemented (i.e., whose library contains the above functions) would have such quotations properly replaced. Otherwise, if the higher level language is not implemented on that particular incremental computer, such quotations would be handled as gaps but would not stop evaluation.

In this way one can think that each time he extends the library of the incremental computer he is implementing an increment of a higher level language.

1.5 The Organizational and Managerial Aspects: Decisions and Policies

In management philosophy a distinction is often made between expressions of *decisions* or *actions* (to buy, sell, hire, fire, etc.) on one side and expressions of *policies* on the other. (Here, by expression of a policy or of a decision, we mean a formal, official, operative statement thereof.) A policy is a *decision rule* which gives the pattern to a set of decisions (abstractly, one can view a policy as an infinite, synthetically defined set of decisions). At higher management echelons, there is distinction between expression of top level policy, which is reserved to top managers or policy makers, and expressions of middle level policy which consists of applying expressions of top level policies to particular circumstances. Thus the relation between top level policy and middle level policy is the same as between the latter and single decisions.

However, in management practice, the above taxonomy does not allow for sharp lines of demarcation. The distinction is based on difference of emphasis and quantity, not of kind, and hence is not dichotomous. What we really have in management is a hierarchized continuum of expressions of policies. (Here include among the expressions of policies also those which are merely being tested or played around with, such as the "what if" questions.) The ones which are the highest in the hierarchy are very general in the sense that they contain many variables, i.e., unknowns or gaps. By filling some of these gaps with information which specifies a particular one among the situations to which a general policy applies, one obtains expressions of special policies for that situation, thus *specializing* the general policy. By filling more gaps, one brings the process of specialization further, until ultimately a point may be reached where there are no gaps left, i.e., what is left is the expression of a fully specified decision or action.

Thus the difference between expressions of policy and expressions of action is one of degree, not of quality. More precisely, it is a difference of *degree of generality*, measured by the number of variables (i.e., gaps on unknowns) present in its expression. The degree of generality is high for top level policies. On the contrary, fully determined, specificactions have zero generality, that is, they have no variables (informally said, the latter have a high *specificity*; specificity is the opposite of generality).

What is important here is that in a formal (theoretical) model of an organization we can measure the level of a policy or decision: Such measure is its degree of generality or number of variables present in its expression. The reason why, in organization theory, one frequently discretizes the above continuum by grouping all policies belonging to a certain bracket of degree of generality, is that such different brackets tend to correspond to different *decision loci*; i.e., they are formulated by individuals or committees having different seniority, amount of responsibility, and access to information. Still, however, such grouping is very flexible, and loci and levels of policy formulation, as well as the flow of information, can be easily shifted. Such flexibility derives directly from the fact that, as stated, the difference between classes of policies is one of degree, not of kind.

Decentralization, one of the characteristic features of modern management, stipulates an on-going downward trend in the movement of decision loci, i.e., a permanent process of specialization of policies. In computational terms, decentralization can be defined as an on-going process of gradually filling gaps in expressions of policies.

However, such flexibility is no longer kept when automatic information systems based on conventional computers take over some phases of the metabolism of information which occurs as part of the life of an organization. In fact, the adoption of conventional computers requires introducing a dichotomy which separates the lowest echelon (i.e., one of the expressions with no variables) from the others. This need for a separation stems from the fact that conventional computers require two different kinds of *languages*. One of them, usually called *programming language*, is used only to encode policies which do have variables. The other one, usually called *data language*, can be used exclusively for expressions which no variables, such as contents of punched cards, magnetic records, lines of print, or displays on a screen. In conventional computation two such languages are incompatible. For example, a line of output print from an inventory listing is generally not an executable piece of program.

If we assume that an organization structure is invariant in time, this is no problem (more generally, under such a hypothesis conventional computers would provide a perfectly satisfactory vehicle to automation). But such a hypothesis is unrealistic: managers know by now that the main drawback ensuing from the introduction of computer-based management information systems is that they tend to cause a sluggishness in the organization's response to changes of policy, structure, methods, or environment. One of the reasons for such shortcomings is this duality of languages.

> For a simple example consider a case of shipment orders, which consist of a printed line, with no variables. At a certain time management decides to change its methods in order to allow decisions concerning the carrier to be made down the line of the issuance of the shipment orders, based, for example, on the current availability of trucks at the shipping point. We will assume that the method of choosing the carrier, given such parameter (i.e., the number of trucks) depends on the particular item being shipped. Before the change of methods, each order contained the identification of the carrier. Instead, after the change, it must contain an expression of the policy to be followed in connection with this particular item in order to select the carrier as soon as the number of available trucks is known.
>
> With a conventional computer, there are two solutions of this problem. The first consists of replacing each order by a piece of executable code which, when executed, will produce a shipment order. The second, more common, solution consists of writing a new separate program which covers all policies referring to all items to be shipped. In this case, the orders would only contain parameters for such program. However, both of these solutions require rewriting from scratch the programs for shipment ordering. This is extremely costly and time consuming, and involves a delay of weeks or months in the implementation of the change.

With the incremental computer, on the contrary, the same language is used for both data and programs. In particular, a piece of code with no unknowns is equivalent to a datum (line of print, etc.) of a conventional computer. Thus the incremental computer eliminates the need for dual language, and hence the ensuing sluggishness in the automation of management information systems. Consequently, the shortcomings deriving from the inflexibility of the automatic system are eliminated to a large extent.

> If the system were based on the incremental computer, in the above example of a change occurring in the way orders for shipments are handled, no special action whatsoever would be necessary to implement the change. In fact, the underlying assumption behind such change is that the number of available trucks is not known (or not informative) at the time when the shipment order is first prepared. Thus, all that would be necessary would be to withhold such information during the preparation of the shipment order (if such information is not available, withholding is automatic due to the mode of operation of the incremental computer, discussed in Section 4). As a consequence of such withholding, the shipment orders would be *automatically* issued each containing an expression of the policy

to be followed in order to select the carrier. Such expression of policy will be a form (i.e., an algorithm) in a variable or unknown or gap, say,

(x, NUMBER OF AVAILABLE TRUCKS)

which, evaluated in a context that provides a value (or a way of computing the value) of the above unknown, would yield the identification of the carrier. All this is done automatically as a matter of course, without special programming, by the incremental computer.

Thus, implementation of changes of policy do not require any reprogramming of the incremental computer. All they require is to modify the context in which forms are being evaluated. In management applications, such modifications of the context are obtained simply in terms of a suitable *control of the data flow*.

In summary, it is a well-known fact that the adoption of conventional computers and programming systems for the automation of management information systems often introduces rigidity. This shortcoming is due to peculiarities of such conventional systems, and will be completely removed once computers and programming systems with incremental characteristics are developed to a point making their use in management possible. This follows directly from the fact that the processes which take place in the incremental computer bear considerable relations to (or better, are a theoretical model of) those which take place in human organizations. More precisely, the organization of the incremental computer, although it is far less diversified and sophisticated, shares a critical feature with human organizations, namely, open-endedness to evolution.

1.6 Techniques Involved: On-Line Computation and List Processing

The natural habitat of the incremental computer is in close man-computer interaction, where human users sit on *on-line* terminals and interact directly with the computer.

The technology of on-line computation has been developed quite extensively in recent years on conventional computers. Several on-line systems, some of which provide for multiple terminals (multiaccess) on a single large computer (which is hence *time-shared* between simultaneous users) are presently being considered. This work in on-line computation has consisted mainly of applied programming and engineering focusing on developing sophisticated subroutines and some hardware features which make the approach practical. But no revision of the theoretical formulations of computations has been attempted in this connection.

In on-line computation with a conventional computer the human being can interrupt the machine, and the machine can call the human being at any time during processing. One might ask if on-line conventional computers do no already fulfill the purposes set forth in Sections

1.1 and 1.2. They do not. On-line, multiple-access, time-shared, interactive computers cannot completely make up for the inadequacies of conventional programming systems. With on-line computation, changes in programs being developed can be made only by interrupting *and breaking up* working programs, altering them, and then resuming computation; no evolutionary characteristics are inherent in the underlying system of an on-line conventional computer. Thus, as preliminary usage confirms, multiple-access time-sharing of conventional computers is useful mainly in

(1) facilitating debugging of programs, and
(2) running certain particular programs which have fully specified, preprogrammed, and permanently built-in interactive features, after they have been completely written and debugged.

While such physical means for close man-computer interaction are necessary for progress in information systems, their development is not sufficient alone to produce any substantial expansion of the services provided by automation into the new area of formalization of thought and command.

What we need, instead, is a simple principle for designing a computer in a way which allows the user the option to execute programs without attaching any special significance to the extent to which a program is complete—a computer in which the operation of bringing to evidence gaps and relationships is taken for granted, as opposed to being something that the user has to program in each case. This justifies the need for complementing the current extensive development work on man-machine interaction with the present piece of theoretical research.

But there is more. Any version of this incremental computer (even if simulated interpretively on a conventional one) would allow for man-computer interaction without all of the extra *ad hoc* features of conventional on-line computers. It would be sufficient to provide it with automatic display and interruption upon the occurrence of either or both of the following two types of events:

(1) A gap is found (a gap may be an unknown for which no value is assigned in the data or a quotation for a form which is not in the library).
(2) The evaluation of a function quotation, which occurs within the form that the computer is given to evlauate, is completed.

Upon interruption, the human being may want to extend the data by assigning values to more unknowns, extend the library, and/or resume evaluation.

In essence, on-line computation is the natural mode for the incremental computer, and the incremental computer is a "natural" for on-line computation. (On the contrary, on-line computation can be thrust onto conventional computers, which are basically designed with a different purpose in mind, only to some extent and with great effort, expense, and operational overhead.) In particular, simulative implementations of this increment computer as interpretive language for a conventional one should be done on machines with on-line facilities.

As described in the previous section, the operation of the incremental computer relies heavily on the possibility of replacing a form, say, a, occurring within another form b, with a form c. Now a and c may be of different and unpredictable length. Thus, for allocating memory, the incremental computer has to use a well-known technique which was developed for this specific purpose ten years ago: the *association list* memory organization. Section 3 is devoted to describing the particular version of this technique that we think is suitable for this particular incremental computer. This successful technique allows for eliminating all difficulties in terms of complication of machinery (or programming) and waste of time or memory space connected with replacing certain forms for other forms of different length by paying a fixed overhead cost.

The lengths of forms to be substituted for each other may vary. For example, a may be
$$(x, A)$$
while c is the matrix
$$\left\| \begin{matrix} 7 & 2 \\ 4 & (x, Q) \end{matrix} \right\|$$
which, in the formal language of the incremental computer, is
$$((7, 2), (4, (x, Q)))$$
Thus, five characters are replaced by seventeen. If b is designed in a way to direct, by its evaluation, the computation of the determinant of such matrix, which, *incrementally* computed, becomes the function
$$7 \times (x, Q) - 8$$
of the free variable (x, Q), this last form of nine characters will have to replace all of b, which has certainly more than seventeen.

That part of memory which is not used in always batched in a pool, called *free storage list*. If two or more users are time-sharing an incremental computer (physical or simulated) they can use a common free storage list; in addition, the forms that they are processing can be read, developed, and stored in lists in memory which are intertwined, thus achieving maximum utilization of memory space to meet their needs independently without overhead. Hence, the memory of a time-shared incremental computer need not be partitioned in advance among the simultaneous users, as is necessary (and costly) to do in conventional time-shared computers.

A list processing technique is also used in LISP. Independently of this, users of LISP at MIT consistently report that LISP is by far the handiest computer or programming system for on-line usage. This establishes two connections between the incremental computer and LISP. A third connection, to wit, the non-time-sequenced representation of algorithms (which, however, is optional in LISP but mandatory in this incremental computer) was referred to in Section 1.2. This did not happen by chance: This incremental computer derives directly from the work done on LISP.

1.7 Where We Stand Now and What Remains to Be Done

The basic research reported herein deals with a computer which can process information regardless of whether or not it is complete. Elements of incompleteness, or gaps, are left indicated symbolically by the process of evaluation of the forms in which they occur. Such gaps can be unknowns, denoted

$$(x, \ldots)$$

or (library) functions, denoted

$$(f, \ldots)$$

where, in either case, the dots stand for an identifier (e.g., a descriptive sentence in English).

Thus the incremental computer can be used by human beings to build models, complex command and control systems, or retrieve information without having to follow a preplanned sequence of efforts for specifying the algorithms. The human being can supply the information in the order that he prefers, and the computer will draw his attention to relevant gaps. But a gap can be handled by this incremental computer if, and only if, the very fact that there is a gap in a given form is realized when a form is first written.

To give an oversimplified example, an aircraft engineer can use the incremental computer to start designing a form which is a general model for an airplane without being willing, at the moment, to think of the details of the rudder drag. Thus, he will leave the design of the rudder open by denoting its drag, e.g.,

$$(x, \text{RUDDER DRAG}) \qquad (1.7)$$

and thus he will obtain a model of the airplane which is a function of the unknown (1.7) that is used as a free variable. Such model of the airplane is amenable to accommodate any model of rudder drag (for evaluation of alternative designs, for instance) which can be formally represented by any form. Still, the engineer, while modeling the airplane, had to remember that it must have a rudder drag, and although he does not know what its quantitative formula will be, it is necessary for him to know where such drag fits into the general model of the aircraft. If he disregards including (1.7) in all places of the model of the airplane which depend on the rudder drag, he will no longer be able to later include formulas for computing such drag quantitatively in the model.

Thus, this incremental computer is incremental only in one direction: Information can be added freely, but only upon having anticipated *where* there might be a need for new information.

This can be partly remedied by breaking up a form and changing it by including new gaps when it is already written and perhaps already evaluated with a context. But this is exactly the undesirable way in which incrementality of any kind can be obtained from a conventional computer. Such an approach is undesirable because, in essence, it requires the user to do an amount of coding and debugging which, no matter how well facilitated by effective (but time- and space-consuming) software, will waste his time, hamper man-computer interaction, and divert the user's attention from his main problem to menial bookkeeping tasks.

This is a serious problem of basic research. It consists of designing a new incremental computer which has "gap opening" as a basic feature. We have done no substantial amount of research on it, so we leave it open to question.

Sections 2, 3, and 4 present the basic design and language of the incremental computer. They give enough information to orient us in the development of an interpretive simulation of the incremental computer on a conventiona one. A simulation of a reduced version of this incremental computer has been successfully written (in LISP) by Raphael (see Lombardi and Raphael [8]). Possibly, it is wise to use list processing languages for full interpretive implementations, although some versions of ALGOL, JOVIAL, and PL/1 are also legitimate candidates.

However, these partly untested, early specifications are bound to contain mistakes and leave important problems unsolved. In particular, here data are always assumed to be in memory, and there are no specifications for input-output from or to tape, disk, card reader, or printer. (The same is true for all versions of LISP except the last one to date.) At this preliminary stage the design of such features can be postponed. They can be added later. In fact, they do not involve changing the language, and hence the basic operation. All they require is to implement a special behavior for such self-explanatory unknowns as

$(x, \text{CARD READER})$

for the input, and self-explanatory functions such as

$(f, \text{PRINTER})$

for the output. Thus, the nonprocedural mode of operation can be extended without compromises to cover the input-output.

But there is more incompleteness than that. In fact, this article is only concerned with the internal processing of forms, and stipulates that the value of forms is simply made available to the human being by displaying them as they are. In this way the human being would have to scan dull and uniform information in order to detect gaps, and make a painstaking parenthesis count in order to visualize relationships.

So, essentially there is another aspect of incremental computation which is not discussed here: How to display the result of computations to human beings in order to readily give them a synopsis of the current status of the forms and of the location and interrelationships of gaps. This can be done, for example, by having the computer issuing a separate listing of all unknowns and functions (i.e., all gaps) found in the result of an evaluation. The human being may specify which unknowns he means to be free variables of the output, and the computer will list these unknowns separately from the others (for this distinction see Section 1.2). Moreover, the computer may display the form as *trees* (making obvious use of the parentheses and commas) as opposed to sequential lines, and use a special format (or intensity or colour of light if the display device is a cathode ray tube) for gaps (and maybe for different kinds of gaps).

This problem is probably intellectually less difficult but practically as important as the design of the internal structure of the computer. Again, not having been studied so far, it is open to question.

2. Syntax

2.1 General

This section is devoted to introducing a primitive alphabet of symbols or *marks*, establishing rules by means of which marks can be assembled to form those particular aggregates—the *forms*—which constitute the basis for the definition of the functions that the incremental computer can evaluate, and studying properties of such forms. Additional and more highly technical material, such as the possibility of their *canonical decomposition* within the space of all forms, is given in the Appendix.

The alphabet presented in this section is restricted to a preliminary set of marks which is necessary for introducing formation rules and elementary evaluation methods. Later the alphabet will be extended in order to allow for more compact representation of functions and more general evaluation methods.

2.2 Primitive Alphabet

The primitive alphabet consists of three kinds of marks: *constants*, *operative marks*, and *punctuation marks*. Constants are:

(1) The *truth values* $\mathfrak{T}$ and $\mathfrak{F}$.
(2) Finite sequences of decimal digits and capital characters of the

English alphabet, with at least one character of the latter kind (*alphanumeric constants*). Examples: BUMBLEBEE, A11.

(3) *Integer constants* or *integers*, represented as finite sequences (of any length) of digits followed by the lower case character b followed by the indication (in binary) of the base, everything being preceded by a minus sign if the integer is negative. If the character b and the indication of the base are omitted, the base is taken to be ten.

For example,
$$-240, \quad 137b1000 \quad \text{and} \quad 82$$
are integers. The first is the decimal negative integer -240. The second is the octal positive (or absolute) integer 137 (which, in decimal, is 95). The third is the positive (or absolute) decimal number 82.

(4) *Rational constants* or *rationals* are denoted like integers, with the only difference being a radical point in the sequence of digits.

For example,
$$-101.11b10 \quad \text{and} \quad 938.64$$
are rationals in the binary and decimal system, respectively. As stated, there is no bound to the number of digits in the representation of a rational constant.

In order to represent large or small numbers by scaling, we will introduce the well-known option of adding to the right of a number the character e followed by an integer (with or without minus sign) in the same base, which denotes the power of the base by which the remaining number should be multiplied.

Thus, instead of
$$.000000001b10$$
we can write
$$1b10e - 1001$$

There are three operative marks in the primitive alphabet: x, f, and f^*, called *unknown mark*, *function mark*, and *direct function mark*, respectively. Operative marks will be used to define important types of aggregates of marks, viz., the *unknown*, the *function letter*, and *direct function letter*, respectively.

The six punctuation marks are the comma, the production mark ::=, the open parenthesis, the closed parenthesis, the open brace, and the closed brace, i.e.,
$$, ::= ( ) \{ \}$$

Italics, when present in forms, will always denote items specified in the text: They are only informal notations of the metalanguage in which the incremental computer is described here, as opposed to constituents of the notation used to represent forms.

2.3 Forms

A finite ordered sequence of one or more constants separated by one space (which sometimes for clarity will be filled by a hyphen) is called *extended constant*, and the marks of which it consists are referred to as the *elements* of the extended constant. The purpose of introducing extended constants is to be able to use full natural language phrases to identify descriptively elementary information items on which the incremental computer operates, thus obtaining a notation for the machine representation of relations and processes which is as close to human direct understandability as is compatible with simple and unambiguous representations. By this compromise solution, elements of information within the computer are always immediately reducible to intuitive contents because their representation in human natural language is also used by the computer. On the other hand, as will be explained in the following, the syntax of the language of the incremental computer is not like the one of natural language; on the contrary, it is based on a fairly formal use of punctuation analogous to the one of grammar school algebra.

One may bring up the question of whether or not, in general, it would be both feasible and desirable to devise means of translating natural language into the mixed notation of the incremental computer. Substantial progress toward this end has been achieved by numerous researchers in the field of artificial intelligence. As for desirability, natural language is not the best way to represent complex relations or processes, not even for communication between human beings; for example, scientists, engineers, and military men would be practically unable to work and communicate if they had to use natural language as the only notation, as opposed to using it as metalinguistic complement to their artificial, conventional notations. Thus complex relations are rarely thought or expressed in natural language, which makes such language of little use to system design.

An *aggregate* is any finite ordered sequence of one or more operative marks, punctuation marks, and extended constants (without separating spaces), where the following two conditions are met:

(i) There are no occurrences of the production mark "::="
(ii) Two extended constants never occur consecutively

The number of marks in an aggregate e will be denoted by $L(e)$.

An extended constant contained in an aggregate e is said to *occur strongly* in e if it is not part of any other extended constant contained in e.

A particular kind of aggregate, referred to as *forms*, plays a more important role and needs a thorough discussion. The first and simplest kinds of forms are those covered by the following.

Definition 1: Extended constants and operative marks are forms. It should be noted that punctuation marks are not forms. According to this first definition,

2.5

x

2.5 PLUS T3 AB 1b101

are forms. An aggregate which can be proved to be a form on the basis of definition 1 alone will be referred to as *atomic form* or *atom*.

Let a and b be aggregates. Then the aggregate

$$a, b$$

is called *concatenation of a and b*. Clearly the concatenation is an associative, although not necessarily commutative, operation.

Definition 2: The concatenation of two forms is a form. Let $a_1, a_2, \ldots, a_n$ be atoms. Then, by a total of $2n - 1$ instances of definitions 1 and 2 it can be proved that the aggregate

$$a_1, a_2, \ldots, a_n \qquad (2.1)$$

is a form. Conversely, any aggregate which can be proved to be a form only by applying definitions 1 and 2 a finite number of times has the structure of (2.1), where a_1 are atoms and n is an integer.

Definition 3: The enclosure in parentheses of a form is a form. For example,

$$(x) \qquad (2.2\text{a})$$

$$(-3, \text{ALPHA}, f, 2) \qquad (2.2\text{b})$$

$$(x, 2, (-3, \text{ALPHA}, f, 2)) \qquad (2.2\text{c})$$

are forms.

Definition 4 (conditional forms):
Let a, b, and p be forms. Then the aggregate

$$(a\{b\}p) \qquad (2.3)$$

is a form, called *conditional form*. In (2.3), a is called *true alternative*, b is called *false alternative*, and p is called *decision predicate* of the conditional form.

Definition 5 (recursion clause): No aggregate is a form unless its being such follows from a finite number of instances of definitions 1, 2, 3, and 4. For example, neither $)x($ nor f nor $(5$ are forms, because one can easily prove that no finite sequence of instances of definitions 1, 2, 3, and 4 could prove them to be forms.

Using the well-known metalinguistic notation called *Backus normal form*,[1] the definitions of constant, extended constant, operative mark, and form can be presented as follows:

⟨constant⟩ ::= ⟨integer⟩|⟨rational⟩|⟨alphanumeric⟩|$\mathfrak{T}$|$\mathfrak{F}$

⟨extended constant⟩ ::= ⟨constant⟩|⟨constant⟩
⟨one separating space⟩⟨extended constant⟩

⟨operative mark⟩ ::= $x|f|f^*$

⟨atom⟩ ::= ⟨operative mark⟩|⟨extended constant⟩

⟨form⟩ ::= ⟨atom⟩|⟨form⟩, ⟨form⟩|(⟨form⟩)|
(⟨form⟩{⟨form⟩}⟨form⟩)

⟨conditional form⟩ ::= ⟨form⟩{⟨form⟩}⟨form⟩

An aggregate consisting of the leftmost (rightmost) n occurrences of marks of a form having at least n marks is referred to as *left* (*right*) *partial form*. If a form a_1 consists of a sequence of successive marks within an aggregate a_2, a_1 is called *subform* of a_2.

Some properties of forms are discussed in the Appendix.

2.4 Unknowns and Synthesis

Let e and b be aggregates, and let a be another aggregate consisting of a sequence of consecutive marks in e (i.e., *a subaggregate* of e). Then the aggregate obtained by replacing a by b in e will be called *substitute* of b for a in e and denoted $S(b, e, a)$. Using the concept of undecomposable forms, introduced in Appendix A.3, one can prove the following theorem.

Theorem 1—*If e and b are forms and a is an undecomposable subform of e, then $S(b, e, a)$ is a form.*

A proof is given in Appendix A.4.

An *unknown* is the enclosure in parentheses of the concatenation of the unknown mark x and an extended constant, called *identifier* of the unknown. For example, the unknown

(x, ARC OF SINE)

has ARC OF SINE as identifier.

Let e be a form such that the number $M(e)$ of its canonical components[2] is even. Suppose further that each odd canonical component

$$e_{2i-1}, (i = 1, 2, \ldots, M(e)/2)$$

consists of an extended constant. Then e is called a *parameter sequence*.

[1] Compare with the report on ALGOL 60 in *Commun. ACM* **3** No. 5 (1960).
[2] For definition of *canonical component* see Appendix A3.

Its odd components e_{2i-1} are called *parameters* and the even components e_{2i} are called *values*, so that e_{2i} is the *value of the parameter* e_{2i-1}.

For improving readability in this write-up, the commas occurring between a parameter and its value in a parameter sequence will sometimes be replaced by a colon, which, for all intents and purposes, is equivalent to a comma. Thus, instead of writing a parameter sequence

$$A, (x, \text{HAVE A MARLBOUROUGH}), Y\ 25, \text{NO}$$

we may write

$$A: (x, \text{HAVE A MARLBOUROUGH}), Y\ 25: \text{NO}$$

Let g be a form and e a parameter sequence, and let us consider a new aggregate metalinguistically denoted

$$g|e \tag{2.4}$$

consisting of the form g, where all occurrences of any unknown whose identifier is identical to at least one parameter of e are replaced by the value of the first such parameter. The aggregate (2.4), which is a form by theorem 1, is called *synthesis* of g and e. For example, if e is

$$A:8, D:((f, Q), R), C:3, A:2,$$

and g is

$$((x, A)\{(x, D)\}(x, F))$$

then $g|e$ is

$$(8\{((f, Q), R)\}(x, F))$$

Synthesis is the principal symbol manipulating action which the incremental computer performs. In a sense, it plays a role equivalent to the "execution of an instruction" in a conventional computer. Its result can be described as being the development of a form g into a new form $g|e$ consisting of integrating in g all the information contained in e which is both relevant to g and not available in g. Such assimilation takes place by *filling blanks* of g, i.e., by substituting appropriate forms for occurrences of unknowns.

In particular, if g contains no occurrences of unknowns, then g and $g|e$ are identical.

To define synthesis, so far, g has been allowed to be any form, while e has been required to have the format of a parameter sequence. However, this restriction can be removed by simply saying that if $M(e) = 1$, then, for all g, $\{g|e\}$ is g; if $M(e)$ is odd but other than 1, e's last canonical component is ignored in the synthesis. Finally, if some one of the odd components of e, say e_{2i-1}, is not an extended constant, then, in the synthesis, e_{2i-1} and e_{2i} are ignored. By this generalization, synthesis $g|e$ is defined for all forms g and e.

Synthesis is the basic operation by which the incremental computer applies algorithms to particular situation by *specializing* forms to contingent sets of arguments.

Synthesis is not in general associative, so that the forms

$$(a|b)|c \tag{2.5}$$

and

$$a|(b|c) \tag{2.6}$$

may differ.

In terms of conventional computation, (2.5) is analogous to a precompilation of a form

$$k = a|b$$

whereby the second synthesis, $k|c$, recalls the *execution* of k at object time with c as data. As far as (2.6) is concerned, the synthesis

$$h = b|c$$

reminds us of the execution of a *subroutine* which performs a first stage of computations on the data c and prepares them as input to a *main program*, which is the synthesis $a|h$.

3. Memory Organization

3.1 General

The memory of the incremental computer is organized in *association lists* or, briefly, *lists*. Each list is a sequence (without repetitions) of words, which contains a form. Each word is divided into two parts. One part, called *center part*, contains a mark or a fraction thereof, while the other, or *left part*, contains the address (in the conventional sense) of the word whose center part contains the following mark or another fraction of the same one. The incremental computer scans forms sequentially by jumping from one word to the next by following the contents of their left part. This way of associating one word to another will be referred to as *first level association*. Scanning of a form by first level association will yield a right-to-left scan of the form (this choice is arbitrary).

Some words (precisely those whose center part contains a punctuation mark) will have a third part, called *right part*, which contains the address of another word whose center part carries a mark or fraction thereof of the same form. This other association, called *higher level association*, is aimed at expediting the scan of forms by allowing for skipping aggregates contained in them, as discussed later.

The basic concept of list-organized memory has been common in information systems design for a decade, but still gives rise to controversies and misunderstandings. The purpose of this technique is dual, namely:

(1) To allow for a systematic way of storing and locating information which has a complex structure, especially when such structure varies in time in an unpredictable fashion.

(2) To allow for a systematic approach to dynamic storage allocation for items of information whose length varies unpredictably. By means of association lists, a fixed price (approximately 50%) in terms of storage is payed as overhead. In

return, every single word of storage is always available to honor requests for storage space. It is often believed that list organization has two shortcomings, namely:

(a) It implies a waste of storage for information other than the "quantitative" data to be stored, namely, for association addresses. This is not true. The association addresses have as much right to be viewed as part of the stored information as have the quantitative data; they are the information about the *structure* of the quantitative data (marks), which is as important as the quantitative data themselves. The only reason why list organization is not advisable for programming mathematical problems in conventional computing is that such problems have by and large a fixed, extremely simple data structure, to wit, a sequence of words, which does not vary in time, for the program, and single words or multidimensional (rectangular, triangular, etc.) arrays for the data. But this is not the case for the kind of problems (incremental formalization) for which the incremental computer is designed.

(b) It is not amenable to efficient sequential scans. This is also false. A conventional computer which scans by first-order association would be as fast as one which (as many do) uses index registers. It would probably be less expensive by present electronic standards, because indexing requires the services of an adder.

Still, list organization does have one inherent comparative shortcoming (and only one, as far as we can see); namely, the fact that it often does not allow for immediate location (*random access*) of information in the middle of a list without scanning the whole list or parts thereof. This can be speeded up only case by case, depending on the particular problem that one has. For the problem of designing an incremental computer, we have adopted the method of higher order association, which allows for immediate, or almost immediate, access to all those parts of a list that the single operation performed by the incremental computer (i.e., evaluation of forms within a contest) can possibly require.

3.2 Lists

As previously stated each memory word is divided into three parts: left, center, and right. The contents of the three parts of a word w will be denoted

$$\mathfrak{L}w, \quad \mathfrak{C}w \quad \text{and} \quad \mathfrak{R}w,$$

respectively.[3] The left part must have the capacity of an address (i.e., the number of digits (base k) that it must be able to contain must be the $\log_k$ of the number of words in the memory).

We do not want to give any specifications for the capacity of the center part, which is devoted to containing the "quantitative" information. But whatever its capacity, say h characters ($h \geq 1$), we will specify how marks longer than h characters are represented.

---

[3]The notations $\mathfrak{L}$, $\mathfrak{C}$, and $\mathfrak{R}$ and their powers will be used as operators. So, for example, $\mathfrak{L}^2\mathfrak{R}w$ denotes "the contents of the left part of the word whose address is contained in the left part of the word whose address is contained in the right part of w."

Each such mark is divided into strings of h characters, called *submarks*, starting from its right end. The leftmost submark may have less than h characters. Each submark is assigned to the center part of one of a sequence of words of storage linked by first-order association. Each word must have a special bit, the *mark end bit*, which is set to the value 1 for those words which carry the last (i.e., the leftmost) submark of a mark, and to 0 for all others. Thus, one can read a mark right to left by following first level association and stopping as soon as he finds a mark end bit whose value is 1. By means of this policy marks of any length (and, consequently, numbers of any "precision") can be uniformly stored.

If a mark can be stored in a single word, then we will call the address of that word *address of that mark*. If the length of the mark exceeds the capacity of a word, and it has to be broken into submarks, then by *address of that mark* means the address of the word which carries its rightmost submark. The right part of the words must be able to carry an address; it should be as long as the left part.

However, in the incremental computer, only those words whose center part carries a punctuation mark need a right (higher level association) address; all other words have an empty right part. This suggests consolidating and collapsing the information contained in the center and right part as follows: In each word, besides a full left part, there will be:

(1) A quadruplet of bits, 12 of whose 16 different value combinations correspond to the seven punctuation marks introduced so far (that is, production mark, comma, open parenthesis, closed parenthesis, open brace, closed brace, and colon) and to the three additional ones (i.e., square brackets and *flagged integers*), which will be introduced in the next section, while two more denote the fact that the word does not carry a punctuation mark or a flagged integer. The alternative between the latter two combinations is used as mark end signal.

(2) A set of bits capable of carrying at least one address which, in case the above quadruplet indicates the presence of a punctuation mark or flagged integer, carries a higher level association address. Otherwise, it carries a submark.

Once these conventions are made, we will forget about the actual distribution of information within words and refer to the three parts of a word as if they were actually separate. We will also forget about marks which need to be chopped into submarks: Thus, in the following, when we say "mark contained in (the center part of) a word," unless otherwise specified we refer to the whole mark, one submark of which is contained in that word.

In the incremental computer the utilization of memory is always maximum in the sense that all memory words are returned back to a common pool (the *free storage list*) as soon as their contents become irrelevant to further processing. Maintenance of this pool is carried out automatically by the incremental computer.

The percentage of memory space devoted to organizational overhead is constant with respect to the length of the aggregates stored there. As will be seen in the following, the percentage of time devoted to overhead operations, such as addressing, is also constant with respect to the length of the aggregates operated upon. This constant ratio of overhead space and time is an important peculiar feature of this incremental computer, and many aspects of its design have been devised in order to provide it with this feature. The study of computation schemes where the ratio between average organizational overhead in space or time and total space or time, respectively, increases and tends to 1 when the length or the complexity of the information to be processed increases may have a certain mathematical interest but cannot possibly give good indications for the advancement of computation methodology. In fact, while a constant overhead ratio, even very high, can potentially be reduced by skillful tailoring, this is not the case for overhead ratios not bounded above by a number < 1. This is, in essence, the angle from which the design of the memory organization of this incremental computer should be viewed.

A *list*, as stated previously, is a sequence without repetitions of a finite number of memory words. Each word, with the exception of the last one, contains as left part the address of the following one (*first-order association address*). The last word contains a 0 as left part to tag it as last word.

If a list is denoted S, $N(S)$ denotes the number of its words. In order to represent lists in this article, that is, in a *metalanguage*, we shall divide the representation into a narrow left margin for the addresses, and a wider space for the significant part of the contents of the word. This wider space is divided into three columns, each of which represents one part of the words in the list. Each word of a list will be represented on a separate line, along with its address in memory, and a list is represented by sequence of such lines.

A list is said to be *empty* if none of its center parts contain information. This concept must be distinguished from the one of *0 list*, that is, a list which has no words. The center and right parts of the words of empty lists are always regarded as not containing significant information. The left part of the last word in a list contains a 0 (assuming that the memory addresses are numbered from 1 up) so that the end of a list can be sensed by finding a 0 in its left part.

In the metalanguage of this article, the contents of the three parts of the words of a list are written in three columns separated by some space. For example, the following is the representation of an empty list of 4 words:

200	51
51	2
2	100
100	0

The address of the first and last word of a list (200 and 100, respectively, in the case of the above example) will be referred to as *initial address* and *final address* of the list, respectively. The former is sufficient to identify a list.

Let S_1 and S_2 be two lists having no words with common addresses. The *junction of S_1 to S_2* is a new list S_3 of $N(S_1) + N(S_2)$ words consisting of the first $N(S_1)$-1 words of S_1, followed by the last word of S_1 with the initial address of S_2 replacing the contents of its left part, followed by all words of S_2. The initial and final address of S_3 are the ones of S_1 and S_2, respectively. Junction of lists, whenever possible, is clearly associative.

Let S be a list. The n_1-n_2 *section* ($1 \leq n_1 \leq n_2 \leq N(S)$) of S is the list consisting of the words of S from the n_1th to the n_2th, inclusive, where the contents of the left part of the n_2th word has been replaced by 0. The initial and final address of such section is the one of the n_1th, and n_2th word of S, respectively. Let S' denote the n_1-n_2 section of S. The n_1-n_2 *remainder* of S is a list consisting of all words of S not belonging to S' where, if $n_1 > 1$, the contents of the left part of the $(n_1 - 1)$th word are replaced by the address of the $(n_2 + 1)$th word or by a 0, depending on whether or not $n_2 < N(S)$. The initial address of the n_1-n_2 remainder of S is the one of S or the one of its $(n_2 + 1)$th word, depending on whether or not $n_1 > 1$, while its final address is the one of S or the one of its $(n_1 - 1)$th word, depending on whether or not $n_2 < N(S)$.

If both $n_1 = 1$ and $n_2 = N(S)$, then it will be convenient to say that the n_1-n_2 remainder of (S) is a *0 list*.

If w_1 and w_2 are the addresses of the n_1th and n_2th word of a list S, respectively, w_1-w_2 *address section* or w_1-w_2 *address remainder* will be ways of referring to n_1-n_2 section or remainders, respectively, in those cases where w_1 and w_2 are known while n_1 and n_2 are not. The notations *n section*, *n remainder*, *w address section*, and *w address remainder* are abbreviations for denoting sections, etc., going from the nth word, or the word of address w, to the end of the list involved.

Certain lists (which ones exactly will be discussed later) need a permanent reference to their first and last address in order to be processed by the incremental computer. If this is the case for a list S, two extra words, *control word* and *end pointer* denoted by s_0 and s_∞, respectively, will be assigned to it. These words will also have three parts, of which the leftmost contain the initial and final address of the list, respectively. In the metalanguage the control word and end pointer are displayed on a separate line preceding and following, respectively, the lines containing the words of the lists to which they refer, and separated from them by a horizontal line. For example, if the list exhibited earlier in this section has a control word located in address 29 and an end pointer in address 45, then it will be represented as follows:

29	200
200	51
51	2
2	100
100	0
45	100

The control word of a 0 list contains a 0 in its left part. In the following, s_i will denote the ith word of the list S.

3.3 Aggregates in Lists

Let S be a list, a an aggregate, and n a positive integer such that

$$L(a) \leq N(S) - n \qquad (3.1)$$

Let a_i ($i = 1, 2, \ldots L(a)$) denote the ith mark in a, counting from the left. If for each i the mark a_i is located in the center part of the $(n + L(a) - i)$th word of S, then the aggregate a is said to be n-allocated in the list S. If w is the address of the nth word of S, and a is n-allocated in S, it may also be said to be w-address allocated in S. (Remember that aggregates are allocated in lists in reverse order, in the sense that the rightmost mark goes into the first word, etc.) If n is not mentioned it is taken to be 1.

Given an aggregate a, we want to extend the definition of *depth* of an occurrence a_i of a mark in a given in the Appendix, to the case of parentheses. The intuitive meaning of this extension should be that the depth in a of the occurrence a_i of an open or closed parenthesis, respectively, should equal the one of an imaginary additional mark which were introduced to the immediate right or left, respectively, of a_i in a.

In order to extend this concept formally, let us first think in terms of left depth $D_l(a_i, a)$. If $i = 1$, then its left depth is -1 or $+1$, depending on whether a_i is a closed or open parenthesis. For $i > 1$, if a_i is an open parenthesis, its left depth is defined as $D_l(a_{i-1}, a) + 1$. If it is a closed parenthesis, $D_l(a_i, a)$ is either $D_l(a_{i-1}, a) - 1$ or $D_l(a_{i-1}, a)$ depending on whether or not a_{i-1} was a closed parenthesis. Conversely, $D_r(a_{L(a)}, a)$ is 1 or -1 whenever $a_{L(a)}$ is a closed or open parenthesis, respectively. If a_i is an open parenthesis, for $i < L(a)$, $D_r(a_i, a)$ is $D_r(s_{i+1}, a)$, depending on whether or not a_{i+1} is an open parenthesis. If a_i is a closed parenthesis, then $D_r(a_i, a)$ is $D_r(a_{i+1}, a) + 1$. If a is a form, left and right depths thus defined are always equal and never negative. Note that the right depth of marks in partial forms can never be negative. Let a_i be an open parenthesis at right depth d in the partial form a. Then there must be closed parentheses or commas at depth d to the right of a_i in a, and let us call *mate* of a_i the leftmost of them.

Let us extend this concept of mate to the case where a_i is an occurrence at depth d of a comma in a. If there are in a and to the right of a_i occurrences of commas or closed parentheses of depth d, then the leftmost of them is the mate of a_i. Otherwise, a_i is said to be *unmated in a*. If a_j is the mate of a_i, then a_i will be called the *antimate of a_j*. If a contains commas of depth 0, the leftmost of them in a is called the *initial mate* of a. Otherwise, a is said to be *initially unmated*. Furthermore, if a_i is an occurence of depth d of a closed parenthesis in a, then, if there exist in a to the left of a_i open parentheses at depth d, then the rightmost of them is the mate of a_i.

For example, in the form

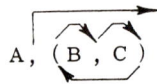

where the arrows indicate transition from punctuation marks to their mates, the mate of the open parenthesis is the second comma (from the lef), the mate of the second comma is the closed parenthesis, while the first comma is unmated. The initial mate of this form is the first comma. The antimate of the closed parenthesis is the second comma, while its mate is the open parenthesis.

By means of an argument similar to the one used in Appendix A3 to prove the canonical decomposition theorem, one can easily prove that the aggregate consisting of all marks in a form included between a mark and its mate, exclusive of extremes, or of all marks preceding an unmated comma are forms.

Let the partial form a be n-allocated in the list S with control word and end pointer. Let us develop a set of rules for filling the right parts of the words of S which contain punctuation marks of a. If $n = 1$, then the right part of the control word T_{s_0} contains the address of the initial mate of a, provided that it exists. Otherwise it contains the address of the end pointer s_∞. If $n > 1$, this address will be contained in the right part of the $(n - 1)$th word of S. In either case, all words of S carrying punctuation marks of a will have in their right part the address of the respective mate, if it exists, or else the address of s_∞.

Then, the partial form a is said to be n-embedded in the list S. If w is the address of the nth word of S, a can also be said to be w-address embedded in S. If n is not explicitly mentioned it is taken to be 1.

For example, the form of 13 marks

can be 2-embedded in a list of 15 words with control word and end pointer as given in Table I (where w_i denotes the ith word of the list).

INCREMENTAL COMPUTATION

TABLE I

O (Control word)	Address	$\mathfrak{L}(w_i)$	$\mathfrak{F}(w_i)$	$\mathfrak{N}(w_i)$
	21	28		17
1	28	15		
2	15	10	)	5
3	10	20	ARITHMETIC	
4	20	30	,	15
5	30	5	-3	
6	5	7	(	20
7	7	6	,	40
8	6	12	)	11
9	12	9	x	
10	9	16	,	6
11	16	11	421108600	
12	11	17	(	9
13	17	13	,	7
14	13	26	107.2	
15	26			
∞ (End pointer)	40	13		

A representation of the same form 1-embedded in a 13 word list with control word and end pointer can be as given in Table II. Both of these tables exhibit 15-address embeddings.

TABLE II

O (Control word)	28	15		17
1	15	10	)	
2	10	20	ARITHMETIC	
3	20	30	,	15
4	30	5	-3	
5	5	7	(	20
6	7	6	,	21
7	6	12	)	9
8	12	9	x	
9	9	16	,	6
10	16	11	421108600	
11	11	17	(	9
12	17	13	,	7
13	13	0	107.2	
∞ (End pointer)	21	13		

If one starts from the word s of a list S containing the initial mate of a form a which is n-embedded in S, moves from this word to the one whose address is contained in the right part of the first one, and repeats this operation r-1 times (that is, one computes $\mathfrak{R}^r(s)$) assuming that a closed parenthesis is never encountered except possibly at the last step, one is brought to a word whose left part contains the list address of the last (rightmost) mark of the rth canonical component of a. If one performs the same operation starting from a word containing a mated occurrence a_i of depth d of an open parenthesis in a, then one is brought to a word containing in its left part the address of the rightmost mark in the $r-1$th component of the form included between a_i and its mate, extremes excluded. The contents of the right parts of lists where forms are embedded contain this information relevant to their canonical decompositions, and allow for a direct rapid access to the components of forms, to the components of the *interior* of components, etc. (If an undecomposable form a has the format (a'), where a' is a form, then a' is called *interior* of a.) The contents of these right parts are called *higher order association* of the list. In contrast, the contents of the left parts, or first-order association, allow for scanning forms in sequence, one mark after the other. While the average time of accessing a mark through the higher order association is roughly proportional to the depth of the mark and does not depend on the length of the form involved, the average time of doing it through first-order association is proportional to the length of the form. The only purpose of adopting first-order association in this incremental computer is that it allows for efficient utilization of storage in this machine, in which the units of processed information, namely, the forms, have an unpredictably time-varying length, and they are therefore not very suitable for efficient sequential storage allocation. The reason for adopting higher order association is quite different; in fact, this feature of this computer allows it to reach canonical components of forms directly and thus perform syntheses efficiently. Because of higher order association, the ratio of overhead operations due to addressing in the incremental computer is independent of the size of the aggregates on which it operates, so that complex forms are treated as easily as simple ones. In contrast, addressing of components of forms based on first-order association, while logically much simpler, would imply a ratio of overhead operations for addressing purposes strongly increasing with the size of the aggregates operated upon.

3.4 Free Storage List and Logical Lists

At any time of its operation the incremental computer will have one, and only one, special list with control word, called *free storage list F*, in no section of which any aggregates are allocated. Its purpose is to serve as a reservoir of space (words) to build new lists. At the beginning of operations all memory words are in the free storage list. Memory space is always appropriated by taking 1-n sections from the free storage list where n is the required number of words. When the aggregate allocated in any list S is no longer needed, this list is *erased* by simply adding it to the free storage list (after having added the control word and end pointer of S to S itself, if there were such words); the aggregates allocated in lists thus logically erased need not be physically erased, but are simply ignored. As will be seen in Section 4, this incremental computer provides for immediately returning to the free storage list any other list as soon as the aggregate that it carries is no longer needed, so that, should a step of computation attempt to appropriate a section from the free storage list which exceeds it in length, this would mean that the incremental computer is inherently unable to perform such computation unless provided with a larger memory, that is, with a longer initial free storage list.

The initial order of the words in the free storage list is irrelevant. By *taking n words of free storage* one means considering a 1-n section of the free storage list and replacing the free storage with its 1-n remainder. By *joining an aggregate a to the beginning of a list S*, one means taking $L(a)$ words of free storage, and 1-allocating (or 1-embedding, if a is a partial form) a in the list obtained by joining this new list to S. By *joining an aggregate a to the end of a list S*, one means the same operation, with the only differences that S is joined to the new list and a is $N(S)$-embedded. If case a and the contents of S are partial forms, the contents of the right part of s_0 and of words carrying unmated marks must be adjusted. By *removing n_1 marks from the beginning, from n_2 or from the end* of a list S, one means taking a 1-n, n_2, n_2-$(n_2 + n_1)$, or $(N(S) - n_1)$-$N(S)$ section of S, respectively extracting the aggregate contained in it, adding this section of S to the free storage list, and replacing S with the remainder of this section.

The notation *removing n marks from address w of the list S* has analogous meaning.

From here and until the end of Section 3.5, all aggregates will be assumed not to contain any braces unless otherwise specified. The extension of all concepts presented here to aggregates of the most general kind is then performed in Section 3.6.

A *logical list* is a list S with control word and end pointer with a partial form a embedded in it, such that $L(a) = (Ns)$.

The $\mathfrak{L}\mathfrak{R}s_0$-section of S, that is, the sublist of S consisting of all words following the one whose address if $\mathfrak{R}s_0$, is called *top* of the logical list. If a logical list S contains a form a embedded in it, the rth canonical component of a is $\mathfrak{L}\mathfrak{R}^r s_0$-embedded in S. The first component of a is embedded in the top of the logical list.

The reason why the top of logical lists has been defined to consist of the intuitive end of the list (according to the first-order association) is that aggregates are allocated in lists in the reverse order, and the end for first-order association is the beginning for higher order association. The units of information on which the incremental computer operates are forms and their canonical components, not marks: When canonical components of a form a embedded in a logical list S are to be operated upon, the ith of them is found immediately, since its rightmost mark is $\mathfrak{CLR}s_\infty$. The addressing system of the incremental computer is based on higher order association, and one should think of a logical list S in terms of lists of lists (or list structure) linked by the higher order association rather than in terms of a list of words linked by first-order association. The sole purpose of first-order association is to achieve maximum utilization of physical storage, and the reason why it goes backward with respect to higher order association lies only in the mode of operation of this particular incremental computer which, as will be explained in Section 4, reads the forms backward in order to evaluate them.

In the following, a list other than a logical list will be referred to as a *physical list*. Physical lists are not suitable for carrying structured information such as partial forms, and their main use is connected with storing and addressing special sequence marks, mainly constants.

3.5 Embedding with an Auxiliary List

Under the assumption that all storage available for allocating marks is originally in the free storage list, no problems should arise as far as the maintenance of first-order association is concerned. In fact, joining, forming of sections and remainders of lists, as described above, are all operations which preserve first-order association. But this is not the case for higher order association, unless something is done about it. The scheme discussed in this section allows for solving this problem by associating with each logical list S another (physical) list U, called *sequencing list* of S, such that the logical items allocated in it are not aggregates but isolated marks (so that first-order association can be efficiently used also for addressing purposes in U). An algorithm to produce the higher order association of partial forms embedded in logical list S is thus defined in terms of the allocation of marks into a physical list.

The concept of sequencing list is a variation of a device sometimes called *push-down list* or *stack*, which is present in programmed form in most program compilers for conventional computers and in wired form in some conventional computers. Push-down lists are lists of marks, not of structured information, and therefore can be effectively addressed by first-order association. On the other hand, the logical lists used by this incremental computer are a more general concept for which there is no intuitive equivalent in conventional or semiconventional machines.

Let a be a right partial form and a_i the ith mark from the right of a. First, mainly as an exercise, we will devise a simple algorithm for associating to each a_i its right depth. For this purpose, one utilizes a sequence b_i $(i = 0, 1, \ldots L(a))$ of numbers and a sequence c_i of truth values defined recurrently as follows:

$b_0 = 0$

$b_i = \begin{cases} b_{i-1} + 1, & \text{whenever } a_i \text{ is a closed parenthesis} \\ b_{i-1} - 1, & \text{whenever } c_{i-1} \text{ has the value } \mathfrak{T} \\ b_{i-1} & \text{otherwise} \end{cases}$

while

$c_0 = \mathfrak{F}$

$c_i = \begin{cases} \mathfrak{T} & \text{whenever } a_i \text{ is an open parenthesis} \\ \mathfrak{F} & \text{otherwise} \end{cases}$

The purpose of these definitions is to be able, for all i, to compute the integer $D_r(a_i, a)$, which equals b_i, on the basis of information pertaining to a_i and a_{i-1} alone. The value of b_i will be kept in a special register denoted R_d for right depth register.

Let us consider the problem of proceeding from the partial form a to generating a logical list Q with end pointer q_∞ and control word q_0 such that $N(S) = L(a)$, in which a is 1-embedded. The basic tool for this operation is the list U, with end pointer and control word. The list S is initially a 0 list, consequently, both

$$\mathfrak{L}s_0 = \mathfrak{R}s_0 = 0$$

and

$$\mathfrak{L}s_\infty = \text{address of } s_0$$

The algorithm consists of $L(a)$ steps, the ith of which starts with the computation of b_i and c_i and the addition to the end of Q of the mark a_i: This implies the replacement of $\mathfrak{L}s_\infty$ by the previous contents of the left part of the control word of the free storage list.

In addition, if a_i is a parenthesis or comma, the following two steps are taken:

(1) If a_i is a closed parenthesis, then a word is joined to the beginning of U. The center part of this word contains a closed parenthesis, and its right part the address of the word which has just been joined to Q (whose address is now $\mathfrak{L}q_\infty$).

(2) If a_i is a comma and U is other than a 0 list, $\mathfrak{R}u_1$ is copied into $\mathfrak{L}s_\infty$ (i.e., into the right part of the word just joined in Q). Otherwise, the address of q is placed into $\mathfrak{L}s_\infty$. Then two cases are possible:

(a) If $\mathfrak{C}u_1$ is a closed parenthesis, a new word is joined to the beginning of U. Its center part contains a comma and its right part contains $\mathfrak{L}q_\infty$.

(b) If a_i is an open parenthesis, $\Re u_1$ is copied into $\mathfrak{L}q_\infty$. Then, if $\mathfrak{C}u_1$ is a comma, the first word of U is removed (so that the second word of U becomes the first). Now $\mathfrak{L}q_\infty$ is copied into the right part of the word of address $\Re u_1$. Finally, the present first word of U is removed.

Consider the problem of proceeding from the above logical list, with the right partial from a 1-embedded in it, to another logical list Q' resulting from adding a left partial from a' to the end of Q. This operation can be easily performed provided that the status of U at the end of the generation of Q, the integer $b_{L(a)}$ (which incidentally is always the length of U minus one) and the truth value $c_{L(a)}$ (which is $\mathfrak{T}$ iff $a_{L(a)}$ is a closed parenthesis) are available. In fact, Q' can be generated just by continuing the operation of forming Q beyond the $L(a)$th step, considering a' as extension of a.

The above basic procedure can be trivially extended to n-embeddings of partial forms a into logical lists Q such that $N(Q) > n + \mathfrak{L}(a)$.

Memories organized in list forms are one of the answers given to certain questions arising in general category of information processing problems, namely, the problems of *dynamic storage allocation*. Some background on these problems may be obtained from reference [*13*].

3.6 Mating of Braces and Conditional Forms

There will be a need for an addition to the higher order association system, on which the typical way of addressing of the incremental computer is based. This addition is introduced in order to allow for higher over-all efficiency and removal of noninherent uncomputability problems, as will be thoroughly explained in Section 4.

Let us first present the scheme of higher order association of occurrences of braces informally. First, let us make clear what we want to accomplish. As will be explained in Section 4, a conditional form

$$(a\{b\}p) \tag{3.2}$$

is evaluated as follows: If the *value* (whatever this will mean) of p is the constant $\mathfrak{T}$, then the value of (3.2) equals the value of a. If the value of p is the constant $\mathfrak{F}$, then the value of (3.2) equals the value of b (the case in which p has other values need not be discussed here).

Thus the computer, in its right-to-left mode of operation, proceeds first to evaluating p. If the value of p is $\mathfrak{T}$, then it should plainly skip b altogether and proceed by scanning a from the right end. If the value of p is $\mathfrak{F}$, then it should evaluate b and skip all of a.

We want to design higher order association for forms containing braces in a way which allows for performing such decisions with a minimum amount of complication (i.e., with minimum hardware or software). This can be done if we define the mate of occurrences a_i at depth d of a punctuation mark in a form a of the most general kind as follows:

(1) If a_i is an open brace, its mate is the rightmost (i.e., closest to a_i) occurrence to the left of a_i of an open parenthesis of depth d.

(2) If a_i is a closed brace, its mate is the occurrence of a mark immediately preceding (i.e., to the immediate left of) the rightmost occurrence to the left of a_i of an open brace of depth d.

(3) If a_i is a comma or open parenthesis, its mate is the leftmost occurrence of a comma, closed parenthesis, open brace or closed brace at depth d to the right of a_i.

(4) If a_i is a closed parenthesis, its mate is the rightmost occurrence of an open parenthesis at depth d to the left of a_i.

Thus the mate of a_i stays to the right of a_i whenever a_i is an open parenthesis or comma, and to the left otherwise.

Let us clarify the concept with an example of a form, where the arrows stemming from occurrences of punctuation marks point to their respective mates:

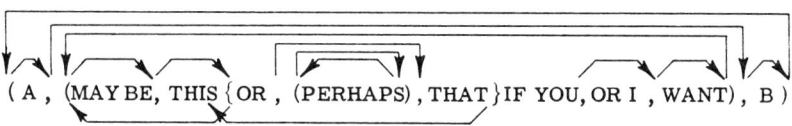

Note that the mate of the closed brace is the mark THIS, while the mate of the open brace is the open parenthesis initiating the conditional form.

Now let us modify steps of the algorithm of the previous section and the operation of the list U in a way to accommodate such extensions. We will have to utilize a special one-bit register, denoted z, whose value at the beginning is 0 and whose value at the end of step i, denoted z_i, is 1 or 0, depending on whether or not a_i is an open brace. In addition, we will use a register called *open brace register* of the capacity of one address. This register contains a 0 at the beginning. Then, at the beginning of the performance of the ith step, if z_{i-1} is 1, the contents of $\mathfrak{L}q_\infty$ is copied into the right part of the word whose address is contained in the open brace register. In addition:

(1) If a_i is a closed parenthesis, then a word is added to the beginning of U. The center part of this word contains a closed parenthesis and its right part contains $\mathfrak{L}q_\infty$.

(2) If a_i is a comma or a closed brace, then, if U is a 0 list, a 0 is placed into the right part of the word of address $\mathfrak{L}q_\infty$. Otherwise, $\mathfrak{R}u_i$ is copied there. Then, in either case, two cases are possible:

(a) If $\mathfrak{C}u_1$ is a closed parenthesis or an open or closed brace, a new word is joined to the beginning of U. Its center part contains a_i and its right part contains $\mathfrak{L}q_\infty$.

(b) If $\mathfrak{C}u_1$ is a comma, $\mathfrak{L}q_\infty$ and a_i replaces the previous contents of $\mathfrak{R}u_1$ and $\mathfrak{C}u_1$, respectively.

(3) If a_i is an open parenthesis,
   (a) If u_1 is a comma, u_1 is removed from U.
   (b) If u_1 is an open brace, or closed parenthesis, $\mathfrak{L}q_\infty$ is copied into the right part of the word of address $\mathfrak{R}u_1$, and u_1 is removed from U.
   (c) (u_1 cannot be an open brace.)

(4) If a is an open brace, then all the actions relative to the case where a_i was a comma or closed brace are performed. In addition, the list U is scanned until a word is found, say, u_j, such that $\mathfrak{C}u_j$ is a closed brace (j can be 1 or 2 only); now $\mathfrak{R}u_j$ is placed into the open parenthesis register, and, if $j = 1$, u_j is removed from U. Finally, as stated, z is put to the value 1.

The basic difference between the operations of mating open parentheses or commas on the one hand and closed parentheses, open and closed braces on the other for embedding purposes is that in the first case one should memorize all addresses of possible mates and place them when the occurrence to be mated is found, while in the second case, since the closed parentheses and braces precede (i.e., are to the right of) their mate, their own addresses are memorized for the purpose of supplementing the word carrying them with the addresses of the words carrying their mates as soon as these addresses become known.

Note also that, for mating commas and parentheses, it is not necessary to memorize the depth of the occurrences of possible mates, because of the way the association list U is being operated.

4. Operation of the Incremental Computer

4.1 The Library

A form of level one consisting of the enclosure in parentheses of the concatenation of the function mark f and a positive integer, is called *function address letter*, and the integer is called *address indication* of the function address letter. A form of level one structured like a function address letter, with the only difference that the address indication is replaced by an extended constant other than an integer, is called *function letter*, and the extended constant is called *identifier* of the function letter. For example,

$$(f, 22)$$

is a function address letter with address indication 22, while

$$(f, \text{SUM})$$

is a function letter with identifier SUM.

The incremental computer has a *library* of forms, each of which is associated with an extended constant, called *name* of that form, such that two forms have different names if, and only if, they differ by at least one mark. The library cannot contain two forms having the same name, or, in other words, it cannot contain the same form twice. The library should be viewed as a logical list. However, for practical purposes it is most effectively stored sequentially, on tapes, drums, or disks.

Forms contained in the library must be of level ≥ 1 and undecomposable. A further requirement on forms contained in the library is that no one should contain as subform a function address letter. One of the operations of the incremental computer is to update its own library on the basis of new forms written by human beings.

New forms for the library are presented along with their identifier. More precisely, a new form a having as identifier I_a should be presented by writing a preceded by I_a, with a production mark in between; that is, according to format

$$I_a ::= a \qquad (4.1)$$

which is called a *form definition*. For example, the following notation can be adopted for presenting to the incremental computer library a new form, whose identifier is to be FACTORIAL, in the unknown (x, N):

FACTORIAL $::= (((f, \text{PRODUCT}), (x, N), ((f, \text{FACTORIAL}),$
$N:((f, \text{DIFFERENCE}), (x, N), 1)))\{1\}((f, \text{EQUALITY}), (x, N), 0))$ (4.2)

In the library, any form e is represented by a *library item*, that is, a form of two (canonical) components, the second of which is e itself, while the first, called *label*, consists of the identifier of e. The library is a logical list W with control word and end pointer where the concatenation of all library items corresponding to all forms available for computation is embedded. More precisely, if the forms to be embedded in the library are the forms $a_1, a_2, \ldots, a_n$, having identifiers $I_{a_1}, I_{a_2}, \ldots, I_{a_n}$, respectively, then the library is a list embedded in which there is the form

$$I_{a_1} ::= a_1, \quad I_{a_2} ::= a_2, \quad \ldots, \quad I_{a_n} ::= a_n,$$

For embedding purposes, the production mark (like the colon) is considered and processed exactly like a comma. In fact, both the colon and production mark could be replaced by commas even in the language of the incremental computer The only reason why we chose not to do so is to make the language clearer to read by human beings.

The addition of a new item to the library consists of replacing the library's contents by the concatenation of its previous contents and the new item to be added.

As specified above, forms are embedded in lists in the direction opposite to the one of first-order association, so that they can easily be scanned mark-by-mark in reverse order. In particular, this applies to the library, and it allows for efficient searching of forms on the basis of their identifiers by simply following the sequence of second-order associations. Indeed, the initial mate of the contents of the library is the production mark which separates the first form from its identifier. If w_0 is the control word of W, which carries in its right part the address of this initial mate, the word containing the last mark of the label of the first form has address $\mathfrak{L}\mathfrak{R}w_0$, while $\mathfrak{R}^2w_0$ is the address of the word w' carrying the comma between the first form and the label of the second one. The address of the word carrying the last mark of the first form is $\mathfrak{L}\mathfrak{R}w_0$: In case the first library item is the one which is searched for, it can be extracted in reverse order by following the first-order association starting from this address. In case the first library item is not the one looked for, $\mathfrak{L}\mathfrak{R}w'$ is employed to check the second library item exactly like the address of the initial mate, contained in the right part of the control of the library, was used to check the library item. An analogous procedure applies to all library items. This search procedure allows for scanning in sequence all labels and for skipping the corresponding forms.

4.2 Evaluation by Synthesis

The basic operation of the incremental computer consists of:

(1) *Loading*, i.e., embedding into a list, called, for reasons explained later, *library abstract list* L a given undecomposable form a.

(2) *Evaluating* a with respect to the currently available context of information, i.e., the current contents of the library, and putting its value (which is again an undecomposable form b) into another list, the *main list* M.

(3) *Editing*, i.e., either *displaying* b or *joining it to the library*, or both, according to the choice of the operator. Junction to the library is possible only if a is initially supplied along with an identifier which becomes the label of b in the library. (For simplicity, we will assume that the identifier is always provided.) The computer will also check that the label of the new library item is not identical with any existing one: If any such identity is found a diagnostic must be issued.

The first and third operations are performed in an obvious manner. Upon simplification, the second one is performed by the incremental computer by scanning a right to left and progressively generating b in M. We will assume that a is embedded in L preceded by the given identifier of a [as in (4.2), Section 4.1] so that the address from which to initiate the scan is $\mathfrak{L}\mathfrak{R}^2 l_0$.

The value b of a is defined operationally by the operations described in this section. Before going into detail, the following definition is given:

A function quotation is the enclosure in parentheses of a function letter or of the concatenation of a function letter and a parameter sequence.

For example,
$$((f, \text{SINE}))$$
and
$$((f, \text{SINE}), \text{ARC}: (x, \text{ABC}))$$
are function quotations.

In the left-to-right scan, a function quotation can be easily recognized by detecting the sequence

$$((f \qquad (4.3)$$

and verifying whether or not the subform following the comma in (4.3) is an extended constant other than an integer: The latter operation requires a further scan by first-order association starting from the address contained in the right part of the word carrying in its center part the second parenthesis in (4.3).

We can now define a *value d* for function quotations c (which are a particular case of forms) as follows: *The value d of c is c if the library does not contain an item whose label equal the identifier of the function letter of c. Otherwise, d is the synthesis of the library form whose label coincides with the identifier of the function letter of c and the parameter sequence of c (if such parameter sequence is not present, the value of c is the library form).*

In its scan, the computer replaces all function quotations that it finds with their values, which it computes.

Now this way of operating would be inefficient, because it would require scanning the library each time a function quotation is encountered. Thus the incremental computer does not directly operate on function letters, but on *function address letters*, discussed in Section 4.1, whose format is

$$(f, q)$$

where q is a positive integer connoting a memory address. Accordingly, the above replacement is not performed on function quotations, but on *function address quotations*, analogous to function quotations except for the fact that the function letter is replaced by a function address letter. The computer maintains a list P, called *library control list*, embedded in which there is the concatenation of all function identifiers that it has already encountered during the evaluation of a, followed by a comma and by the address of the word of L carrying the rightmost mark in a. So the form in P might look like

ABC, 125, SINE, 25, FUNCTION ABC, 0, SQUARE ROOT, 1024

Whenever, during the scan involved in the evaluation of a, a function letter v is encountered, P is sequentially scanned in order to find out whether or not the identifier of v matches any odd-numbered canonical component of the contents of P. If it does, v is replaced (in the list where it is found) by the function address letter

$$(f, p)$$

where p is the integer to the right of the matching odd-numbered canonical component of the contents of P.

If the search for a match is not successful, a comma, the identifier of v, and another comma are joined to the end of P. Then the library is searched for an item whose label matches the identifier of v. If this is not found a 0 is added to the end of P (so that the function address letter

$$(f, 0)$$

identifies functions which are not available in the library).

If such library item is found, then both its label and its form (called *reference* of v) are joined to the end of L, and the address of the word of L carrying the rightmost mark in the reference is joined to the end of P.

In this way, the computer scans the library at most once for each item quoted during the evaluation of a, regardless of whether or not the search is successful.

Notice that, during the evaluation of a, L will progressively augment its contents: While initially it only contains a, later it will contain several library forms quoted in a. This is similar to what happens on conventional computers, under many monitor systems, where the subroutines and the main program (which corresponds to a), are loaded in sequence. The only difference here is that the loading of the equivalent of subroutines takes place *while* the equivalent of the main program is being run (*dynamic loading*) rather than *before* (*preplanned loading*). The replacement of function letters by function address letter can be viewed as a kind of "relocation."

At the end of the operation, when the computer is supposed to store in the library and/or display the value b of a, which is the contents of M, it should take care of eliminating from b all occurrences of function address letters and replacing them with the corresponding function letters, whose identifiers it can find by scanning P (or, more easily, by operating directly on the contents of L, which involves no searching). Thus the form b is made "relocatable" again, and, in addition, the intuitive connotation of the identifiers of the function letters is restored.

Once this point has been made clear, in the following we will often take as understood the fact that the incremental computer actually does not handle function quotations directly, but replaces them by function address quotations the first time that it encounters them. But for the sake of simplicity of presentation, we will always refer directly to treatment of function quotations.

At the beginning of the evaluation the main list M is a 0 list, or, in other words, it is represented by its control word and end pointer, whose left parts contain a 0 and the address of the control word, respectively. Furthermore, a register called *sequence pointer* and denoted R_c whose contents will be denoted $\mathfrak{L}R_c$, is reserved to the evaluation process. At the beginning of the evaluation, R_c contains the address of the word of L which carries the last mark in a. The basic *cycle* of the evaluation process begins by adding to the end of M the mark contained in the center part of the word of L whose address is contained in R_c, that is, $\mathfrak{CL}R_c$, and then replacing the contents of the sequence pointer by the contents of the left part of that word. This means moving the sequence pointer one step down the list a in the direction of the first-order association. If all cycles are performed that way, the result after as many steps as there are marks in a is to have the form a embedded in M; such embedding is still in the reverse order as required for all embeddings, in the sense that if one follows the direction of the first-order association of M he would read a backward. In other words, the performance of $L(a)$ basis cycles would simply duplicate the contents of the list L into M (a, however, is not erased from L).

If a does not contain any occurrences of function letters, the synthesis value of a is a. This suggests building into the incremental computer a way of checking when undecomposable forms have been completely scanned: This can be done best by using the register R_d, discussed in Section 3.5, which, when the ith rightmost occurrence of a mark of a is placed into M, is set to a value equal to the right depth of such occurrence. Since a is undecomposable, a is completely scanned when for the first time either the list L is ended or a comma of right depth 0 is found and detected by the vanishing value of R_d.

Consider now the case in which a contains occurrences of function letters, and let v be the first one from the right. In the right-to-left scanning operations v is detected when its rightmost open parenthesis comes up and is joined to M. Let m be the (last) word of M which carries it. At this time, the parameter sequence (unless it is empty), is already embedded in M. To check whether or not it exists and to access it, the easiest way is to embed into the end of M an open parenthesis preceding v and then, following for one step the higher order association of M, moving to the word of M which carries either a comma or a closed parenthesis, depending on whether or not there is an argument sequence to the immediate right of v in the form embedded in M. Let m_v denote that word. If there is a first argument, that is, if $\mathfrak{C}m_v$ is a comma, $\mathfrak{L}\mathfrak{R}m_v$ is the address of the word of M carrying the last mark in the first parameter, while $\mathfrak{L}\mathfrak{R}^{2i}m_v$ is the corresponding address relative to the ith parameter ($i = 1, 2 \ldots$) of v in M, and the total number of parameters of v is the smallest integer i such that $\mathfrak{L}\mathfrak{R}^{2i}m_v$ is a closed parenthesis. The address of the word carrying the rightmost mark of the ith parameter value is $\mathfrak{L}\mathfrak{R}^{2i+1}m_v$. For performing a synthesis, one needs the address of the word of M carrying the last mark of each argument value, which allows extracting if from M, mark after mark, from right to left by following first-order association. This address is exactly the one which is supplied by this procedure.

At the time $\mathfrak{L}R_c$ is the open parenthesis of v, the address of the word of L carrying the rightmost mark of the reference of v is $\mathfrak{L}\mathfrak{C}\mathfrak{L}\mathfrak{R}\mathfrak{L}R_c$ (remember that v is actually a function address letter). Now the action retake (except when $\mathfrak{C}\mathfrak{L}\mathfrak{R}\mathfrak{L}R_c = 0$, in which case no action is needed) is, after entering into M an open parenthesis, to continue operating from this new address, that is, placing this address into the sequence pointer R_c, with the only difference that when an unknown (x, q) comes up it is to be replaced by the $(i + 1)$th argument value to the right of v, where i is the smallest integer such that the ith argument to the right of v is q.

Before going into the details of this operation, however, let us see what data should be memorized before entering into this stage: first of all, the resumption address $\mathfrak{L}R_c$, from which the embedding of a should be resumed after the processing of v is accomplished; second, the current contents $\mathfrak{L}m_\infty$ of the end pointer of M (this address, called *linkage address*, is also needed to rapidly compute through higher order association the addresses of the arguments and argument values of v, which are found in M); third, the contents of the depth register R_d, which carries the right depth in the partial form contained in M of the mark carried by its last word (see Section 3.5); and fourth (though not absolutely necessary because it could also easily be recomputed each time it is needed), the number n of arguments following v.

> Note that the argument values to be substituted for unknowns are taken from M rather than from L, where they would also be available. This is possible because the right-to-left scan places argument sequences and arguments into M before a function quotation is recognized as such. The advantage of considering the argument sequences in M is that when they are in M they may already have been processed and transformed, because the computer evaluates them before placing them into M. Thus, for example, odd-numbered canonical components of the argument sequence in L of the format (x, Q), which are not arguments because they are not extended constants, might have been replaced by extended constants

before being placed in M: This may happen if the function quotation under consideration is a subform of another function quotation. Also, argument values in L which themselves contain occurrences of function quotations and/or unknowns may have these replaced by other forms by the evaluation process before they are placed into M. Thus, the use of the argument sequences in M, rather than in L, always gives an argument sequence which is at the most advanced stage of incremental processing.

It may happen that the reference of v also contains occurrences of function letters, so that its embedding into M is also likely to be interrupted, as v had interrupted the embedding of a. In this case a new set of four numbers, analogous to the previously considered one, should be memorized. However, the previous quadruple should by no means be destroyed. This need for *stacking* information suggests the introduction in the incremental computer of a list S, called *linkage list* (which, not containing structured information, does not need to carry higher order association addresses and can be addressed word-by-word through first-order association). Each time the processing of a newly occurring function quotation is begun, a new list of four words is added to the beginning of S: Their center parts contain the linkage address, the contents of the end pointer of M, the current contents of R_d, and the number of arguments in the function quotation, respectively. When the processing of a function quotation is ended (this is signaled by the embedding into M of a mark at *relative* right depth 0), the contents of the center part of the first and third word of S are copied into the registers R_c, and R_d, respectively, and the first four words of S are erased. (Note that some structuring, viz., separating quadruples of words by commas, might take advantage of second-order associations to get the incremental computer to work faster.)

The list S is operated as a so-called *push-down list*, that is, items are taken out of it only in the reverse of the order in which they are put in (first in–last out). This well-known technique is used for most of the lists of the incremental computer, including those described in Section 3, whose purpose was to help embedding forms in other lists. As a matter of fact, only W, L, and P are other than push-down lists.

The main list M can also be viewed as a push-down list. The elements placed in it, however, are not marks but forms. The top of M (which, following first-order association, comes toward the end) is the part where the most recent form is embedded.

To make the operation of the incremental computer more uniform, a quadruple of words of S is also associated with a, that is, the list S initially consists of four words whose center parts contain the address of the first word of L, a 0 to signify the fact that M is a 0 list, a 0 for the right depth reached before entering into a, and a third 0 to denote the number of arguments given to a. This a is formally treated like the reference of a hypothetical initial function letter having no arguments. This feature also allows for realizing when the value of a is computed and embedded in M: In fact, this happens when an attempt is made to erase four words from the list S when S contains only four words.

Let us analyze the operation carried out by the incremental computer in order to compute the value of a. First of all, the initial setting of the list S is constituted: This consists of four words, the center parts of which contain the contents of the left part of the control word of L, and three zeroes, respectively. The contents of the left part of the control word of L is also placed into the sequence pointer R_c, and the right depth register R_d is cleared.

Then repetitions, called *cycles*, of a sequence of actions, take place as follows:

(i) The contents of $\mathfrak{L}R_c$ is replaced by $\mathfrak{L}^2 R_c$.

(ii) The mark $\mathfrak{CL}R_c$ is added to the end of M and the right depth of this mark is computed and placed into R_d (the algorithm for this computation has been discussed in Section 3.5).

(iii) If (first case) the right depth of this last mark is 0, or (second case) if this mark is an open parenthesis at depth 1, $\mathfrak{C}s_1$ is placed into R_c, $\mathfrak{C}s_2$ and $\mathfrak{C}s_4$ are placed into the left part of a special register R_s and into R_d, respectively, and the first four words of S are erased. At this point, in the second case, $\mathfrak{L}R_s$ is the address of the word of M carrying in its center part the open parenthesis which terminates to the left the function quotation currently being processed. Using this information, the occurrence of a function address quotation which caused the processing of the last reference form is removed form M. The first case, instead, corresponds to encountering the left end of a, i.e., the evaluation of a is complete.

(iv) If $\mathfrak{CL}R_c$ is an open parenthesis of right depth >1, then three cases are possible, and correspond to the options (v), (vi), and (vii):

(v) $\mathfrak{C}R_c$ is the open parenthesis occurring as the leftmost mark in an unknown. At this point, this unknown is already allocated in M. Its identifier is readily available, its last mark being $\mathfrak{CLRCL}R_c$ and, if $\mathfrak{C}s_2 > 0$, the odd canonical components of the argument sequence are scanned starting from address $\mathfrak{C}s_2$; if one is found which matches the identifier, the unknown is replaced by the corresponding argument value; otherwise it is left there.

(vi) $\mathfrak{CL}R_c$ is the open parenthesis which starts a function address letter. In this case, $\mathfrak{CL}R_c$ is added to the end of M and a unit is subtracted from the contents of R_d, which is then placed into the center part of s_3, which thus carries the right depth of the mark immediately preceding this function address letter. Then R_d is cleared, the number n of arguments is computed as specified above, and $\mathfrak{L}R_c$, the contents of the right part of m_0, a zero and the integer n are allocated into a list of four words which is added to S. Then, after replacing the contents of $\mathfrak{L}R_c$ by $\mathfrak{L}\mathfrak{R}\mathfrak{C}\mathfrak{L}R_c$ a new cycle is performed.

(vii) In any other case, a new cycle is performed.

4.3 Primitive Evaluation

So far the incremental computer, if only allowed to carry out synthesis evaluation, would expand forms indefinitely. But assimilation of information involves reducing it after absorption. The first tool to achieve this is to allow it to have particular ways of handling some particular function letters, which will be called *primitives*. Function quotations whose function letter is one of these should be replaced during the evaluation process by another form—generally a simple mark. For example,

$$((f, \text{SUM}), \text{ADDEND } 1:4, \text{ADDEND } 2:5)$$

might be replaced by the form

$$9$$

while

$$((f, \text{EQUALITY}), \text{FIRST TERM: A}, \text{SECOND TERM: B})$$

might be replaced by the form

$$\mathfrak{F}$$

It is not necessary nor wise to stipulate that all incremental computers in a computer network should have the same set of primitives. Instead, the persons in charge of each computer should be free to decide which primitives should be available and which other form identifiers should correspond to library forms or maybe not be present in the computer's information context at all. These decisions will strongly influence the computer's efficiency in performing particular computations. Thus, in order to keep full compatibility between the machine languages of computers with different sets of primitives (similar to "instruction codes" of conventional computers) it is necessary to avoid using different notations for primitive and regular function identifiers; Instead, each particular incremental computer should be able to recognize those identifiers which correspond to its own primitives when it encounters them in function quotations.

In this way, full language compatibility is maintained between incremental computers of different power. Those which have a wider set of primitives will be able to evaluate certain forms faster than those which do not, but they all will be able to accept any form for evaluation.

By *local information context* available to an incremental computer at a given time we will denote the union of its library and its set of primitives (or, more strictly speaking, the set of mappings of the subspace of the space of all forms into itself to which its set of primitives gives rise).

Here we will leave this basic set of primitives *a priori* undefined, and introduce new primitives as soon as the need arises. No attempt will be made to conserve redundancy by reducing the number of primitives.

Before introducing the first examples of primitives, the general philosophy by which primitive function quotations are handled should be discussed. Let

$$(v, a_1:b_1, \ldots, a_n:b_n) \tag{4.4}$$

be a function quotation, where v is a primitive function letter with identifier m, and $a_1:b_2 \ldots a_n b_n$, $(n \geq 0)$ be the argument sequence. There is always a decision policy called *threshold policy* associated with m. If such policy is two-way, it will be called *threshold predicate*. Let us discuss an example, namely, the one where m is SUM, n is 2, and the threshold policy is the predicate: *Both b_1 and b_2 are integer or rational constants.* The value of

$$((f, \text{SUM}), \text{FIRST ADDEND}: b_1, \text{SECOND ADDEND}: b_2) \tag{4.5}$$

when the threshold predicate is satisfied, is the constant mark resulting of the sum of b_1 and b_2 where the summation is performed for integers or rationals, depending on whether or not both a_1 and a_2 are integers (or possibly, intergers enclosed in parentheses or in sets of nested parentheses).

For example, the value of

$$((f, \text{SUM}), \text{FIRST ADDEND}: 5, \text{SECOND ADDEND}: -1.2)$$

is 4.3, and the value of

$$((f, \text{SUM}), \text{FIRST ADDEND}: (3.14), \text{SECOND ADDEND}: ((1)))$$

is 4.14, while the value of

$$((f, \text{SUM}), \text{FIRST ADDEND}: 1, \text{SECOND ADDEND}: (x, A)) \tag{4.6}$$

is again (4.6), because the threshold predicate is not satisfied. Similarly, other arithmetic primitive letters with identifiers such as DIFFERENCE, PRODUCT, RATIO, etc., can be defined with the same threshold predicates as SUM and values defined in an obvious way.

The class of the propositional primitives (AND, OR, NOT, etc.) call for threshold policies other than predicates. For example, the threshold policy for

$$((f, \text{AND}), a_1:b_1, a_2:b_2) \tag{4.7}$$

is four-way:

(a) If both b_1 and b_2 are truth-valued constants (possibly enclosed in nested parentheses), then (4.7) should be replaced by $b_1 \wedge b_2$ (i.e., its value is $b_1 \wedge b_2$).

(b) If b_1 or b_2 is the constant $\mathfrak{F}$, then (4.7) should be replaced by the constant $\mathfrak{F}$.

(c) Otherwise, if b_1 or b_2 is the constant $\mathfrak{T}$, (4.7) should be replaced by b_2 or b_1, respectively.

(d) If none of the previous three conditions is met, (4.7) should not be replaced (i.e., its value is (4.7)).

Another widely used class of system functions is the one of the *relational* functions of two arguments. A typical example is

$$((f, \text{EQUALITY}), a_1:b_1, a_2:b_2) \qquad (4.8)$$

whose threshold predicate is *both b_1 and b_2 are atoms* (perhaps enclosed in nested parentheses) and whose value is the truth-valued constant $\mathfrak{T}$ or $\mathfrak{F}$ depending on whether or not b_1 is mark-by-mark identical to b_2. Other possible system functions of the same class would be INEQUALITY, MAJORITY, NONMAJORITY, MINORITY, NONMINORITY.

This choice of the threshold policy pattern for the relational system functions is largely arbitrary. In fact, other choices may be more effective from different viewpoints.

Slightly improperly, one could say that, by evaluating forms, the incremental computer "executes" the alogorithms relative to unknowns to which a value is assigned in the argument sequence, while at the same time it "compiles" the algorithms relative to the unknowns whose value is left unassigned. The concept of threshold predicate has been introduced for the specific purpose of implementing this unified approach to all kinds of computations in the incremental computer. Threshold predicates allow, for example, for substituting the directly meaningful constant 9 for any occurrence of $((f, \text{SUM}), 1:5, 2:4)$ in a larger form, while any occurrence of (f, SUM) in a function quotation with argument values other than constants is left the way it is.

If an undecomposable form a consists of the enclosure in parentheses of another form b, then we say that a is *normal*. The normality of

$$(b) \qquad (4.9)$$

can be easily checked by the computer, by determining that the mate of an open parenthesis in (4.9) is a closed parenthesis. Then b will be called *interior* of a, and the transformation of a into b will be called *peeling*.

We will assume that every incremental computer has at least three basic primitives, INTERIOR, COMPONENT, and DIMENSION. The value of

$$((f, \text{INTERIOR}), \text{FORM}: d) \qquad (4.10)$$

is (4.10) when d is other than a normal form; otherwise the value of (4.10) is the interior of d.

The value of

$$((f, \text{COMPONENT}), \text{ORDER}: c, \text{FORM}: d) \qquad (4.11)$$

is (4.11) when either c is not a positive integer or d is not a normal form, or when the interior of d has less than c canonical components. Otherwise, it has as value the cth canonical component of d.

The value of

$$((f, \text{DIMENSION}), \text{FORM}: d) \qquad (4.12)$$

is (4.12) if d is not a formal form, or else it is an integer constant equaling the number of canonical components of the interior of d.

In order to handle both synthesis and primitive evaluation, the computation procedure discussed in the preceding section should be provided with a further option to the case (iv), namely:

(viii) If the last word of M contains the open parenthesis of a function letter, and if the function quotation which would be contained in the end of M by joining to it $\mathfrak{CL}R_c$ (which is an open parenthesis) has a function letter with an identifier which corresponds to one of the primitive functions of the particular incremental computer under consideration, then such function quotation is removed from M and its value (computed by the logico-arithmetic unit of the computer) is joined to the end of M.

4.4 Infixes and Prefixes

The format of function, function address, and primitive function quotations requires writing the function letter to the left of the sequence of arguments. For certain system function letters such notation is awkward, both because one would prefer to write established special signs such as $+$ or $=$ instead of (f, SUM) or $(f, \text{EQUALITY})$, respectively, and because everyone is accustomed to writing such signs between the two arguments rather than to the left of them, that is, as infixes rather than prefixes. It will therefore be wise to extend the notation to be used by the human designer of algorithms to allow for a finite selection of commonly accepted infixes by extending the alphabet and syntax of the incremental computer to take care of them by reducing them to the standard notation discussed above, on the basis of which the incremental computer can evaluate forms. The solution to this problem presented here is an adaptation to functions of structured arguments of the original methods developed (for the particular case of functions whose argument values are atoms) by Samelson and Bauer [12] and Pacelli and Palermo [11].

The (arbitrary) selection of infixes that we will consider is listed in Table III.

TABLE III
SELECTION OF INFIXES

Infix	Order	Agglutinating strength	Corresponding function letter
d	1	12	$(f, \text{DIMENSION})$
@	1	11	$(f, \text{INTERIOR})$
$\downarrow$	2	10	$(f, \text{COMPONENT})$
$\sqrt{}$	1	9	$(f, \text{SQUARE ROOT})$
$/$	1	9	$(f, \text{INVERSE})$
$\times$	2	8	$(f, \text{PRODUCT})$
$\cdot/\cdot$	2	8	(f, RATIO)
$\oplus$	1	7	(f, PLUS)
$\ominus$	1	7	(f, MINUS)
$+$	2	6	(f, SUM)
$-$	2	6	$(f, \text{DIFFERENCE})$
$>$	2	5	$(f, \text{MAJORITY})$
$<$	2	5	$(f, \text{MINORITY})$
$\geq$	2	5	$(f, \text{NONMAJORITY})$
$\leq$	2	5	$(f, \text{NONMINORITY})$
$=$	2	4	$(f, \text{EQUALITY})$
$\neq$	2	4	$(f, \text{INEQUALITY})$
$\rightarrow$	1	3	$(f, \text{NEGATION})$
$\vee$	2	2	$(f, \text{DISJUNCTION})$
$\wedge$	2	2	$(f, \text{CONJUNCTION})$

The first column displays the infixes, the second column the number of operands or *order* involved, the third column the *relative agglutinating strength* or *binding power* as considered in common mathematical conventions, and the fourth column the function letter that they stand for.

Here, $\oplus$, $\ominus$, and $/$ denote the *unary* or *monadic plus, minus,* and *inverse*, respectively, $\cdot/\cdot$ denotes (binary) division, while the denotation of all others is standard. This list is arbitrary and only given as an example; what will be said in this section can be extended to any other preferred list of infixes.

We will here introduce a simplifying convention: Since the nature of the argument of functions usually represented by infixes is universally accepted, it is not necessary to quote the arguments in the argument sequences of function quotations whose function letter corresponds to an infix; instead, such argument sequences will simply consist of the argument value or concatenation of the argument values (given in the appropriate order, in case a function of order 2 is not commutative). The incremental computer must be able to recognize such function letters, of which there is only a limited number, and behave accordingly.

For example, instead of writing
$$((f, \text{SUM}), \text{FIRST ADDEND}: a, \text{SECOND ADDEND}: b) \qquad (4.13)$$
we will simply write
$$((f, \text{SUM}), a, b) \qquad (4.14)$$
or
$$a + b$$

This is the only case in which the incremental computer differentiates between colons and commas: in fact, only on this basis could it tell that (4.14) has two argument values instead of just one. Otherwise, it might interpret a as being an argument and b its corresponding argument value.

To handle infixes, the incremental computer needs a further list V with control word and end pointer which is a 0 list at the beginning. Let us suppose that during a certain cycle V is not a 0 list and $\mathfrak{CL}v_0$ is an infix m (that is, the first word of V carries m), and let us describe an operation, which will be referred to as *conversion of an infix*. The notion is the following: Conversion of m is a replacement of m by a function letter; such replacement occurs after the operand(s) to which m refers is (are) joined at the end of M; more precisely, conversion of m consists of joining to the end of M the function letter corresponding to m, and then enclosing such function letter and its operands in parentheses to form a function quotation.

Conversion is started by inserting the closed parenthesis which will then be the end of the quotation under construction. This closed parenthesis should be inserted between $\mathfrak{R}s_0$ and $\mathfrak{LR}s_0$ or between $\mathfrak{R}^2s_0$ and $\mathfrak{LR}^2s_0$, depending on whether m is of order 1 or 2; insertion has been discussed previously and no difficulties should arise in arranging either first- or second-order association in this connection. Then, a comma, namely, the one separating function letter from argument sequence in any quotation, is added to the end of M; after that, the marks (in the reverse order) of the primitive function letter corresponding to m and an open parenthesis are successively joined to the end of M. At this point, conversion is completed by removing the first word of V (thus erasing m) and by replacing the function quotation at the end of M.

The basic modifications to the logic of the incremental computer involved in removal of infixes affects only those cycles where $\mathfrak{CL}R_c$ is a parenthesis or an infix. Let us discuss the three cases separately.

(i) $\mathfrak{CL}R_c$ is a closed parenthesis. Then $\mathfrak{CL}R_c$ is joined to the beginning of V, and the cycle is continued normally.

(ii) $\mathfrak{CL}R_c$ is an infix m'. Then, if V is not empty and $\mathfrak{C}v_1$ is an infix with agglutinating strength higher tham m', $\mathfrak{C}v_1$ is converted and hence removed from V. This operation is repeated as many times as necessary either to exhaust V or to find at the beginning of V a closed parenthesis or an infix of agglutinating strength not exceeding the one of m'. Then, m' is joined to the beginning of V, and the cycle stops here.

This implies that an infix is never allocated to M. Note also that among infixes with equal agglutinating strength this procedure implies association to the left so that, for example, $1 + 2 - 3 + 4$ would be treated as

$$(((1 + 2) - 3) + 4)$$

(iii) $\mathfrak{CL}R_c$ is an open parenthesis. Then, if $\mathfrak{C}v_1$ is an infix, it is converted; such conversion is repeated as many times as necessary in order to find a closed parenthesis at the beginning of V. (There must be one, otherwise the aggregate under evaluation would not be a form.) When it is found, the word carrying it, which at that time is v_1, is removed from V, and then the cycle is continued as usual, thus joining $\mathfrak{CRL}R_c$ to the end of M.

Note that the antimate of $\mathfrak{CRL}R_c$ is already in M, because of the way case (i) above was treated.

When writing forms, human beings have the option of using infixes such as $a + b$, or regular function quotations [like (4.13)], or shortened function quotations [like (4.14)]. The second option remains the only one available in connection with function quotations with fewer arguments than the order of the corresponding infix.

When a form is loaded in L from the outside of the computer, all infixes have to be converted by the loading routine. (During evaluation, this routine is not active.)

For the purpose of storing forms in the library there is no need to restore infixes for the corresponding function letters. We therefore assume that the library contains no infixes. But they are needed for the purpose of displaying forms contained in M since infix notation is more compact and readable. Of course, infixes should replace function quotations if, and only if, they have a number of arguments which matches the order of the corresponding infix.

The operation of *reinstatement of infixes* should be handled by the display routine. It only requires scanning the contents of M looking for function quotations the identifier of whose function letter corresponds to an infix, and whose argument sequence contains as many arguments as the order of the infix. For each such function quotation the first and last mark (two parentheses), the function letter, the comma following the function letter, and all arguments (if any) must be removed and the infix inserted in the appropriate position between (or preceding) the argument value(s). This can be readily handled by using higher order association.

4.5 Conditional Forms and Their Threshold Policies

Conditional forms of the format

$$(a_1\{a_2\}p) \tag{4.15}$$

allow the incremental computer to "make decisions or choices" in terms of selecting between alternatives. The philosophy to implement in the evaluation of (4.15) is that, when within the current information context the value of p is a truth-valued constant, either only a_1 or only a_2 should be evaluated (depending on whether the value of p is $\mathfrak{T}$ or $\mathfrak{F}$) and taken as the value of (4.15) while a_2 or a_1, respectively, should simply be skipped so that no time is wasted.

The format (4.15) has been preferred over other alternative formats, such as, for example,

$$((f, \text{CONDITIONAL}), \text{TRUE ALTERNATIVE: } a_1, \text{FALSE ALTERNATIVE: } a_2,$$
$$\text{DECISION PREDICATE: } p) \tag{4.16}$$

because, in the right to left scan of (4.16), the computer would first have to evaluate all three expressions, p, a_2, and a_1 before realizing that it is handling a conditional form. This does not happen using the format (4.15), since such realization occurs at the appropriate time, namely, when a closed brace is encountered: At that time the computer has just terminated the evaluation of p but not yet started the one of either a_1 or a_2.

The threshold policy for conditional forms clearly depends on whether or not p is a truth-valued constant.

Let us define a *parenthesized truth value* as either a truth-valued constant or the enclosure in parentheses of a parenthesized truth value.

We want the computer to ignore parentheses surrounding truth-valued constants in a decision predicate, so that, e.g.,

$$(a_1\{a_2\}((\mathfrak{F})))$$

would be handled exactly as

$$(a_1\{a_2\}\mathfrak{F})$$

The philosophy for evaluating (4.15) is the following: If the value of p is a parenthesized truth value, then, as we said, the value of (4.15) is either the value of a_1 or the value of a_2. Otherwise, the value of (4.15) is the form

$$(a'_1\{a'_2\}p')$$

where a'_1, a'_2, and p' are the values of a_1, a_2, and p, respectively. Thus, here again, a choice which cannot be made because there is not enough information available in the context is left symbolically indicated.

Now let us see how to implement such a philosophy. If p is a parenthesized $\mathfrak{F}$, the computer does not add the closed brace to the end of M, and just continues with the scan, i.e., it substitutes $\mathfrak{L}^2 R_c$ for $\mathfrak{L} R_c$. If p is a parenthesized $\mathfrak{T}$, again it does not add the closed brace to the end of M, and it jumps directly to the true alternative by substituting $\mathfrak{R}\mathfrak{L} R_c$ for $\mathfrak{L} R_c$ (thus skipping both the false alternative and the open brace). When the computer encounters an open brace, it does not join it to the end of M (except for a case considered later) and replaces $\mathfrak{R}\mathfrak{L} R_c$ for $\mathfrak{L} R_c$, thus skipping the true alternative.

When p is not a truth value, this has been determined before the closed brace is encountered. (Let us recall that closed braces are joined to the end of M if, and only if, p is not a parenthesized truth value.) The most obvious action that the incremental computer can take in this case is then to join to the end of M the aggregate

$$a_1 \{ a_2 \tag{4.17}$$

This can be accomplished by providing the incremental computer with an additional list Λ with control word and end pointer, which is a 0 list at the beginning of the evaluation of a. When a closed brace for which the decision predicate p is the constant $\mathfrak{T}$ (possibly parenthesized) is encountered, a new word, containing a closed brace in its center part and the mark 1 in its right part, is joined to the beginning of Λ. Then $\mathfrak{L} R_c$ is replaced by $\mathfrak{R}\mathfrak{L} R_c$ so that the false alternative is skipped. If, in contrast, p is not a parenthesized truth value, the same action is taken, with the only difference that this new word will contain a 0 in its right part, while if p is $\mathfrak{F}$ (possibly parenthesized) no action is taken on Λ.

When an open brace is encountered, then two cases are possible:

(1) The open brace corresponds to a closed brace whose p equals $\mathfrak{T}$. This case is identified by the fact that the right part of the first word λ_1 of Λ contains a 1. The action to be taken is to remove the first word of Λ and then to replace $\mathfrak{L} R_c$ (which contains the address of the open brace) with $\mathfrak{R}\mathfrak{L} R_c$, so that a_1 is plainly skipped.

(2) The open brace just encountered corresponds to a closed brace whose p is not a parenthesized truth value. This case is identified by the fact that λ_1 contains a 0. The action to be taken is to replace $\mathfrak{C}\lambda_1$ by an open brace, join an open brace to the end of M, and continue the scan (i.e., replace $\mathfrak{L}_1{}^2\mathfrak{R}_c$ for $\mathfrak{L} R_c$). While performing the cycle, the incremental computer always checks if $\mathfrak{C}\lambda_1$ is an open brace, in which case it adds a unit, subtracts a unit, or does not make any change to $R\lambda_1$, depending on whether $\mathfrak{C}\mathfrak{L} R_c$ in the considered cycle is a closed parenthesis, an open parenthesis, or any other mark, respectively. In this way, the occurrence of the left end of a_1 is detected by simultaneously

$\mathfrak{R}\lambda_1$ being 0 and $\mathfrak{C}\lambda_1$ being a closed brace. When such detection takes place λ_1 is removed from Λ.

Now we are faced with the following problem: If, in (4.15), p is other than a truth value, we should somehow restrict the extent to which a_1 and a_2 are evaluated. Otherwise the incremental computer would risk wasting time (and even get deadlocked in infinite recursions) in attempting to compute both alternatives, one of which would be discarded by future information contexts. More precisely, in this case we still want to evaluate primitive function quotations occurring in a_1 and a_2. But we do not want to evaluate function quotations other than primitive.

In order to implement this behavior let us associate with Λ an initially cleared register R_λ (which can be located, for example, in the right part of the end pointer of Λ). Each time a closed brace for which p is not a parenthesized truth value comes up, a unit is added to R_λ; each time λ_1 is removed because both $\mathfrak{C}\lambda_1$ is a closed brace and $\mathfrak{R}\lambda_1$ vanishes, a unit is subtracted from R_λ. If R_λ contains n during a given cycle, this denotes that $\mathfrak{C}\mathfrak{L}R_c$ is an occurrence of a mark which is part of n nested conditional forms whose decision predicate is not a parenthesized truth value. Now the first criterion of threshold policies is the implementation of the common sense rule: "Do not evaluate either a_1 of a_2 in any conditional form for which p is not a parenthesized truth value." This is easily implemented by requiring the incremental computer to perform the replacement in M of a function quotation (as described in (v) in Section 4.2), only if this quotation does not occur within either of the alternatives of a conditional form whose decision predicate is other than a parenthesized truth value; that is, conditional upon R_λ containing a 0.

This condition, however, should not affect the replacement of primitive function quotations. Furthermore, other careful relaxations of this condition can be studied in order to enable the incremental computer to *rewrite* both a_1 and a_2 in a more convenient way whenever p is not a parenthesized truth value, for cases where this is deemed desirable.

One could also consider another approach to the problem of devising a threshold policy for function quotations. This is based on a *pattern* $P(b)$ associated with each form b in the library (an appropriate way of storing it can easily be devised). This pattern is a form which expresses certain conditions on the argument sequences of quotations such that any quotation is replaced in M only if the conditions are met. There are several orders of generality on which one can work in trying to define classes of such conditions and the way of handling them for the purpose of giving a decision rule to tell, for each function, which formats of arguments warrant carrying computation further. A general approach is to allow as $P(b)$ forms defined in such a way that their value is always a truth value. Then, the incremental computer, when confronted with a quotation referring to b, should first evaluate $P(b)$ for the argument sequence of that quotation, and proceed to replacing that quotation only if this first evaluation yields $\mathfrak{T}$. This method would enable one to determine with considerable flexibility and detail the argument sequences for which replacement should be undertaken.

The main shortcoming of the above philosophy is that for most cases the form $P(b)$ would be fairly cumbersome to write. Consequently, we will sketch a second alternate method, which stays at the other extreme in the sense that it is far from general, but is easy to use. This method allows for building $P(b)$ directly and simply on the basis of the one single factor in the argument sequence of a quotation which is most likely to affect computability directly: the difference between the number of different unknowns occurring in the argument sequence and the number of arguments. According to this method, $P(b)$ should be an integer constant, expressing the maximum number of different unknowns occurring in the argument sequence of a quotation, minus the number of arguments present in the quotation, for which it should be substituted. For example, for the case of FACTORIAL, this integer would be -1.

4.6 Looped Lists

Replacement of function quotations by the synthesis of the reference and the argument sequence requires joining the reference to the end of M while replacing the unknowns. In particular, the substitutes for unknowns having a corresponding item in the argument sequence are argument values of the quotation, which consequently need to be copied from one section of M to another. Effective representation of processes sometimes requires argument values of function quotations consisting of extremely large forms: In some cases, the whole *machine status* has to be used as argument value. This is the case, for example, in a library of functions for collinear data base operations (see Lombardi [4]). On the other hand, replacement of function quotations is a major part of the processing performed by the incremental computer; therefore, in order to operate efficiently, it is necessary to eliminate this copying of arguments. With such modification, the number of cycles necessary for evaluating forms will no longer be directly affected by the length of the argument values of the function quotations involved. In order to avoid duplicating arguments by copying them from one section to the end of M, one should be able to refer or *point* to them by some kind of compact notation ad hoc, which will now be established, and provide for interrupting the regular sequence of scanning aggregates allocated in a list in order to be able to scan other aggregates when they are referred to.

Now lists, as presented in Section 3, do not allow such forming of loops: First-order association establishes a complete order of the words of any list. Consequently, we have to introduce an extension of the concept of list in the sense of introducing *looped lists*, where, while first-order association is still utilized, it is no longer being exclusively utilized as word-by-word addressing method, and hence no longer yields a complete ordering.

Additions to the alphabet of Section 2.2 necessary for the present purposes are two new punctuation marks, namely, the *open* and *closed square bracket*, and a new kind of constant mark, namely the *flagged integer*, denoted by a positive integer constant with a bar, called *flag*, such as $\overline{20}$. (Flags are an adaptation of a long-established concept of conventional computation.) The connotation of a flagged integer $\bar{n}$ is that, for all computational purposes, it should be regarded as representative of another, generally longer form, the right end of which can be accessed by resuming scanning through first-order association from the address n in the computer memory (in other words, flagged integers are addresses).

Brackets and flagged integers are present only inside the computer. They cannot be used by human beings in writing forms, and they are not used for displaying the output.

Let a' be an aggregate contained in a form a, which is embedded in a list Y; y_l and y_r denote the words of Y (control word and end pointer inclusive) carrying the occurrence of a mark in a, if any, to the immediate left and right of a', respectively. Let us call *bracketing* the operation consisting of inserting between y_l and the sequence of words of Y carrying a', and between this sequence and y_r, two new words containing in their center parts an open and a closed bracket, respectively, thus enclosing a' in brackets. The removal of such brackets from around an aggregate will be called *debracketing*. When bracketing, the right part of the word carrying the closed bracket will be used to store the address of the word carrying the open one. The right part of this latter word will be used to store the constant 1, which will be utilized as explained below.

Brackets are used when the incremental computer, in the course of evaluating a function quotation, encounters an unknown for which there is an argument value in the argument sequence, and this argument value is long enough to make it desirable not to copy it (e.g., it is neither a constant nor an operative mark). If such argument value is already bracketed, a unit is added to the contents of the right part of the open bracket (which can be reached as $\Re\mathfrak{L}y_{\text{comma}}$, where y_{comma} is the word carrying a comma or closed parenthesis to the immediate right of the argument value). Otherwise, the computer brackets such argument value. In either case it replaces the whole unknown with one mark, namely, a flagged integer which is the address of the closed bracket.

Thus the right part of the word carrying the open bracket serves to keep track of how many flagged integers *point* to that particular bracketed form.

Let us now see which adaptations of the operation of the incremental computer this solution to the problem of redundant reproducing of argument entrains. In order to handle this solution, the incremental computer must have another (*push-down*) list B with control word and end pointer, which is a 0 list at the beginning. As stated, when $\mathfrak{C}\mathfrak{L}R_c$ is a flagged integer, it is interpreted as an address. In this case two words are successively joined to the beginning of B; the first of them contains $\mathfrak{L}R_c$ in its right part and a comma in its center part, while the second (which becomes the first word of B) contains a 1 in its right part and some mark different from a comma in its center part. Then $\mathfrak{L}R_c$ is replaced by $\mathfrak{L}\mathfrak{C}\mathfrak{L}R_c$ (the flag need not be reproduced) so that the scan is resumed from the right end of the bracketed form.

Whenever, during evaluation, B is not a 0 list and $\mathfrak{C}\mathfrak{L}R_c$ is a closed bracket, a unit is added to $\mathfrak{R}b_1$, while, when $\mathfrak{C}\mathfrak{L}R_c$ is an open bracket, a unit is subracted from $\mathfrak{R}b_1$. In this last case it may happen that as a consequence of such subtraction $\mathfrak{R}b_1$ becomes 0: This means that we have encountered the open bracket which forms the left end of the aggregate related to the flagged integer which had caused the addition to B of its current first two new words. Consequently, scanning should be resumed from the immediate left of that flagged integer; i.e., we have to replace $\mathfrak{L}R_c$ by $\mathfrak{R}b_2$ and then remove the first two words of B.

A problem which needs special handling in this connection is that of the free storage list. In normal operation, after the replacement of a function quotation, the quotation is deleted. However, if some of its argument values have been bracketed, they are still useful, and the words carrying them should not be returned to free storage. One could solve this problem by scanning the function quotation and sorting out obsolete from useful information; however, any such solution would be highly inefficient.

A satisfactory solution can be found by extending the mode of operation of the free storage list, and by taking advantage of the fact that when a list is returned to free storage its contents are not physically erased. The fact that when storage space is needed it is taken from the storage list word by word, by following first-order association, also plays an important role. In fact, while doing this, the aggregates allocated in the free storage list F will be scanned right to left. When, in taking words from free storage, one is found (say, f_1) whose center part contains an open bracket, then such open bracket is replaced by any other mark (e.g., a comma). Now two cases are possible: Either the right part of the word carrying the corresponding open parenthesis (of address $\mathfrak{R}f_1$) contains a positive number, or it contains a 0. In the first case the reutilization of words from free storage is resumed with the word of address $\mathfrak{L}\mathfrak{R}f_1$, thus skipping the whole bracketed form. Otherwise, the reutilization continues without interruption (also, f_1 is reutilized).

When the center part of f_1 is a flagged integer, then, before clearing this word for further utilization, a unit is subtracted from the right part of the word of address $\mathfrak{RC}f_1$, which, in its center part, carries the open bracket corresponding to the flagged integer.

Two cases are possible now: If either the result of such subtraction is positive, or $\mathfrak{C}^2 f_1$ is a closed bracket, retrieval of words from free storage proceeds normally. Otherwise, the list whose first and last words have addresses $\mathfrak{C}f_1$ and $\mathfrak{RC}f_1$, respectively (which contains exactly the bracketed form including the open bracket and the closed bracket), is added to the end of the free storage list F (so that it will eventually be utilized), and the retrieval of words from free storage proceeds.

The philosophy implied by these operations is the following: When the right part of the word carrying the open bracket has become zero, this means that there are no flagged integers left pointing to the closed bracket. When the closed bracket is changed into another mark, this signifies that the bracketed form is not part of any other bracketed form which should be saved (because otherwise the closed bracket could not have been reached from the right by the process of reutilizing free storage). Hence, reutilization of a list carrying a bracketed form takes place immediately as soon as both of these conditions are met.

Finally, when, at the end of evaluation, the contents of M is to be stored in the library and/or displayed, flagged integers must be removed from it. Hence the ad hoc (editing) routine must take care when scanning the contents of M to interrupt the scan each time it finds a word, say, m_1, whose center part carries a flagged integer. Upon such occurrence the editing routine should not include the flagged integer in the edited output, but rather join to the beginning of an ad hoc list C (which is a 0 list at the beginning of editing) a new list of two words, which contain in their center parts the constant 1 and the address of m_1, respectively, and then resume the scan from the address $\mathfrak{LC}m_1$. When the routine encounters closed or open brackets, it again does not include them in the edited output, but it adds or subtracts, respectively, a unit from the center part of c_1. If the result of such a subtraction is zero, the scan is resumed from the address $\mathfrak{C}c_2$ and the first two words of c are removed.

Such operations complement the ones described in Section 4.2 which were aimed at making relocatable all forms which leave the incremental computer.

4.7 Recursive Functions and Discharge Lists

Conventional computers based on procedural representation of algorithms require iterative description for representing procedures which should be repeated several times, each time on data produced by the previous repetition, in order to produce the required final results. The declarative representation of functions by means of forms, on which the presentation of problems to this incremental computer is

INCREMENTAL COMPUTATION   313

based, requires providing for forms which allow us to define functions by referring to the value of the same forms for other appropriate arguments, so that the value of the required function can be computed by means of a sequence of *materializations* of a single form, that is, a sequence of evaluations for different arguments.

For example, a procedural representation of the computation of $y!$ for a conventional computer can be informally phrased as: *Place y into two words w_1 and w_2. Subtract 1 from the contents of w_2 and then multiply the contents of w_1 times the contents of w_2, placing the product in w_2; repeat until w_2 contains a 1. At this time w_1 contains the factorial of y.*

In contrast, the same function should be informally presented to the incremental computer as: *The factorial of 0 is 1, while the one of any other positive integer y is y multiplied by the factorial of $y-1$.*

Let us discuss as an example the particular problem of enabling the incremental computer to compute factorials of positive integers, without adding any new ad hoc primitive. This can be done by adding to the library a new form, whose identifier is FACTORIAL. The factorand, which in the above informal discussion was referred to as y, cannot practically be introduced as a contant mark, because in this case a separate form would be needed to define the factorial of each integer. Consequently, y must be represented in that form by something for which the incremental computer can substitute other forms, that is, an unknown. Since there are no other unknown elements in the definition of this form, for compactness this unknown will be denoted (x, N).

Now, the definition of the factorial function can be presented to the library of the incremental computer in various ways, among which one can think of selecting

$$\text{FACTORIAL} ::= (((f, \text{FACTORIAL}), N:(x, N) - 1) \times (x, N) \{1\}(x, N) > 1) \quad (4.18)$$

If then one wants to compute the factorial of, say, 5, one should have the computer read from the card hopper and allocate into L the form

$$\text{FACTORIAL OF 5} ::= ((f, \text{FACTORIAL}), N:5) \quad (4.19)$$

Let us now discuss this approach in detail in order to bring to light one of its major shortcomings. In its operation, the incremental computer would start embedding (4.19) into M by scanning it right to left. When an open parenthesis to the left of f is found, the form (4.18) is added to the end of L; an appropriate entry is added to P, and the rightmost occurrence of the mark FACTORIAL in (4.18) is replaced by an appropriate address, both in L and in M. After entering four additional words to the linkage list S, the incremental computer proceeds now to scanning right to left and embedding into M the part of (4.18) to the right of the production mark. When the rightmost occurrence of (x, N)

is encountered, it is replaced by a 5 coming from M, and when a function letter corresponding to $>$ is met, the function quotation $((f, \text{MAJORITY}), 5,1)$ is removed from the top of M and the scanning of (4.18) resumes from the immediate left of the open brace. When the function quotation related to the function letter $(f, \text{FACTORIAL})$ comes up, the incremental computer joins the linking information to S and starts again adding to the end of M the part of (4.18) right of the production mark, with the only difference that this time all occurrences of (x, N) are replaced by 4 in M.

Here, two problems arise: First of all, one sees that in order to compute in this way the factorial of 5, one has to embed into M slight variations of the right side of (4.18) five times, and only then can one proceed to carry out the multiplications necessary to obtain the required result, which is 120. Consequently, the incremental computer causes the computation of 5!, which should be reduced to five multiplications, sums and comparisons, and should not require storing more intermediate information than two marks at any time, to be preceded by the embedding of a long aggregate in M. Second, S will wind up consisting of up to $5 \times 4 = 20$ words.

This time- and space-consuming aspect would be quite general in the operation of the incremental computer. We therefore proceed to another solution to this problem based on the technique of *external quotations* and *external recursive functions*.

The root of the problem is that the recursive metalinguistic definition of factorial given above has an inherent element of inefficiency, namely the fact that when one applies that definition to compute $n!$, before being able to start performing the sequence of n multiplication yielding the result, the computer should count backward from n to 1, making a comparison at each step. To avoid this shortcoming, one can redefine the factorial by using an auxiliary function *factorial 3* of three variables as follows:

The function factorial 3 *of the three positive integers y_1, y_2, y_3 has the value y_3 or factorial 3 $(y_1, y_2 + 1, y_3 \times (y_2 + 1))$ depending on whether or not $y_1 = y_2$. The function* factorial 1 *of one integer η has the value of the function* factorial 3 *for $y_1 = \eta$, $y_2 = 0$ and $y_3 = 1$.*

To the incremental computer, this new definition should be presented as

FACTORIAL 3 ::= $((x, \text{CURRENT})\{((f, \text{FACTORIAL 3}),$
COUNT: COUNT $+ 1$, CURRENT: $(x, \text{CURRENT}) \times (x, \text{COUNT})$,
FACTORAND 3: $(x, \text{FACTORAND 3}))\}(x, \text{COUNT})$
$> (x, \text{FACTORAND 3}))$ \hfill (4.20)

FACTORIAL 1 ::= $((f, \text{FACTORIAL 3}), \text{COUNT}: 1,$
CURRENT: 1, FACTORAND 3: $(x, \text{FACTORAND}))$ \hfill (4.21)

Let us briefly examine what happens when the incremental computer is asked to evaluate

$$\text{FACTORIAL OF } 8 ::= ((f, \text{FACTORIAL } 1), \text{FACTORAND}: 8) \qquad (4.22)$$

assuming that (4.20) and (4.21) have been stored in the library.

After embedding in M and scanning the part of (4.21) right of the production mark, the incremental computer will do the same with the analogous part of (4.20). At the first scan the decision predicate is found to have the value $\mathfrak{F}$, because $8 > 1$, so that a further quotation of FACTORIAL 3 is encountered and should be evaluated: At this time a new set of four words is entered into the linkage list S. This process is repeated eight times, until finally the decision predicate is found to be $\mathfrak{T}$ and the true alternative (x, CURRENT) is taken as value. At this point the value issued is already 8!

However, computations are not finished, because the incremental computer must, for eight consecutive times, extract the contents of the first four words of the linkage list S, remove those words, and resume scanning each one of the eight materializations of the form FACTORIAL 3 from its left end, in order to realize that the scanning of such materialization is ended. Consequently, despite the fact that (4.20) and (4.21) do not indicate any need for such additional useless count, the incremental computer still has to perform it. Furthermore, eight materializations of the part of (4.20) right of the production mark and eight sets of four words each for the linkage list S are saved, thus taking storage space, without really being used for accomplishing any useful operation.

One could think of defining FACTORIAL 1 in a way different from (4.20) and (4.21). However, other definitions generally yield similar shortcomings. The waste of time and storage space in computing FACTORIAL 1 is only one example of a general phenomenon occurring during the evaluation of recursive functions: So far, the incremental computer is not able to avoid storing forms after all of their significant information has been exploited, nor to avoid storing linkage information for resuming work on the forms nor later actually resuming such useless work. However, certain simple extensions of the logic of the incremental computer, presented in this section, are sufficient to remove this drawback.

Let

$$((f, \text{ADDRESS}), a_1: \ldots : a_n) \qquad (4.23)$$

be a function address quotation occurring during the evaluation of a form e. Hence, (4.23) must be a subform of a normal form a which either coincides with e or is the reference of a function address quotation [a and (4.23) may coincide]. Form (4.23) comes up when the second occurrence of an open parenthesis (from the left) is joined to the end of

M. Assume that the threshold policy of the reference of (4.23) allows for replacement of this particular occurrence of (4.23). We wish to establish a criterion to determine whether or not a is of any further interest after (4.23) is replaced. If the right depth d of the leftmost open parenthesis in (4.23) is 1 (d is $\mathfrak{C}s_2$), then this must be the leftmost mark in a: therefore a is no longer useful. If $d > 1$, the computer uses two ad hoc registers, R_r and R_s, which initially contain[4] the address of the word carrying this leftmost open parenthesis in (4.23) and its depth d, respectively. Then the computer proceeds as follows:

(i) The contents of $\mathfrak{L}R_r$ are replaced by $\mathfrak{L}^2 R_r$. Three cases are possible now, namely:

(ii) $\mathfrak{L}R_r$ is an open parenthesis. In this case a unit is subtracted from R_s. Then, if the result of the subtraction is >1, (i) is repeated. Otherwise the procedure is halted.

(iii) $\mathfrak{L}R_r$ is an open brace. In this case the contents of R_r are replaced by $\mathfrak{L}R_s$, and cases (ii), (iii), and (iv) are considered again.

(iv) $\mathfrak{L}R_r$ is neither an open parenthesis nor an open brace. In this case the procedure is halted.

Now this procedure can terminate in two ways: either on (ii) or (iv). If it is terminated on (ii) or if $d = 1$ we say that (4.23) is an *external function quotation*: the fact of (4.23) being external implies that there is no reason for the computer to go back to a after having replaced (4.23). Hence, the part of a left of (4.23) is of no further interest. When a recursive function is presented to the library, then, if all quotations referring to itself occurring in its definition form are external, this function will be referred to as an *externally defined* recursive function. Finally, if all functions of the library for an incremental computer (except primitives) are externally defined, each will be referred to as an *external recursive function*.

This last definition implies that a recursive function is external if it is externally defined and, in addition, all functions in terms of which it is defined are also externally defined.

In the following, only external recursive functions will be used to represent processes.

External function address quotations can be recognized by the incremental computer on a local basis. It remains to discuss what the incremental computer should do when it is confronted with the external function quotation (4.23) whose threshold policy allows for replacement, in order to take advantage of the fact that a is of no further interest. First of all, it will join $d-1$ open parentheses to the end of M, thus completing a form in the top of M. From this point, let us just see

[4] We keep denoting the contents of a register R by $\mathfrak{L}R$.

how its action should differ from the one discussed earlier. In the first place it will not join any new four words to the linkage list S. In fact, of the first four words of S, all but the first one now contain information which is useful only to resume scanning e, and is therefore no longer needed. Therefore, the information carried by the center part of these three words will be replaced by the current value of $\mathfrak{L}m_\infty$, a 0 for the right depth, and the number of arguments pertaining to the currently considered quotation, respectively. Note, however, that $\mathfrak{C}s_2$ contained the address of the argument sequence of a function quotation whose reference is e. Before erasing it, this information is utilized right now to remove this quotation from M, thus achieving the main savings in space (in M) allowed by the extensions of the incremental computer now under discussion.

As far as $\mathfrak{C}s_1$ is concerned, it is the resumption address of the quotation of a; since the incremental computer should not return to a, no new linkage address should be set, and $\mathfrak{C}s_1$ should be left unchanged, so that after handling the current quotation the incremental computer will directly resume considering the form which contained a quotation for a. In other words, after external quotations are completely processed the forms containing them are "short circuited" in the sense that they are cut off from further scanning.

This device, added to the logic of the incremental computer, was first presented by this author [3] under the name *discharge accumulator*. It allows savings in time and space in connection with the evaluation of externally defined functions. For example, in the case of factorial, both shortcomings pointed out before are eliminated.

4.8 Literal Functions

So far, appropriate notations and evaluation methods have been provided only for those forms which are written by human beings, stored as part of the library, and embedded in L each time they are needed to perform a computation. However, the flexibility of the incremental computer could not be considered adequate unless the latter were also able to evaluate forms of rather different origin; namely, forms which are generated during the course of the evaluation of other forms and/or come up as arguments of other forms. The characteristic feature of such forms, which renders special treatment necessary, is the fact that when they are evaluated they are in M, while all forms considered so far were in L. So far, R_c has always been the address of a word of L, but now it is necessary to allow for its being the address of a word of M as well. The forms discussed up to now were referred to by means of functions or function address letters, consisting of the function mark f, the purpose of which is to introduce the identifier or the address of the form involved. In the present case, in contrast, a new operative mark, the *literal function mark f^**, is to be used for introducing the forms itself, in the format of a *literal function letter*

$$(f^*, b) \tag{4.24}$$

where b is the form involved. It will be required that b is undecomposable. Literal function letters are mainly used to compose *literal function quotations* in the format

$$((f^*, b), a_1: \ldots :a) \tag{4.25}$$

where $a_1: \ldots :a_n$ is an argument sequence formally identical to those of function quotations introduced in Section 4.2.

The *value* of (4.25) is the value of the synthesis of b and the form $a_1, \ldots, a_n$. The evaluation process for literal function quotations requires only a trivial extension from the process discussed so far, namely, the fact that when (4.25) comes up (in the sense that the closed parenthesis preceding f^* is joined to the end of M) the new mark to be placed in R_c is not b (which, unlike the function address letters, is not necessarily a mark but may be any undecomposable form) but rather the address of the word of M carrying the rightmost mark in b, that is, $\mathfrak{LRm}_0$.

All concepts discussed for function address quotations such as, for example, the one of conditional forms of external quotation and threshold policies apply to literal function quotations without any change.

Let us clarify this by means of the example of a form representing a *functional*, that is, a function one of whose variables is a variable element of a space of functions. The example chosen here is a simple approximation of the Riemann integral of a real function of one real variable on a given interval, obtained by selecting 100 equidistant points of the interval, averaging the values of the integrand at those points, and multiplying the average by the length of the interval.

The new form, whose identifier shall be INTEGRAL, involves four unknowns (x, A), (x, B), $(x, \text{INTEGRAND})$, and (x, DX), the first and second of which represent the lower and upper bound of the domain of integration, respectively, while the third stands for a form in one variable, that is, the integrand function, and the fourth for the bound (dummy) variable of integration.

To define INTEGRAL using only externally defined recursive functions, it is convenient to utilize an auxiliary recursive form INTEGRAL 6 of 6 unknowns, whose evaluation process essentially consists of computing the above average. The six unknowns of this form stand for the upper bound of the interval of integration (to be used in order to check when the summation process is ended), the distance Δ between the points where the integrand is evaluated, the form representing the integrand function, the (current) partial sum of the values of the integrand computed by the preceding materializations of INTEGRAL 6, the abscissa of the point at which the value of the integral should be computed as part of the current materialization and added to the previous partial sum, to be used by the following materialization, and the bound variable of integration.

Formally expressed,

INTEGRAL $::=$ ((f, INTEGRAL 6), UPPER: (x, B), DELTA:
$.01 \times ((x, B) - (x, A))$, INTEGRAND: $(x,$ INTEGRAND$)$, CURRENT: 0,
ABSCISSA: (x, A), DX: (x, DX)) (4.26)

is the definition of the integral. The part of (4.26) right of the production mark is a quotation for the above discussed function, INTEGRAL 6, defined (recursively) as

INTEGRAL 6 $::= (.01 \times ((x, B) - (x, A)) \times (x,$ CURRENT$)\{((f,$ INTEGRAL 6$),$
UPPER: $(x,$ UPPER$)$, DELTA: $(x,$ DELTA$)$, INTEGRAND: $(x,$ INTEGRAND 6$)$,
ABSCISSA: $(x,$ ABSCISSA$) + (x,$ DELTA$)$, CURRENT: $(x,$ CURRENT$) +$
$((f^*, (x,$ INTEGRAND$), (x, DX): (x,$ ABSCISSA$))$, $DX: (x, DX)))\}(x,$
UPPER$) \leq (x,$ ABSCISSA$))$ (4.27)

Suppose that the incremental computer is asked to approximate

$$\int_{\pi/2}^{2\pi} \frac{\sin y}{y} dy$$

that is, to evaluate

((f, INTEGRAL), $A: 1.57$, $B: 6.28$, $DX: Y$,
INTEGRAND: $(((f,$ SIN$),$ ARC: $(x, Y))/(x, Y)))$ (4.28)

when $(f,$ SIN$)$ is a function of the unknown $(x,$ ARC$)$ already in the library, and let us sketch the crucial points of the process that it carries out. For simplicity of presentation, as always, we will disregard the conversion of infixes. First of all, (4.28) is scanned right to left and joined to the end of M, without performing the division or computing the sine, for which the threshold policy does not allow. When $(f,$ INTEGRAL$)$ is encountered, the right hand side of (4.26) is joined to the end of L, where it is then also scanned right to left and joined to the end of M. In doing this, however, each occurrence of (x, A) and (x, B) is replaced by the constants 1.57 or 6.28, respectively, and the form

$$((x, B) - (x, A))$$

is replaced by .0471; the only occurrence of $(x, \text{INTEGRAND})$ is replaced by

$$(((f, \text{SIN}), \text{ARC}: (x, Y))/(x, Y)) \tag{4.29}$$

so that occurrences of (x, Y) are entered into M.

When the function letter $(f, \text{INTEGRAL } 6)$ is encountered, the external function quotation to be considered, after joining the right-hand side of (4.27) to the end of M, is thus

$((f, \text{INTEGRAL } 6), \text{UPPER}: 6.28, \text{DELTA}: .0471, \text{CURRENT}: 0, \text{ABSCISSA}: 1.57,$
$DX: Y, \text{INTEGRAND}: (((f, \text{SIN}), \text{ARC}: (x, Y))/(x, Y)))$ \hfill (4.30)

Then, the right-hand side of (4.30) is scanned and joined to M, and while doing this all occurrences of (x, UPPER), (x, DELTA), (x, DX), $(x, \text{INTEGRAND})$, $(x, \text{CURRENT})$, and $(x, \text{ABSCISSA})$ are initially replaced by 6.28, .0471, Y, $(((f, \text{SIN}), \text{ARC}: (x, Y))/(x, Y))$, 0 and 1.57, respectively. Since the occurrences of $(x, \text{ABSCISSA})$ are replaced by 1.57, the threshold condition for the conditional form, whose decision predicate is now

$$6.28 < 1.57$$

that is, $\mathfrak{F}$, is satisfied. The occurrence of the form

$$(x, \text{ABSCISSA}) + (x, \text{DELTA})$$

is replaced by 1.6171. When the literal function quotation is encountered, its reference is the form (4.29). The only argument value of this quotation is 1.57, and the form by which this notation is replaced is a constant, numerically close to .637, which is the ratio between the sine of the right angle and its measure in radians.

The next quotation concerning INTEGRAL 6 considered will be

$((f, \text{INTEGRAL } 6), \text{UPPER}: 6.28, \text{DELTA}: .0471, \text{INTEGRAND}: (((f, \text{SIN}),$
$\text{ARC}: (x, Y))/(x, Y)), \text{ABSCISSA}: 1.6171, \text{CURRENT}: .637, DX: (x, DX))$
\hfill (4.31)

[Here we have taken the approximate value .637 for (sine 1.57)/1.57.] The two quotations (4.30) and (4.31) differ only for the values of the CURRENT and ABSCISSA arguments, which represent the partial sum so far computed and the value of y for which $\sin y/y$ should be computed as part of the next materialization of INTEGRAL 6, respectively. There are a total of 100 such materializations, and in the ith of them the two argument values are

$$1.57 + .0471 \times i$$

and

$$i \int_{\pi/2}^{2\pi} \frac{\sin y}{y} \cdot dy,$$

respectively, while all other argument values always remain the same. After 100 such materializations, finally the decision predicate of (4.27) is found to be $\mathfrak{T}$, and the negative option is chosen. Since the quotation for INTEGRAL 6 in (4.26) and for INTEGRAL in (4.28) both occurred externally, the constant replacing this 100th quotation is the only mark in M, and is thus directly recognized as solution of the given problem, that is, as approximate value of the given integral.

4.9 Shorthands

It may happen that a form definition, as discussed in Section 4.2, contains as subforms repeated occurrences of one or more undecomposable forms. One can extend the notation for forms and the language of the incremental computer in order to allow the human being to write each of these forms only once, and to refer to it indirectly by means of a *shorthand* which replaces it in each of its occurrences, in order to save both human effort and storage space. (This feature will recall the "macroinstructions" of conventional computations.) For this purpose, we will use an additional operative mark, z, called *shorthand mark*.

A *shorthand* is a normal expression consisting of the enclosure in parentheses of the concatenation of the shorthand mark and a positive integer constant, called *identifier* of the shorthand. For example, $(z, 4)$ is a shorthand whose identifier is 4.

The use of shorthands will be restricted to the replacement of normal forms occurring repetitively in a form definition. When a human being writes a form definition and expects that a subform, say, a, will occur repeatedly, he replaces each of its occurrences within that definition by the shorthand $(z, 1)$. When he finds a second such form, say, a_2, he uses $(z, 2)$ in the same way, and so on. Then, to the end of the form definition, he adds a comma and a normal form, consisting of the enclosure in parenthesis of the concatenation of the forms $a_1, a_2, \ldots, a_n$. Thus, a form definition has the format

$$identifier ::= form, (a_1, \ldots, a_n). \qquad (4.32)$$

The part $(a_1, \ldots, a_n)$ of (4.32) is called *shorthand reference sequence* of the function defined in (4.32).

The order of the identifiers of the shorthands is irrelevant, but the form a_i must correspond to the symbol (z, i), and will be called *reference* of (z, i). Any of the forms a_i may contain occurrences of any shorthand $(z, 1), \ldots (z, n)$ except, of course, (z, i). All forms contained in the library have the format (4.32) (though the reference sequence may be missing for some items) and the modifications to the library search process described in Section 4.2 to handle this new format are trivial.

New form definitions, presented in the format (4.32), are embedded in L as they are. Similar action is taken for all forms coming from the library.

Note that, unlike "macroinstructions," the meaning of shorthands hold only within the context of the form where they are used.

When the incremental computer, while scanning a form e, encounters occurrences of a shorthand, it should start scanning the corresponding reference, which is in L, and resume with e after it is all through with such shorthand. In order to do so, it needs two new lists with control word and end pointer, D and G. Both are 0 lists at the beginning of operations. When evaluation of the form e is started either because e is the form whose evaluation the problem consists of, or because e is the reference of a function quotation, then a new word carrying in its center part the address of the word carrying the comma between e and the shorthand reference list pertaining to e, is joined to the beginning of G. When an occurrence of a shorthand, say (z, i), is encountered, two new words are successively joined to the beginning of D, carrying in their center parts the current $\mathfrak{L}R_c$ and a 1, respectively, and R_c is replaced by the address of the word of L carrying the rightmost mark of the ith canonical component of the interior of the shorthand reference list of the form being scanned, which can be computed as $\mathfrak{L}^2\mathfrak{R}^i\mathfrak{C}g_1$. Whenever D is not empty and a closed or open parenthesis is encountered, a 1 is joined to or subtracted from $\mathfrak{C}d_1$, respectively. Whenever D is not empty and $\mathfrak{C}d_1$ is zero, the open parenthesis is not joined to the end of M, $\mathfrak{L}R_c$ is replaced by $\mathfrak{C}d_2$ and the first two words of D are removed. Whenever G is not empty and the process of scanning a form is completed (as discussed in Section 4.3), the first word of G is removed.

This extension to the logic of the incremental computer saves both storage space and human effort in repeated use of subforms. This is accomplished by using shorthands to depart from the sequence in which marks are normally scanned and to direct the control register R_c to point to the place in memory carrying the reference which is common to that shorthand and to all those identical to it within the same form. A reference is thus completely scanned and processed each time the corresponding shorthand is encountered.

One could hence consider the problem of enabling the incremental computer to achieve some savings in time in connection with shorthands by scanning each reference to a shorthand only the first time it is encountered, and, for each subsequent occurrence of the same shorthand, referring to the position in M where the results of the processed reference can be found. The study of such an extension is left to the reader; some of the problems to which such extension gives rise are briefly outlined here.

In order to carry out such extension, one can think of utilizing again the brackets, flagged integers, and concept of looped lists, which were introduced in Section 4.7 for the purpose of enabling the incremental computer to avoid copying arguments. The use of brackets and flagged integers can be directly extended from unknowns and argument values to shorthands and shorthand references. Shorthands, like unknowns, have a meaning which is uniquely defined within the context of a materialization of the normal form given by a function definition, but not outside of such limits. But unlike unknowns, which refer to argument values which are already in M when the materialization of the form to which they belong is considered, shorthands stand for forms whose value, at that time, must still be embedded in M at least once. This is a first problem which, however, admits a straightforward solution.

A more difficult problem is created by the fact that, unlike argument values, references of shorthands may contain other shorthands as well as unknowns, both with meaning defined within the same context. If the computer evaluates references of shorthands only once during a given materialization, some occurrences of shorthands and unknowns within the considered materialization may never be directly scanned, in the sense that $\mathfrak{L}R_c$ may never be the address of any one of their marks. This makes it rather difficult to assess how many times each shorthand or unknown occurs within a materialization of a form. The number of occurrences of a given unknown, which is to be contained by the right part of the word which carries the open bracket to the immediate left of the corresponding argument value (or references of shorthand, if we want to make this extension), is needed in order to enable the incremental computer to tell when the memory space carrying such argument value or reference is again available as free storage: This, according to the logic scheme presented in Section 4.7, occurs when all active occurrences of the corresponding unknowns (or shorthands) are in turn back in free storage. Thus, without such information, the computer would not easily know exactly when a sublist of free storage carrying a bracketed form can be scrapped and reutilized.

4.10 Processes in Abstract Spaces

This section is devoted to giving some selected examples of representation of points of elementary abstract spaces in a way meaningful to the incremental computer. The main goal is to give the reader more familiarity with using the incremental computer by showing how classes of processes, such as standard operations with vectors or polynomials, can be represented within the framework of its language by building on the infrastructure so far described. The purpose of this section is to indicate, without carrying the study to any completeness, some areas of potential application of the incremental computer and the way one should face the problems of formalizing the processes typical of such areas.

Vectors of n real elements can be represented as enclosure in parentheses of the concatenation of $n + 2$ marks, namely,

$$(\text{REAL VECTOR}, n, c_1, \ldots, c_n) \qquad (4.33)$$

where c_i is the ith component of the vector. It is well understood that c_i does not have to be a number: It can be any undecomposable form. Let us recall that the binary infix $\downarrow$ with binding strength 10 is a substitute

for the function letter (f, COMPONENT) in a way such that the value of
$$i \downarrow a$$
is the ith canonical component of the interior of a. A reasonable threshold predicate for $\downarrow$ would be *i is a positive integer*. Let the function IS UNDECOMPOSABLE of the unknown (x, FORM) have the value $\mathfrak{T}$ iff an undecomposable form replaces the unknown. Then the predicate in the unknown (x, POSSIBLE VECTOR)

IS REAL VECTOR ::= (((f, IS UNDECOMPOSABLE), FORM: (x, POSSIBLE VECTOR)) $\wedge$ (1 $\downarrow$ (x, POSSIBLE VECTOR) = REAL VECTOR))

is $\mathfrak{T}$ only if a real vector is replaced for the only unknown, while

ORDER ::= 2 $\downarrow$ (x, POSSIBLE VECTOR)

is the order of the only unknown. Let us also recall that the value of the primitive function (f, INTERIOR) of the unknown (x, FORM) is the interior of the (normal) form which replaces the unknown, and that the prefix @ stands for (f, INTERIOR).

To represent the sum of two vectors, we will utilize the auxiliary form $A411$ defined as

$A411$ ::= ((f, $A411$), FIRST: (x, FIRST), SECOND: (x, SECOND), COUNT: (x, COUNT) + 1, ORDER: (x, ORDER), CURRENT: (@(x, CURRENT), (x, COUNT) $\downarrow$ (x, FIRST) + (x, COUNT) $\downarrow$ (x, SECOND)){(x, CURRENT)}(x, COUNT) $\leq$ (x, ORDER)) (4.34)

Then the sum of two real vectors (x, FIRST) and (x, SECOND) is expressed by

REAL VECTOR SUM ::= (REAL VECTOR, 2 $\downarrow$ (x, FIRST), ((f, $A411$), FIRST: (x, FIRST), SECOND: (x, SECOND), COUNT: 3, ORDER: 2 $\downarrow$ (x, FIRST), CURRENT: 3 $\downarrow$ (x, FIRST) + 3 $\downarrow$ (x, SECOND))) (4.35)

To better understand (4.34) and (4.35), keep in mind that the interior of the form representing a vector of n elements has $n + 2$ canonical components, of which the third one is the first component of the vector. Both in (4.34) and (4.35) the two addend vectors are (x, FIRST) and (x, SECOND): This (unnecessary) coincident notation has been selected by the writer for explanatory purposes. In (4.34) the unknown (x, COUNT) is a count of the number of materializations, the unknown (x, ORDER) is a reminder of the total number of components of the vectors $+2$, and the unknown (x, CURRENT) at the ith materialization is the enclosure in parentheses of the concatenation of the sums of the first i pairs of corresponding elements of the added vectors.

A polynomial in one indeterminate of degree n with real coefficients can be represented according to the format

(POLYNOMIAL, n, a_0, a_1, . . . , a_n) (4.36)

where a_i is the coefficient of the power $n\text{-}i$, that is, the a_i are in decreasing order of power.

The sum of two such polynomials, not necessarily of equal degree, can be represented by using the auxiliary form A4112 defined as

$A4112 ::= (((f, A4112),$ ORDER: $(x,$ ORDER$),$ COUNT: $(x,$ COUNT$) + 1,$ FIRST: $(x,$ FIRST$),$ SECOND: $(x,$ SECOND$),$ DEGREE $1:(x,$ DEGREE $1),$ DEGREE $2:(x,$ DEGREE $2),$ CURRENT: $(@(x,$ CURRENT$), ((x,$ COUNT$) \downarrow (x,$ FIRST$)\{(x,$ COUNT$) \downarrow (x,$ SECOND$)\}((x,$ ORDER$) - (x,$ DEGREE $2)) > (x,$ COUNT$))))\{((f, A4112),$ ORDER: $(x,$ ORDER$),$ COUNT: $(x,$ COUNT$) + 1,$ FIRST: $(x,$ FIRST$),$ SECOND: $(x,$ SECOND$),$ DEGREE $1:(x,$ DEGREE $1),$ DEGREE $2:(x,$ DEGREE $2),$ CURRENT: $(@(x,$ CURRENT$), (x,$ COUNT$) \downarrow (x,$ FIRST$) + (x,$ COUNT$) \downarrow (x,$ SECOND$)))\}(((x,$ ORDER$) - (x,$ DEGREE $1) > (x,$ COUNT$)) \wedge ((x,$ ORDER$) - (x,$ DEGREE $2) > (x,$ COUNT$)))\{(x,$ CURRENT$)\}$ $(x,$ ORDER$) \geq (x,$ COUNT$))$ (4.37)

Let
$$\text{MAX} ::= ((x, 1)\{(x, 2)\}(x, 1) > (x, 2)) \quad (4.38)$$
then

SUM POLYNOMIAL $::=$ (POLYNOMIAL, $@((f, A4112),$ ORDER: $((f,$ MAX$),$ $1:2 \downarrow (x,$ FIRST$), 2:2 \downarrow (x,$ SECOND$)) + 2),$ COUNT: $3,$ FIRST: $(x,$ FIRST$),$ SECOND: $(x,$ SECOND$),$ DEGREE $1:2 \downarrow (x,$ FIRST$),$ DEGREE $2:2 \downarrow (x,$ SECOND$),$ CURRENT: $((f,$ MAX$), 1:2 \downarrow (x,$ FIRST$), 2:2 \downarrow (x,$ SECOND$)))$

(4.39)

where the addends have identifiers FIRST and SECOND, respectively. (However, this particular definition of the sum of polynomials ignores the possibility that leading zero coefficients in the sum may diminish its degree.) To represent the sum of two polynomials p_1 and p_2, instead of using the notation

$$((f, \text{POLYNOMIAL}) \text{ FIRST}: p_1, \text{SECOND}: p_2) \quad (4.40)$$

one might prefer to use

$$p_1 + p_2 \quad (4.41)$$

Still more generally, one might use $+$ as common identifier of commutative group operation in any abstract algebra. The advantage ensuing from this is that one would be able to represent processes by forms which are invariant with respect to the spaces in which the variables are defined, provided that the functions quoted are defined in such spaces. Such representations, filed in the library of the incremental computer, would give rise to different processes, depending on the arguments of the quotations referring to them. To show the reasoning by which this can be achieved, we will exhibit as an example the simple case in which $+$ should be used for referring both to the primitive function $(f,$ SUM$)$

of two integers or rationals, and to (f, SUM POLYNOMIAL). This can be achieved by using the form definition

FORMAL SUM ::= (((f, SUM POLYNOMIAL), FIRST:(x, A), SECOND:(x, B)){(((f, SUM), FIRST:(x, A), SECOND:(x, B))}(1 ↓ (x, A) = POLYNOMIAL)) (4.42)

To make FORMAL SUM[5] available, the incremental computer should convert the infix $+$ occurring in

$$a + b \qquad (4.43)$$

into the prefix (f, FORMAL SUM) occurring in the quotation

$$((f, \text{FORMAL SUM}), A:a, B:b) \qquad (4.44)$$

Similarly, more general extensions of the capability of an incremental computer to handle commutative binary operations in other groups, while still keeping the validity of the notation (4.43) throughout its present and future library, can be implemented by simple variations of (4.42)

In order to simplify the representation of forms, we may introduce the following convention concerning the argument sequences of function quotations: When an argument value consists of an unknown whose identifier coincides with the corresponding argument, the unknown will be replaced by the ampersand. For example, the notation

$(($f$, a), b:(x, b))$ will be replaced by $(($f$, a), b, \&)$

Upon adding the ampersand to the alphabet of the incremental computer, trivial modifications to the operations above described will cause it to take appropriate care of this convention.

So far, we have considered polynomials from a strictly formal standpoint, that is, as elements of a ring of which the SUM defined above is one of the basic operations. Let us now define *polynomial functions* of one real variable, and represent in a way meaningful to the incremental computer the relation between polynomials and polynomial functions. The important property to have is the polynomial function of the formal sum of two polynomials, as defined above, which must coincide with the point-by-point arithmetic sum of the polynomial functions of the addends. Let

$A4113$ ::= ((x, CURRENT){(((f, $A4113$), COUNT:(x, COUNT) $+ 1$, ORDER: &, FREE: &, POLYNOMIAL: &, CURRENT:(x, COUNT) ↓ (x, POLYNOMIAL) $+$ (x, CURRENT) $\times$ (x, FREE))}(x, COUNT) $>$ (x, ORDER)) (4.45)

and

[5] Here FORMAL SUM is restricted to two interpretations. An open ended definition may be worked out as an exercise by the reader.

POLYNOMIAL FUNCTION ::= ((f, 4113), FREE: (x, FREE VARIABLE),
ORDER: $2 + 2 \downarrow$ (x, POLYNOMIAL), POLYNOMIAL: &, COUNT: 3, (4.46)
CURRENT: $3 \downarrow$ (x, POLYNOMIAL))

In (4.46) the unknown (x, POLYNOMIAL) stands for a (*formal*) polynomial [which could be displayed according to the format (4.36)] while the unknown (x, FREE VARIABLE) stands for a rational number. The value of the right-hand side of (4.46) within a context of full information is a rational number consisting of the application of the formal polynomial (x, POLYNOMIAL) to the rational variable (x, FREE VARIABLE): a well-known procedure for the computation is formalized in (4.45). If p is a formal polynomial, the polynomial function in the free variable y associated with it can be written

$((f,$ POLYNOMIAL FUNCTION$),$ POLYNOMIAL: $p,$ FREE VARIABLE: $y)$ (4.47)

Let p_1 and p_2 be two formal polynomials. The sum of their corresponding polynomial functions in the variable y can be represented in two formally different but numerically equivalent ways, namely,

$((f,$ POLYNOMIAL FUNCTION$),$ POLYNOMIAL: $((f,$ SUM POLYNOMIAL$),$
FIRST: $p_1,$ SECOND: $p_2),$ FREE VARIABLE: $y)$ (4.48)

or else

$((f,$ POLYNOMIAL FUNCTION$),$ POLYNOMIAL: $p_1,$ FREE VARIABLE: $y) +$
$((f,$ POLYNOMIAL FUNCTION$),$ POLYNOMIAL: $p_2,$ FREE VARIABLE: $y)$ (4.49)

Appendix: Properties of Forms

A.1 Structural Proofs

Definition 5 of Section 2.3 states that for each aggregate which is a form there must be at least one proof, called *structural proof*, of its being a form, consisting of a finite sequence of *statements*, i.e.; instances of definitions 1, 2, 3, and 4, such that each instance of definition 1 is always applied to an extended constant or an operative mark, and each instance of definition 2, 3, and 4 is applied to aggregates which have been proved to be forms as a result of instances of definitions 1, 2, 3, or 4 preceding it in such proof. Thus, each statement of a structural proof has the format:

> "The aggregate a is a form because of definition 1, or of definition 2, 3, or 4 applied to the aggregates $b_1, b_2, \ldots,$ which are *outputs* of previous statements."

Here a and $b_1, b_2, \ldots$ are called *output* and *input(s)* of the statement, respectively.
 We shall always assume that the last statement of any structural proof of a form e has e as output. Furthermore, we shall assume that in a structural proof there are never two statements whose output is identical.

Let us call *chain* a sequence of statements of a structural proof of e such that

(1) The last one has e as output.
(2) The first one is an instance of definition 1.
(3) The output of each, except the last one, serves as input for at least one subsequent statement in the chain.
(4) At least one of the inputs of each of them, except the first one, is the output of a previous statement of the chain.

If a statement does not belong to any chain, it is irrelevant to the proof. We shall always assume that structural proofs do not contain such irrelevant statements.

A.2 Levels of Forms

Let us associate with each form an integer, called *level*, as follows:

(1) The level of an atom is 0.
(2) The level of a form a obtained by concatenation of two other forms a_1 and a_2 is the higher of the levels of a_1 and a_2.
(3) The level of a form a_1, obtained by enclosing in parentheses the form a_2 of level j, is $j+1$.
(4) The level of the conditional form $(a\{b\}p)$, where a, b, p, have levels j_1, j_2, j_3, respectively, is the highest among the three numbers j_1+1, j_2+1, j_3+1.

For example,
$$x, 3$$
is a form of level 0,
$$(\text{A}\{(f), \text{SUM}, (2)\}3.14, -2)$$
is a form of level 2, and
$$((f), \text{SUM}, 3.14, (12, \text{S}, x, 7))$$
is a form of level 2.

Defined in this way the level of a form depends on its particular structural proof that one has in mind; consequently, the level is not *a priori* unique because there can be several structural proofs of the same form. It will be shown later in this appendix that the level is really independent of the structural proof, and unique. But until then its uniqueness will never be stipulated.

Let us consider the following:

Lemma 1—The difference between the total number of open and closed parentheses in a form is always 0.

Proof. Obvious, by definition 5, Section 1.2. In fact, the only provision for introducing parentheses in the structural proof of a form is given by definitions 3 and 4, Section 2.3, which require introduction of parentheses in couples of an open parenthesis and a closed parenthesis.

Similarly, *Lemma 2—The differences between the number of open and closed braces in a form is always 0.*

Now let e be an aggregate, and let a be a mark other than a parenthesis in e. Let $O_l(a, e)$ and $C_l(a, e)$ denote the total number of open and closed parentheses, respectively, to the left of a in e and $O_r(a, e)$ and $C_r(a, e)$ the total number of open and closed parentheses, respectively, to the right of a in e. Let us prove the following:

Lemma 3—If e is a form, then, for all a

$$O_l(a, e) - C_l(a, e) = C_r(a, e) - O_r(a, e). \tag{A1}$$

Proof. In fact, by lemma 1, since the mark occurring in a is not a parenthesis

$$O_l(a, e) + O_r(a, e) = C_l(a, e) + C_r(a, e) \tag{A2}$$

from which (A1) immediately follows.

Theorem 4a—If e is a form, then, for all a,

$$O_l(a, e) - C_l(a, e) \geq 0 \tag{A3a}$$

Proof. By induction with respect to the level n of e.

First of all, (A3a) is true for $n = 0$, because in this case (e) has the format (2.1) of Section 2.3, where all a_i are atoms, and there are no occurrences of parentheses. Assume now that the theorem has been proved for all integers t such that $0 \leq t < n$ and let us consider, in a structural proof of a, the first instance of definition 2, 3, or 4, Section 2.3 stating that an aggregate, say, e^*, containing a, is a form of level n contained in e (e^* and e may coincide). The remainder of the structural proof cannot contain instances of definition 3 or 4, Section 2.3, having as input forms containing e^*, because otherwise e would be of a level greater than n. Consequently, e has the structure

$$e_1, e_2, \ldots, e^*, \ldots, e_{s-1}, e_s \tag{A4}$$

where e^* is

$$e_1^*, e_2^* \tag{A5a}$$

or

$$(e_2^*) \tag{A5b}$$

or

$$(e_1^*\{e_2^*\}e_3^*) \tag{A5c}$$

Let i be such that a occurs in e_i^*. Then,

$$O_l(a, e_i^*) - C_l(a, e_i^*) \geq 0 \tag{A6}$$

by hypothesis, because the level of e_i^* is n. The contribution to both members of (A3a) of all e_j different from e^* vanishes by lemma 1, as well as the one of all e_j^* where $j \neq i$.

Let us consider the case $i = 2$. In this case, if (A5a) holds,

$$O_l(a, e) = O_l(a, e_i^*) \tag{A7a}$$

If (A5b) or (A5c) hold

$$O_l(a, e) = O_l(a, e_i^*) + 1 \tag{A7b}$$

and in both cases

$$C_l(a, e) = C_l(a, e_i^*) \tag{A8}$$

If i is either 1 or 3, then (A7b) and (A8) hold in any case. Thus, by subtracting (A8) from either (A7a) or (A7b), we have

$$O_l(a, e) - C_l(a, e) \geq O_l(a, e_i{*}) - C_l(a, e_i{*}) \tag{A9}$$

Hence, (A3a) follows immediately by (A9) and (A6).

Analogously, one can prove

Theorem 4b—*If e is a form, then, for all a,*

$$O_r(a, e) - C_r(a, e) \leq 0 \tag{A3b}$$

So far, the concept of level of a form has been envisaged as dependent of the proof that one can give that an aggregate is such. This proof is not necessarily unique, and it is easy to give examples where more than one proof is possible. Consequently, the level of a form is not *a priori* unique. It is now necessary for further development to give a proof of its uniqueness. This can be done, among other ways, by introducing a new auxiliary concept: We shall call *left depth* and *right depth*, respectively, of a mark a different from a parenthesis in an aggregate e the integers

$$D_l(a, e) = O_l(a, e) - C_l(a, e)$$

and

$$D_r(a, e) = C_r(a, e) - O_r(a, e)$$

By theorem 4, neither depth is ever negative, whenever e is a form.

Theorem 5—*The maximum depth of occurrences of marks in a form e is the level of e.*

The main consequence of this theorem is the fact that it assures the uniqueness of the level of any form.

Proof. Let a be an occurrence of a mark at maximum depth d in e. Consider a chain (Section 2.3) of statements of structural proof of e one of whose inputs always contains a and whose first statement is an instance of definition 1, Section 2.3 (such chain must necessarily exist).

The level of e is the maximum among the levels of all outputs of the statements of such chain, while the depth of a in e is the maximum depth of a in such outputs. Let us prove the theorem by showing that level and depth of a are equal for all such outputs.

In fact, it is certainly true for the first one, whose output has no parentheses. Let us assume that it is true for the first $n - 1$ statements. Then, if the nth is an instance of definition 3 of Section 2.3, its output has both level and depth of a which exceed by 1 the ones of its input. These two are equal because this input must be the output of a previous statement.

If the nth statement is an occurrence of definition 2 of Section 2.3, let us show that a cannot occur in one of the inputs having a level lower than the other one. In fact, since the property is true for both inputs, if that happened the input with higher level would also contain a mark, say, $a{*}$, of depth higher than the one of a in the output of the nth statement. The depth of $a{*}$ in e will also be higher than the one of $a{*}$ in e, because all statements of the chain following the nth statement will raise both of their depths equally: This cannot be because of the way a has been chosen. Hence, the depth of a in the output of the nth statement equals its depth in the input to which it belongs, and thus the level of its output.

An argument consisting of combining those expounded for definitions 2 and 3 holds in case the nth statement is an instance of definition 4. Hence, the theorem is proved.

If a denotes an aggregate, let a^{-1} denote the *inverse* aggregate of a consisting of marks which compose a but in reverse order, where open parentheses and braces are replaced by closed parentheses and braces and vice versa, then the following holds:

Theorem 6—If a is a form, so is a^{-1}.

Proof. In fact, a structural proof for a^{-1} can be constructed by simply inverting the order of all couples or triplets of forms which serve as inputs to occurrences of definitions 2 and 4, Section 2.3, in the structural proof of a.

A.3 Canonical Decomposition

Let e be a form of level n and let us define the *canonical decomposition* of e, consisting of writing e as

$$e_1, e_2, \ldots, e_{M(e)} \tag{A10}$$

where each e_i is an aggregate containing no occurrences of commas at depth 0 in e, called ith *canonical component of e*, and $M(e)$ is a positive integer, called *number of canonical components* of e. The canonical decomposition of e is based on the occurrences of commas of depth 0 in e. If there are no such occurrences, then $M(e) = 1$ and the canonical decomposition of e is e, and e is said to be *undecomposable*. If there are $m - 1 > 0$ such commas, then $M(e) = m$, and e_1 and $e_{M(e)}$ are the aggregates consisting of all marks preceding the first of such occurrences or following the last of them, respectively, while e_i ($i = 2, 3, \ldots, M(e) - 1$) is the aggregate consisting of all marks following the $(i-1)$th and preceding the ith of such occurrences.

The canonical decomposition thus defined is obviously unique. In the case $M(e) > 1$, however, it remains to prove the following:

Theorem 1 (canonical decomposition theorem)—All canonical components of a form are forms.

Proof. Let us prove this theorem for the canonical component e_j. If e_j is an atom the result is immediate. Otherwise, let us consider a structural proof of e, and assert that it must contain the statement that e_j is a form. Let t be the first statement of such structural proof having as output a form e^* containing e_j as subform. There must be an occurrence of a comma of depth 0 either to the left or to the right of e_j in e, which we will call c. Let us show that e^* and e_j are identical, which would prove the theorem. In fact, suppose they were not: In this case t cannot be an instance of definition 3 or 4, Section 2.3, because, if it were, c could no longer have depth 0 in e.

Assume that t is an instance of definition 2, stating that e^* is a form because it is the concatenation of two forms e_1^* or e_2^*. Let us call c^* the occurrence of a comma linking such concatenation, which must be in e_j, otherwise either e_1^* or e_2^* would contain e_j, and hence t would not be the first statement yielding a form containing e_j. Furthermore, c^* has depth 0 in e^*. Let us show that c^* also has depth 0 in e. In fact, each statement of the structural proof of e raising the depth of c^* would also raise that of c. Consequently, c^* and c must have the same depth in e, which is 0. But e_j cannot contain commas of depth 0 in e, so that t cannot be an instance of definition 2. Thus the theorem is proved.

A.4 Substitutes

We present here a proof of theorem 1 of Section 2.4.

Proof. Since a is undecomposable, every structural proof of a must contain a statement t having a as output: This can be proved by considering the first statement whose output a^* contains a, and showing that $a = a^*$ with an argument similar to the one used in the canonical decomposition theorem. We must construct a structural proof of $S(b, e, a)$. We can do so by starting from the one of e, and adding a complete structural proof of b right after t. Let us denote e^A the inputs of statements of the structural proof of e which contains one or more (say, n) occurrences of a. Let us call $e^A{}_j$ ($j = 1, \ldots, n$) the aggregate obtained from e^A by replacing b for the jth occurrence of a. Then right after each statement which uses a e^A as input, we will insert a sequence of j statements which have the input e^A replaced by a $e^A{}_j$, and the output has the corresponding occurrence of a replaced by b. If a statement has two or three e^A as input, two or three such sequences need to be inserted.

At this point, every $e^A{}_j$ is the output of a statement that together with all statements preceding it forms a structural proof for $e^A{}_j$ (which, however, may need to be weeded from irrelevant statements). And $S(b, e, a)$ is one of the $e^A{}_j$. This proves the theorem.

Acknowledgments

Some paragraphs of Section 1 were written jointly with Dr. Bertram Raphael, now at the University of California, Berkeley, and Dr. Zenon S. Zannetos of the MIT Sloan School of Management. The subject matter of this report has provided the material for half of the two-week course "Man-Computer Information Systems" offered by the author and Dr. Bertram Raphael at the Physical Sciences Extension–Engineering Extension, University of California, Los Angeles, California, July 20–30, 1964, organized by Dr. Clifford Bell and Mr. Harold L. Tallman. The author is indebted to Dr. James C. Emery and Dr. Martin Greenberger, MIT Sloan School of Management, and to Dr. Michel A. Melkanoff and Dr. R. Clay Sprowls, UCLA, for their advice, sponsorship, and encouragement.

References

1. Berkeley, E., and Fredkin, E., in *The LISP Programming Language, its Operation and Applications*. Information International, Needham, Massachusetts, 1964.

2. Lombardi, L. A., Nonprocedural data system languages. Invited paper, reprints of papers presented at the 16th National Conference of the Association for Computing Machinery, Los Angeles, California, 1961.
3. Lombardi, L.A., Zwei Beiträge zur Morphologie und Syntax deklarativer Systemsprachen. Akten der 1962 Jahrestagung der Gesellschaft fur angewandte Mathematik und Mechanik (GAMM), Bonn, 1962; *Z. Angew. Math. Mech.* (42) Sonderheft (1962), T27–T29.
4. Lombardi, L. A., On the control of the data flow by means of recursive functions. *Proc. Symp. "Symbolic Languages in Data Processing," Intern. Computation Center, Rome, 1962.* Gordon & Breach, 1962.
5. Lombardi, L. A., On table operating algorithms. *Inform. Process., Proc. 2nd IFIP Congr., Munich, 1962* Sect. 14. North-Holland Publ., Amsterdam, 1963.
6. Lombardi, L. A., Prospettive per il calcolo automatico. *Scientia* [4] **57**, 2 and 3 (1963) (in Italian and French).
7. Lombardi, L. A., A general business-oriented language based on decision expressions, in ACM Symposium on the Structure of Mechanical Languages. *Commun. Assoc. Computing Machinery* **7**, No. 2 104–111 (1964).
8. Lombardi, L. A., and Raphael, B., LISP as a language for an incremental computer, in *The LISP Programming Language, its Applications and Operation.* Information International, Maynard, Massachusetts, 1962.
9. McCarthy, J., *LISP 1.5 Manual.* MIT Press, Cambridge, Massachusetts, 1964.
10. Newell, A., and Tonge, F. M., An introduction to the information processing language V. *Commun. Assoc. Computing Machinery* **3**, No. 4, 205–211 (1960).
11. Pacelli, M., and Palermo, G., Sequential translation of a problem-oriented programming language, *Proc. Symp. "Symbolic Languages in Data Processing," Intern. Computation Center, Rome, 1962.* Gordon & Breach, 1962.
12. Samelson, K., and Bauer, F. L., Sequential formula translation, *Commun. Assoc. Computing Machinery* **3**, No. 2, 76–83 (1960).
13. Papers presented at ACM storage allocation symposium, June 1961. Princeton, New Jersey. *Commun. Assoc. Computing Machinery* **4**, 103, 416–464 (1961).

Author Index

Numbers in parentheses are reference numbers and indicate that an author's work is referred to although his name is not cited in the text. Numbers in italic show the page on which the complete reference is listed.

A

Abrahams, P., 54(37), *101*
Adams, C. W., *42*
Allen, T. R., *42*
Alt, F. L., 155(1), *186*
Andrews, E. G., 6(*3*), *42*
Archer, R., 105(1), *151*
Arden, B. W., *42*
Armenti, A. W. 37(51) *44*
Auslander, M., 53(5), 78(6), 80(5), 92(6), *99*

B

Backus, J. W., 242(1), *244*
Balmer, H. A., 70(1), 95(1), 97(1), 98, *99*
Bar-Hillel, Y., 154(2), *186*
Barnett, M. P., 67, 70(28), 95(20, 55), 97(20, 28, 55), *100*, *102*
Bartlett, J. M., 156(49), *188*
Basu, S. K., 206, *244*
Bauer, F. L., 249, 302, *333*
Berkeley, E., 249, 258, *332*
Bernick, M. D., 53(2), *99*
Blackwell, F. W., 65(3), 78, *99*
Bleiweiss, L., 86, *99*
Bloomfield, L., 154(3), *186*
Bobrow, D. G., 156, *186*
Bobrow, R. J., 58(53), 78(53), 83(53), 85(53), 92(53), 95(53), *101*
Boilen, S., 7(5) *42*
Bolinger, D. L., 156, *186*
Bond, E. R., 53(5, 43), 78, 80, 92, *99*, *101*
Boys, S. F., 97, *99*
Brayton, R., 74(36), *101*
Brooker, R. A., 155(6), *186*
Bross, I., 155(7), *186*
Brown, W. S., 53(9, 10), 58, 70(9, 10), 78(9), 95(9), 97(9), 98(9), *99*
Burks, A. W., 193, *244*

C

Callender, E. D., 53(2), *99*
Caviness, J. S., 60(21), 65(21), 78(21), 97(21), *100*
Chomsky, N., 154, 155(12), 156(8, 9, 10), *186*, 230, *244*
Clapp, L. C., 63, *100*
Clark, W. E., *44*
Codd, E. F., *42*
Coffman, C., *45*
Comfort, W. T., 19(7), 32(7), *42*
Cook, G. B., 97(8), *99*
Corbato, F. J., 6(10), 7(10), 13(11, 77), 18(77), 29(10), 32(11), *42*, *43*, *45*
Couleur, J. F., 13(33), 19(33), *43*
Crisman, P. A., 7(12), *42*
Critchlow, A. J., *42*
Culler, G. J., *42*
Cundall, P. A., 80, 86(4), *99*
Cunningham, J. A., 24(59), *44*
Cuthill, E., 97, 98, *100*

D

Daggett, M. M., 6(10), 7(10), 29(10), *42*
Daley, R. C., 6(10), 7(10), 29(10), 34(15), *42*
Darley, D. L., 37(25), *43*
David, E. E., Jr., *42*
Davis, M. R., *42*
Dennis, J. B., 7, *42*, *43*
Dijkstra, E. W., 193, *244*
Dobzhansky, T., 105(2), *151*
Dougherty, C. Y. 156(11), *186*
Dunn, T. M., *43*
Dunten, S. D., *44*, 63, *100*

E

Edwards, D., 54(37), 74(36), *101*

AUTHOR INDEX

Edwards, D. B. G., 18(38), *43*
Efimba, R., 70(28), 97(28), *100*
Ellis, T. O., *42*
Engelman, C., *43*, 57(16), 63(16), 66(16), *100*
Evans, T. G., 37(25), *43*

F

Fano, R. M., 7(26), 9(26), 32(26), *42*, *43*
Farber, D. J., 61(17), 86(17), *100*
Feldman, G., 34(27), *43*
Feurzlig, W., 155(29), *187*
Fletcher, R., 98, *100*
Fodor, J. A., 229, *244*
Foote, J. E., *42*
Forgie, J. W., *43*
Fotheringham, J., *43*
Fox, P., 74(36), *101*
Fredkin, E., 7(5), *42*, *43*, 249, 258, *332*
Fried, B. D., *42*

G

Galler, B. A., *42*
Gerard, J. M., 70(28), 95(20), 97, *100*
Gill, S., 29(31), *43*
Gilman, H., 34(27), *43*
Glaser, E. L., 13(33), 19(33), *43*
Goldstein, M., 54(32), 60(32), 95(32), 97, 98, *100*
Gorn, S., 109(9), *152*, 193, *244*
Graham, R. M., 13(77), 18(77), *45*
Gray, H. J., 6(57), 34(57), 37(57), *44*
Green, B. F., Jr., 155(12), *186*
Greenberger, M., *43*
Grisoff, S., 53(5), 78(6), 80(5), 92(6), *99*
Griswold, R. E., 61(17), 86(17), *100*
Gross, M., 154, *186*

H

Hanson, J. W., 60(21), 65(21), 78, 97(21), *100*
Harman, G. H., 156(14), *187*
Harris, Z. S., 154(17, 18), 155(15, 20), 156(16, 19), *187*
Hart, T., 54(37), *100*, *101*
Hartt, K., 70(23), 78(23), 95(23), *100*
Hays, D. G., 154(21, 22, 23), *187*
Herget, P., 97, *100*
Hirschkop, R., 86(4), *99*
Hiż, H., 154, *187*
Hockett, C. F., 105(1), *151*, 154(27), *187*

Hodes, L., 74(36), *101*
Hooke, S. H., 106(5), *152*
Humphries, D. E., 24(59), *44*
Hyde, J. P., 53(10), 70(10), *99*, *100*

I

Ingerman, P. Z., 155(28), *187*
Irons, E. T., 155(29), *187*
Iturriaga, R., 54(41), 61(41), *101*
Izsak, I. G., 70(28), 95(20), 97(20, 28), *100*

J

Jesperson, O., 106(3), *151*
Joseph, C., 60(21), 65(21), 78(21), 97(21), *100*
Joshi, A. K., 156, *187*

K

Kahrimanian, H. G., 49, 64, 65(29), *100*
Kain, R. Y., 63, *100*
Kaluznin, L. A., 194, *244*
Katz, J. J., 229, 230(9), *244*
Keller, J. M., *43*
Kelley, K. R., 70(30), 78(30), *100*
Kenney, R., 53(5), 78(6), 80(5), 92(6), *99*
Kilburn, T., 18(38), *43*
Kinslow, H. A., *43*
Kirsch, R. A., 226(10), 228(10), *244*
Klerer, M., 67, *100*
Kotok, A., 37(40), *43*
Kuno, S., 155, *187*

L

Lamb, S. M., 156, *187*
Lambek, J., 154(37), *188*
Lampson, B. W., *43*
Landin, P. J., 194, *244*
Lanigan, M. J., 18(38), *43*
Lapidus, A., 54(32), 60(32), 95(32), 97, 98, *100*
Laughery, K., 155(12), *186*
Leagus, D. C., 58, *99*
Lecerf, Y., 154, *188*
Lederman, D., 97(33), 98, *101*
Ledley, R. S., 226(13), 243(13), *244*
LeShack, A. R., 95(50), 98(49, 50), *101*
Levin, M., 54(37), *101*
Lichtenberger, W. W., 6(42), 12(42), 19(42), *43*
Licklider, J. C. R., 7(5), 41, *42*, *44*
Lock, K., *44*

AUTHOR INDEX

Loden, W. A., 70(1), 95(1), 97(1), 98(1), *99*
Lombardi, L. A., *44*, 249, 261, 268, 309, *333*
Luckham, D., 74(36), *101*

M

McCarthy, J., 7(5, 47), *42*, *44*, *45*, 54(37), 74(36), *101*, 190, 194, *244*, 249, 258, *333*
McCullough, J. D., *44*
Maling, K., 65(35), 74(36), *101*
Martin, J., *44*
Martin, S. E., 156(11), *186*
Martin, W. A., 63, 67, *101*
Matthews, G. H., 156, *188*
May, J., 67, *100*
Melnitsky, B., 115(12), *152*
Mikus, L. E., *44*
Mooers, C. N., *44*
Morris, D., 155(6), *186*
Morris, J., 154(45), 163(45), *188*
Morrissey, J. H., *43*
Musen, P., 97, *100*
Myszewski, M., 53(5), 78(6), 80(5), 92(6), *99*

N

Narashimhan, R., 226(17), 228(17), 243 (16, 17), *244*
Naur, P., 233(18), 237, *244*, *245*
Nerode, A., 194, *245*
Neumann, P. G., 34(15), *42*
Newell, A., *333*
Nievergelt, J., 243(16, 17), *244*
Nolan, J. F., 37(51), *44*, 49, 64, 65(40), *101*

O

O'Brien, T. C., *42*
Oettinger, A. G., 155(34, 40), *187*, *188*
Oliver, G. A., 13(33), 19(33), *43*
Opler, A., *44*
Ossanna, F. J., *44*

P

Pacelli, M., 302, *333*
Palermo, G., 302, *333*
Park, D., 74(36), *101*
Patel, N. R., 29(54), *44*
Patrick, R. L., *44*
Perlis, A. J., 54(41), 61(41), *101*
Peter, R., 194, 206, *245*

Petrie, W. M. F., 108(7), *152*
Pirtle, M. W., 6(42), 12(42), 19(42), *43*
Polonsky, I. P., 61(17), *100*
Postal, P. M., 230(9), *244*
Prywes, N. S., 6(57), 34(57), 37(57), *44*
Pyke, T. N., Jr., 6(58), 12(58), 28(58), 32(58), *44*

R

Radbill, J. R., 73(4), *108*
Raphael, B., 249, 268, *333*
Raze, C., 154(45), 163(45), *188*
Reeves, C. M., 97(8), 98, *99*, *100*
Rhodes, I., 155(1, 41, 42), *186*, *188*
Rippy, D. E., 24(59), *44*
Robinson, J., 154(43, 45), *188*
Rom, A. R., 70(42), *101*
Rosenberg, A., 4, *44*
Russell, S., 74(36), *101*

S

Sager, N., 154(45), 155(46), 163(45), *188*
Salkoff, M., 154(45), 163(45), 166(47), *188*
Saltzer, J. H., *44*
Salzman, L. F., 108(8), *152*
Samelson, K., 193, *245*, 249, 302, *333*
Sammet, J. E., 50(45), 51(45, 46, 47), 53(5, 43), 78, 80, 92(6), 94(45), *99*, *101*
Samuel, A. L., *44*
Sanford, J. R., 53(2), *99*
Schorr, H., 61, 65(48), *101*
Schwartz, J. I., 6(66), 9(65, 66), *44*, *45*, 217(24), *245*
Sconzo, P., 95(50), 98, *101*
Shavitt, I., 97(8), *99*
Shaw, J. C., 5(69), 11(68), *45*
Sherr, A. L., *45*
Shortell, A. V., Jr., *45*
Simmons, R. E., 156, *188*
Simmons, R. F., *45*
Skinner, F. G., 106(6), *152*
Slagle, J. R., 60(51), 66, 78, *101*
Sommerfelt, A., 106(4), *152*
Standish, T. A., 54(41), 61(41), *101*
Steel, T. B., 141(14), *152*
Strachey, C., 6, *45*
Strum, E. C., *43*
Sumner, F. H., 18(38), *43*

T

Tague, B. A., 53(10), 70(10), *99*

Teager, H. M., *45*
Tobey, R. G., 53(5), 58, 78, 80(5), 83, 85(53), 87(54), 92(6, 53, 54), 94, 95, 97, 98(49, 50, 52), *99, 101*
Tonge, F. M., *333*

V

VanHorn, E. C., *43*
Vazsony, A., *45*
Vyssotsky, V. A., 13(11, 77), 18(77), 32(11), *42, 45*

W

Wactlar, H. D., 67, 70(30), 78(30), 95(55), 97(55), *100, 102*
Walker, D. E., 156, *188*
Walton, J. J., 95(56), 98 (56), *102*
Weissman, C., *45*
Weizenbaum, J., 39, *45*
Wells, M. B., 67, *102*

Wells, R., 154(51), *188*
Westervelt, F. H., *42*
Wilkes, M. V., 21(80), *45*
Williams, L. H., 70(58), *102*
Winett, J. M., *45*
Witmer, E. A., 70(1), 95(1), 97(1), 98(1), *99*
Wolf, A. K., 155(12), *186*
Woodger, M., 193, 233, *245*
Woods, W. E., *45*
Wooldridge, D., *102*

Y

Yang, G. H., *43*
Yngve, V. H., 156, *187, 188*

Z

Zilles, S. N., 53(5), 58(53), 78(6, 53), 83(53), 85(53), 92(6, 53), 95(53), *99, 101*
Zurcher, F. W., *44*

Subject Index

A

Abstract algebra, abstract spaces, 323–327
Acceptance *see* General Acceptance Method
Adaptation, 38
Address indication, 290
Aggregates, 272, 281–284
ALGOL, 125, 143–147, 195, 224, 229, 233–238, 254, 269
  deficiencies, 238
  Formula ALGOL, 54, 55, 60, 61
Algorithm for scheduling, 27
ALGY, 53
Allocation of memory, 18
ALPAK, 53, 54, 56, 70, 98
Alphabet, 226, 270, 271
Alphanumeric constants, 271
Ambiguities
  permanent predictable, 176, 177
  syntactic, 157–163
American
  Engineering Standards Committee, 110
  Society for Testing and Materials (ASTM), 112
  Standards, 109–115, 138, 139
  Standards Association *see* ASA
APT, 149
Arithmetic, types of, in formula manipulation, 57, 58, 82
ARPA-SDC Time Sharing System, 9, 10, 34
Artificial intelligence, 243
ASA, 104, 109–115, 120, 121; *see also* Sectional Committees, X, Z
Assemblers, 53, 215, 241, 250
Assignment, 200, 237
Associative registers, 20
Association (of lists), 284
  address, 279
  list *see* List
Atoms, atomic forms, 273
Automata, 190

B

Backus normal form, 273, 274
Baseball, 155
BASIC, 11
Bell Telephone Complex Computer, 6
Berkeley Time-Sharing System, 12, 19
Blocked program, 28
Bound names, 198, 199
  formal, 203
Business Equipment Manufacturers Association (BEMA), 128, 134–137

C

CALL (system command), 33
Cambridge Polish, 74
Canonical component, c. decomposition of forms, 274, 331, 332
Carnegie Tech System, 11
Cathode ray tube display, 24
CCITT, 115, 122
Central processor, 14–16
Centralization, 31
Chaining of commands, 34
Charges, 31
Choreography, 226
Clock, 15
COBOL, 62, 125, 143, 149, 150
CODASYL, 150
Combining rules, 157
COMIT, 61
Command and control, 253
Commands
  chaining, 34
  macro, 34
Committees *see* Sectional, Standardization
Technical (TC) *see* ECMA, IEC, ISO
Comparative conjunctions, 157, 167, 173–175

339

340   SUBJECT INDEX

Compatible Time-Sharing System (CTSS), 7–10, 29, 32–34, 63, 86
Compilers, 53, 250, 255, 256, 261
Compiler-compilers, 241, 242
Complex numbers, 61, 62, 85
Components *see* Canonical
Computable functions, c. predicates, 201
Concatenation (of aggregates), 273
Conditional evaluation (of expressions), 259
Conditional forms *see* Forms
Constants, 198, 270
  extended, 272
Constituent analysis, 183
Conversational mode, 38
Coordinate conjunctions, 157, 160, 167, 171, 172
CORD System, 12, 28, 32
Control *see* Command
Control word, 280
Conversion of infixes, 304
Criteria for standardization, 150, 151
Critical real time, 4
CRT display, 24
CTSS *see* Compatible Time-Sharing System

D

Dartmouth Time-Sharing System (DTSS), 11, 12, 32
Datanet-30, 12
Dataphone, 8, 24
Debugging, 35, 38
Decentralization, 263
Decisions, d. rules, 262–265, 306, 309
Declarative computation, 249
Decomposition *see* Canonical
Dedicated systems, 5
Degraded service, 30, 35
Depth of occurrence, 281, 330
Dictionary, 215, 216, 227
Differentiation, 64, 65, 78, 86, 87
Direct function, 271
Discharge list, 312–317
Discontinuous elements in linguistic structure, 156, 183, 184
Disk file, d. memory, 21
Display, 24
Drum memory, 21
Duplex, full, 26
Dynamic linking of segments, 19

E

ECMA (European Computer Manufacturers Association), 115, 123–125
  TC-5 (ALGOL), TC-6 (COBOL), TC-8 (FORTRAN), TC-10 (PL-1), 125
Editing, 37, 66–68, 88
Electronic Industries Association (EIA), 136
Electrotechnical Commission, International *see* IEC
Embedding
  in a language, 53, 224
  in lists, 282, 286–288
End pointer, 280
Error detection and correction, 25
European Computer Manufacturers Association *see* ECMA
Evaluation
  of expressions, 257, 292–302
    conditional, 259
  of labels, 199
Evolution of time sharing, 6
Executive, e. program, 33, 224, 234
Existing Standards Method, 111, 112
Expressions
  comparison of, 67, 68, 89
  evaluation of, 257, 292–302
    conditional, 259
  representation of, 73–75, 92
  separation into components, 71
  simplification, 58–60, 83–85, 95
  types of, 55–57, 80, 81
  well-formed *see* Forms
Extended constants, 272
External
  quotations, 314, 316
  recursive functions, 314, 316
  storage, 32, 77, 78, 93, 94

F

Factoring, 66, 88
Failsoft capability, 16, 35
FAP, 163, 166, 176, 186
Federation of National Standardizing Associations (ISA), 115
Flagged integers, 310–312
Flow charts, 194, 214
  basic, 197–201
  formal, 203, 220
  general, 202–206, 221

SUBJECT INDEX

FORMAC, 53, 55, 78–95, 98
  applications, 98
  capabilities
    general, 80–86
    specific, 86–92
  general-purpose system, 79
  implementation, 92–95
  language level, 79
Forms, 248, 258, 260, 267, 272–274
  atomic, 273
  Backus normal, 273, 274
  conditional, 273, 288, 306–309
  levels of, 328–331
  partial, 274
  synthesis of, 274–276
  undecomposable, 274, 318, 331
Formula ALGOL *see* ALGOL
Formula manipulation
  applications, 95–98
  capabilities
    general, 55–63
    level of, 54, 55
    specific, 64–71
  definition, 47–49
  general-purpose systems for, 52
  implementation, 72–78
  importance, 49–51
  level of language, 53, 54
  on-line, 63
Formula translation, 47–102, 249
FORTRAN, 62, 79, 81, 82, 125, 143, 147–149, 254
Free (storage) list *see* List
Full duplex, 26
Functional programming, 258
Functionals, 318
Function
  address letter, 290
  letter, 271, 290
  mark, 271
  represented by a flow chart, 201
Functions
  basic, 197
  computable, 201
  direct, 271
  literal, 317–321
  of gaps, 256
  polynomial, 324–327
  primitive, 300
  recursive, 312–317

G

Gaps in computer programs, 252, 254, 262, 266, 268
  functions of, 256
  interrelationships of, 270
  see also Open-ended, Unknowns
Garbage collection, 77
GE-235, 12
  -635, 13
  -645, 13, 14, 19
General Acceptance Method, 111
General-purpose time-sharing system, 5
Graceful degradation, 35
Grammar *see* Syntax
Grammatical restrictions, 157, 162, 166, 168, 169

H

Hardware, for time-sharing systems, 31–33
Harvard Predictive Analyzer, 155
Hierarchical computation, 195, 216–225, 234
Hierarchy of storage devices, 16
History of standardization, 104–109

I

IBM-1050, 12, 24
  -7030 (STRETCH), 63
  -7044, 12
  -7090, 7, 80
  -7094, 7, 80, 155, 163, 249
  -7750, 8, 32
  Selectric, 9, 24
  System/360 Model 67, 19
Identifier, 274, 290
IEC (International Electrotechnical Commission), 115, 121
  TC-53 (Computers and Information Processing), 121, 122
IFIP (International Federation for Information Processing), 125–127
  TC-2 (Programming Languages), 127, 141
    WG-2.1, 143, 144
Immediate constituent analysis, 183
Infixes, 75, 250, 302–305
  conversion of, 304
  reinstatement of, 305

342 SUBJECT INDEX

Information Processing Systems Standards Board *see* IPSSB
Information retrieval, 34
  on-line, 37
Information storage, 34
  on-line, 37
Input/output for formula manipulation, 66, 67, 88
Integer constants, 271
Integration, 66, 78, 87
Interface, 26, 27
Interleave, 17
International
  Advisory Committee of X-3, 131
  Electrotechnical Commission *see* IEC
  Federation of National Standardizing Associations (ISA), 115
  Federation for Information Processing *see* IFIP
  Organization for Standardization *see* ISO
  Standard, 119
  Telecommunications Union (ITU), 115, 122
  Telegraph and Telephone Consultative Committee (CCITT), 115, 122
Interpreter, 249, 250, 261
Interrupt, 15
Interval timer, 15
IPL V, 163, 175
IPSSB (Information Processing Systems Standards Board), 127
ISA (International Federation of National Standardizing Associations), 115
ISO (International Organization for Standardization), 104, 115–121
ISO Recommendations, 119–121
ISO Technical Committees, 120
  TC-95 (Office Machines), 119
  TC-97 (Computers and Information Processing), 116–119, 142, 143, 146, 149
  Subcommittees, 117–119
ITU (International Telecommunications Union), 115, 122

J

JOHNNIAC Open Shop System, 11, 12
JOSS, 11, 12
JOVIAL, 217, 269
Junction of lists, 279, 285

L

Labels, 198, 199
  address, 208
  formal, 203, 219
  vertex, 205
Language *see* Natural language
Languages, computer (machine)
  model, 207–211
  specification of, 225–229
  translation, 211–217
Languages, hierarchical, 217–225
Languages, picture, 226
Languages, programming
  design, 238–240
  levels, 52–54, 79, 261
  model, 197–207, 241
  processors, 193
  specification of, 225–229, 231
  system command, 33
  universal, 239
  see also under names of individual programming languages
Levels of forms, 328–331
Library control list, 293
Library of forms, 290–292
Linguistic theory *see* Natural language
Linkage list, 315, 317
LISP, 54, 74, 77, 80, 249, 258, 261, 267, 269
List processing, 48, 249, 250, 262–265
Lists, 276–281
  association, 249, 267, 276
  discharge, 312–317
  free (free storage), 76, 77, 93, 267, 278, 284–286, 311
  linkage, 315, 317
  logical, 284–287
  looped 309–312
  physical, 286
  pushdown, 249, 250, 286, 297, 311
  sequencing, 286
Literal functions, 317–321
Logical lists, 284–287
Logical memory address, 20
Looped lists, 309–312

M

MAC, 9, 13, 249; *see also* M.I.T., Compatible Time-Sharing System
Macrocommands, macroinstructions, 34, 54, 321–323

SUBJECT INDEX 343

MAGIC, 24
Magnetic tape (in time-sharing systems), 21, 22
Man-computer (man-machine) interaction, 36, 38, 39, 41, 192, 225, 240, 242, 249, 265; *see also* On-line
  in formula manipulation, 62, 63, 85, 86
Man-machine interface, 22
Management information system, 38, 262–265
Mapping, 19
Marks, 270, 271; *see also* Function, Operative, Punctuation, Unknown mark
Master mode, 15
Materialization of forms, 313, 315
MATHLAB, 57, 63
Mating of punctuations, 281, 288–290
Memory, 16–22, 77; *see also* Storage
  external, 77
  multiple banks of, 17
  primary, 16, 17
  virtual, 19
Memory allocation, 18, 212, 216, 234; *see also* Storage allocation
Memory relocation, 18
Memory relocation register, 7
Metalanguage, 189, 279
Metric system, 107, 108
M.I.T., 63, 86, 249, 250, 267; *see also* MAC, Compatible Time-Sharing System
Mode
  conversation, 38
  master, 15
  slave, 15
Models
  of computer (machine) languages, 207–211
  of programming languages, 197–207, 241
MULTICS, 12–14, 19, 29
Multiple banks of core memory, 17
Multiplexed Information and Computing Service *see* MULTICS
Multiprocessing, 4, 32, 192
Multiprogramming, 4

N

National Bureau of Standards, 12, 24, 155
Natural languages, 196, 229–231, 242, 243
  string analysis of, 154, 155, 157–162
    computational economy of, 184, 185

Network of computers, 40
Noise, 25
Nonnumerical computer applications, 50
Nonprocedural programming, 258

O

ODIN, 34
On-line
  formula manipulation, 63, 261, 265–268
  users, 3
  see also Man-computer interaction
Open-ended computer programs, 252, 254, 257
Operative marks, 270
Overhead, 27, 276
Overlap, 17

P

Paging, 18–20
Parameter sequence, 274
Parity check, 25
Partial forms, 274
Pattern matching, in formula manipulation, 60, 61, 71, 85, 89
Pattern recognition, 243
PDP-1, 8, 10, 63
PDP-6, 63
Physical lists, 286
Picture languages, 226, 243
PL/1, 14, 125, 143, 151, 254, 269
Policies (expressed as open-ended programs), 262–265
Polish notation, 73–75, 250; *see also* Cambridge Polish
Polynomials, 55, 56, 70, 78, 89, 324–327
Predicates, 197
  computable, 201
  formal, 202, 204, 220
Predictive analysis, 155
Prefixes, 302–305
Primitives, 299
  of computer languages, 207–209
  of hierarchical languages, 219–223
  of programming languages, 195, 197
Priority scheduling, 29
Privacy, 31
Processors, for programming languages, 2, 193
Production mark, 271, 313

Program, 4
  blocked, 28
  sentence analysis, 155
  swapping, 18
  testing, 37
Project MAC, 9, 13, 249; *see also* M.I.T., Compatible Time-Sharing System
Protected mode of operation, 7
Punctuation marks, 270
Pushdown
  lists, 249, 250, 286, 297, 311
  store, 225

Q

Quantum time, 28
QUICKTRAN, 12
Quotation, 293

R

Rational
  constants, 271
  arithmetic, 57, 58, 82
Real-time system, 3; *see also* Man-computer interaction
  critical, 4
Recursive
  computation, 217, 218
  functions, 233, 312–317
    classification of, 194
Redundancy, 33
Register, memory relocation, 7
Reinstatement of infixes, 305
Reliability, 17, 33–36, 40
Relocation of memory, 18
Relocation register, 7
Remote terminals, 22–24
Representation of expressions, 73–75, 92
Resources, 2, 31
Resumption address, 296
Round robin, 28
Rules for combining, 157

S

SAINT, 66
Scheduling, 27–30
  priority, 29
SDS-930, 12
SDS-940, 12, 19

Sectional Committee Method, 111–114
Sectional Committees of ASA, 112–114; *see also* X, Z
Segments, dynamic linking of, 19
Selectric, 9, 24
Semantics, 198, 199, 230–233
Semiotics, 193
Sentence analysis, 155
Separating of expressions into components, 71
Sequencing list, 286
Shorthands, 321–323
Simplification of expressions, 58–60, 78, 83, 95
Slave mode, 15
SNOBOL, 61
Specification of languages and processors, 193, 194
Standardization
  committees, 108; *see also* Sectional Committees
  criteria, 150, 151
  early examples of, 104
  history of, 104–109
  International Organization for, *see* ISO
  see also Existing Standards, General Acceptance, Sectional Committee
Standards, American, 109–115, 138, 139; *see also* ASA
  existing *see* Existing Standards Method
Standards Boards, 111, 127
Storage allocation, 72, 75, 76, 92, 93, 276, 284; *see also* Memory allocation
Strategies, incremental updating of, 253
STRETCH *see* IBM
String
  analysis, linguistic, *see* Natural languages
  decomposition, 186
  processing, 48
  program, 155, 163, 171–177
Subforms, 274
Substitution, 332
  automatic, in formulas, 68–70, 71, 89
  in flow charts, 202
Supervisor *see* Executive program
Swapping of programs, 18
Symbiosis, man-computer, 41; *see also* Man-computer interaction
Symbol manipulation, 48
SYMBOLANG, 54
Syntactic ambiguity, 157, 163

SUBJECT INDEX

Syntax, 153–188, 197, 228, 230–233
   of incremental computer, 270–276
Synthesis of forms, 274–276
System
   ARPA-SDC Time-Sharing, 9, 10
   Berkeley Time-Sharing, 12
   call, 33
   Carnegie Tech, 11
   command, 33
   Compatible Time-Sharing (CTSS), 7–10, 29, 32–34, 63, 86
   CORD, 12
   critical real-time, 4
   Dartmouth Time-Sharing, 11, 12
   dedicated, 5
   FORMAC, 78–95
   general-purpose time-sharing, 5
   Johnniac Open-Shop, 11, 12
   language, 33
   management information, 38
   real-time, 3
   resources, 2, 31

T

Tape, 21, 22
TC (Technical Committee) *see* ECMA, IEC, ISO
Teaching machines, 37
Telecommunications Union, International (ITU), 115, 122
Telegraph and Telephone Consultative Committee, International, 115, 122
Teletype, 9, 12, 24
Teletypewriter, 23
TELEX, 23, 24
Threshold policy, threshold predicate, 300, 306–309
Time-of-day clock, 15
Time-Sharing, 1–45, 92, 240, 265; *see also* System
   utility, 40, 41
Timer, interval, 15
Transformational
   analysis, 156, 185, 186
   decomposition, 186
Translation
   for hierarchical computation, 225
   of programming languages, 195, 211–217
   syntax-directed, 241, 242
   see also Natural languages
Trees, 270

Truth values, 270
   parenthesized, 306, 307
TSS *see* System, time-sharing
Turing machines, 190, 194, 227, 259
TWX, 8, 23
Typewriter terminal, 9, 12, 23, 24

U

Undecomposable forms, 274, 318, 331
United States of America Standards Institute (USASI), 104; *see also* ASA
Univac, 64, 155
University of Pennsylvania, 155, 157
Unknowns, 255, 259, 265, 268, 274–276, 313
Unknown letter, unknown mark, 271
Unraveling *see* Substitution
Utility, time-sharing, 40, 41

V

Variables *see* Unknowns
   free, 255, 256, 268
Variary operators, 74
Vectors, 323, 324
Vertices, of flow charts, 199
Virtual memory, 19, 20
Vocabulary *see* Alphabet

W

Weights and measures, 106; *see also* Metric system
Well-defined computation, 201
Well-formed expressions *see* Forms
Western Union, 8, 24
Whirlwind, 64

X

X-3 (ASA Committee), 116, 127–134, 141
   International Advisory Committee, 131
   Subcommittees, 140
   X-3.4, 141–151
X-4, 119, 127, 134, 135
X-6, 127, 136

Z

Z-39 (ASA Committee, Library Work and Documentation), 127